Multidisciplinary studies presented to
Edgar Zurif
on his 60th birthday

LANGUAGE AND THE BRAIN

FOUNDATIONS OF NEUROPSYCHOLOGY

A Series of Textbooks, Monographs, and Treatises

Series Editor

LAIRD S. CERMAK

Memory Disorders Research Center, Boston Veterans Administration, Medical Center, Boston, Massachusetts

LANGUAGE AND THE BRAIN
Representation and Processing

Edited by

Yosef Grodzinsky
Aphasia Research Center
Department of Neurology
Boston University School of Medicine
Boston, Massachusetts, and
Department of Psychology
Tel Aviv University
Tel Aviv, Israel

Lewis P. Shapiro
Department of Communicative Disorders
San Diego State University
San Diego, California

David Swinney
Department of Psychology
University of California, San Diego
La Jolla, California

ACADEMIC PRESS
A Harcourt Science and Technology Company

San Diego   San Francisco   New York   Boston   London   Sydney   Tokyo

Academic Press
A Harcourt Science and Technology Company
525 B Street, Suite 1900, San Diego, California 92101-4495, USA
http://www.apnet.com

Academic Press
24-28 Oval Road, London NW1 7DX, UK
http://www.hbuk.co.uk/ap/

Library of Congress Catalog Card Number: 99-67289

International Standard Book Number: 0-12-304260-7

PRINTED IN THE UNITED STATES OF AMERICA
99   00   01   02   03   04   EB   9   8   7   6   5   4   3   2   1

Contents

Chapter 7   *Sentence Memory in Amnesia*
             Laird S. Cermak

Part IV   *The Lexical–Structural Interface*

Chapter 8   *Toward a Neurochemistry of Naming and Anomia*
             Martin L. Albert

Chapter 9   *Language Deficits in Broca's and Wernicke's Aphasia:*
             A Singular Impairment
             Sheila E. Blumstein and William P. Milberg

Chapter 10   *Right Hemisphere Contributions to Understanding Lexical*
             Connotation and Metaphor
             Hiram Brownell

Contributors

Numbers in parentheses indicate the pages on which the authors' contributions begin.

Martin L. Albert (157) Aphasia Research Center, Department of Neurology, Boston University School of Medicine, Boston Veterans Administration Medical Center, Boston, Massachusetts 02130.

Sergey Avrutin (295) Department of Linguistics, Yale University, New Haven, Connecticut 06520.

Sheila E. Blumstein (167) Department of Cognitive and Linguistic Sciences, Providence, Rhode Island 02912.

Hiram Brownell (185) Department of Psychology, Boston College, Chestnut Hill, Massachusetts 02467; and Harold Goodglass Aphasia Research Center, Department of Neurology, Boston University School of Medicine, Boston, Massachusetts 02130.

Enriqueta Canseco-Gonzalez (229) Department of Psychology, Reed College, Portland, Oregon 97202.

David Caplan (315) Neuropsychology Laboratory, Massachusetts General Hospital, Boston, Massachusetts 02114.

Alfonso Caramazza (203) Department of Psychology, Harvard University, Cambridge, Massachusetts 02138.

Laird S. Cermak (143) Center for Memory Disorders, Boston University School of Medicine, Boston, Massachusetts 02130.

Merrill Garrett (31) Department of Cognitive Science, University of Arizona, Tucson, Arizona 85721.

Anat Geva (123) Department of Psychology, University of Michigan, Ann Arbor, Michigan 48109.

Harold Goodglass (267) Department of Neurology, Boston University School of Medicine, Boston, Massachusetts 02130.

Yosef Grodzinsky (73) Aphasia Research Center, Department of Neurology, Boston University School of Medicine, Boston, Massachusetts 02130; and Department of Psychology, Tel Aviv University, Tel Aviv 69978, Israel.

Gregory Hickok (87) Department of Cognitive Sciences, University of California, Irvine, Irvine, California 92697.

Ray Jackendoff (3) Center for Complex Systems, Brandeis University, Waltham, Massachusetts 02324.

Tracy Love (105, 273) The National Center for Neurogenic Communication Disorders, University of Arizona, Tucson, Arizona 85721; and Department of Psychology, University of California, San Diego, La Jolla, California 92093.

Joan Maling (351) Volen Center, Brandeis University, Waltham, Massachusetts 02454.

William P. Milberg (167) Geriatric Research, Education and Clinical Center, Veterans Administration Medical Center, West Roxbury, Massachusetts 02132.

Janet L. Nicol (105) Department of Cognitive Science, University of Arizona, Tucson, Arizona 85721.

Maria Mercedes Piñango (327) Linguistics and Cognitive Science Program, Department of Psychology, Brandeis University, Waltham, Massachusetts 02254.

Penny Prather (273) Boston Veterans Administration Medical Center, Boston, Massachusetts 02130.

Lewis P. Shapiro (357) Department of Communicative Disorders, San Diego State University, San Diego, California 92182.

Edward E. Smith (123) Department of Psychology, University of Michigan, Ann Arbor, Michigan 48109.

David Swinney (273) Department of Psychology, University of California, San Diego, La Jolla, California 92093.

Preface

Language, a core intellectual ability, is supported by complex neural and psychological mechanisms. In this book, we offer a state-of-the-art multidisciplinary perspective on the inner workings of these mechanisms. This book encompasses work ranging from the latest neuroimaging techniques to detailed syntactic argumentation, from considerations of the brain bases of online lexical access to discourse processing, from memory to metaphor. This type of mix is typical of our field today: to be a player, one must have one's fingers dipped in linguistic theory (at all its levels), cognitive psychology, cognitive neuroscience, communicative disorders, and experiments "wet" and "dry." This volume represents this mix. We feel, therefore, that it is most appropriate to dedicate this book to Edgar Zurif, whose work has touched upon all these themes.

We have organized the book along the lines of functional interfaces between levels of language representation and processing. We begin with considerations of the architecture of the language system. Jackendoff (Chapter 1) addresses the fundamental issue of mental modularity, proposing a different (non-Fodorian) approach to "representational modularity," which focuses on two putative kinds of modules—integrative and interface—and the roles they may play in language processing. Garrett (Chapter 2) addresses the conflicts between evidence that appears to support interactive accounts and evidence supporting modular accounts of structural processing. He argues that resolution of these conflicts may be found in a "filtering model" that holds that an essentially modular production system is the source of the apparent interactive constraints on parsing.

We next move to consideration of the comprehension–production interface in language. Grodzinsky (Chapter 3) examines apparently separate linguistic descriptions of production and comprehension deficits in aphasia and attempts to derive one from the other in support of an "overarching agrammatism." Hickok (Chapter 4) argues that speech perception systems are organized bilaterally in the posterior supratemporal plane and that these systems participate in both speech perception and speech production; conduction aphasia is linked to damage to these systems. Nicol and Love (Chapter 5) link the impairment in comprehension found in Broca's aphasia to a deficit in rehearsal and hence to production in this population.

Consideration of the memory–language interface begins with Smith and Geva's (Chapter 6) description of neuroimaging and behavioral evidence demonstrating that verbal working memory is implemented by the same neural mechanisms involved in language processing. They describe the level of interdependence of these two functions. Cermak (Chapter 7) examines the language deficits found in amnesic patients and describes how these reveal the role of memory in language processing.

We next consider the lexical–structural interface in language processing. Albert (Chapter 8) proposes that lexical–semantic deficits in anomia result from deficiencies in cholinergic neurotransmission, whereas deficits in phonological/articulatory output result from deficiencies in dopaminergic neurotransmission, providing both clinical and experimental support. Blumstein and Milberg (Chapter 9) connect level of lexical activation to deficits found in both Broca's and Wernicke's aphasia. Broca's aphasics are claimed to underactivate and Wernicke's aphasics to overactivate, effects that are argued to extend to phonological and syntactic processing. Brownell (Chapter 10) considers how the right hemisphere (and different regions within the right hemisphere) contributes to the comprehension of metaphor and connotation. Caramazza (Chapter 11) examines modality-specific lexical processing deficits to inform a model of the general architecture of the lexical processing system. Canseco-Gonzalez (Chapter 12) provides an in-depth review of the electrophysiological (ERP) evidence underlying both lexical and structural (first- and second-pass) processing. Goodglass (Chapter 13) assembles evidence to argue that the ability to identify the grammatical gender of a noun is essentially a semantic operation and is not the same as accessing the syntactic features involved in gender agreement. Swinney, Prather, and Love (Chapter 14) present evidence from both aphasic processing and from left- and right-hemifield studies (with neurologically intact subjects) that support and consolidate a modular view of lexical access.

Our final section deals with the syntax–discourse interface in language processing. Avrutin (Chapter 15) examines the comprehension of both discourse-linked and non-discourse-linked Wh- questions. He argues that children as well as Broca's aphasic patients evince an interface deficiency that emerges during resource-intensive syntax–discourse operations. Caplan (Chapter 16) uses evidence from PET studies to reveal the neural localization of the processing of relative clauses. Piñango (Chapter 17) argues that Broca's aphasics' comprehension deficits are attributable to a mismatch between the ordering of thematic roles and the order of roles in syntactic representation. Maling (Chapter 18) provides linguistic argumentation for string-vacuous movement in subject relative sentences, a ding that underlies experimental evidence demonstrating filler-gap reaccess effects in these constructions. Shapiro (Chapter 19) investigates the time course of processing gap-filling constructions and concludes that lexical, structural, and discourse processing are demonstrably independent.

The volume was written by Edgar Zurif's colleagues and students. Our current knowledge and understanding of the neurological underpinnings of language would not have been as rich as they are today had Edgar Zurif not forcefully entered this field and shared his zeal and insights with us. All of us have benefited from and appreciated Edgar's curiosity and quest for deeper understanding; most of all we value his friendship.

Edgar's career reflects the range of science found in this book. He began his research career with studies of lateralization, proceeded to linguistically informed deficit analyses of aphasia, later encompassed on-line lexical and structural processing, and most recently engaged in studies utilizing advanced neuroimaging techniques. Many of his experiments have become landmark studies in the field; several constitute the background literature to papers in this volume. His numerous contributions have played an important role in shaping this field and making it what it is today. Howard Gardner's dedication is a personal tribute to Edgar, one that captures the flavor of Edgar's contributions to the field and to his colleagues. This volume is a small tribute to an outstanding scientist and friend.

Joyous moments of celebration are sometimes lessened by sad events. As this book was on its way to the printer, we learned of the death of our friend, colleague, series editor, and contributor to this book, Laird Cermak, who passed away at age 57 on November 4th, 1999. Without him this book would never have come into being. Director of the Boston Center for Memory Disorders, Laird was a good friend, neighbor, and partner of the Aphasia Research Center, home to Edgar, as well as to many of this book's contributors at one time or another. We all appreciated his wisdom and good cheer, and we shall always miss him.

Yosef Grodzinsky
Lewis P. Shapiro
David Swinney

In Dedication to Edgar Basil Zurif

Edgar Basil Zurif was born in Montreal on January 9, 1940. This biographical information is readily available in resource books and on the Web (though Edgar is unlikely to look it—or anything else—up there). I did not have to look it up, however, because I will never forget Edgar's birthday. More on that later.

For twenty years, I had the pleasure of working with Edgar, side by side in the same dingy (and that is being generous) office at the Boston Veterans Administration Aphasia Research Center. We shared the space, research assistants, a shower that was converted into a closet, and equipment that did not work most of the time. But beyond these creature comforts and discomforts, I was privileged to grow professionally with Edgar. Roughly the same age and both near the start of our research careers, we had the equivalent of a professional marriage, one that, perhaps not surprisingly in this turbulent age, lasted beyond the marriages in which we were involved when we first joined forces in the fall of 1971.

Truth to tell this was an arranged marriage. Edgar and I had not known each other before, and we had simply been placed in the same space as a convenience by Harold Goodglass, the director of the Aphasia Research Center. But this arranged marriage took. We soon applied for a grant together and shared this grant for the next two decades. We attended courses together, wrote papers together, and gave talks and seminars together. And our relationship became personal as we became good friends. We shared affinities, gossip, prejudices, tall tales, trips, parties, books, movies, trivial pursuits, wonderful ups, and less frequent but no less painful downs. In 1982 we even took a European trip, together with our wives. . . but while we all got along, something told us not to mix professional and personal marriages.

I can't speak for marriages approved by the state or the church, but I can testify to why Edgar is a good partner in research. To begin with, he knows a tremendous amount not only about the areas of his designated expertise, but also about many regions that would seem quite peripheral. He reads, he thinks, he remembers. Edgar is also a compulsive learner. He wants to know more, he writes it down, he asks questions, and he debates with himself and with others. Even more important, Edgar is a wonderfully lucid thinker. He does not tolerate sloppiness in himself or in others—indeed, he insists doggedly on clarity in his own thinking, speaking, and writing.

As is evident from the contributions to this volume, Edgar is a wonderful collaborator in neurolinguistics and allied fields. He has worked with many of the leading figures in the field and has had a strong hand in the formation of the most talented figures in the next generation of workers. (Truth to tell, he has played a "nontrival" role as well in the development of those from rival schools.) He is an enviably effective mentor.

But I am here to affirm that Edgar is an equally skillful collaborator with someone whose interests are complementary to his. Edgar and I worked comfortably in language and cognition for twenty years. Aping the hemispheric specializations that attracted Edgar to the field in the 1960s, he took the phonological and syntactic aspects of language, while I took the semantic and pragmatic components; he favored the brief, carefully timed presentations and processes, while I explored the lengthier, more leisurely forms of processing; he focused on language in a strict sense, while I emphasized communication and other forms of cognition—all right, he (and Dave Swinney and Penny Prather and Yosef and Lew) took the left hemisphere and I (and Hiram Brownell) took the right.

Edgar's contributions to neurolinguisitics are significant and will last. While he neither started the field nor coined the term, he was as important as anyone in ushering the Modern Era of Neurolinguistics and has been as important as anyone in sustaining it and giving it direction and intellectual force. As I write, he is probably the most central figure in the field. And while his own interests have remained true to his first love of syntactic processing and its fate in those with Broca-style aphasias, he has left an imprint on a wide range of topics that run the virtual gamut of cognitive neuropsychology.

To be a central figure, one must have a powerful intellect, strong theoretical interests, and ingenious empirical gifts. These Edgar has in abundance. These do not earn one a Festschrift at age 60, however. Edgar's personal traits have been equally important in sustaining his leadership position: his willingness to discuss, to debate, and even (on occasion) to admit that he has been wrong; his patience in designing studies, explaining concepts, and drawing out the best in colleagues and students, even wayward ones; his enthusiasm for the subject; his fundamental theoretical commitments, coupled with the capacity to change course or argument when the data or new arguments so dictate; his friendship, mentoring, and loyalty to so many "happy collaborators."

You would not know it from his calm and modest demeanor, but Edgar cares about what he wears . . . perhaps almost as much as he cares about the nature of syntactic parsing. Occasionally, he buys new clothing. Because he hates to accumulate things, and because he is by nature generous, Edgar sometimes gives away his clothing. At least 15 years ago, he decided he no longer wanted to wear his black pinstriped winter suit. So he gave it to me, and it fit—very well, in fact. As the new year clicks in every twelve months, I move Edgar's suit to the front of my closet and when January 9 rolls around, I don the suit and give Edgar a call. We confirm our friendship, laugh a little, commiserate as necessary, looking back to the days of glory at the Boston VA and ahead to our "senior moments" as latter-day Sunshine Boys. If one is to grow old—though 60 is not old any more, Edgar—it is good to have collaborators and friends like Edgar Basil Zurif.

Howard Gardner

Part I

Architecture of the Language System

Chapter 1

Fodorian Modularity and Representational Modularity

Ray Jackendoff

Jerry Fodor's overall agenda in *The Modularity of Mind* (1983) is that we should not conceive of the mind as a giant maximally interconnected net, such that, for instance, your language processing can potentially be affected by what you ate for breakfast or the color of the speaker's hair or millions of other ridiculous things. The book is to be taken as an argument against generalized association, cognition as general-purpose problem solver, general connectionism, heavily top-down AI, and top-down "new look" psychology. It is an argument *for* the specialization of mental functional architecture.

I agree completely with Fodor's (1983) overall agenda. But I think that Fodor's realization of this agenda as what has come to be called *the* modularity hypothesis has some serious difficulties that need to be addressed. Unfortunately the issue of modularity has come to be identified with Fodor's realization, so if one does not agree with him in detail one is liable to be thought of as opposed to modularity. However, one can in fact imagine other conceptions of modularity that preserve the basic agenda and that therefore also deserve to fall under the rubric of modularity theory.

In this chapter I work out one such variant, *representational modularity*, and show how it meets my objections to Fodor's (1983) approach while preserving his essential insight. (The essentials of this version of modularity were proposed in Jackendoff, 1987, especially chapter 12; Jackendoff, 1997, works out consequences of this position for linguistic theory.) An important innovation in this approach is a distinction between two kinds of modules: *integrative modules*, which are responsible for integrating particular levels of representation, and *interface modules*, which are responsible for communication among representations. The latter have not been clearly recognized in previous literature with which I am familiar; but they prove to be key in understanding many of the crucial issues.

Language and the Brain

In order to keep terminology clear, I will use the term "Fodorian modularity" or "F-modularity" for Fodor's (1983) theory, leaving the term "modularity" free for related variants.

PROBLEMS WITH FODORIAN MODULARITY ON THE INPUT SIDE

Suppose Fodor (1983) is right (as I think he is) that there is a device for language perception in the brain (or a collection of devices) that is domain specific, that is, devoted to language perception but not to churchbell or symphony or cow perception and not to proving theorems. And suppose he is right that the operation of this device is fast (i.e., measured in milliseconds from input to output) and mandatory (i.e., you can't help hearing appropriately structured sounds as language). Then a basic question is: What exactly does this device do? In particular, what are its input and output, and how does it get from one to the other?

According to Fodor (1983) (at least in the book), the input is the transducers at the ear; the output is some "shallow" representation, perhaps a syntactic structure or a "logical form" [which in current Chomskyan generative theory (government-binding theory and/or the minimalist program) is a part of syntactic structure]. The output is definitely *not* a form of representation in which the internal semantic properties of words are available—what I would call "conceptual structure" and what Fodor would call "narrow content" or the syntax of the language of thought. For the moment let me use the term "propositional structure" as a relatively theory-neutral term for this level; the intent is that it is the level in terms of which rules of inference and/or meaning postulates (take your choice) are stated.

An important part of Fodor's (1983) agenda is that language perception is informationally encapsulated, so that nothing outside the language module can affect the operation of language perception. Much of the fuss about modularity (e.g., Crain & Steedman, 1985; Marslen-Wilson & Tyler, 1987) has been about the semantic end of the system—whether syntactic parsing is influenced by semantics or not. The usual argument goes: such-and-such a property of meaning or context has a measurable influence on syntactic parsing, therefore language perception is not informationally encapsulated, therefore modularity is wrong. The usual reply goes: If you look at the phenomena more subtly and do the following experiments, you find that in fact syntax is *not* influenced by semantics up to a certain point in time, therefore modularity is right. (Representative examples include Altmann, 1987; Clifton & Ferreira, 1987; Frazier, 1987; Fodor, Garrett, & Swinney, 1992.) But notice that the argument really concerns F-modularity, not modularity in general. F-modularity might be wrong without requiring a reversion to indiscriminately general-purpose processing. It might be, rather, that semantic effects are indeed possible, but constrained by a different version of the modularity hypothesis.

Before addressing the issue of the syntax–semantics connection, I want to soften you up by looking at the *input* end of the language perception module, pointing out four cases where the visual system has a robust effect on language perception. This will show either (a) that the language perception module is hardly as informationally encapsulated on the input end as Fodor suggests, or alternatively (b) that the language perception module, if informationally encapsulated, is a great deal more distended than ought to be appealing to advocates of F-modularity. These two alternatives will make more sense after the examples.

1. In his footnote 13, Fodor (1983) himself mentions the McGurk effect (McGurk & MacDonald, 1976), in which lipreading contributes to phonetic perception and can even override the acoustics of the speech signal in creating judgments about what the utterance *sounded* like. In the McGurk effect, subjects have no conscious awareness of the disparity between lip position and acoustic signal—they can't help hearing the sound that would correspond to lip position. This is a classic sort of modularity effect. (Fodor's footnote, significantly, is not in the section on informational encapsulation, where it would be most pertinent.)

2. Mentioned in Jackendoff (1987) is the case of reading, where visual inputs encode quasi-phonological information. This operation is fast, mandatory (try seeing writing as mere design!), and subject to domain-specific brain damage—again hallmarks of modular processes. However, suppose Fodor were right about the scope of the language perception F-module: its input is transducers at the ear, and its output is syntactic representation. The problem is that phonological structure is a level of representation intermediate between these two, hence by hypothesis informationally encapsulated. That means that the visual system should not be able to affect phonological structure and supplant the normal input of the module. In other words, if Fodor were right about the informational encapsulation of the language module, there could be no such thing as reading.

Alternatively, Fodor (1983) might reply (and has done so) that we really don't know the exact extent of the language module, and that a full characterization would include this second class of possible inputs. And certainly within this class of inputs there is domain specificity and informational encapsulation. It doesn't change the phonological content of what you're reading if you change the colors on your computer screen or carve the letters in a tree or realize them in neon lights. That is, the full capabilities of the visual system are not being exploited. Yet—there is certainly interpenetration between the parts of vision involved in reading and in seeing cows. So the alternative of simply viewing reading as another part of the language module has to finesse a serious problem of how orthographic information is segregated and processed differently from the rest of visual input.

A number of papers in Garfield (1987) mention reading, but curiously, none observes this profound challenge to Fodor's position. For instance, Clifton and Ferreira (1987) speak of a "lexical-processing module (which processes both visual and auditory information)" (p. 279), the former of which sneaks in reading without further notice. Yet the visual information involved in reading is not raw visual input: identifying letters and their linear order would appear to require a level of visual processing at which size and shape constancy have been established, and at which shapes can be abstracted away from the peculiarities of typeface. Moreover, the linear order of written words can't be detected by a purely "lexical" module. So much of the "vision module" must be invoked in reading—one input module coupled into the middle of another.

Moreover, this chapter, as well as Carroll and Slowiaczek (1987) and Frazier (1987), discusses the effects of parsing difficulty on eye movements in reading, without noticing that this constitutes a severe violation of the tenets of F-modularity. Within Fodor's conception, how can the inner workings of the domain-specific and informationally encapsulated language module interact with the inner workings of the domain-specific and informationally encapsulated vision module, such that, say, "the eye-movement control system interrupts the word-recognition processor and switches into reanalysis mode, under the control of the language processor" (Carroll & Slowiaczek, p. 234)? Unlike the other two papers, Carroll and Slowiaczek at least recognize vision and language as "two systems that are biologically and functionally distinct" (p. 235); but they neglect the obvious consequence for F-modularity.

3. Also mentioned in Jackendoff (1987) are ASL and other signed languages, in which representations derived from visually perceived gesture substitute in the language module for intimate details of the segmental phonology. Here informational encapsulation is even more compromised than in reading. In reading, visual representations are at least used to derive phonological representations that are part of the language module anyway. In ASL, a whole set of abstract gestural representations is substituted for phonetic content in encoding and accessing lexical items (as well as other linguistic units)—while preserving syntactic structure and rhythmic aspects of phonology. If Fodor were right about the inputs and out-

puts of the (innate) language perception module, and about informational encapsulation, ASL simply couldn't exist.

Again, the alternative could be that there is still another subdivision of the language module that Fodor just neglected to mention. But when does the "additional subdivision" game stop?

4. A more modest case of leaking through the barriers of the language module has to do with the stress-timing of hand movements (beat gestures) signaling emphasis. Consider the sentence in (1), whose emphatic stress is indicated by capital letters. This sentence can be accompanied by the sequence of beat gestures shown in (a) below it (where X is the location of a beat gesture), but certainly not by the sequence in (b). In fact, it is virtually impossible to perform the latter version of the sentence; the reader is encouraged to try it. The overall generalization is that beat gestures may coincide only with emphatic stresses.

(1)   This is the most riDICulous thing I've EVer heard.
      a.   X   X
      b.   X   X   X

Of course, the beats need not be visual—they can be performed by pounding on the table (auditory) or poking the hearer (haptic). The point is that the temporal placement of gesture is determined by the interaction of the language module with a more general process of rhythmic perception. Rhythmic perception in turn crosses modalities and content domains, pertaining, for instance, to gesture and music as well as language. Thus speech rhythm, which is an important part of linguistic representation and linguistic processing, involving complex rules in the grammar and deeply embedded in the grammar's inner workings, is neither entirely domain specific—since it has parallels in other domains—*nor* informationally encapsulated—since it interacts with rhythm in these other domains.

Yet again, a proponent of F-modularity might say this is just another branch of the informationally encapsulated language module that Fodor (1983) didn't happen to think of. But the point this time is that speech rhythm is not entirely domain specific: it bleeds off into various other domains.

More generally, looking at all these exceptions at the input end alone, it is beginning to look like the language perception module not only takes input from the auditory system, but also gerrymanders the visual system in an altogether puzzling way, allowing it access to phonetic perception (through the McGurk effect), phonological encoding (through reading), lexical encoding (through ASL), and stress-timing (through beat gesture). This is far from the possibility of arbitrary visual and inferential influence on language perception that Fodor dreads, but it is also far from the simple input system he lays out in the book. What does informational encapsulation amount to, if every time a putative counterexample appears, the language module is enlarged? Notice too that this move is only open on the input end of the language module. For if Fodor wants to preserve syntax from *semantic* influence, putative evidence for such influence cannot be countered by enlarging the language module to encompass those portions of semantics. That's just what Fodor wants to avoid.

(Curiously, to my knowledge none of the critics of F-modularity attend to potential counterexamples on the input end. For some reason, interaction of language perception with semantics, on the output end, is a much more fashionable issue.)

WHAT IS THE OUTPUT OF LANGUAGE PERCEPTION?

Marslen-Wilson and Tyler (1987) argue (as I did also in Jackendoff, 1987) that the output of language perception is not "a shallow level of structure," as Fodor (1983) claims. They say (p. 38), ". . . what is compelling about our real-time comprehension of language is not so much the immediacy with which linguistic form becomes available as the immediacy with which interpreted meaning becomes available. It is this that is the target of the core processes of language comprehension."

Why would Fodor object to this conclusion? Remember that the main contrast he is trying to make is between the input systems, which are fast, mandatory, domain specific, etc., and the central processes, which are supposed to be concerned with what he calls belief fixation. The latter are supposed to be relatively slow and nondomain specific, isotropic (i.e., potentially drawing on any kind of mental information), and Quinean (i.e., potentially resulting in the revision of any kind of mental information). Fodor's chief example of belief fixation is scientific theorizing and discovery.

Let's grant that this is the character of belief fixation. Put in less grandiose terms, belief fixation is the process of deciding whether you think that what someone tells you is true or not. But what is the input to *this* process?

According to Fodor (1983), the input to belief fixation has to be the output of the input system, namely, some sort of "shallow representation," say a syntactic parse. It is not yet propositional structure. But *in order to be fixed* (i.e., for its truth value to be determined), *a belief has to be formulated in terms of propositional structure.* A syntactic representation is simply the wrong vehicle for belief fixation. Thus some process must convert syntactic structure into the propositional content of what the speaker said. Is *this* process slow, Quinean, and isotropic? Or is it part of the language perception processor? Fodor seems to think it is not part of language perception (or else fails to notice that it is necessary); Marslen-Wilson and Tyler and I think it is.

This conversion certainly is fast and mandatory—one doesn't have a choice whether to interpret potentially meaningful utterances as meaningful. Perhaps it lags a few milliseconds behind syntactic parsing. That's no big surprise, since the proper relations among elements in propositional structure depend in part on syntactic structure, so they can't be determined for sure until syntactic structure is in pretty good shape. But despite this lag, the character of this process is a lot more like parsing than like scientific theorizing.

Let me suggest three examples that in different ways highlight the fast and mandatory nature of the conversion from syntactic structure to propositional structure. First, suppose I utter, "The guy on my right is a jerk." I feel fairly confident that that the guy on my right will experience some immediate affective reaction, measurable by something like a GSR—and that everyone else will experience somewhat less of one. If my guess is right, this means that everybody is deriving the meaning of the sentence and interpreting it contextually to determine whether they are the person being insulted. I might expect a hearer to undergo some GSR just from hearing the lexical item *jerk* in this context, but considerably more if it is understood as being directed at his or her own person. (Has anyone actually done this experiment?)

Now, detecting the meaning of this sentence may lead to a subsequent process of belief fixation that's slow and Quinean: "Am I a jerk? What evidence in my past experience can I bring to bear? Gee, maybe I really am a jerk, contrary to all my past beliefs. . . ." But preceding that, I am pretty sure there will be a fast, mandatory, modulelike reaction to *what is said*. This reaction is not an issue of belief fixation—it's evidently prior to belief fixation, and definitely not a central process in Fodor's sense.

Here is a more intricate example, bearing on the experiments discussed by Marslen-Wilson and Tyler (1987) and by Fodor et al. (1992) concerning the interpretation of the implicit subject (PRO) of a VP. Both papers discuss cross-sentential cases such as (2).

(2)   As John was leaving the theatre he saw Annie walking down the street. He wanted to talk with her. (PRO) following quickly after her, ...

Fodor et al. argue from their experimental results that the assignment of PRO to *John* depends on contextual information and is not a function of the modular language parser per se. However, consider well-known examples such as these, where PRO is interpreted *intra*sententially:

(3) a. Bill asked Harry to leave.
 (Bill asked Harry$_i$ [PRO$_i$ to leave], i.e., PRO = Harry)
 b. Bill asked Harry to be permitted to leave.
 (Bill$_i$ asked Harry [PRO$_i$ to be permitted PRO$_i$ to leave])

What accounts for the difference in the interpretation of PRO? One might initially think it has to do simply with the change from active to passive in the subordinate clause. But the facts are actually more complex. Here are two examples with passive subordinate clauses in which the outcome is different.

(4) a. Bill asked Harry to be examined by the doctor.
 (Bill asked Harry$_i$ [PRO$_i$ to be examined by the doctor])
 b.*Bill asked Harry to be forced to leave.
 (*Bill$_i$ asked Harry$_j$ [PRO$_{i/j}$ to be forced PRO$_{i/j}$ to leave])

In (4a) PRO proves to be *Harry*, not *Bill*; (4b) proves to be ungrammatical. It turns out that the interpretation of PRO is a complex function of the semantics of the main and subordinate verbs—complex enough that there is no completely adequate linguistic theory of it yet (see Sag & Pollard, 1991, and Jackendoff, 1997, pp. 70–73, for recent attempts and literature surveys.) It cannot be determined from a syntactic parse alone.

How does this bear on modularity? The interpretation of PRO and the grammaticality of sentences containing PRO depend on the meanings of two verbs and the combinatorial properties of their meanings, as determined *only in part* by the syntactic parse of the sentence. But certainly the interpretation of PRO *precedes* belief fixation: the interpretation of PRO as Harry in (4a) and as Bill in (4b) isn't a *belief*—it's simply part of what the sentence means. That is, the interpretation of PRO in "controlled" VPs, which has always taken to be within the language processor, involves the semantics of verbs and the combinatorics of propositional structure. It is not part of belief fixation.

Incidentally, using the combinatorial properties of verb meanings to help interpret PRO also violates one of the basic tenets of Fodor's theory of lexical meaning. According to Fodor (1975, 1998; Fodor, Garrett, Walker, & Parkes, 1980), a word meaning is an undecomposable monad in the language of thought. Although such a monad may be connected to others by meaning postulates, meaning postulates cannot compose in such a way as to account for the interactions among verb meanings necessary to compute the antecedent (or lack thereof) for PRO in (3)–(4).

Rather, the verb meanings *must* have internal structure, possibly of the sort proposed by Sag and Pollard (1991).

My final example concerns sentence (5).

(5)　The light flashed until dawn.

The interpretation of this sentence requires that the light have flashed repeatedly. Yet there is no lexical item in the sentence that creates this aspect of the interpretation: in isolation, *The light flashed* implies that it flashed once, so the source of repetition is not *flash*; in *John slept until dawn*, John is not falling asleep repeatedly, so the source of repetition is not *until*. Rather, the source of repetition is the interaction of the meanings of these two words: *until* implies the bounding of a process extended in time, and *flash* alone cannot describe such a process. To remedy this incompatibility, the interpretation reconstrues (or coerces) *flash* as an extended process by taking it to imply a petition of punctual events. (Talmy, 1978, is an early citation of this phenomenon; see discussion and references in Jackendoff, 1997, pp. 51–53.)

Here again the sense of repetition is not part of the syntactic structure of the sentence; rather it is part of the propositional content. Nevertheless, the mental process producing this aspect of the interpretation is not slow, optional, isotropic, or Quinean; it is fast and mandatory. And it must take place before belief fixation gets underway, since it creates the mental expression about which belief is to be fixed, and over which inferences are computed. Arriving at this interpretation has now been shown experimentally to entail some additional processing load; moreover this additional load can be sorted out from syntactic processing (Piñango, Zurif, & Jackendoff, 1999). However, it is emphatically not a matter of slow belief fixation.

Overall then, the conclusion is that the output of language perception is not a syntactic structure but an expression in the Language of Thought/conceptual structure/narrow content.

REPRESENTATIONAL MODULARITY

A lot of the confusion about modularity, I suspect, comes from failing to observe an important property of mental representations, considered as formal systems. This problem, hinted at in the previous section, is embodied in the common practice of drawing diagrams of processing along the lines of (6),

(6)　syntactic processor ⟶ semantic processor

and saying things like "the output of the syntactic processor is sent to the semantics."

Although this makes sense intuitively, it neglects an important step. A domain specific syntactic processor is concerned strictly with syntactic trees, made up of things like nouns (Ns), verb phrases (VPs), complementizers, and case-marking. If it constructs a parse of a sentence, the parse is still made out of syntactic units. Suppose it were to send this parse off to the semantics. What would the semantics do with it? The semantic processor doesn't know anything about noun phrases (NPs) and case-marking; rather it knows about things like conceptualized objects and events, and about claims to truth and falsity. A syntactic parse simply contains no such information.

Let me make this more concrete. The syntactic information that a certain NP is the object of a verb is on its own useless to the semantic processor. Rather, what the semantic processor needs to know is that the individual denoted by this NP plays a certain thematic role (say Patient) in the action denoted by this verb. Similarly, in a classic example of ambiguous PP attachment such as *Fran painted the sign on the porch,* the syntactic processor can say only that the final PP may be attached to either the NP object or the VP. But this is of no use to the semantic processor, which is concerned with whether the speaker is specifying the location of the sign or the location of the action of painting. In both these examples, it is necessary to correlate the syntactic structure with its semantic consequences. In other words, "sending" syntactic information to the semantic processor actually must entail a process of conversion from one format of encoding to another, a nontrivial process. It is not like sending a signal down a wire or a liquid down a pipe. It is rather a computation in its own right.

But this is precisely the step that F-modularity is missing. Leaving the output of the language perception module at "shallow representations," that is, at syntactic structure, leaves it formally unavailable for the process of belief fixation, which requires semantic information. The argument of the previous section amounts to the claim that the conversion of syntactic to semantic information must be part of language perception.

The observation that syntactic and semantic information are formally incompatible provides a key to making sense of all the counterexamples of the preceding two sections, and of why they are problematic to Fodor (1983). We begin by making a distinction between three sorts of mental processes:

1. Processes that construct a full representation in a particular format, given a collection of fragmentary structures in that format. The classic example is a syntactic parser, which is given a sequence of lexical

categories like (7a) and constructs a fully specified syntactic structure like (7b).

(7) a. Determiner^Adjective^Noun^Auxiliary^Verb^Noun
b. $[_S [_{NP}$ Det $[_{AP}$ A] N] Aux $[_{VP}$ V $[_{NP}$ N]]]

Such processes are called *integrative* processes in Jackendoff (1987).

2. Processes that convert one form of mental representation into another. The classic example is the conversion of acoustical information—frequency analysis of a continuously varying speech signal—into a discretely segmented phonetic representation. Another, as just observed, is needed to convert syntactic parses into specifications of semantic roles. Such processes are called *translation* processes in Jackendoff (1987) and *interface* processes in Jackendoff (1997). (The reason for change in terminology is that these conversions do not preserve "meaning." As will be seen later, it is better to think of them as implementing partial homologies between two forms of representation.)

3. Processes that take full representations in a particular format and relate them to or construct new representations in the same format. Classic cases are rules of inference, which derive new propositional representations from existing ones, and principles of mental rotation, which derive new visual representations from existing ones. Another might be checking to see whether two words rhyme, which compares two phonological representations. I'll call these *inferential* processes. Belief fixation in Fodor's sense is an inferential process.

I would like to suggest that the locus of modularity is not large-scale faculties such as language perception (Fodor's view) but at the scale of individual integrative, interface, and inferential processors. That is, the informational encapsulation and domain specificity of a mental process has to do precisely with what representations it accesses and derives. I will call this approach *representational modularity*. Such a view has been espoused not only by Jackendoff (1987) but also by Arbib (1987), Levelt (1989), and Bever (1992) (among others).

In order to flesh this out a bit, let's consider the two forms of mental representation about which the most is known: phonological and syntactic structure. We can see that these are strongly domain specific and encapsulated from one another: notice that phonologists and syntacticians can (and do) go their merry way for years without talking to one another. This isn't a joke—the need for intercommunication is rarely felt, even if less frequently acted on. For instance, the nature of stress rules and of principles of syllabification (phonology) has nothing whatsoever to do with the nature of case-marking or the formulation of the passive (syntax). On the present view, then, the independence of phonological and syntactic representations means that the two representations have separate integrative processors. Let's call them the phonology and syntax modules. Of course, phonological structure is neither auditory nor motor: it represents speech in terms of discrete linearly ordered speech sounds, whereas the auditory and motor signals are continuously varying. Hence there must be separate integrative processors for these latter representations as well (though virtually nothing is known about the formal nature of the representations).

Just having integrative processors isn't very useful. In speech perception, auditory signals have to be transformed or converted into phonological structure; in speech production, phonological representations have to be converted into motor signals. For these purposes we need interface modules.

What about syntax? A moment's thought suggests that syntactic information never has a direct bearing on auditory or motor representations. Rather, the effect of syntax on these latter two is always mediated by phonology. In other words, the architecture of the system is such that syntax is connected to phonology by an interface module, but there is no such module connecting syntax to auditory or motor information. Thus the layout of the modules so far looks like (8); where a diagram like (6) had a simple arrow we must insert an interface module.

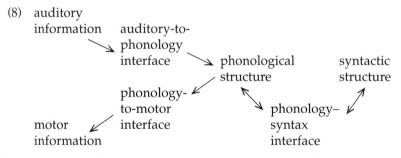

(8) auditory
      information   auditory-to-
                     phonology
                     interface   phonological   syntactic
                                       structure   structure
                     phonology-
                     to-motor
      motor   interface   phonology–
      information   syntax
                                       interface

Mappings are needed in both directions between phonology and syntax, since they are related both in perception and production. Accordingly, I have placed a double-headed arrow between them, suggesting a bidirectional interface module. Alternatively, there might be separate processors for phonology-to-syntax and the reverse. I have no opinions either way, so in what follows, I will use the notation with double-headed arrows to stand for the disjunction of these two hypotheses.

As already intimated, syntactic structure is a distinct level of representation from meaning (a.k.a. propositional structure, Language of Thought, conceptual structure, narrow content). In addition to the argument marshaled above, they must be distinct because (1) syntactic structure has word order, whereas there is no reason to believe thought does; (2) different syntactic structures are used in different languages to express the same thought. So meaning requires an integrative processor of its own. It is therefore necessary for linguistic inputs to be converted into the format of propositional structure before inferential processes can go to work. Hence the system requires an interface module that goes from syntactic structure to propositional structure. Likewise, in speech production, propositional information must give rise to syntactic structure, so that the words can be placed in proper hierarchical order. Incorporating these conversions into the system, we add (9) as a continuation of (8).

(9) phonological   syntactic   propositional
    structure   structure   structure

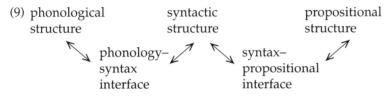

(9) is still an oversimplification. Phonological information having to do with stress and intonation contour interacts directly with the subsystem of meaning dealing with focus and presupposition, with no necessary syntactic intervention, for instance in the contrast between *JOHN hit Bill, John HIT Bill,* and *John hit BILL.* So there is another highly constrained interface module directly from phonology to meaning.

(By the way, some theorists posit a level of "linguistic semantic structure" intervening between syntax and propositional structure. If so, this just adds an extra integrative module and an extra interface module to the picture in (9). It does not change the structure of the theory of representational modularity in any essential way.)

The upshot is that when one perceives language, auditory information drives the modules in (8)–(9) successively from left to right; when one speaks, propositional information drives the modules successively from right to left. Thinking in terms of spreading activation, one could think of language perception as activating and clamping the auditory level, with activation spreading to propositional structure, and of language production as activating and clamping propositional information, with activation spreading to motor signals. But of course this is a relatively crude way of thinking about it; the interest lies in the connections made within modules and between them, such that activation can spread appropriately.

Note in particular that it is not necessary for a level of representation to be completed by its integrative processor in order for the next interface module to start passing information up or down the line; any fragment of representation at one level is sufficient to call into action (or activate) any modules that can make use of this information. That is, this architecture permits "opportunistic" or "incremental" processing [to use Marslen-Wilson & Tyler's (1987) and Levelt's (1989) terms, respectively].

In addition, since interface modules operate in both directions between phonology, syntax, and propositional structure, it is possible to use inter-modular feedback in the course of processing. For instance, a phonetic input, bereft of word boundaries, might well have to wait for evidence of semantic plausibility to arise before word boundary decisions are settled for certain. (10) is a case in point: the existence of a boundary preceding the first contrastively stressed syllable depends on the semantics as well as the syntax of the following contrasting clause.

> (10)   a. It's only a PARent, not a TEACHer.
>   b. It's only apPARent, not REAL.

Here the phonology module must potentially entertain alternative structures, both of which get passed on by the interface processors successively to syntax and semantics. When the semantics processor resolves the ambiguity, thus "clamping" the intended meaning, the interface processors pass down the inhibition of the rejected structure to syntax and phonology.

We see a similar effect in the experimental work of Tanenhaus, Spivey-Knowlton, Eberhard, and Sedivy (1995), where eyetracking shows that visual input interacts with parsing of sentences like (11).

> (11) Put the apple on the towel in the cup.

In order to be able to talk about what we see, interface modules must connect propositional structure to the visual system (Macnamara, 1978; Jackendoff, 1987; Landau & Jackendoff, 1993). To the extent that the visually presented environment affects the course of syntactic parsing, then, it is due to exactly the sort of feedback effect posited for (10), only this time between syntax and visual representations via propositional structure, rather than between phonology and propositional structure via syntax.

Each module thus can be driven by representations derived by others. At the same time it must satisfy its own constraints as well. For instance, as is well known, the mapping from auditory information to phonology is nontrivial—that is, there is serious work for the interface processor to do. However, it is *not* the job of the auditory-to-phonology processor to supply word boundaries where there are no pauses in the auditory signal. In fact, as far as this processor is concerned, the first clauses in (10a, b) are indistinguishable. The possibility of a word boundary after *a* in (10a) must be supplied, rather, by the integrative processor for phonology. That is, part of the job of the phonology module in language perception is to find the word boundaries in the utterance, which are underdetermined by the input. And sometimes, as seen in (10), feedback is needed via the phonology–syntax module and even beyond, in order to solve this problem.

Moving up one level, the phonology-to-syntax interface module provides linear order but underdetermines constituency; so one of the main problems for the syntax integrator is working out a syntactic constituent structure consistent with its own constraints. This is of course the standard problem of parsing; often feedback from the semantics-to-syntax interface module will be needed to sort out the correct parse. Finally, syntactic structure often underdetermines propositional structure. For instance, syntax provides no evidence for the sense of repetition in (5). Rather, this must be provided either by the integrative module for propositional structure or by the syntax–propositional interface module.

Notice how each module is thus domain specific—an integrative processor deals with only one kind of representation, an interface processor with two (we might therefore want to call it "bidomain specific"). Similarly, each module is informationally encapsulated—the only kind of information that can influence it is its designated input level. Through the chaining of integrative and interface processors, we achieve the overwhelmingly complex conversion of acoustic information into meaning. Notice also that if each processor is mandatory and fast, then the chain will be mandatory and (almost as) fast. That is, the effect of Fodor's faculty-sized module is created by the chaining of a series of representation-specific modules.

DIFFERENCES BETWEEN F-MODULARITY AND REPRESENTATIONAL MODULARITY

There are two important differences between this chain of smaller modules and Fodor's (1983) faculty-sized language module. First, it closes a crucial gap in Fodor's conception. As pointed out in the two previous sections, Fodor has no way to get from "shallow representations" (i.e., syntax) to the Language of Thought (i.e., propositional structure). In representational modularity, this function is fulfilled by an interface module that is altogether parallel to the one that mediates between phonology and syntax, which for Fodor falls within the (F-) module for language perception.

A second difference between F-modularity and representational modularity is that the latter permits a single level of representation to be fed simultaneously by multiple interface processors, all of whose outputs are taken into account by the integrative processor in constructing a most coherent representation at that level. A simple case would be the McGurk effect, where an interface processor with visual inputs (specifically mouth configuration) evidently provides information to phonological structure about the composition of phonetic segments. The phonology integrative processor doesn't care which interface processor has provided the input; it just puts the conflicting fragments of information together as best it can. In other words, the phonology processor is still domain specific and informationally encapsulated; it just has a new source of phonological information. But in turn, this new source is an interface processor which (presumably) is likewise constrained; its input is *only* mouth configurations, not hair color or high-level beliefs, and its output is *only* fragments of phonological structure. (We return to the constraints on interface processors in the next section.)

Quite a different case is presented by the sense of body orientation (Lackner, 1981, 1988). Here inputs converge from a wide variety of sensory systems: stretch receptors in the muscles, touch and pressure sensors in the skin, the semicircular canals and otolithic organs in the ear, and of course the visual system and auditory localization. The result is a unified sensation of body position and orientation, which in the present framework can be seen (for a first approximation) as the consequence of a single integrative processor reconciling the inputs from a large number of independent interface modules. Here, if anyplace, is a modular system in Fodor's sense: it is certainly a fast, mandatory, and cognitively impenetrable input system—but with multiple sources of input.

These are cases where multiple processors converge on a single integrative processor. The converse also exists: multiple interface processors that take aspects of the same level of representation as their input. A simple case is auditory representation. Alvin Liberman and colleagues (e.g., Liberman & Studdert-Kennedy, 1977) have argued at length that the auditory-to-phonetic interface processor is a specialized modular device that runs in parallel with ordinary auditory processing (i.e., church-bell and thunder perception), taking the same auditory input and doing different analyses of it. In fact, there appear to be other specialized devices that also use the auditory signal in different ways: voice recognition and auditory affect (tone of voice/emotion) perception. Each of these is known to be subject to differential dissociation due to brain damage (Etcoff, 1986, 1989). That is, the auditory-to-phonetic translation is only one of several specialized devices that diverge from auditory representation.

Likewise, propositional structure is used as input for speaking (via the propositional structure-to-syntax interface), drawing inferences (a process creating new propositional structures from old), and acting (i.e., converting an intention—a kind of propositional structure—into a format of representation that can drive bodily motion such as navigating or reaching). Through the interface to the visual system, its representations can be used to check a verbal claim or an inference against a visual input. Thus propositional structure fulfills its central function by virtue of having many interfaces to different capacities.

A different sort of interface configuration arises in reading aloud. Here visual input drives phonological representation through an interface, but then the information flow goes in both directions: toward pronunciation through the phonology-to-motor interface, but also toward understanding, through the phonology-to-syntax interface (except when reading aloud in a language one does not know!).

Clifton and Ferreira (1987, p. 290) make the cautious hypothesis that "some representational vocabulary—for instance, thematic roles [in my approach an aspect of propositional structure—RJ]—may even be shared between the modules of the grammatical system and the general-purpose system for representing knowledge and beliefs." What I hope to have shown is that it is *necessary* for modules to share information. Total informational encapsulation of a system makes the system totally useless to the rest of the brain. The interaction of integrative and interface modules in the present proposal makes the sharing of information altogether natural.

What about the "slow" central processes posited by Fodor? To the extent that Fodor is correct about belief fixation being relatively slow, isotropic, and Quinean, these properties are now confined to inferential processors which compare newly constructed propositional structures to those present in long-term memory, and which construct further inferences and judgements on the basis of this comparison. If, as I believe, there is a further system of central representations(s) concerned with spatial understanding, this too may well support slow and isotropic inferential processes: consider spatial problems like optimally packing a carton, designing a better mousetrap, and deciding the best route to drive to the other side of the city. That is, inferential processes may well be modular too, though of a different sort than the integrative and interface modules.

THE BIDOMAIN SPECIFICITY OF INTERFACE MODULES

So far I have spoken of an interface module as if it simply has access to its characteristic input representation and produces its characteristic output representation. But we can be more specific, just from looking a bit more closely at the examples presented so far.

Consider the sharing of auditory information among four different interfaces. The auditory-to-phonetic module pays attention to timing and distribution of formant transitions—the information it needs to derive phonetic information. But it is oblivious to the general amplitude and pitch envelope, which are cues to voice and affect recognition. Conversely, the modules for identifying voice and affect are oblivious to the distinctions that identify phonetic segments, but they do detect the cues relevant to their own domains. That is, each interface module makes use of only a subset of the distinctions available in its input representation. Conversely, an interface module need not provide all the sorts of information needed by its output representation: think again of how the auditory-to-phonetic module does not provide word boundaries. Thus, more generally, an interface module can be *more* domain specific than either its input or out- put representation, constrained to deal with only a subset of each.

This characteristic is replicated in other interface modules. The phonology-to-syntax module correlates linear order in its input and output representations. But it knows nothing about aspects of phonological structure such as syllabification, which are relevant to pronunciation but not to syntax, and it knows little about embedding in syntactic structure, which is more relevant to semantics than to phonology.

Similarly, the interface that relates propositional structure to visuospatial understanding knows nothing about such important aspects of propositional structure as scope of quantification, conditionals, illocutionary force, or value. It recognizes only those aspects of propositional structure that deal with objects, their parts, their location, their motion, and perhaps the forces among them. It also does not know everything there is to know about spatial representation: in particular, it probably does not have access to detailed analogue shape information about objects (Landau & Jackendoff, 1993).

In every case, then, the bidomain specificity of the interface processor is limited precisely to those aspects of the two representations that can be directly correlated, while other aspects of each representation are treated as irrelevant, "invisible" to the interface.

A crucial point emerges from this look at the interface modules: we should not think of the mind at all as *translating* or *interpreting* input signals into thoughts. There is no sense, for example, in which syntactic structure is a *translation* of phonological structure; rather, some aspects of it correlate with some aspects of phonological structure, and other aspects of each are independent. That is, we ought to think of the relation between representations created by an interface not as a translation but rather as a sort of partial homology.

In this light, let's consider again the counterexamples to Fodorian modularity mentioned earlier. As suggested in the previous section, the McGurk effect can now be attributed to an additional interface processor that contributes information to the integrative phonology module. But this interface can't tell phonology about all aspects of phonological structure—only those distinctive features that can be detected by visual inspection (lip closure and rounding, and perhaps vowel height) plus perhaps some weak information about degree of stress. Similarly, its input is not all aspects of visual structure, but only those that pertain to the external appearance of the vocal tract. So it implements an extremely limited partial homology between the visual input and phonological structure.

Reading requires a different visual-to-phonological interface. It provides phonology with predominantly segmental information; punctuation gives some information about prosodic bracketing that is also derivable from the auditory signal. However, unlike the auditory-to-phonological interface, reading does not give information about stress (except through use of underlining or italics). And on the other hand, reading gives more reliable information about word boundaries than auditory input. So it too implements a partial homology between visual input and phonological structure—with a quite different selection of visual inputs than the McGurk effect, and with outputs partially overlapping with the auditory-to-phonological mapping.

The timing of beat gestures with stress presents a different partial homology. Basically, beat gestures set up a metrical grid of their own; these must be placed in optimal coincidence with the metrical grid in phonological structure. Every other aspect of phonological structure is irrelevant. A similar though more complex problem occurs in setting texts to music: essentially the musical and linguistic stresses must coincide (within certain degrees of latitude). In each of these cases, all that is required is a highly bidomain specific interface processor that has access to only a subset of phonological information pertaining to rhythm.

Sign language presents a more complex case. Phonological structure is now generally viewed as a collection of semi-independent *tiers*—subsystems that are themselves independent but connected by limited interfaces. These subsystems include segmental sequence, syllabification, morphophonological structure (division into stems, prefixes, and suffixes), stress, and intonation. That is, phonology itself is a microcosm of the larger system. (The same is likely true of propositional structure, where, for instance, information about topic and focus is largely orthogonal to information about thematic roles.) Sign language evidently replaces one of these subsystems—the segmental structure—with a new one linked to visual input, whose distinctive features are things like hand shape and hand movement. But the rest of phonological organization—syllabic, prosodic, and morphological structure, is preserved. Again, it appears that the replacement parts in the system are still highly domain specific and encapsulated.

What begins to bother me here is the proliferation of special-purpose interface processors. The situation is better than an indiscriminate general-purpose processor, because each processor is so limited in what it can do. On the other hand, where do they come from? Do all these pathways of information flow, complete with all their constraints, have to be innate?

I see a couple of possibilities. My inclination is to think that all the levels of representation—the integrative processors—are innate, and that *some* of the interface processors are innate but others are not. The process of reading, for instance, acts like a module in an accomplished reader, but it requires intensive training for most people in a way that the phonology-to-syntax module does not. At this point I don't fully understand the logical and neurological issues involved in making a claim that an interface module is learnable, so I will have to leave it at that.

(A possibly wild suggestion: Suppose there are brain areas for whose use more than one integrative module competes, and which shift allegiances depending on attention. Such an area would be in a position to detect and record fortuitous coincidences in pattern between two modules that are capable of using it. It might therefore be possible for it to *develop* into an interface processor without having any special use for that purpose wired into it from the start.)

THE RELATION OF PROCESSING TO THE LINGUIST'S GRAMMAR

The standard model of generative grammar, handed down in its essentials from Chomsky (1965) and continuing into Government-Binding Theory (GB) (Chomsky, 1981) and the the Minimalist Program (MP) (Chomsky, 1995), conceives of grammar as *syntactocentric* and *derivational*. The central generative capacity of language is concentrated in syntax. An initial stage of syntactic derivation (D-structure in GB, the operation Merge in MP) builds structure, complete with lexical items; then various rules of movement and deletion produce levels of syntactic structure that are subjected to phonological and semantic interpretation. Phonological and semantic structures are conceived of as outputs of a syntactic derivation, with no significant generative capacities of their own.

As has been remarked for decades, this framework of grammatical theory cannot serve directly as a model of processing. We were all taught as graduate students that one should not think of a syntactic derivation as modeling the course of processing: one doesn't think of the initial symbol

S first, then gradually expand it till one chooses the words, then push the pieces around until one finally decides what the sentence means and how to pronounce it. So the notion of derivation has been distanced from processing by calling it "metaphorical"; this term has been applied especially to processes of syntactic "movement."

It seems to me in retrospect that Chomskyan generative grammar could well have seen fit to abandon the syntactocentric assumption in the middle 1970s, but the opportunity was resolutely rejected. At this time phonological theory began to develop autonomously generated tiers of prosodic structure, syllabic structure, and intonation contour, linked by "association lines," and it became clear that these were by no means "continuations" of low-level syntactic derivations. But the autonomy of phonology never came to be recognized in Chomskyan syntax, and today the Minimalist Program (Chomsky, 1995) speaks of "phonological Spell-Out" in terms roughly comparable to those in early generative syntax.

Likewise, by the middle 1970s the extended standard theory had beaten off the challenge from Generative Semantics, which claimed that syntax is just a "continuation" of a derivation whose generative component is made up of semantic elements. Much of this argumentation (Chomsky, 1972; Jackendoff, 1972) concerned the autonomy of syntax from semantics. Yet the next major move in the theory was to institute a syntactic level of Logical Form (LF) (Chomsky, 1979; May, 1985), derived by "covert movement," whose purpose was to make syntax and semantics less autonomous from each other. Before long Chomsky would say (Chomsky, 1986, p. 68) "PF [phonetic form] and LF constitute the 'interface' between language and other cognitive systems, yielding direct representations of sound on the one hand and meaning on the other. . . ."

In this statement, Chomsky (1986) elides the fact on which so much has hinged in the present chapter: an interface has to implement a relationship between two distinct representations. Hence it cannot be derivational in the standard sense, changing one structure into another built out of the same primitives. That is, the interface between syntax and meaning—not to mention that between syntax and phonology—cannot be like moving elements around in a tree, interior to a syntactic derivation. Nor can the systems dealing with meaning and phonology make any sense out of a syntactic tree. So a grammar by necessity needs components that establish relationships among these disparate formats. A syntactic level alone cannot "yield a direct representation of meaning." (Incidentally, I must say that it is hard to believe that Chomsky could be guilty of such an elementary formal error. But, despite a fairly extensive correspondence with him about this issue, I sadly see no alternative.)

Several independent factions in generative grammar have been attracted to a different conception of grammar, a *constraint-based* theory, in which the notion of derivation is replaced by a set of "declarative" constraints on well-formedness of grammatical structures, and which characterize relatedness between constructions by means other than syntactic movement.

Constraint-based frameworks include Head-driven Phrase Structure Grammar (Pollard & Sag, 1994), Lexical-functional Grammar (Bresnan, 1982), Construction Grammar (Fillmore & Kay, 1993; Goldberg, 1995), Role and Reference Grammar (Van Valin & LaPolla, 1997), Autolexical Syntax (Sadock, 1991), Multidimensional Categorial Grammar (Bach, 1983), Autosegmental Phonology (Goldsmith, 1976), and Optimality Theory (Prince & Smolensky, 1993; Grimshaw, 1997); a similar architecture is proposed for musical structure (though involving quite different representations) by Lerdahl and Jackendoff (1983).

An important characteristic of many of these approaches is that they admit multiple sources of generative capacity—multiple autonomous levels of structure, each characterized by its own set of constraints, plus sets of linking (or interface) constraints that establish the connections among the levels. Jackendoff (1997) proposes a general form for such architectures that incorporates the basic insights of these approaches. In such frameworks, a well-formed sentence must have well-formed structures in each component, connected in a well-formed fashion by linking constraints. In other words, the syntactocentric conception of grammar has been abandoned in favor of one in which syntax is but one among several generative components.

The interesting feature of these architectures in the present context is how nicely they map into models of processing. One can see the constraints specific to a particular level as principles applied by the integrative processor for that level; likewise, the linking constraints are the business of the interface processors. The constraints within a level are nondirectional, so that one can use them to build (or activate) structures from the bottom up or from the top down. The interface constraints are likewise nondirectional, so that one can, for instance, use them to build (or activate) partial syntactic structures based on phonological input— or equally well vice versa. Moreover, the interface constraints can be used directly to generate feedback, so that for instance, in perception, semantic-to-syntactic and syntactic-to-phonological constraints can together serve to constrain phonological analysis, as in (10) above.

In addition, the role of the lexicon becomes clearer. In the standard architecture, lexical items are inserted into initial syntactic derivations, then carried through the derivation until they are "interpreted" semantically and phonologically. This of course bears no relation to a theory of processing.

In a constraint-based theory, the account is quite different. A lexical item is a long-term memory association of a phonological structure, a collection of syntactic features, and a meaning (propositional structure). It can therefore be viewed as part of the linking constraints: if, for instance, the sound /kæt/ is present in phonological structure, this licenses a linked singular count noun in syntactic structure and a linked meaning [CAT] in conceptual structure. In other words, a lexical item is a small-scale linking rule, and the lexicon in general is to be thought of as part of the interface components from phonology to syntax and from syntax to semantics.

This said, it is easy to see the role of lexical access in processing. Consider first perception. The auditory-to-phonetic interface dumps a raw sequence of phonetic segments in the lap of the phonology integrative module. In order to figure out where to place the word boundaries, the phonology module sends out a call to the lexicon: "Does anybody out there sound like this?" (i.e., does that phonological structure of any item match this raw input?) And various lexical items pipe up, "Me!" (i.e., become activated). But by virtue of becoming activated, a lexical item doesn't just activate its phonology: it also activates its syntax and semantics, and thus establishes partial structures in those domains and partial linking to the phonology.

Similarly in production: suppose one has a complex conceptual structure one wants to express. Then the semantics-to-syntax processor sends a call to the lexicon: "Does anybody out there mean this?" And various candidates raise their hands: "Me!" and thereby become activated. But by virtue of becoming activated, they also activate their syntax and phonology, and thus establish partial structures in those domains and partial linking to the intended message.

I don't think there is anything new about this idea in processing: it is just that it corresponds so nicely to the view of lexical items that falls out of the constraint-based approach to grammar.

The upshot, then, is that representational modularity is a variant of modularity that, unlike F-modularity, can be brought into a very close and appealing relation to a variant of generative grammar that is independently of interest—though a relation to standard generative grammar is as distant as ever.

DEGREES OF MODULARITY

In talking with people about modularity, I often get the impression that they think of a modular capacity as entirely independent of the rest of the mind. And that is indeed what domain specificity and informational encapsulation seem to imply—just the opposite of isotropic and Quinean (i.e., maximally connected). But, as stressed several times already, an entirely domain-specific and informationally encapsulated module would be functionally disconnected from the rest of the mind, and could therefore serve no purpose in the larger goal of helping the organism perceive and behave.

The view of modularity developed here invites a middle road, because an important part of the hypothesis is how modules communicate with each other, namely, through interface modules. In particular, the means by which the language faculty communicates with central cognition is of precisely the same essential character as the means by which the various subparts of the language faculty communicate with each other. So no module is entirely informationally encapsulated.

To make clearer how Fodor's (1983) original agenda now plays itself out, it is worthwhile reviewing what domain specificity and informational encapsulation mean in the present framework.

The domain specificity of an integrative module has to do with the range of distinctions encoded by the level of representation with which this module deals. The phonology module deals exclusively with phonological distinctions—and its subcomponents are even more domain specific: the stress tier deals only with stress grids, for instance. The propositional structure module deals with propositional organization of thought; the spatial structure module deals with the shape, location, and motion of physical objects (and like phonology it may well divide into subcomponents).

The domain specificity of an interface module is better termed "bi-domain specificity": it has to do with the range of distinctions that the module is sensitive to in both its input and output representations. As we have seen, an interface module may be more domain specific than the integrative modules it connects; the "McGurk" module is an especially good example of a very narrowly specific interface module.

Informational encapsulation is a bit more complex. It seems to me that we can't talk properly about *the* informational encapsulation of a module. Rather, we have to talk about it in relational terms. The original intuition is that the speaker's hair color can't affect phonetic perception—a relational statement. The more general question is: to what degree does a distinction D_1 in one representation R_1 have a bearing on a distinction D_2 in representation R_2? For instance, word boundaries in phonology have a direct reflection in syntactic structure; so syntax is not at all encapsulated with respect to this aspect of phonology. Similarly, embedding in syntactic structure is closely related to embedding in corresponding propositional structure, so there is little encapsulation here.

For a more distant case, motion detected in the visual field (or detection of someone's hair color, for that matter) *can* affect propositional structure through the spatial-to-propositional interface, and, if expressed in language, have an indirect effect on produced phonological structure through the chain of interfaces. Even the output of the semicircular canals may have an effect on phonological structure (the speaker may say "I'm dizzy!"), but the effect is distant, mediated by a long chain of intermediate representations and interfaces.

On the other hand, the motion of the speaker's *lips* may have a *direct* effect on phonological structure, through the "McGurk" interface. So here, in a very small domain, gerrymandered in both input and output components, we have more information flow, and more direct information flow, than in random aspects of vision and phonology.

In other words, the presence of an interface between two representations is what makes them *not* informationally encapsulated from each other. The extent of the information flow depends on the degree to which the interface module is more domain specific than the representations it connects. The phonology-to-syntax interface is relatively rich; the "McGurk" interface is not.

In principle, an interface module might be precisely as domain specific as its input and output representations. This would mean that every distinction in the input representation could make a difference in the output representation, and every distinction in the output representation could be affected by something in the input representation. In such a case, though, it would hardly make sense to speak of two distinct "modules" any more: their interactions would be more or less unconstrained. We might as well see the union of their domains as a single larger domain, and we might as well see the interface module just as a part of the principles involved in integrating this larger domain.

It therefore begins to make sense to speak of "degrees of modularity" rather than absolute modularity. Two domains connected by a narrow "information bottleneck" will be relatively modular: not very many parts of each domain can affect the other. As the interface becomes richer, more parts can interact. If communication between the two domains is wide open, it is impossible to say where one leaves off and the other begins. Given the gradual nature of this transition from relatively modular to nonmodular, it is impossible to say exactly where modularity leaves off.

A cynic might say therefore that the issue of modularity is dissolved. I would disagree. Rather it develops into a more nuanced set of questions: What families of distinctions form richly interconnected and well-integrated domains, and where are there more restricted "informational bottlenecks"? The correlates in processing are as they always have been:

Can one identify particular stages of informational integration, enhanced by priming or disrupted by concurrent load in the same domain? Can these stages be identified with discrete levels of representation in the formal theory? To what extent can these stages be temporally distinguished in the course of processing and/or spatially distinguished by brain imaging? To what extent can they be differentially disrupted by brain damage? It seems to me that this slightly more nuanced viewpoint on modularity leaves unaffected all the standard issues in processing. Perhaps it can spare us continuation of some of the needless debate of the 15 years.

ACKNOWLEDGMENTS

It is a pleasure to be able to honor Edgar Zurif by contributing to the present volume. I'm not sure how to translate my admiration of Edgar into the medium of cold public print. Suffice it to say that, although he has elevated whining into an artform (and is happy to acknowledge it), you don't have to go very deep before you encounter a thoroughgoing mensch of the greatest professional and personal integrity. I have been honored to have him as a colleague and friend for these last 15 years.

This paper originated in remarks on Fodorian modularity presented at an MIT Cognitive Science colloquium in fall 1991, which explains the datedness of many of the references. Nevertheless, I believe that many of the misunderstandings enumerated here still persist, so that despite the passage of time the discussion is still pertinent. In particular, almost everything said here about F-modularity applies as well to the version of modularity in Fodor (2000).

REFERENCES

Altmann, G. (1987). Modularity and interaction in sentence processing. In J. Garfield (Ed.), *Modularity in knowledge representation and natural-language processing* (pp. 249–258). Cambridge, MA: MIT Press.

Arbib, M. (1987). Modularity and interaction of brain regions underlying visuomotor coordination. In J. Garfield (Ed.), *Modularity in knowledge representation and natural-language processing* (pp. 333–364). Cambridge, MA: MIT press.

Bach, E. (1983). On the relation between word-grammar and phrase-grammar. *Natural Language and Linguistic Theory, 1*, 65–90.

Bever, T. (1992). The logical and extrinsic sources of modularity. In M. Gunnar & M. Maratsos (Eds.), *Modularity and constraints in language and cognition* (Vol. 25 of the Minnesota Symposia on Child Psychology, pp. 179–212). Hillsdale, NJ: Erlbaum.

Bresnan, J. (Ed.). (1982). *The mental representation of grammatical relations.* Cambridge, MA: MIT Press.

Carroll, P. J., & Slowiaczek, M. L. (1987). Modes and modules: Multiple paths to the language processor. In J. Garfield (Ed.), *Modularity in knowledge representation and natural-language processing* (pp. 221–248). Cambridge, MA: MIT Press.

Chomsky, N. (1965). *Aspects of the theory of syntax.* Cambridge, MA: MIT Press.

Chomsky, N. (1972) *Studies on semantics in generative grammar.* The Hague: Mouton.

Chomsky, N. (1979). *Language and responsibility.* New York: Pantheon.

Chomsky, N. (1981) *Lectures on government and binding.* Dordrecht: Foris.

Chomsky, N. (1986) *Knowledge of language.* New York: Praeger.

Chomsky, N. (1995) *The Minimalist Program.* Cambridge, MA: MIT Press.

Clifton, C. & Ferreira, F. (1987). Modularity in sentence comprehension. In J. Garfield (Ed.), *Modularity in knowledge representation and natural-language processing* (pp. 277–290). Cambridge, MA: MIT Press.

Crain, S. & Steedman, M. (1985). On not being led up the garden path. In D. Dowty, L. Kartunnen, & A. M. Zwicky (Eds.), *Natural language parsing: Psycholinquistic, computational, and theoretical perspectives.* Cambridge: Cambridge University Press.

Etcoff, N. L. (1986). The neuropsychology of emotional expression. In G. Goldstein & R. E. Tarter (Eds.), *Advances in clinical neuropsychology* (vol. 3). New York: Plenum.

Etcoff, N. L. (1989). Asymmetries in recognition of emotion. In F. Boller & J. Grafman (Eds.), *Handbook of neuropsychology* (vol. 3, pp. 363–382). New York: Elsevier Science Publishers.

Fillmore, C., & Kay, P. (1993). *Construction grammar coursebook.* Berkeley, CA: University of California, Copy Central.

Fodor, J. (1975). *The language of thought.* Cambridge, MA: Harvard University Press.

Fodor, J. (1983). *The modularity of mind.* Cambridge, MA: MIT Press.

Fodor, J. (2000). *The mind doesn't work that way: The scope and limits of computational psychology.* In press.

Fodor, J., & Lepore, E. (1998). The emptiness of the lexicon: Reflections on James Pustejovsky's the generative lexicon. *Linguistic Inquiry, 29,* 269–288.

Fodor J., Garrett, M., Walker E., & Parkes, C. (1980). Against definitions. *Cognition, 8,* 263–367.

Fodor, J., Garrett, M., & Swinney, D. (1992). A modular effect in parsing. Unpublished manuscript.

Frazier, L. (1987). Theories of sentence processing. In J. Garfield (Ed.), *Modularity in knowledge representation and natural-language processing* (pp. 291–308). Cambridge, MA: MIT Press.

Garfield, J. (1987). *Modularity in knowledge representation and natural-language processing.* Cambridge, MA: MIT Press.

Goldberg, A. (1995). *Constructions: A Construction Grammar approach to argument structure.* Chicago: University of Chicago Press.

Goldsmith, J. (1976). *Autosegmental phonology* (Doctoral dissertation, MIT) Indiana University Linguistics Club, Bloomington.

Grimshaw, J. (1997). Projection, heads and optimality. *Linguistic Inquiry, 28,* 373–422.

Jackendoff, R. (1972). *Semantic interpretation in generative grammar.* Cambridge, MA: MIT Press.

Jackendoff, R. (1987). *Consciousness and the computational mind.* Cambridge, MA: MIT Press.

Jackendoff, R. (1997). *The architecture of the language faculty.* Cambridge, MA: MIT Press.

Lackner, J. (1981). Some contributions of touch, pressure, and kinesthesis to human spatial orientation and oculomotor control. *Acta Astronautica, 8,* 825–830.

Lackner, J. (1988). Some proprioceptive influences on the perceptual representation of body shape and orientation. *Brain, 111,* 281-297.

Landau, B. & Jackendoff, R. (1993). "What" and "where" in spatial language and spatial cognition. *Behavioral and Brain Sciences, 16,* 217–238.

Lerdahl, F., & Jackendoff, R. (1983). *A generative theory of tonal music.* Cambridge, MA: MIT Press.

Levelt, W. J. M. (1989). *Speaking.* Cambridge, MA: MIT Press.

Liberman, A., & Studdert-Kennedy, M. (1977). Phonetic perception. In R. Held, H. Leibowitz, & H. L. Teuber (Eds.), *Handbook of sensory physiology: Vol 8; Perception.* Heidelberg: Springer-Verlag.

Macnamara, J. (1978). How do we talk about what we see? Manuscript, McGill University.

Marslen-Wilson, W., & Tyler, L.K. (1987). Against modularity. In J. Garfield (Ed.), *Modularity in knowledge representation and natural-language processing* (pp. 37–62). Cambridge, MA: MIT Press.

May R. (1985). *Logical form: Its structure and derivation.* Cambridge, MA: MIT Press.

McGurk, H., & MacDonald, J. (1976). Hearing lips and seeing voices. *Nature (London), 264,* 746–748.

Piñango, M. M., Zurif, E., & Jackendoff, R. (1999). Real-time processing implications of enriched composition at the syntax-semantics interface. *Journal of Psycholinguistic Research, 28,* 395–414.

Pollard, C., & Sag, I. (1994). *Head-driven Phrase Structure Grammar.* Chicago: University of Chicago Press.

Prince, A., & Smolensky, P. (1993). *Optimality Theory: Constraint interaction in generative grammar.* Piscataway, NJ: Rutgers University Center for Cognitive Science.

Sadock, J. M. (1991). *Autolexical syntax.* Chicago: University of Chicago Press.

Sag, I., & Pollard, C. (1991). An integrated theory of complement control. *Language, 67,* 63–113.

Talmy, L. (1978). The relation of grammar to cognition—A synopsis. In D. Waltz (Ed.), *Theoretical issues in natural language processing 2* (pp. 14–24. New York: Association for Computing Machinery.

Tanenhaus, M. K., Spivey-Knowlton, M. J., Eberhard, K. M., & Sedivy, J. C. (1995). Integration of visual and linguistic information in spoken language comprehension. *Science, 268,* 1632–1634.

Van Valin, R. D., & LaPolla, R. J. (1997). *Syntax: Structure, meaning, and function.* Cambridge: Cambridge University Press.

Chapter 2

Remarks on the Architecture of Language Processing Systems

Merrill Garrett

THE GOALS OF THE DISCUSSION

I will note some of the recurrent conflicts among experimental outcomes that rely on behavioral indices of parsing (various response time and error measures). These controversies may be understood in terms of two additional data classes: a recent series of eye-movement studies that supports strong interactive claims re parsing, and an equally recent series of event related potential (ERP) studies that supports modular systems. I will argue that the various conflicts between empirical findings require a resolution in terms of a filtering model, and sketch the outline of such a proposal. The essential feature of the resolution lies in using the language production system as the source of the apparent conceptual and discourse level constraints on parsing. Further, because the evidence from language production itself indicates a modular architecture, this approach is one that embeds the full range of interactive processing claims in an architecture that preserves the essential correspondence between the informational structure in formal grammar and the processing types in real-time language performance systems.

A BACKGROUND ASSUMPTION

When we contemplate language processing questions, there are multiple sources that we draw on to constrain theoretical claims. These begin with formal grammars, and should in a quite real sense, end with formal grammars. When we ask how words are learned, recognized, pronounced, integrated in utterance, or interpreted in their discourse ensembles, we pose those questions in terms of structural features that grammars associate with words as a function of their embedding in grammatical rule systems.

We know at the outset that the classes of structure that capture the major distributional features of language expression will govern our attempts to discover real-time information processing accounts of language comprehension, production, acquisition, evolution, and dissolution. The vocabulary of processing descriptions incorporates phonetic, phonological, morphological, lexical, syntactic, and semantic variables. Formal grammars array these facets of language structure in somewhat variable ways, modulo some variation in the goals of linguistic theory embraced by different theoretical camps (see Newmeyer, 1998, for an enlightening historical reprise of the contemporary scene in linguistics). But, withal, the major threads are woven in impressively similar design: aspects of form and content lead intertwined but distinct lives. Grammatical structure is diverse across languages in this regard, but it is not haphazard. The theories of real-time language use that our research generates must afford an answer to the question of how languages could display the structure they do, given the processing account we offer. Processing accounts that fail such a test require amendment, extension, or abandonment.

SOME EXPERIMENTAL EXAMPLES AND PERSPECTIVES FROM PARSING STUDIES

Research in comprehension has played out against a background of claims for the centrality of syntax in the architecture of processing systems. Modular systems theory has assigned a central role to the construction of syntactic representations for sentences during the comprehension process (e.g., Forster, 1979; Foder, 1983; Frazier, 1990; Gorrell, 1995; Crocker, 1996). By contrast, some accounts that emphasize interactive processing perspectives eschew specifically syntactic representation in favor of a direct mapping from lexical inputs to a discourse model via a mixed computation that combines syntactic, semantic, and pragmatic constraints (e.g., Marslen-Wilson & Tyler, 1987). Interaction can be described in several different ways, and not all interactive proposals treat relations among the potential information types in the same ways—see, for example, Altman and Steedman (1988) for a discussion that highlights important distinctions. More recently, some varieties of constraint based parsing rely on an ensemble of statistically based conditions on the use of lexical items that includes a range of linguistic and nonlinguistic properties, without principled distinctions among the types (McClelland, St. John, & Taraban, 1989; MacDonald, Pearlmutter, & Seidenberg, 1994; Spivey & Tannenhaus, 1998). Interpretation is based on the lexical string and the bundle of interacting constraints associated with each element; interpretation is direct and without an identifiable mediating syntactic representation. There is, of course, theme and variation among these positions, with varying takes on the relevance of syntactic representations and on the relation of the processing claims to grammatical theory. I mean here only to swing a broad brush.

The first thing to note is that all theoretical camps have their ammunition. We do not lack for observations that testify to seemingly systematic aspects of the language comprehension profile. They do not line up in sterling orderly rows, however.

On the one hand, numerous studies report findings that parsing performance is unresponsive to clearly available semantic bias: research with rapid serial visual presentation (RSVP), self-paced reading, cross-modal priming, naming and lexical decision latency, and several cousins and variants of these provide examples of processing circumstances in which plausible construals of sentence contents would dictate analyses other than the one listeners or readers appear to (momentarily at least) embrace. Frazier (1999) in a recent book remarks on the import of the intuitions we have about our processing of this example:

a gift for a boy in a box

Intuition testifies what systematic experiment affirms: the boy is initially in the box. Why indeed is the plausible attribution not the governing one? Evidently because the processes of phrasal assignment and interpretation of the consequent structure are "faster" than the inference that gifts are more likely to be in boxes than are boys. Various answers can and have been offered, and we will touch on some in later sections. But, examples like this one show that rather general terms *(boy)* linked to structurally versatile elements *(in)* may resist the influence of specific and available commonsense relations *(gift in box)* while accepting uncommon ones *(boy in box)*. The message that this conveys to many observers is that interpretive constraints on the processing of sentence form are distinct from syntactically driven ones. The experimental literature provides a variety of illustrations implicating a wide range of structures [see references cited above; see also Frazier & Clifton (1996) for pertinent further discussions]. The example cited above implicates prepositional phrase attachment—a favorite stalking horse for debates about syntactic and semantic/pragmatic interaction to which we will return. I will say little more about indicators that available semantic and conceptual constraint have limited impact on parsing decisions and will spend more ink on evidence for the contrary position for reasons that will become obvious.

So, on the other hand, we may likewise cite a variety of rather similar studies reporting results supporting the claim that lexical recognition and parsing procedures are intrinsically subject to semantic bias. To illustrate briefly, a long-running experimental attack on the modularity question is represented in the work of Marslen-Wilson and Tyler (their 1987 paper reviews several relevant findings). A representative example (Tyler & Marslen-Wilson, 1977) illustrates an important point about the sort of contextual constraint they tested. It focused on the likelihood of interpreting an ambiguous phrase like "landing planes" as a plural noun phrase (NP) ("Landing planes are very noisy near an airport") or a singular gerundive nominal ("Landing planes is dangerous in a storm"). The experimental effect of an immediately prior context ("If you are standing near the runway . . . " vs. "If you are not a trained pilot . . .") was evaluated by reaction time for choice between the variants of the linking verb "is/are" following the ambiguous phrase. Reaction time (RT) was faster for targets compatible with the prior context sentence. The significant point is that the interpretive force of the context was available within the few hundred millisecond time frame required for a lexical choice that fit one of two competing syntactic analyses of the ambiguous phrase. The contextual constraint is at the sentence/discourse level.

Work by Crain and Steedman (1985) and others also implicates interpretation of discourse structure in parsing. That influential work indicates that the likelihood of interpreting a verb phrase as a relative clause modifier rather than as a main verb is influenced by the discourse setting: contrasts between single protagonist settings versus dual protagonist settings (for NP interpretation) shows the latter promotes relative clause analyses [i.e., fitting with continuation (a) rather than (b) in the example].

the teachers *taught by the Berlitz method* . . .

(a) . . . were very successful   /   (b) . . . but couldn't get jobs anyway

The significant observation is that the tendency to analyze the material following the initial NP (e.g., "the teachers") as a relative modifier is enhanced by appositeness to the discourse (i.e., when a relative is needed to distinguish among potential referents in the discourse). This work is one of several to address the analysis of garden paths in reduced relatives of the venerable "horse raced past the barn" ilk (Bever, 1970). Other work by Trueswell and Tannenhaus (1994) with the same structure reports that an inanimate NP eliminates the garden path effect so generally observed; for example:

the *fossil* examined . . . versus the *archeologist* examined . . .

Here the focus is on lexical effects rather than the broader scale of the discourse.

Of particular interest to the discussion here are studies of lexical constraints that evaluate argument structure effects (see Carlson & Tanenhaus, 1988). These implicate a combination of subcategorization frames and thematic structure, namely, the structural configurations that can be associated with a lexical item and the semantic/conceptual roles (agent, theme, . . .) occupied by the NPs in the structure. With respect to the first variable, subcategorization frames, questions may be posed both regarding the extent to which detailed subcategorization information is immediately recruited and, to the extent that it is, how the information is deployed. There is evidence for effects that seem to ignore subcategorization (e.g., postulation of a trace following an intransitive verb; see, for example, Mitchell, 1994, among others), and evidence that supports early availability and application of such information. These latter are combined with assessment of whether different verbs have different preference orderings for the class of structural options that can be associated with them. So, for example, a comparison may involve verbs that prefer a direct object versus those that prefer a sentence complement (from Trueswell & Kim, 1998):

The man accepted the prize.

The man accepted (that) the prize was not going to him.

For the example pair, the direct object analysis with *prize* as theme is preferred over the sentence complement analysis. By contrast, for a verb like "expected", the preference would be shifted more into balance between the two options, and for a verb like "realize," the sentence complement analysis would be strongly dominant. Self-paced reading tasks and eye-movement studies show reprocessing effects for the complement versions that are interpretable as reflections of these differences (e.g., reprocessing in the disambiguating regions following verbs like "accept" and "expect," but not verbs like "realize"). One may, as Trueswell and Tanenhaus (1994) and several others have done, profitably combine subcategorization bias with thematic role assignment, for the latter reflect plausibility factors: the readiness with which available NPs for argument slots suit their thematic roles affects processing time. The demonstration of lexical biases and of the interaction of plausibility with those biases is a matter to which we will return.

A considerable body of work on parsing examines the analysis of prepositional phrases, namely, the structure with which we began this brief excursion, and which, by the observation made there, clearly may run counter to locally available practical knowledge derivable from the lexical elements in the target sentence. But, work by various investigators (see, e.g., McClelland et al., 1989) argues that the likelihood of interpreting a prepositional phrase as an instrumental adverbial phrase ("they saw the man with the binoculars but couldn't recognize him") or as a reduced relative clause modifier ("they saw the man with the binoculars had a red hat on") can be influenced by the relative plausibility of the relations among the lexical constituents. Clearly, the matters of timing and measurement, plus the nature of the constraint type will bulk large in sorting through the experimental space. In these and other examples, we see different kinds of nonsyntactic interpretive constraint at work. Note the very important differences between the application of constraints that inhere in the meaning of individual lexical items and those that depend on contingent facts merely associated with the interpretation of a word, or that cannot be determined from an individual lexical entry at all but instead arise via the interpretation of phrase, sentence, and discourse. One will see the import of a processing effect that relies, for example, on the fact that dogs are animate physical objects in a different light than one that relies on our knowledge that they may tend to bite, or do not read newspapers, or that one may be alleged to have only three legs. This is true both in terms of practical matters such as the likely time course of access to different informational classes and in terms of the import of observed effects of the various constraints vis-à-vis the rationalization of relations between grammars and parsers.

A particularly salient example of this is the following: recent studies of eye movement suggest that mere observation of the layout of a visual array can directly affect the attachment preferences for prepositional phrases. Using eye-tracking measures, Tanenhaus et al. (1995) report that attachment follows the implied contrasts in a visual array: "put the apple on the napkin" is variously interpreted—and immediately so, re the eye pointing measure—depending on whether an unambiguous locative analysis or a relative modifier is apposite. To observe that the mere experience of a visual scene directly translates to a linguistic bias seems the very epiphany of nonmodularity. Were it so in just those terms, what would be left of the notion of *informational encapsulation* of linguistic representation? A less tendentious way to put the matter is that some mechanism brings the conceptual force of the visual information to bear on language with great rapidity. Is it a parsing influence? I set this aside for the moment, but note that such a case highlights the need for an account of why constraints are variously effective. If the informational representations that drive language processing were, in fact, genuinely integrated as some interpretations of the eye-movement data would have it, what stops the seamless workings of this in other experimental situations?

Overall, outcomes are mixed and the picture is one that defies easy summary. Multiple structural types have been evaluated. Some appear to be more susceptible to interpretive manipulation than others. So, for example, prepositional phrase attachments have come in for a great deal of attention—in part because of the substantial variation one can induce in attachment preference as a function of the interpretation of the sentence. By contrast, the effects of semantic constraint on direct object/sentence complement ambiguities (as in "the child knew the answer to the problem was in the book") are murkier. Experiments that focus on implicit structural elements (e.g., empty categories or structural traces of varying sort) present still another variable scene (see, e.g., Nicol & Swinney, 1989, for some general commentary).

Given the state of affairs just described, one might suppose that we are not in a position to draw confident conclusions about how modular or nonmodular syntactic processes in language comprehension may be. Why does the biasing work sometimes and not others? For some tasks, but not others? And what does it mean vis-à-vis the general question of the underlying architecture if we accept that there are significant materials and task specificity to these effects? Lots of folk would argue they can provide the answers to such questions strictly within the domain of design and paradigm. But I doubt that the answer lies in systematic incompetence on either side. At the center of this is the question whether the primary determinants of the variability are principled in terms of processing types, or merely adventitious—accidents of strength and timing.

A paper by Bever, Sanz, and Townsend (1998) puts the matter in terms of a set of *propositions of the debate* (here, slightly rephrased):

If syntax is modular, nonsyntactic information can't affect it.

Syntax processing is absolute rather than probabilistic.

Sentence comprehension could rest solely on distributed cues of diverse type, without recourse to sentence level syntax.

If syntax is necessary for comprehension, syntactic assignment must precede interpretation.

Syntactic properties of sentences are not affected by conceptual beliefs.

All are denied under their analysis for various reasons—some of which I will take note of here. The resolution of the contrasting views as suggested by Bever et al. incorporates the constraint satisfaction approach into a system of strategies that is applied for initial analysis. But, the proposal preserves syntactic processing as a backup and confirmatory system, and as a system that provides deeper and more sophisticated analysis of sentence form. Detailed syntax is a *late processing* phenomenon on this view. This constitutes at bottom an analysis-by-synthesis (ABS) procedure that embeds the grammar as a generative source (see, e.g., Fodor, Bever, & Garrett, 1974, for an early but still useful exposition). The solution that is pursued structures the architecture of the comprehension system so that it accommodates the interactive observations, while preserving a role for specifically syntactic representation in the ABS system.

This proposal seeks to avoid the "mystery" of why we need a grammar in the context of comprehension mechanisms that ignore the typology of information that grammars robustly display. It does so by postulating that grammars are necessary psychological components in two senses: First, they are essential to account for language acquisition. Bever et al. (1998) note with some justice that development of a distributed network representation of grammatical targets requires targets to train on. There is no bootstrap to be fished out of the constraint sea for this purpose. And, second, they afford a principled resource for evaluation and revision of analyses delivered by the constraint satisfaction comprehension system. This seems cogent, but I am inclined to be even more exigent. Aspects of this approach are quite attractive as a synthetic effort. But, there are some features of the proposal that I have reservations about, and some empirical observations that suggest the need for specifically syntactic processes that are earlier than a late stage cleanup and elaboration function. Various experimental findings suggest that basic syntactic structure is assigned very rapidly (e.g., differences in the recovery of sentence content for syntactically well formed and ill formed sentences presented in RSVP and same–different matching modes; see Forster, 1979, for an instructive analysis of some rate issues). It may be that here, as has from time to time been suggested, one should distinguish between early stage parsing that is of rather limited scope and later stage parsing that has deeper structural issues to resolve. The Bever et al. treatment has that logical character, but treats the early stage as genuinely different in kind from the later stage, namely, an "approximate, strategic mode"—done in whole or in part by constraint satisfaction methods versus a "rule mode" of symbolic calculation.

Though I think the behavioral evidence for early stage, specifically syntactic operations, is quite relevant, I will not pursue it here, in part because there is lots of discussion available without my two cents worth, and in part because I want to focus on evidence of similar import that derives from electrophysiological studies of language processing. The convergence of such data with the behavioral patterns that show modular architecture is quite forceful.

THE ELECTROPHYSIOLOGICAL RECORD

Recording systems using scalp electrodes for detection of electrical activity in the brain have been with us for some decades (*eeg systems*). But the most recent decade has seen the culmination of many years of patient effort by a relative handful of very able investigators who were seeking to develop the necessary technology and methodology to examine cognitive processes with this tool. Their work has combined with the advent of new microelectronic and computational tools to make the approach much more generally available to the scientific community. Much of the resulting research of relevance to our purpose here uses event related potential (ERP) techniques to look for characteristic patterns of brain activity elicited by informationally (e.g., linguistically) defined stimulus classes. Electrical records are time-locked to stimulus onset, and the records for many instances of a given stimulus type are averaged across trials to extract the regularities of response to the type. Evidence from that work and from related studies using brain imaging technology indicates the existence of brain systems responsive to specifically syntactic properties of sentence structure. These syntactically driven ERP patterns can and have been quite systematically compared and contrasted with electrophysiological complexes that show selective response to interpretive aspects of sentence structure. The structural properties that give rise to the former are readily associated with conventional grammatical distinctions. The central presumption for interpretation of these patterns is straightforward: If one presumes that the linguistic analyses we work with in language are partly or largely artifacts of linguistic analysis and not representative of the computational structures that are responsible for language use, then we would not expect to find uniform brain consequences of the distinctions drawn by such artifice.

Several reviews provide excellent introductory treatments of the methodology for language studies and summary descriptions of recent findings. I, therefore, provide little such assistance here; see, for example, Coulson, King, and Kutas (1998); Friederici (1998a); Hagoort, Brown, and Osterhout (1999). Some salient points are cited below for brief illustration of the range of observation in play for purposes of the argument underway in this essay; reference to "N400," "P600," and "LAN" follows current labeling practices for the major response types of interest.

ERP responses to semantic congruity were established by Kutas and Hilyard (1980), namely, variation in the N400 response to "goodness of fit" of a lexical item to its sentential context. And from the outset, and in many subsequent studies, N400 was shown to be indifferent to syntactic well-formedness. Neville et al. (1991) reported syntactically specific effects in a direct comparison of semantic and syntactic violations in closely matched sentence pairs visually presented. They reported an early negative polarity complex largely focused on left anterior recording sites and emerging around 250–300 ms poststimulus (i.e., timed from the point of first logically possible detection of the deviance in the string), with maximum amplitude around 400 ms (a pattern now generally referred to as an LAN response for *left anterior negativity*). It was elicited by major category violations and by a wh-movement violation. That pattern is similar in timing and configuration to the N400 response elicited by semantically implausible lexical targets, but it appears at quite different recording locations from those associated with the N400. In fact, when the two violation types were contrasted in the same sentence frames (as Neville et al. did), the two responses were complementarily distributed vis-à-vis recording sites: for semantic violations, primarily posterior sites were activated, with greater prominence on the right, but for syntactic violations, sites were strongly left anterior. On that evidence, distinct patterns of neural activity arise from the two types of violations.

Osterhout and colleagues in several publications have reported a strong and sustained positive polarity shift observable bilaterally and at most recording sites starting around 500 ms and peaking at 600–700 ms after the point of a syntactic violation. A group at the Max Planck Institute in Nijmegen led by Hagoort and Brown has also provided extensive analysis of this ERP complex for Dutch language materials. This response (P600) is observed for agreement violations and subcategorization violations as well as for phrasal violations (Hagoort, Brown, & Groothusen, 1993; Osterhout & Holcomb, 1992; Osterhout, Holcomb, & Swinney, 1994); this prominent positive shift response was also observed for Neville et al.'s (1991) phrase structure violations. Though it is rather later than either the LAN or the N400, it is well to keep in mind that the temporal indicators with this methodology, while powerful and affording considerable precision, have some limitations. In particular, we are not entitled to assume that the processing events that cause the ERP pattern did not arise until the point of our ability to detect it with our measure. We can be confident they arose no later than that point but the possibility exists that a chain of events is set in motion by the stimulus features at some earlier point (but does not immediately "surface" for our observation), and is detectable for us only after some delay. Having said this, I will nevertheless at a later point entertain some intriguing speculations that use the observed temporal order of the various semantic and syntactic responses as their base.

Two additional features of work by the Nijmegen group on P600 patterns for Dutch language materials are of special interest here. One is their observation of an N400 complex that often appeared at ends of syntactically deviant sentences. They suggested this might reflect a kind of interference (arising from the earlier occurring syntactic analysis problems) with closure or interpretive "wrap-up" processes of semantic integration for the sentence as whole. On that understanding, this effect is an indication of some contingent relations among the hypothesized processing types. Yet another demonstration of this from their work uses "syntactic prose" (much in the manner of earlier word monitoring experiments by Marslen-Wilson & Tyler, 1980) in which the test "sentences" mirrored the syntactic organization of their initial experimentation (including all the violation types) but lacked semantic coherence. In such sentences, structure is signaled only by sequence of grammatical class and inflection because the major content items are randomly substituted for (with preservation of grammatical class), and hence no sensible interpretation is supportable for the successive constituent groups of the structure—nor, of course, for the string as a whole. Under these circumstances, they observed the same P600 patterns as for the matched normal and syntactically deviant but interpretable stimuli, but did not observe the N400 wrap-up response (Hagoort & Brown, 1994; see also Hagoort, Brown, Vonks, & Hoeks, forthcoming). This reinforces the claim for a syntactically driven P600 and the general impression of linked but distinct processing types.

Friederici and collaborators have reported several similar outcomes in studies of German that have looked at phrasal violations, subcategorization violations, and gender effects among others. But, that work has focused greater attention on the earlier language components and indeed some of their work has indicated both an LAN pattern at around 400 ms and an LAN pattern for some violations arising with somewhat shorter latency—an "early, left, anterior negativity" (ELAN) (Friederici, Hahne, & Mecklinger, 1996). An early left negativity has also been remarked by Neville in her work (see below). I will not further pursue the ELAN/LAN distinction here, but it is one of substantial interest. A revealing feature in some of these studies in German is the comparison of E/LAN and P600 responses to variations in strategic responses by subjects (viz., as effected by instruction to attend to or ignore sentence interpretations, or by changes in the relative proportions of the violation types). In a number of instances, P600 responses were modified by such manipulations, indicating some greater sensitivity to the comprehender's processing priorities and/or attentional commitments, but the E/LAN responses were not so affected, indicating no such dispositional capacity (Hahne & Friederici, in press). Further, when violations were constructed at a given point in the test string such that there were either semantic only, syntactic only, or both semantic and syntactic violations, interactions were observed. When occurring separately, each elicited its characteristic wave form (LAN and P600 for the syntactic violations, and N400 for the semantic violation), but when combined, only the LAN appeared (Friederici, Hahne, & von Cramon, 1998). Again, as in several other result patterns already mentioned, there is an indication of contingent relations among the processing types. Exactly how one should seek to reconstruct these might vary, but the message is that the observational base has the potential to tell us about this kind of issue, and these types of investigations hold the prospect of significantly finer discriminations among parsing processes with this methodology than we might have anticipated. See Friederici (1998b) for a proposal that associates the E/LAN responses with automatic syntactic analysis and the P600 with processes of reanalysis and repair of syntactic structure (e.g., temporary ambiguity and garden path effects).

There are many other quite fascinating clusters of observations available and/or rapidly developing with ERP measurements. For example, Coulson et al. (1998) review evidence for the view that there are multiple LAN effects, some of the sort I have noted above, but others better understood in terms of working memory mechanisms that are involved in dealing with discontinuous dependencies in sentence processing. Recent observation also suggests that the P600 may reflect multiple aspects of sentence processing that can be distinguished in terms of responsible recording sites (Hagoort & Brown, in press). In another vein, reports by Neville, Mills, and Lawson (1992) on ERP tests of deaf readers of English reveal some systematic differences in ERP responses to vocabulary classes that are correlated with major contrasts in syntactic function ("closed class" and "open class" elements). Neville's work also combines this observation with functional magnetic resonance imaging (fMRI) studies that bear on issues of localization, and these outcomes are congruent with both ERP and imaging based claims for localization in classic areas of language specialization. Work by a number of the cited investigators and others likewise pursues convergence of ERP and imaging results as well as extensions of these techniques to the study of patients with brain injury who display aphasic patterns of selective loss of grammatical capacity (see, e.g., Brown, Wassenaar, & Hagoort, 1999; Friederici, von Cramon, & Kotz, 1999). There are, in short, many more aspects of the electrophysiological and imaging findings that can be brought to bear on the effort to identify the contributing processes to real-time language use. So, I emphasize that the sketch that I have provided here is just a sketch, and is to be understood as a (representative) sample taken to illustrate the basis for the argument I am pursuing in this essay, not as a systematic representation of the field of enquiry being drawn on.

Observations based on correlations of brain response and language processing performance provide persuasive evidence for distinct brain systems associated with several different structural domains, and these domains have a natural interpretation within the framework of grammatical theory: phrase structure, inflection, movement and binding, and lexical semantics. And, there is good reason to consider some of the processing evidence derived from such study as indicating strategic and dispositional responses to both semantic and syntactic task priorities. These latter may be distinguished from the former in terms of both electrode location (and plausible construal of that data in terms of brain generator location), and in terms of time course of processing. So, one may remark a system response to syntactic configuration within 200 ms or less, and reflections of the integrative effects that unite syntactic and semantic factors following closely, but with variable relation to the initial syntactic response. Some salient conclusions that seem indicated by data of the type just reviewed are as follow:

Semantic integration of lexical elements into their context is distinct from syntactic integration of lexical elements into their structural frame.

More than a single syntactic signature is demonstrable and they span a substantial time range—approximately 150 ms to 700+ ms.

Early responses to syntax are inflexible and are localized to a substantial degree in classic language processing areas associated with syntactic processing (viz., based both on language impairment data and brain imaging data).

Later responses to syntax show greater sensitivity to interpretive factors than do the early responses and are much more broadly distributed.

Though the dissociation of the processing types cannot tell us how syntactic processing fits into the overall language processor, it does rather convincingly indicate that the identification of such a structural type is not an artifact of linguistic analysis.

LANGUAGE PRODUCTION STUDY

Any general evaluation of the architecture of language processing systems must address not only the character of language comprehension, but also that of language generation. Several issues immediately present themselves, not the least of which are important differences between production and comprehension regarding the intrinsic relations between conceptual, semantic, syntactic, and phonological processes. And, as I will momentarily review, given such differences in the way the two classes of processing tasks relate to conceptual and semantic systems, the production evidence shows a surprising degree of modular structure. This is central to the current discussion, for I wish to argue that linkages between production and comprehension systems may rationalize some conflicting results outlined in the discussion of parsing studies, and thus may lend support to a somewhat more uniform treatment of the processing relations between syntactic structure and various classes of interpretive constraint.

Language production models must account for the real-time integration of utterance form in the service of the specific force of the meaning that a speaker wishes to convey on a given occasion of utterance. So, language production models are driven in the first instance by an interpretation of conceptual content that gives rise to the communicative intent of a speaker. Language comprehension models, by contrast, are driven in the first instance by the acoustic or orthographic input that is the target of interpretation. Given these differences, one might, with no other facts available, expect the primary processes of sentence analysis/construction, and particularly those for phrasal structures, to directly and pervasively reflect the nature of the controlling inputs in the two cases. But the apparent case is somewhat different.

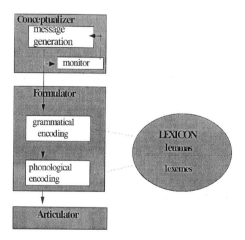

Figure 1   A model of production processes, adapted from Levelt (1989).

Diverse strands of investigation underlie claims for models of the language production system. Levelt (1989) provided an admirable summary of the evidence then available as well as a comprehensive interpretation and elaboration of language production theory. Research in the ensuing decade has extended the observational base and tested the general architectural claims he laid out in a variety of ways. Figure 1 provides a summary picture of the organization of the production system. Modular processing in both lexical and phrasal domains is represented.

My own work and that of a number of others examining the distributional character of spontaneously occurring speech errors indicates such a multistage process. It is one in which abstract lexical representations (i.e., phonologically uninterpreted objects, referred to as *lemmas* in Figure 1) are integrated into a syntactic representation, followed by processes in which the phonological form of utterance components and associated prosodic structures is developed. Semantic control is exercised in the initial stage of lexical and phrasal selection, but is not directly implicated in the mechanisms of phrasal integration or phonological interpretation. Data used to motivate this picture include patterns of word substitution errors, as well as various movement errors of sound and word exchange or anticipation or shift in location that allow one to infer what the computationally effective descriptions sentence elements may be at different points in the encoding sequence. Many detailed constraints of syntax, morphology, phonology, and prosody may be remarked in the error patterns (Fromkin, 1971), but semantic constraints on the interaction of sentence elements at syntactic and phonological levels are not readily discerned (Bierwisch, 1982). Certainly, one may see powerful semantic influences on certain word substitution errors, but these appear to be best characterized as errors in the initial selection of lexical content, that is, errors prior to the operation of the mechanisms that take semantically selected elements and incorporate them into syntactic and prosodic structures (see, e.g., Garrett, 1980, 1993a, for a summary review of these arguments).

Experimental work by Levelt and colleagues (see Levelt, Roelofs, & Meyer, 1999, for a review and citation of many relevant research reports) has addressed a variety of issues in this area, with special force in the domain of lexical retrieval for syntactic integration. So, for example, a series of experimental investigations with picture–word interference tasks has explored the interfaces between the conceptual/semantic levels, lemma levels, and word form levels depicted in Figure 1. That work has provided the basis for quite detailed accounts of the time course of activation of the different classes of structure associated with lexical targets, with rather compelling indications for staged recovery of semantic and phonological description. A related line of reasoning applies to the study of tip of the tongue (TOT) states, in which one sees a prima facie sharp dissociation between semantic and phonological information. Recent experimental work with TOT states has indicated that more precise boundaries may be drawn that correspond to the experimentally certified structure based on the picture–word interference paradigm and the spontaneous word substitution patterns noted above: in TOT states, distinguishable access to semantic, syntactic, and phonological representations may be identified (see, e.g., Vigliocco, Antonini, & Garrett, 1999). To this list, one may add a convergence of the reaction time and error profile studies with ERP investigations. In picture naming tasks, it has been demonstrated that syntactically constrained responses precede phonologically constrained responses as evidenced by differences in timing of motor readiness potentials (van Turennout, Hagoort, & Brown, 1998). I should, however, not leave this brief discusion without emphasizing that I have set aside many interesting and important issues regarding the internal structure of the processes just outlined, and in particular issues concerning the degree and role of feedback relations between phonological, syntactic, and semantic processing stages. The general architectural contrasts under discussion are well attested; the detailed relations among the component systems are the focus of considerable debate. For example, a paper by Dell, Schwartz, Martin, Saffran, and Gagnon (1997) reports some combined modeling and experimental work that is important to our understanding of the conditions that underlie potential interactions between levels. Against that background, they provide an insightful perspective on the general issues of modular systems in networks. There is also in the earlier cited Levelt et al. (1999) review a carefully considered assessment of various experimental problems as they relate to the picture–word interference paradigm and the dynamics of lexical recognition and retrieval.

Work by Kathryn Bock and colleagues is particularly revealing with respect to ways in which interpretive and lexical constraints interact with sentence construction (see Bock, 1990; Bock & Levelt, 1994, for reviews). Several aspects of this program of study are relevant, including work on memory (e.g., Bock & Warren, 1985), agreement processes (e.g., Bock & Eberhard, 1993), and work on "syntactic priming" (Bock, 1986), and my brief remarks will not do justice to the breadth and subtlty of the inquiry. I will focus for illustration on aspects of the syntactic priming work. In such experiments one can affect the relative likelihood of producing a given syntactic type in a picture description episode (e.g., active vs. passive, or double object constructions vs. to-datives) by manipulating the syntactic form of a sentence generated on the just preceding trial; for example, passives are more likely to be used for the picture description task if preceded by a passive prime than an active prime. N.B.: The prime sentences and the picture description targets are unrelated in content vis-à-vis objects referred to and the cover task used in the experiments obscures the experimenter's interest in the successive trial relations. This work provides a clear demonstration of a processing stage/representation that is sensitive to phrasal configuration but not to lexical content, and more particularly, not to the semantic force of the lexical content. So, for example, work by Bock and Loebell (1990) showed that syntactic priming effects treat as equivalent objects the by-phrases in sentences like these:

the plane landing *by the control tower* versus the plane landed *by the pilot*

Thematic roles differ but syntactic configuration is preserved. By contrast, when configuration changes, though prosody and superficial sequencing of words is preserved, priming is lost (as for the pair: "Susan took a book to read"; "Susan took a book to class"). Note that these findings do not arise via the use of techniques that are not demonstrably sensitive to influence by interpretive variables. So, for example, animacy and thematic role have been examined in similar tasks (Bock, Loebell, & Morey, 1992) and shown to have clear effects on the relative likelihood that a given NP will occupy a particular argument slot, but such effects do not interact with the priming of phrasal configurations. This is a kind of outcome that is similar in spirit to the idea derivable from speech error distributions that there is some degree of computational separation between the selection of lexical elements that are embedded in a sentence structure and the integration of the structure itself. Note that this claim does not run counter to lexically driven encoding schemes, but it does not fit versions that do not countenance a distinguishable syntactic representation. Quite the contrary, as the priming patterns provide a prima facie case for the existence of an abstract structure that encodes syntactic configuration but not lexical content.

These several kinds of findings indicate a significant degree of modular structure in the language generation system, with global outline as in Figure 1. With these observations about language production in hand, let us return to the problem we began with—that of how one should deal with the contrasting patterns of evidence for interaction and modularity in the domain of comprehension as discussed in the previous two sections.

ANOTHER PATH: LANGUAGE PRODUCTION AS A COMPREHENSION FILTER

It surely looks as though one should grapple with the idea that in comprehension studies there is simultaneous good reason to aver both

modular and nonmodular processing profiles. If one agrees, there are
several pretty puzzles that present themselves in trying to do this. So, if
one were to accept at face value the claims for constraint based processing that is genuinely nonmodular (in the relevant informational structure sense), one must find some way to account for the experimental
circumstances in which semantic, conceptual, and idiosyncratic distributional factors seem to have little impact. The constraint system is well
suited to generate interactions. But, its capacity to account for circumstances in which such are not forthcoming is less obvious. Similarly, the
emerging electrophysiological and brain imaging profile of language
processing, as well as long-standing observations of language impairment that show selective losses vis-à-vis information type must find an
explanation that does not rely on a comprehension model in which informational sources are combined statistically and without regard to
type. The line taken by Bever et al. (1998) addresses some of the experimental studies of parsing that show interaction and brings them into an
accord with some of the evidence for abstract syntactic representations
as relevant to processing. But that avenue does not in my judgment as
readily deal with instances in which interaction does not manifest itself
in early stage parsing, nor with the electrophysiology patterns, or the
structure of language impairments. My inclination in these circumstances is to pursue an accommodation that is similar in general character to Bever et al.'s proposal, but without the assumptions of centrality
for constraint based sentence analysis and "slow syntax," and with a
different source for the interpretive constraints that appear in parsing
performances. That accommodation calls for an integration of the language comprehension and language production systems in ways that
preserve the identity of both, but assigns production processes a prominent role in the routine function of the comprehension system.

We are quite accustomed to agree that language generation and language comprehension systems are intimately linked via monitoring functions of the latter on the former. That is, we are quite accustomed to think
of the comprehension system as providing a continual error control mechanism via monitoring of production processes (see Levelt, 1989, for a review). It has occasionally been briefly noted (Forster, 1979; Jackendoff,
1989; Garrett, 1993b) that production systems should be viewed as having a functionally similar role with respect to comprehension, namely,
that they provide a continual error control mechanism via the production
monitoring of partial products of the recognition system. A somewhat
broader way of putting this point is to think of the production system as
a filter on the generation of multiple analyses by the recognition system.
There is considerable reason to take seriously the view that recognition

systems respond to local ambiguity in the analysis of input strings by maintaining, at least temporarily, multiple analysis paths that are pruned in terms of information gleaned either from posterior context or in terms of higher order interpretive constraints. The idea that I wish to pursue is that the production system should be understood as the major factor in the application of such interpretive constraints in sentence comprehension. It is, in fact, quite plausible to assume that the language production system can rapidly incorporate the initial lexical elements and elementary phrasal structures identified by the recognition system with existing discourse constraints to give rise to candidate sentence structures. On the production hypotheses sketched in the previous section, lexically driven sentence encoding under message control is what the production machinery is specifically designed to do. What reasons, apart from mere possibility, do we have to pursue this line? Here are some straws in this theoretical breeze:

• **The lexically based character of production routines** matches many features of current parsing study (e.g., subcategorization and thematic structure; computational efforts at merging parsing and generation systems).

• **The speed of lexical recognition and structure projection** is compatible with quite early context effects via production.

• **Experimental demonstrations of conceptual and discourse projection** are compatible with a production base.

• **Production performance profiles** can be used to predict comprehension performance (agreement error and lexical biases used in comprehension tests are usually indexed by production bias).

• **The electrophysiological patterns for comprehension** have a plausible fit to a production based processing component.

• **Language disorders** show interesting evidence for the articulation and codependence of comprehension and production systems.

• **Language acquisition profiles** apparently differ for production and comprehension.

Lexically Driven Encoding

Lexically driven encoding in the modeling of production processes is quite in keeping with a number of current "lexically driven" approaches to parsing. In thinking about this, it is well to keep in mind that "lexically driven parsing" comes in several varieties. To embrace such a view is not thereby to embrace a view of parsing as interactive in the relevant sense when one is speaking of comprehension any more than it requires such for production. One may pursue a parser in this mode with as much or as little reliance as one chooses on the lexical semantic, conceptual, or other information associated with a given lexical target. And, one may, of course, exploit in similarly varying ways the linkage between lexically driven parsing and "lexical preferences" as a principle of choice dictating parsing options—as contrasted with general principles of configural economy or structurally driven choice (minimal attachment, late closure, etc.). This latter move is sometimes taken as the opening wedge in a general frequency of usage argument that leads one down the path to claims that processing is fundamentally a matter of the statistical likelihoods of co-occurrence relations between successive words and groups of words. Whether one takes these kinds of statistical properties of words to be an overlay on a syntactically specific parsing architecture or as a central determinant of processing in a system that does not single out grammatical category as a special type is an entirely open matter. The use of probability in parsing can be implemented in ways that preserves the separability of information types or ways that do not.

In this same general vein, one may remark on the place of argument structures associated with lexical elements—the subcategorization frames and thematic structures discussed in the section entitled Some Experimental Examples and Perspectives from Parsing Studies. A very productive line of investigation of the role of semantic variables in sentence comprehension has been the examination of ways in which the thematic roles associated with the structure of verbs interact with subcategorization biases in the structure of verbs. In language production modeling, the lemma driven systems that have been proposed incorporate argument structures (e.g., see Levelt, 1989, chapter 2) in ways quite in keeping with the appeal to argument structures that one finds in parsing studies. From a related but different perspective, one might cite a discussion by Kim, Srinivas, and Trueswell (1998), though in so doing, I'm turning it a bit on its head since it is meant to advance the case for constraint based parsing—which it ably does. That discussion is focused on development of parsing systems based on lexicalized tree adjoining grammar (LTAG: Joshi & Schabes, 1997), and it lends itself to my current point simply because the elementary trees in the LTAG representations encode the syntactic information in ways reminiscent of the properties of lemmas and their invocation. Indeed, these observations simply emphasize the potential for overlap in some machine parsing proposals and systems for generation. The similarity of the compositional operations required of a parser and those required for the lexically driven sentence encoding model has not escaped attention. Computational efforts to develop systems that will support both analysis and generation are thus of particular interest. So, for example, work on production by Stone and Doran (1997) with tree adjoining grammars is illustrative vis-à-vis the general classes of representation alluded to by Kim et al. in the parsing context above. And, work by Vosse and Kempen (1999) and by Kempen (1999) likewise lays out ways to exploit common devices for parsing and production. (I choose these as recent interesting references that bear on the point pursued here, but several useful discussions of this general issue are to be found in the computational literature. It is a matter of long-standing interest.)

Note, however, that though the operations of phrasal composition may be very similar, the controlling inputs to the processors may be treated in distinct ways, particularly as one thinks in terms of the nature of the human production and comprehension systems rather than machine systems. In the case of normal production exercise, the lexical nomination is via message level constraint. In the case of normal first stage comprehension, it is via the outputs of the lexical recognition system. If the parser is to be driven primarily by lexical recognition outputs, without immediate appeal to higher order constraint, then it is here in particular that one can see the useful force of a production architecture that separates the semantic control process from direct involvement in the phrase building operations. That move in the production domain enables phrasal composition systems that can operate with the more "limited" inputs that a recognition parser might deal in. This connects to two additional observations.

First, one may remark on the fit this provides to the empirical warrant of the production data discussed in the previous section. For example, in speech error data one finds indication that phrase building errors do not arise out of the kind of semantic similarity that, for example, gives rise to meaning based lexical selection errors. So, if one examines word exchange errors (e.g., "Cats are a good place for barns"; "This idea had the guy . . . "), one finds the meaning similarity of the interchanged elements is not comparable to that holding between the target and intrusion in a meaning based word substitution error (e.g., "He shot him through with a sword" / arrow; "You can just go jump in the river!" /lake). This and other evidence noted in the previous section invites a view of semantic control of phrasal integration for production as indirect in ways that may facilitate the intersection with comprehension systems.

The other observation turns on whether we should interpret this design feature as enabling the phrase building system of the *producer* to be directly engaged by lexical inputs either from conceptual/semantic or form driven systems. This way of talking would suggest that it is literally the same machinery that computes the phrasal structures for both production and comprehension. There are at least two reasons to be cautious about accepting that notion. First, it would defeat the purpose of an error checking system. If a benefit to be got from the interaction of production and comprehension is their mutual error monitoring functions, then independent sources for the compared signals is rather a necessity. So, the systems of construction might be identical—but there better be two of them, and with different drivers. Second, there is some evidence from language pathologies indicating the selective preservation of comprehension when production is compromised and vice versa. The detail of structural compromise in each of these complementary cases is, however, not sufficient for a fully confident application of that dissociation to the present question. And, it should be noted that such a dissociation is both a virtue (on the error checking mode) and a potential problem for the proposal I'm advancing since it requires that we look for dependencies between the use of production resources and success in comprehension and vice versa. I will return to this point.

The speed of lexical recognition and structural projection is compatible with support for production based processing as a contributor to comprehension. The proposal under evaluation requires early and accurate identification of lexical targets and the recovery of their structural burden within a window that is plausibly supportive of recognition and comprehension performance time constants. These processes are the fodder for the production system as well as the comprehension system and must work in a timely way if any of this is to succeed. We can begin by noting a phenomenon that might be taken as a kind of approximate "existence proof" for such capacity—though it has not been recruited quite to the purposes I intend here. Here I have in mind the "close shadowing" performances documented by Marslen-Wilson (1973), in which some few (perhaps 1 in 5) persons show the ability to sustain repetition latencies for normal connected prose of 250–300 ms with quite good accuracy. What levels of representation are recovered may be not entirely clear, but the reported work certainly showed some clear engagement of the syntactic and semantic force of the shadowed materials. Other examples, of many that might be cited, will remind readers of well-known related evidence. Long since, Marslen-Wilson and Tyler (1987, for review) have argued for a very rapid process in the recognition of lexical targets in the spoken language domain and for the assimilation of the information associated with lexical entries to the comprehension process. How fast? Very. Work by Zwitserlood (1989) is instructive. Using a cross-modal priming paradigm, she provided evidence for the multiple activation of words compatible with the initial phonetic segments of test words and an effective linking of lexical targets to sentence environments at a moment contemporaneous with the occurrence of the terminal phonetic segments of the test words. A related phenomenon is lexical ambiguity resolution. In a variety of experimental studies, multiple activation and rapid contextually appropriate resolution is observed (Swinney, Zurif, Prather, & Love, 1996, for review). Recent ERP results reported by Van Petten et al. (1999) show N400 responses to sentence incongruous words arising prior to the point in the acoustic input at which the word becomes phonetically identifiable. So, lexical information on which encoding as well as decoding could rely is indeed rapidly accessible. Particularly interesting in this regard is an experiment by Trueswell and Kim (1998) using a "fast priming" technique that indicates the subcategorization features of a verb are rather immediately available for the constraint of syntactic analysis. In this procedure, prime words are presented at rates too fast for conscious report. The prime words contrasted those with a direct object bias (e.g., "obtain") and those with a sentence complement bias (e.g. "realize"). Sentences appeared with and without an overt complementizer signal [the man accepted (that) . . .], followed by an implausible target NP ("the fire"), followed by the words of the verb phrase of the complement sentence.

The man accepted (that) the fire could not have started in the attic.

Results showed interference from primes with structures incompatible with the required sentence analysis (i.g., direct object structure primes induced a slow down at the NP and at the first element of the verb phrase), and possible facilitation for compatible primes.

In production terms, access to the representation for, for example, "obtain," if implemented at the lemma level as a procedural call, would activate a package with direct object subcategorization and patient thematic role. This package is compatible with the verb "accept" but in fact would lead to the wrong analysis for the target sentence. That analysis is, on the Trueswell and Kim (1998) results, implemented and then abandoned only at the locus of the verb phrase in spite of the information contained in the immediately preceding NP which constitutes an implausible filler for the theme role in the direct object structure for "accept". Interpreting the pattern of effects in light of a production application is not difficult, but it is not decisive either. But, at very least, it suggests that the projection of a lexically based syntactic frame as a constraint on analysis of immediately following input is very rapid and may proceed before thematic appropriateness of the NP can be evaluated (see also McElree & Griffith, 1995, 1998).

Context, Discourse, and Plausibility Effects

The kind of information available and the time needed to extract it are sharply in focus throughout. The just prior discussion focused on lexical recovery questions. Here we look at more global sorts of information for which impact on comprehension is reported. Ideally, the production system will have some sort of scenario to work from—and isolated sentences with no context are not the best candidates for the operation of production based constraint mechanisms. It is, however, a rather striking fact that a major methodological feature of experimentation designed to evaluate the contribution of various interpretive and discourse factors on comprehension is the use of more elaborated contextual presentations for target sentences. So, in variations of, for example, the Marslen-Wilson and Tyler (1987) and Crain and Steedman (1985) studies adverted to earlier (and many similar not cited), a consistent feature of experimentation has been the use of minidiscourse settings as context for the test sentences. Such a circumstance is necessary to the manipulation of discourse factors and is, therefore, also quite plausible for the application of production based constraints on the analysis of target structures. Sentences in isolation are less readily accommodated by the production hypothesis except insofar as the relevant structure is immediately projectable from lexical entries (e.g., in the manner discussed earlier). From this, one may derive the prediction that well established discourse based influences on parsing may be among the fastest acting such sources of constraint, and in particular, faster than inferentially driven constraints based on the contextually derived meaning of the lexical content of sentences. The eye-pointing studies noted in the earlier section in which I discussed experimental examples from parsing studies (e.g., Tanenhaus et al., 1995) may likewise be plausibly construed from this production perspective. Indeed, in that case, perhaps an even stronger claim might be worth consideration, for we might suppose that the eye movement data arise in significant measure from the primary production system, situated as it is in a highly structured environment and dealing in commentary of a structurally regular range. So, in that task, the visual input is prime production fodder and the mission to match auditory input and potential description high on the priority queue. However one might sort out such a possibility, the rapid assimilation of a visual input to language performance may fall more naturally in the performance domain of production than of comprehension mechanisms.

Work by Forster and colleagues (Forster, 1979) established a prima facie case for an impact of what he dubbed "plausibility" factors on comprehension in a variety of processing tasks—acceptability, RSVP, and same–difference matching. Those materials were not presented in context, but Forster characterized the nature of the plausibility variation as reflecting the relative ease with which a scenario apposite to a test sentence could be constructed. Consider examples like the following:

The pretty minister cried while cannons roared.

Sweating lightly, he walked under the snake.

The effect (controlled for a variety of nuisance factors) is robust under conditions of repetition and instruction. That is, it does not appear to be the case that the consciously available strategic resources of listeners or readers are particularly useful in resolving the computational difficulty posed by sentences like those in the examples. Forster's work generally did not reveal an interaction between syntactic complexity and plausibility variation (Forster, 1979; but see also Forster, 1987). The import of this is fairly clear for the position I'm advancing. If the locus of plausibility effects were in primary parsing operations, one would be forced to affirm what many experimental outcomes do not support, namely, that very general knowledge based constraints are involved in the immediate projection of phrasal geometry during sentence comprehension. If, on the other hand, one attributes the effects quite literally to the ease of generation of a possible construal of the relations implied by the sentence, the production based description is a natural one. This is an area in which some empirical leverage on the hypothesis might be profitably looked for.

Production Profiles Predict Comprehension Performance

It is worth noting that in many experimental Comprehension investigations that look for effects of frequency of structural configuration or other collocational factors, test material has been constructed using procedures that use sentence completion tasks as a basis for estimation of preferences—here I cite no references since the practice is so commonplace. In other instances, the appeal is to statistical measures of relative frequency of occurrence in large corpora. In both cases, the conflation of production and comprehension proclivities is clear. Thus, there is, other things being equal, no necessary problem in the application of a production based parsing filter to existing accounts of putatively comprehension based performance reflecting preference data.

There is an interesting caveat, however. It should be borne in mind that in the case of production, the preferences for one or another structural path will have the full conceptual resources associated with lexical content, but a strictly bottom-up driven parser that operates off the phonological form and grammatical category information may not—to the extent that such cooccurences in generation may reflect conceptual contingencies not available to the recognition parser. That is, the frequency effects may be different in the two domains if the picture I am suggesting is correct: effective recognition frequencies might collapse across factors that affect production. The use of production data to test recognition parsing in paradigms that do not segregate production and recognition influences on task performance may this obscure a contrast of interest. Questions about which class of statistical constraints to apply in parsing systems have been a recent topic of interest (e.g., Mitchell, 1994; Gibson & Tunstall, 1999; Kim & Trueswell, 1998) and there may be scope for pursuit of a production/comprehension based analysis couched in terms of availability of the different types of information in the two systems.

Another, and more detailed example of the convergence of performance profiles in the two domains is provided by work based on studies of agreement error patterns in speaking. Work by Bock and Miller (1991) and several followup studies demonstrated some stable patterns in the breakdown of mechanisms for number agreement in English (since extended with some interesting modifications to several other languages; see Bock, Nicol, & Cutting, 1999; Vigliocco & Zilli, 1999, for more recent treatments). For our purposes, the significant facts are these: number mismatch between a head noun and a local noun, for example, as italicized in the example

The *baby* on the *blankets* . . . (*is*/*are playing with a puppy.)

enhances the likelihood of number error in a sentence completion task compared to a control with no mismatch. Further, the error rate is substantially greater when the mismatch is one in which the local "distractor" is plural and the head singular—the reverse mismatch is often not significantly different from baseline—though this varies a bit. The same effect can be observed in a "recognition" task. Nicol, Forster, and Veres (1997) used a timed reading task to evaluate the same contrasts. A particularly significant aspect of their approach is that they did not use test sentences with errors in them. Rather, they used fully grammatical sentences, but with NPs located in ways that mirrored the position and structural roles of interfering NPs in the production task. They found elevated reading times for the sentences with interfering NPs compared to those without NPs mismatching number; moreover, these effects were limited to mismatches involving a plural interfering NP—just as the case for production performance. Evidently, some processing difficulty in the coordination of number marking arises in production and in comprehension that is of rather striking similarity.

Profile of Electrophysiological Responses to Sentence Processing

The profile of electrophysiological responses to sentence processing presents another area in which one might speculate about the production hypothesis. The ERP components focused on in the section in which I discuss electrophysiological evidence may be fitted to this picture, though at the price of taking seriously a feature of the profiles that I have already noted is at least questionable, namely, the observed time frames for the various syntactic and semantic responses so indexed. The various patterns (E/LAN, P600, N400) do not, we noted, all relate to syntax and interpretation in the same way, and we can ask whether these differences in structural sensitivity are commensurate with assumptions one might make about the drivers for primary syntactic processing and/or production based filtering or adjustment. For good or for ill, the obvious move here is to examine the differences between E/LAN and P600, as both of these have been linked to syntactic processing as primary factors in their elicitation. If the P600 is, as has been suggested by several observers, the reflection of processing that is aimed at "fixing" the deviant structure, that is, it is at least in part the "patchup/backup" system that we are seeing, and if the production system is taken to be the source of the structures used for that function, then we are commited to the view that the P600 is, in part at least, a production reflex. The further observation that the E/LAN is focused on "language specific" areas whereas P600 reflects a much wider distribution of activity fits this general line of speculation, as does the further observation that P600 is responsive to strategic control and to certain semantic interactions. On the production construal, P600 should be responsive to semantic constraint in a way that the ELAN and LAN are not—if the former reflects production system control and the latter does not. And, indeed, that appears to be supportable on current observation. From this, and from observations of how the production system responds to semantic control, one might essay the "prediction" that there is structure in the P600, that is to say, differences in structural sensitivity reflected in its distribution or time course. In particular, one might expect to distinguish responses that are primarily syntactic from those that reflect semantic constraint. Recall from the discussion of the production system that there is a stage of the production process for which it appears that semantic influence is only indirectly manifest and configurational syntax is a major factor. I wish that I could claim to have had such a thought before knowing that such claims have begun to appear, but, alas, I cannot. So call it a "hybrid postdiction." In fact, we do not know how this expectation might fare. Hagoort et al. (1999) do note some indication of a difference in the P600 response to outright syntactic violation (a more posterior distribution) and the recovery from misanalysis traceable to syntactic bias (more equal or more frontal distribution), but it is not obvious exactly how, if at all, that might relate to the production structure noted. What is clear, is that one may bias parsing preferences with semantic constraint and that this is measurable with P600 (e.g., Hagoort, Brown, Vonk, & Hocks, forthcoming).

It would be worth knowing with some precision how similar constraint affects E/LAN (if at all) and whether syntactic bias and semantic bias can be distinguished in the topography of the P600.

Language Disorders

One of the parade cases of dissociation of language production and language comprehension comes in the study of agrammatism, seen (typically) in Broca's aphasia. Clinically, agrammatism is an expressive disorder and is often remarked in conjunction with what seemed to be clinically fairly well preserved comprehension capacity. In an important paper, Caramazza and Zurif (1976) reminded people that this was indeed a matter of relative success in test circumstances not precisely focused on the detail of syntactic factors supporting comprehension, and then provided several experimental demonstrations that such patients did in fact suffer from apparently syntactic limitations (see Caplan, 1987, for review). This was variously interpreted as an indication of a compromise of grammatical knowledge, specifically the syntactic component of the processing/ knowledge system. Preserved lexical semantic capacity, and inference based on such, was offered as the basis for the apparent preservation of comprehension performance in the face of syntactic impairment. Much more has been written about this aspect of agrammatism and its reconstruction (see, e.g., papers in Fromkin, 1995, for wide ranging discussions) and it is a rich area of study. For present purposes, the first important feature lies in the observation of preserved inferential capacity vis-à-vis the lexical semantic base and a significant syntactic impairment that in many patients manifests itself in both structurally compromised production and syntactically limited comprehension. Such a confluence of limitations/capacities is unproblematic for the production hypothesis under examination here.

But, the matter is, of course, by no means so simple. There are a variety of complications, only two of which I will comment on here. First, some agrammatic producer/comprehenders are capable of syntactic processing that is sufficient to support substantial success in well-formedness judgment tasks (Linebarger, Schwartz, & Saffran, 1983); that is, they have a "paradoxical syntactic capacity" if one takes their comprehension problems as syntactically based. Second, there are attested cases of patients who display agrammatic speech but do not display a comprehension limitation; that is, they are "paradoxical comprehenders" if one takes their production as the index of their potential. A brief look at each of these circumstances will have to suffice here.

The ability to make judgments that successfully distinguish syntactically well-formed from ill-formed sequences has been observed in agrammatics who fail diagnostic comprehension tests (e.g., a limited understanding of passives or center branching relatives) and this implies what I wish to affirm: the input parser may deliver a wff product that is disconnected from reliable semantic interpretation. But, the failure of such patients could take several underlying forms given the framework being considered here. If the mechanism for integrating/comparing a recognition based representation with a production based representation is impaired, an erroneous semantically driven production target may be accepted even if the input representation is accurate (i.e., an analysis driven by lexical semantic constraints will have no "recognition brakes"). That circumstance may or may not be combined with a failure in the production machinery itself that uses semantic constraint to engage phrasal construction mechanisms. This is a mechanism that, once engaged, may operate without immediate semantic control (viz., as the production evidence reviewed in the previous section suggests). The picture invited is of a breakdown in the mechanisms that insure a link between syntax and interpretation, not of a breakdown in the mechanisms of phrasal construction—which are by the assumptions of the production model, capable of some independent (of semantic direction) operation and that operation might be exercised in either comprehension system, production system, or both. In brief, there is not much help here. The main message is that the association of meaning with syntax is potentially loose at both ends, and that a syntactic representation could conceivably be available from either source that might mediate successful well-formedness judgments. We do have some evidence that the application of interpretive constraints in ambiguity resolution (Swinney, Zurif, & Nicol, 1989) and in binding (Zurif, Swinney, Prather, Solomon, & Bushnell, 1993; Swiney et al., 1996) is compromised in agrammatics. See also Nicol and Love (Ch. 5, this volume) for an analysis of certain comprehension failures in agrammatism that are traceable to production limitations. That is, we can assert that the loss of productive capacity is sometimes linked with the loss of timely access to integration of interpretive constraints on sentence analysis (see Swinney and Zurif, 1995, for one statement of this perspective). And we have reason to believe that the semantic capacities are intact, at least based on success in tasks that depend on lexical semantic inference.

The production hypothesis is compatible with some dissociation of production and comprehension capacities, but is committed to the view that compromise of basic production capacity should be accompanied by reduced ability to use interpretive constraints to correctly constrain syntactic

analysis. This idea is most directly challenged by those reported agrammatics (see, e.g., Miceli, Mazzucchi, Menn, & Goodglass, 1983; Kolk, Van
Grunsven, & Keyser, 1985) who display no comprehension deficit, that is,
they show evidence of production compromise without an apparent concomitant loss of comprehension function. But, the kinds of information
about compromise in those patients that would bear on the production
hypothesis is not readily available. Production driven syntax is assumed
to play a significant role in the normal functions, but purely form driven
syntactic representations, if constructed by the "data driven" parser are
nevertheless interpretable. Thus, it would be instructive to determine
whether the successful performance of such patients is responsive to the
same range of contextual constraints and to the same course of processing
as normal listeners. In this context, we may consider an observation from
ERP experimentation with agrammatic patients by Brown et al (1999).
These patients were all Broca's aphasics as indexed by the Aachen Aphasia test and all were characterized by effortful production and ommisions
of morphosyntactic elements in their output—so, broadly speaking, all
were agrammatic producers. These were divided into a group of five patients with chance performance on syntactically demanding comprehension tests and a group of five who, though somewhat impaired, scored
above chance on the test, thus indicating significant syntactically based
comprehension capacity. All 10 patients displayed a normal semantic integration effect (N400) to semantically implausible targets in test sentences,
but the five patients with poor comprehension performance showed no
P600 ERP signature to syntactically deviant sentences; by contrast the patients with above chance comprehension scores did show a reduced but
unmistakable P600 response to syntactic deviance (agreement violations
and word order violations). Interestingly, the poor comprehenders who
showed no P600 did show an N400 for the word order violations—that is,
absent the P600 response, they nevertheless showed sensitivity to the semantic oddity produced by the word inversion.

We cannot further interpret these interesting findings for the issues here
addressed beyond saying they give additional evidence that significant
comprehension capacity, is, as the earlier case studies indicated, observable in presence of impaired production, and, additionally, based on the
ERP evidence, that this capacity includes the processes that drive the late
syntactic component. No E/LAN results were observed in this experiment in either normal controls or patients. This kind of study, however,
represents the kind of inquiry that will be needed in order to evaluate the
import of aphasic compromise for the production hypothesis. So, for example, would such patients show the same delay in on line ambiguity
processing or in binding tests for reactivation of potential antecedents

that the larger class of agrammatics displays based on the evidence cited above? And can the performance of the patient groups be distinguished in terms of responsiveness to early and late syntactic components? Quite apart from these matters, it would be important to discover in some detail whether performance compromise in the *production* domain is the same for agrammatics with relatively preserved comprehension as for those whose syntactically mediated comprehension is deficient. "Agrammatism" is a term with considerable latitude of application and there is significant variation in the character of such compromise across patients. Add to this the certain fact that we do not know just how any given agrammatic output symptom relates to an underlying production limitation, and it should be obvious that the existence of the "paradoxical comprehenders" is the call to a research program rather than a prima facie disconfirmation of the role of production in comprehension processing.

Acquisition Profiles

It's pretty clear on the basis of contemporary studies of language acquisition that kids understand a lot that is syntactically quite sophisticated before they talk much and before their own spontaneous speech displays a similar degree of syntactic sophistication (see McKee, Mac-Daniel, & Snedeker, 1998, and references therein). Indeed, when they do talk at early stages, many investigators have taken children's utterances to be quite aberrant re adult syntactic targets. Such a condition, taken at face value poses something like the problem of the agrammatic aphasics noted in the preceding section: they are individuals (children or aphasic) whose production output is "impoverished" or "deviant," but whose understanding seems to draw on significantly greater resources of the syntax. If production plays the role I have ascribed to it in the proposal for an integrated production and comprehension system, how can such a circumstance exist? Several observations and ideas suggest themselves. First, with respect to children, one may question the extent to which their underlying production system is in fact lacking in resource or discriminative capacity. We can note (McKee & Emiliani, 1992) that children's productions are more complex than superficial appearance would suggest, and that elicited production tasks can bring to light evidence of adult grammatical models driving the child's production at the stage when only two or three words are being generated. It may be quite feasible to defend the view that the observed production profile is reduced in range not because the child's ability to bring conceptual content to bear on linguistic representation is limited, and in particular not because of limited access to abstract syntactic devices of the language, but rather because of fairly late stage processes in the encoding cycle. Moreover, there is a complementary point: very young children may not appreciate or control discourse structure and some of the associated implicational devices required to fully exploit it. If so, the apparent dissociation of production and comprehension capacity may have roots other than in the components needed to exercise the production hypothesis I have been pursuing. Overall, it does seem clear that examination of relations between children's developing production and comprehension capacities has the potential to contribute significantly to an evaluation of dependencies between the two systems and their bearing on the production/comprehension hypothesis.

SUMMARY REMARKS

This is in several respects a potentially frustrating proposal for those who like their argument space to draw nice sharp distinctions—as most of us do. And from time to time I think of myself that way, so the production hypothesis makes me a little nervous. For, one might wish to argue that all this conversation about production is merely a funny way to talk about comprehension processes since the assimilation of lexical and phrasal inputs into discourse formats in order to drive production might just be the very process that Marslen-Wilson and Tyler (1987) wished to invoke when they averred that mapping is "direct" from speech input to mental models, and encompassing no intervening representation of syntactic form. Syntax on that view is just another information class embedded in the mapping procedure. That embedding might be done in various ways. How human heads do it remains to be determined. For the hypothesis I have in mind, a lot will turn on whether and how it works out that a partial analysis of the input delivered primarily by data driven processes can be integrated with a preexisting discourse framework, and thus give the production machine a suitably constrained input so as to deliver a useful matching and control signal for integration with the later products of the syntax recognition device. How detailed and accurate can that data driven analysis be if it has no semantic crutches? Accurate enough that the production machine can achieve the necessary convergence with the recognition system within a useful time frame given richer lexical information and an existing discourse frame? I don't know, but I think it's a pretty good bet—certainly one worth close inspection. If such is the case, the picture of the recognition/comprehension component would remain dominantly form driven from beginning to "end" (viz., at match/merge of the top-down production structure with the final bottom-up parsing product). Of course, here's the other end of the possible spectrum: it may be that the devil in these details could turn out to be something like a constraint satisfaction machine of the sort that Bever et al. (1998) adopted as a front end to the ABS system in their proposal. If so, the differences between that proposal and my own would diminish. But, I think there would remain some useful leverage in the production hypothesis even in that scenario; I note some that obtain on either outcome.

It is well to remember another point in this context, namely, that the perspective I'm pursing holds that the recognition based parsing system and the production based phrase building systems are complementary—and the recognition device in particular must be independently capable of achieving richly elaborated structure if it is to serve in its turn as an error correction device and source of constraint on the production system. The production hypothesis offers distinct drivers for the determination of sentence form under comparable time constraints that fits naturally into a scheme of error control requirements on each of the major performance systems. Beyond that, we do know that the production system must be designed to start from conceptual inputs that will drive linguistic outputs. And it looks like a part of the way the human production system works is to put a little space in between the semantic and syntactic engines in the process of doing that job. This is a point worth dwelling on for a moment. We expect production processes to have conceptual/semantic drivers. That is the nature of the input to the system. Nevertheless, the production data indicates that this is compatible with a significant degree of separation in the system for semantic, syntactic, and phonological processing—the system does not manifest itself as a set of "mixed representations." Why aren't we just a little amazed by this? If there is computational advantage to mixed mode processing, why not here if anywhere? It's an interesting thought to ponder: if the direct use of semantic guidance for phrasal construction is essential to real-time success in the compositional operations of language processing, one might reasonably expect to see this strongly manifest in the organization of the phrasal representations computed for language production. The relevant information is indisputably activated therein. But, instead, one sees considerable evidence indicating components of the production system that involve grammatical category and phonological representation but that do not display a similarly striking dependence on the semantic force of the lexical elements (see references in the section entitled Language Production Study). Various reasons might be offered for such a condition. One might even speculate that a motivation for this condition in production arises out the utility of interactions with a system (recognition) that does its processing work on a more limited information base.

The incorporation of the range of interpretive constraints typically appealed to in strongly interactive treatments of parsing for comprehension can be accomplished without abandoning architectures with significant modularity. Production architectures are demonstration cases of that possibility. But, given that assumption, the question I posed for an integrated constraint satisfaction mode of comprehension is fair to pose here for the production proposal. Namely, why on the production view is the effect of interpretation variable across experiments? I have suggested a couple of reasons in preceding remarks vis-à-vis differences in the availability of the necessary lexical and contextual information as it arises in a given communicative situation or from the interaction of production and comprehension processes. The production architecture account must appeal to variations in informational availability just as all interactive accounts must do. The principal added ingredient is provided by the need for production structure itself. The account is explicit about assigning the source of conceptual, semantic, and discourse factors to a language processing system for which interpretive factors are expected—indeed, necessary—components. A variety of factors may be brought to bear: expectations and intentions that can control production decision should be present and determining for comprehension; discourse structure when present should be determining, and may well be so with greater immediacy than virtually any other constraint type; whatever aspects of lexically coded information are not recoverable from first pass recognition will be effective, but only within the time constraints required for application of the constraints via production mechanisms. For this latter point, the relation between subcategorization and thematic role information will be instructive. But, the lexical structure issues will be irritatingly malleable until such time as arguments about the relative availability of the different classes of information about lexical elements are better fleshed out. There are further arguments to be made along these lines, I think—some of them certainly already underway in the context of the picture–word interference task alluded to in the section entitled Language Production Study where some interesting efforts to link word recognition and word production processes seem the best way to deal with conflicting experimental outcomes in that paradigm (see, e.g., Roelofs, forthcoming).

The treatment of the overall comprehension process as involving an "interaction" between production system syntax and data driven recognition devices has some appeal in terms both of the task of linking processors to grammars and the general interest of identifying and motivating commonalities in the two major performance modes. The virtues of this move as a way to rationalize incompatible aspects of the experimental landscape are threefold: it simplifies the comprehension scheme by eliminating the need to try to enfold a layer of semantically and pragmatically driven mechanisms; it advances an interesting set of claims about relations between the two major performance systems; and it makes it easier to preserve a picture of recognition processing that corresponds to the informational structure of grammars. In short, because the architecture of the production system is arguably one in which the conceptual, discourse, and semantic factors are also broadly distinguishable from the mechanisms of phrasal construction and phonological interpretation, the overall picture of processing is one in which one may more readily see both a general fit of production and comprehension processes to each other and of each of these to the character of grammatical systems.

ACKNOWLEDGMENTS

This work was supported in part by National Multipurpose Research and Training Center Grant DC-01409 from the National Institute on Deafness and Other Communication Disorders. I wish also to express appreciation for comments from audiences at UCLA Linguistics, at the University of Pennsylvania I.R.C.S., and at a colloquium, MPI for Pyscholinguistics in Nijmegen, all of which helped me in thinking about the matters presented here.

REFERENCES

Altman, G., & Steedman, M. (1988). Interaction with context during human sentence processing. *Cognition, 30,* 191–238.

Bever, T. G. (1970). The cognitive basis of linguistics structures. In J. R. Hayes (Ed.), *Cognition and the development of language.* New York: Wiley.

Bever, T. G., Sanz, M., & Townsend, D. (1998). The emperor's psycholinguistics. *Journal of Psycholinguistic Research.*

Bierwisch, M. (1982). Linguistics and language error. In A. Cutler (Ed.), *Slips of the tongue* (pp. 29–72). Amsterdam: Mouton.

Bock, J. K. (1986). Syntactic persistence in language production. *Cognitive Psychology, 18,* 355–387.

Bock, J. K. (1990). Structure in language: Creating form in talk. *American Psychologist, 45,* 1221–1236.

Bock, J. K., & Eberhard, E. (1993). Meaning, sound, and syntax in English number agreement. *Language and Cognitive Processes, 8,* 57–99.

Bock, J. K., & Levelt, W. J. M. (1994). Language production: Grammatical encoding. In M. Gernsbacher (Ed.), *Handbook of psycholinguistics.* San Diego: Academic Press.

Bock J. K., & Loebell, H. (1990). Framing sentences. *Cognition, 35,* 1–39.

Bock, J. K., Loebell, H., & Morey, R. (1992). From conceptual roles to structural relations: Bridging the syntactic cleft. *Psychological Review, 99,* 150–171.

Bock, J. K., & Miller, C.A. (1991) Broken agreement. *Cognitive Psychology, 23*, 45–93.

Bock, J. K., Nicol, J., & Cutting, J. (1999). The ties that bind: Creating number agreement in speech. *Journal of Memory and Language, 40*, 330–346.

Bock, J. K., & Warren, R. (1985). Conceptual accessibility and syntactic structure in sentence formulations. *Cognition, 21*, 47–67.

Brown, C., Wassenaar, M., and Hagoort, P. (1999). *Functional plasticity in aphasic patients with agrammatic comprehension.* Manuscript, Max Planck Institute for Psycholinguistics, Nijmegen, The Netherlands.

Caramazza, A., and Zurif, E. (1976). Dissociation of algorithimic and associative processes in language comprehension: Evidence form aphasia. *Brain and Language, 3*, 552–582.

Caplan, D. (1987). *Neurolinguistics and linguistic aphasiology: An introduction.* Cambridge: Cambridge University Press.

Carlson, G., & Tanenhaus, M. (1988). Thematic roles and language comprehension. In W. Wilkens (Ed.), *Thematic relations syntax, and semantic* (vol. 21, pp. 263–300). New York: Academic Press.

Crain, S., & Steedman, M. (1985). On not being led up the garden path: The use of context by the psychological processor. In D. Dowty, L. Kartutunen, and A. Zwicky (Eds), *Natural Language Parsing*, Cambridge University Press.

Coulson, S., King, M., & Kutas, M. (1998). Expect the unexpected: Event related response to morphosyntactic violations. *Language and Cognitive Processes, 13*, 21–58.

Crocker, M. (1996). *Computational Psycholinguistics.* Dordrecht: Kluwer.

Dell, G., Schwartz, M., Martin, N., Saffran, E., & Gagnon, D. (1997). Lexical access in aphasic and nonaphasic speakers. *Psychological Review, 104*, 801–838.

Fodor, J. A. (1983). *The modularity of mind*, Cambridge, MA: MIT Press.

Fodor, J. A., Bever, T. G., & Garrett, M. (1974). *The psychology of language: An introduction to psycholinguistics and generative transformational grammar.* New York: McGraw-Hill.

Forster, K. I. (1979). Levels of processing and the structure of the language processor. In W. Cooper and E. C. T. Walker (Eds.), *Sentence processing.* Englewood, NJ: Erlbaum.

Forster, K. I. (1987). Binding, plausibility, and modularity. In J. Garfield (Ed.), *Modularity in knowledge representation and natural-language understanding.* Cambridge, MA: MIT Press.

Frazier, L. (1987). Theories of sentence processing. In J. Garfield (Ed.), *Modularity in knowledge representation and natural-language processing.* Cambridge, MA: MIT Press.

Frazier, L. (1999). *On sentence interpretation.* Dordrecht: Kluwer.

Frazier, L., & Clifton, C. (1996). *Construal.* Cambridge, MA: MIT Press.

Friederici, A. (1998a). The neurobiology of language comprehension. In A. Friederici (Ed.), *Language Comprehension: A Biological Perspective*, (pp. 263–301). Berlin/Heidelberg/New York: Springer.

Friederici, A. (1998b). Diagnosis and reanalysis. In J. D. Fodor & F. Ferreira (Eds.), *Reanalysis in sentence processing.* (pp. 177–200). Dordrecht: Kluwer.

Friederici, A., von Cramon, Y., & Kotz, S. (1999). fMRI studies of patients with froto-temporal lesions. Manuscript, Max Planck Institute for Cognitive Neuroscience, Leipsiz, Germany.

Friederici, A., Hahne, A., & von Cramon, Y. (1998). First pass vs second pass parsing processes in a Wernicke's and a Broca's aphasic: Electrophysiological evidence for a double dissociation. *Brain and Language, 62*, 311–341.

Freiderici, A., Hahne, A., & Mecklinger, A. (1996). Temporal structure of syntactic parsing: Early and late Event Related Potential effects. *Journal of Experimental Psychology: Learning, Memory, and Cognition, 22*, 1219–1248.

Fromkin, V. (1971). The non-anomalous nature of anlomalous utterances. *Language, 47*, 27–52.

Fromkin, V. (Ed.) (1995). *Special Volume: Linguistic Representational and Processing Analysis of Agrammatism. Brain and Language, 50.*

Garrett, M. (1980). Levels of processing in sentence production. In B. Butterworth (Ed.), *Language production: Vol 1. Speech and talk* (pp. 177–220). London: Academic Press.

Garrett, M. (1993a). Errors and their relevance for theories of language production. In G. Blanken, J. Dittmann, H. Grimm, J. Marshall, & C. Wallesch, (Eds.), *Linguistic disorders and pathologies: An international handbook.* Berlin: de Gruyter.

Garrett, M. (1993b). The structure of language processing: Neurophsychological evidence. In M. Gazaniga (Ed.), *Cognitive neuroscience,* pp. 881–889. Cambridge, MA: MIT Press.

Gibson, E., & Tunstall, S. (1999). *The parser need not keep track of contingent frequencies: A lexical account of the English determiner/complementizer ambiguity.* Manuscript Department of Brain and Cognitive Sciences, Massachuseets Institute of Technology. Poster: 12th annual CUNY Conference on Sentence Processing, March 18–20, New York: CUNY Graduate School.

Gorrell, P. (1995). *Syntax and parsing.* Cambridge: Cambridge University Press.

Hagoort, P., and Brown, C. (1994). Brain responses to lexical ambiguity resolution and parsing. In C. Clifton, L. Frazier, & K. Rayner (Eds.), *Perspectives on Sentence Processing,* (pp. 45–80). Erlbaum: Hillsdale, NJ.

Hagoort, B., & Brown, C. (in press). Semantic and syntactic ERP effects of listening to speech compared to reading. *Neuropsychologia.*

Hagoort, P., Brown, C., & Groothusen, J. (1993). The syntactic postive shift as an ERP measure of syntactic processing. *Language and Cognitive Processes,* 8, 439–484.

Hagoort, P., Brown, C., & Osterhout, L. (in press), The neurocognition of syntactic processing. In C. Brown & P. Hagoort, (Eds.), *The neurocognition of language.* Oxford: Oxford University Press.

Hagoort, P., and Brown, C., Vonk, W., & Hoeks. J. (forthcoming). *Syntactic ambiguity effects in coordination structures; ERP evidence.* Manuscript, Max Planck Institute for Psycholoinguistics, Nijmegen.

Hahne, A., and Friederici, A. (in press). Language comprehension: The brain dissociates early automatic and late controlled processes. *Journal of Cognitive Neuroscience.*

Jackendoff, R. (1989). Consciousness and the computational mind. Cambridge, MA: MIT Press.

Joshi, A., and Schabes, Y. (1997). Tree adjoining grammars. In G. Rozenburg & A. Salomma (Eds.), *Handook of formal languages and automata: Vol. 3, Beyond words.* Berlin: Springer-Verlag.

Kempen, G. (1999). Human grammatical coding. (forthcoming). Cambridge: Cambridge University Press.

Kim, A., Srinivas, B., & Trueswell, J. (1998). The convergence of lexicalist perspectives in psycholinguistics and computational, linguistics.

Kolk, H., Van Grunsven, J., & Keyser, A. (1985). On parallelism between production and comprehension in agrammatism. In M. L. Lean (Ed.), *Agrammatism.* New York: Academic Press.

Kutas, M., & Hilyard, S. (1980). Reading between the lines: Event related potentials during sentence processing. *Brain and Language,* 11, 354–373.

Levelt, W. J. M. (1989). *Speaking: From intention to articulation.* Cambridge, MA: MIT Press.

Levelt, W., Roelofs, A., and Meyer, A., (1999). A theory of lexical access in speech production. *Behavioral and Brain Science,* 22, 1–75.

Linebarger, M., Schwartz, M., & Saffran, E. (1983). Sensitivity to grammatical structure in so-called agrammatic aphasics. *Cognition, 13,* 361–392.

MacDonald, M., Pearlmutter, N., & Seidenberg, M. (1994). Lexical nature of syntactic ambiguity resolution. *Psychological Review, 101,* 676–703.

Marslen-Wilson, W. (1973). Linguistic structure and speech shadowing at very short latencies. *Nature* (London) 244, 522–523.

Marslen-Wilson, W., & Tyler, L. (1980). The temporal structure of spoken language understanding. *Cognition, 8,* 1–71.

Marslen-Wilson, W., & Tyler, L. (1987). Against modularity. In J. Garfield (Ed.), *Modularity in
knowledge representation and natural-language understanding.* (pp. 37–62). Cambridge, MA:
MIT Press.

McClelland, J., St. John, M., & Taraban, R. (1989). Sentence comprehension: A parallel
distributed approach. *Langauge and Cognitive Processes, 4,* 287–335.

McElree, B., & Griffith, T. (1995). Syntactic and semantic processing in sentence comprehension: Evidence for a temporal dissociation. *Journal of Experimental Psychology: Learning,
Memory, and Cognition, 21,* 134–157.

McElree, B., & Griffith, T. (1998). Structural and lexical constraints on filling gaps during
sentence comprehension. *Journal of Experimental Psychology: Learning, Memory, and Cognition, 24,* 432–460.

Mckee, C., McDaniel, D., & Snedeker, J. (1998). Relatives children say. *Journal of Psycholinguistic Research 27,* 573–596.

Mckee, D., & Emiliani, M. (1992). *Il Clitico: Cé ma non si vede. Natural Language and Linguistic
Theory, 10,* 415–437.

Miceli, G., Mazzucchi, A., Menn, L., & Goodglass, H. (1983). Contrasting cases of Italian
agrammatic aphasia without comprehension disorder. *Brain and Language, 10,* 65–97.

Mitchell, D. (1994). Sentence parsing. In M. Gernsbacher (Ed.), *Handbook of Psycholinguistics.*
San Diego: Academic Press.

Neville, H., Nicol, J., Barss, A., Forster, K., & Garrett, M. (1991). Syntactically based sentence
processing classes: Evidence from event related potentials. *Journal of Cognitive Neuroscience, 3,* 151–165.

Neville, H., Mills, D. & Lawson, D. (1992). Fractionating language: Different neural sub-
sytems with different sensitive periods. *Cerebral Cortex, 2,* 244–258.

Newmeyer, F. (1998). *Language form and language function.* Cambridge, MA: MIT Press.

Nicol, J., and Love, T. (2000). Overarching agrammatism: When comprehension involves
production. In Y. Grodzinsky, L. Shapiro, & D. Swinney (Eds.), *Language and the Brain,*
pp. – . Academic Press: San Diego.

Nicol, J., & Swinney, D. (1989). The role of structure in coreference assignment during sentence processing. *Journal of Psycholinguistic Research: Special Issue on Sentence Processing,
18,* 5–24.

Nicol, J., Forster, K., & Veres, C. (1997). Subject-verb agreement processes in comprehension.
Journal of Memory and Language, 36, 569–587.

Osterhout, L., & Holcomb, P. (1992). Event related brain potentials elicited by syntactic anomaly. *Journal of Memory and Language, 31,* 785–806.

Osterhout, L., Holcomb, P., & Swinney, D. (1994). Brain potentials elicited by garden-path
sentences: Evidence of the application of verb information during parsing. *Journal of Experimental Psychology: Learning, Memory and Cognition, 20,* 786–803.

Roelofs, A. (forthcoming). *Speaking while hearing or seeing words.* Unpublished manuscript,
University of Exeter, England.

Spivey, M., & Tannenhous, M. (1998). Syntactic ambiguity resolution in discourse: modeling
the effects of referential context and lexical frequency. *Journal of Experimental Psychology:
Language, Memory and Cognition, 24,* 1521–1543.

Stone, M., & Doran, C. (1997). Sentence planning as description using tree-adjoining grammar. *ACL,* p. 198–205.

Swinney, D., & Zurif, E. (1995). Syntactic processing in aphasia. In V. Fromkin (Ed.), *Special
Volume: Linguistic Representational and Processing Analyses of Agrammatism. Brain and Language, 50.*

Swinney, D., Zurif, E., E Nicol, J. (1989). The effects of focal brain damage on sentence processing: An examination of the neural organization of a mental module. *Journal of Cognitive Neuroscience, 1*, 25–37.

Swinney, D., Zurif, E., Prather, P., & Love, T. (1996) Neurological distributuion of processing operations underlying language comprehension. *Journal of Cognitive Neuroscience, 8*, 174–184.

Tannenhaus, M., Spivey-Knowlton, M., Eberhard, K., & Sedivy, J. (1995). Interpretation of visual and linguistic information in spoken language comprehension. *Science, 268*, 1632–1634.

Trueswell, J., and Kim, A. (1998). How to prune a garden-path by nipping it in the bud: Fast priming of verb argument structure. *Journal of Memory and Language, 39*, 102–123.

Trueswell, J., & Tannenhaus, M. (1994). Toward a lexicalist framework for constraint based syntactic ambiguity resolution. In C. Clifton, K. Rayner, & L. Frazier (eds.), *Perspectives in sentence processing*. Hillsdale, NJ: Erlbaum.

Tyler, L, & Marslen-Wilson, W. (1977). The on-line effects of semantic context on syntactic processing. *Journal of Verbal Learning and Verbal Behavior, 16*, 683–692.

Van Petten, C., Coulson, S. Rubin, S. Plante, E., & Parks, M. (1999). Timecourse of word identification and semantic integration in spoken language. *Journal of Experimental Psychology: Language, Memory and Cognition 25*, 394–471.

Van Turennout, M., Haggort, P., & Brown, C. (1998). Brain acitivity during speaking; From syntax to phonology in 40 msec. *Science, 280*, 572–574.

Vigliocco, G., Antonini, T., & Garrett, M. (1997). Grammatical gender is on the tip of Italian tongues. *Psychological Science, 8*, 314–317.

Vigliocco, G., and Zilli, M. (1999). Syntactic accuracy in sentence production: Gender agreement in Italian and Spanish. In T. Jacobsen, A. Friederici, & M. Garrett (Eds.), *Special Issue: Journal of Psycholinguistic Research*.

Vosse, T., & Kempen, G. (1999). *Syntactic stucture assembly in human parsing: A computational model based on competitive inhibition and a lexicalist grammar.* Manuscript, Leiden Univeristy, The Netherlands.

Zurif, E., Swinney, D., Prather, P., Solomon, J., & Bushnell, C. (1993). An on-line analysis of syntactic processing in Broca's and Wernicke's aphasia. *Brain and Language, 45*, 448-464.

Zwitserlood, P., (1989). The locus of effects of sentential-semantic context in spoken word processing. *Cognition, 32*, 25–64.

Part II

The Comprehension–
Production Interface

Chapter 3

Overarching Agrammatism

Yosef Grodzinsky

If there is a single neuropsychological term that is most closely associated with Edgar Zurif (in terms of both content and style), it is "overarching agrammatism." Zurif was the first to document the comprehension deficit in Broca's aphasia systematically (cf. Zurif, Caramazza, & Myerson, 1972; Zurif, Caramazza, Myerson, & Galvin, 1974; Zurif & Caramazza, 1976), and show that this deficit has a syntactic character. These pioneering studies launched a new era in the neuropsychology of language, as they shifted the focus of research both to syntax, and to comprehension—two areas that are intensely investigated today, with non-negligible success, one might add. Indeed, a significant body of valuable data, as well as a corresponding mass of theoretical work, was initiated by these early discoveries made by Zurif and colleagues.

Conceiving of agrammatism as an "overarching" deficit was the next step. The discovery of syntactic deficits in Broca's aphasia led to the (then unconventional) belief that the deficit in Broca's aphasia was not linked just to speech production, but rather, was generalized, spanning all communicative activities or channels. Moreover, the new findings indicated that the correct descriptive vocabulary for the deficit was linguistic. Thus, if previous accounts of Broca's aphasia viewed it as a channel-specific disturbance (cf. Geschwind, 1970; Goodglass & Kaplan, 1972; Goodglass, 1976), the emerging position was that this syndrome manifests as a severe loss of syntax that cuts across all linguistic activities. This claim has an important consequence: it suggests that the neural tissue implicated in the deficit—Broca's area and its vicinity, were the neural substrate for human syntactic capacity. The underlying reasoning was not unsound: some had already believed that speech production in Broca's aphasia was syntactically impaired; now a syntactic impairment was discovered in comprehension as well. It thus followed, apparently, that the right unit of analysis for neuropsychologists of language was linguistic. On this view (argued for vigorously in Zurif, 1978, and Zurif, 1980), one must "rede-fine" the cerebral language centers, reject the activity-based account of the nineteenth century, according to which Broca's area subtends speech production; instead, a linguistic account is proposed, in which Broca's area is the home of syntactic resources, recruited for both production and comprehension. The linguistic deficiency in Broca's aphasia was, from now on, overarching agrammatism (OAA).

Overarching agrammatism was an innovative and interesting idea. Its appeal, moreover, was in its simplicity. New data from structured experiments that began coming in at the time (mostly from the work of Zurif and colleagues), indicated that the modality-based account was not entirely true, and that receptive aspects of language were also implicated in Broca's aphasia. These data flew in the face of the traditional account, as they demonstrated that the functional deficits subsequent to damage to Broca's area is not restricted to productive aspects of language. A modality-based theory of the language centers had to give way to another, which was a proposal to view language as neurally represented, rather than according to linguistic levels. Syntax, on this view, was anterior, whereas the semantics was taken to be in and around Wernicke's area. A move toward "redefining" the cerebral language centers had begun (Zurif, 1980).

Yet there were problems with the new OAA account. First, apparent counterexamples were soon presented. Certain cases were reported, in which patients disruptions did not span all modalities. There were studies in which Broca's patients scored "poorly" on production tests, yet thrived when their receptive skills were examined (Miceli, Mazzucchi, Menn, & Goodglass, 1983; Kolk & van Grunsven, 1985). And though at least some of these were later discredited (Zurif, 1996), they seemed (at least initially) to indicate that the OAA could not cover all cases. Further, they served as a basis for those who later attacked the concept of syndrome–complex in neuropsychology, and argued that the patient category Broca's aphasia is incoherent (e.g., Caramazza, 1986), partially because of these apparent inconsistencies in the data.

Still, problems with OAA actually seemed to run deeper. To see that, we need to consider what it takes to be convinced of the validity of such an idea. Recall that by overarching agrammatism one meant a specific disruption in language processing, that did not just span all modalities; the pattern of selectivity in the disruption was expected to exhibit cross-modal uniformity. OAA, then, was taken to be roughly the following:

(1) Overarching agrammatism (OAA)
     The language disruption in agrammatism (a) spans all modalities, and (b) the selective pattern of impairment and sparing is identical cross-modally.

Such a version of OAA underlies the psycholinguistic account of agrammatism of Bradley, Garrett, and Zurif (1980). They proposed a comprehension/production parallelism, in that the deficit to both modalities involved closed versus open class vocabulary items. Their account promoted a particular view of the mental lexicon, whose disruption manifests in OAA. Although this proposal was later abandoned for various reasons, it did meet the requirements posited by the OAA hypothesis: it purported to provide uniform cross-modal evidence regarding the selectivity of the aphasic deficit.

Bradley, Garrett, and Zurif's (1980) account was based on meager empirical evidence: all they had available were spontaneous speech data in English, and one set of results from reaction time (RT) experiments that they ran with normal and aphasic subjects. Further, the linguistic basis of their account was rather shaky. Linguistic analyses of agrammatism that were proposed later, taken in conjunction with the massive body of experimental data that has since accumulated, enable us to evaluate the OAA account more seriously than ever before. Yet the type of data they considered underscored the existence of a receptive deficit in Broca's aphasia, and thus from that moment on, OAA was to be true or false not depending on comprehension deficit per se, but rather, on the degree of similarity between it and the deficit in production. Based on the current state of the evidence, I propose to do such an evaluation below. My examination will consist of several steps: first, I will go over the current state of the art in studies of agrammatic speech production. Second, I will summarize the situation in the comprehension domain. Next, differences and similarities between the two will be examined, to evaluate the current validity of the OAA. Finally, I will try to look at points of connection.

PRODUCTION: A TREE-PRUNING HYPOTHESIS

Consider the structural properties of the agrammatic speech production deficit: Recent investigations indicate that, contrary to traditional views, inflectional categories are not all equally impaired. Rather, it turns out that inflectional elements are impaired or preserved depending on their structural position on the syntactic tree. The first piece of evidence for this claim came about through a Hebrew speaking patient studied by Friedmann (1994), who was selectively impaired in the production of inflection: she had problems with tense, but not agreement. This finding runs contrary to common belief, according to which agrammatic aphasics have equal problems with all functional categories. Friedmann also showed, through a retrospective literature review, that cross-linguistic evidence goes in the same direction: a significant group of patients reported in the literature also showed impairment in tense but not agreement (Nespoulous et al., 1988; Miceli, 1989; Silveri, Romani, & Caramazza, Saffran, Schwartz, & Marin, 1980) yet the opposite (impaired agreement but not tense) is never found:

(2) *Speaking English:* The kiss . . . the lady kissed . . . the lady is . . . the lady and man and the lady . . . kissing.

(3) *Reading French aloud:*
Target: Bonjour,   grand-mere, je **vous ai apporte'**
good morning, grandma,   I to-you have bring (pres.-perf.)
Read: Bonjour, grand-mere, je **portrai** euh je /pu/ /zeda/ a-aporte'
bring (future)

Seeking to obtain a detailed error analysis, Friedmann then created a set of tests to track the exact nature of the impairment in tense versus agreement in speech production. The distinction made by the patients was especially important in light of developments in linguistic theory: the split inflection hypothesis (Pollock, 1989) proposes structural differences between tense and agreement, and argues that they each form a distinct functional category. This hypothesis not only provides a powerful and precise descriptive tool, but also presents a host of related issues to be examined. So, the tests were first conducted on one patient (Friedmann, 1994; Friedmann & Grodzinsky, 1997) and then extended to a group of 13 Hebrew and Arabic speaking patients (Friedmann, 1998; Friedmann & Grodzinsky, in press):

(4)   Yesterday the boy walked;

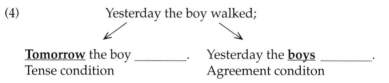

Tomorrow the boy _____.   Yesterday the **boys** _____.
Tense condition   Agreement conditon

The results were remarkable: While agreement was normal, tense was severely impaired, even though the patient's perception of time, as well as comprehension of temporal adverbs, was shown to be intact. Tense errors were mostly substitutions of inflection (with no prefered "unmarked" form, observed in repetition (5), and in completion (6) tasks. In (7) a numerical representation of error rates is presented:

(5) Target: ha'anashim **yixtevu**   mixtav la-bank
the-people write-**future**-3-m-pl letter   to-the-bank
Repeated: ha-anashim **katvu**   mixtav la-bank
the-people write-**past**-3-m-pl letter   to-the-bank

(6) <u>Target</u>: axshav   ata holex.   etmol   'ata ____ (expected: halaxta)
    now you go-pres-2-m-sg Yesterday you ___ (go-**past**-2-m-sg)
<u>completed</u>: axshav ata holex.   etmol   ata <u>telex</u>
    now you go-pres-2-m-sg. Yesterday you go-**future**-2-m-sg.

(7)	Agreement errors	Tense errors
	4% (28/642)	44% (353/805)

This dissociation suggests a deficit that implicates tense, but not agreement features. This, in itself, is new, for agrammatic aphasia has always been thought to implicated all functional elements equally, and the striking asymmetries we observe appear to have been overlooked.

Further, the impairment touches on a cluster of syntactic properties related to the tense node (according the split-inflection hypothesis), which are also disrupted: Observed are subject omissions, difficulties with copulas, and specific word order problems that pertain to nodes in the syntactic tree that are beyond the tense node, but nothing below this node is impaired. Moreover, the impairment is associated with problems in yet higher parts of the tree (CP). As a result, questions and embedded clauses are nonexistent or completely ill formed.

By contrast, other properties that are related to agreement, and lower parts of the tree, are left intact. The distinction that linguists have posited receives direct neurological support. Moreover, the disruption affects the tree from the tense node and above, and leaves whatever is below it intact.

This rather rich cluster of cross-linguistic facts has led to a description of agrammatic speech production that is stated over trees, not elements. That is, unlike every previous statement, which looked at functional elements regardless of their position in the sentence, the currently available data lead to the view that agrammatic aphasic patients produce trees that are intact up to the tense node and "pruned" from this node and up (Friedmann, 1994; Friedmann & Grodzinsky, 1997):

(8) <u>Tree-Pruning Hypothesis (TPH, Friedmann & Grodzinsky, 1997, *simplified*)</u>: Broca's aphasics cannot represent T; higher branches of the tree are pruned (Figure 1).

Interestingly, this claim receives empirical support from yet another direction: there is a salient cross-linguistic difference in the production of verbs by Broca's aphasics. In English, the speech output of Broca's aphasics contains verbs that are bare stems, yet these are in their proper position in the sentence — always after the subject. In verb-second (V2) languages (e.g., Dutch, German), however, where inflected verbs undergo

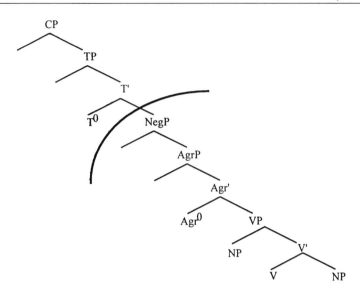

Figure 1 Tree-pruning hypothesis.

movement, the situation is different. In these languages verbs start out in sentence-final position, and must raise to pick up its tense features, and the result is subject-verb-object (SVO) order. A nonfinite verb in a main clause (e.g., in a clause that contains an inflected auxiliary), will remain in final position, and its finite counterpart will be in second position. In a patient whose syntactic tree is pruned, verbs will fail to raise, and the result will be as is observed in Dutch: in aphasic speech verbs in main clauses not only appear uninflected, but also, are in sentence final position, resulting in ungrammatical strings (Bastiaanse & Van Zonnenfeld, 1998; Friedmann, 1998). Dutch agrammatics make no errors on infinitives in subordinate clauses, but have major difficulties with inflecting main verbs, which they mostly produce not only as infinitives, but, critically, in final position.

So, in sum, the deficit in speech production in Broca's aphasia is strongly linked to structural factors: they fail to represent parts of the syntactic tree from a certain node up, and given that these underspecified nodes usually house inflectional categories, it was believed, until more recently, that all inflections are impaired; the current cross-linguistic evidence, however, suggests a partial deficit as described above. Next, we will examine comprehension patterns in Broca's aphasia, and see whether these parallel those in production. As we have seen, for the OAA to be true, such a parallelism is a must.

RECEPTIVE ABILITIES: A RESTRICTIVE
TRACE-DELETION HYPOTHESIS

A syntactic deficit to receptive abilities on Broca's aphasia has been shown time and again over the past three decades. That there is selectively within the syntax is a more recent claim. Thus Caramazza and Zurif (1976) attempted to ascribe "asyntactic comprehension" to these patients, which implied a total loss of syntax. This suggestion, which gave rise to OAA, was clearly too strong. It was only later experimentation that indicated that the impairment was not as widespread: certain syntactic structures gave rise to normal comprehension, whereas others were impaired. The issue has been the stability of these patterns, and their precise description. As matters currently stand, the comprehension patterns of Broca's aphasics appear stable; moreover, it may very well be that cases whose comprehension had previously been thought to be deviant (like the apparent counterexamples to OAA that are mentioned above) in fact conform to the pattern, in that they fall within the allowable variation (cf. Grodzinsky, Pinango, Zurif, & Drai, 1998). As this pattern is currently described, the deficit mainly affects syntactic movement. That is, patients mostly fail (a) to comprehend movement-derived structures (Grodzinsky, 1986, 1990, 1995); (b) to detect violations of grammaticality when movement rules are involved (Grodzinsky & Finkel, 1998); and (c) to properly process movement derived structures on-line (Zurif, Swinney, Prather, Solomon, & Bushell 1993; Swinney & Zurif, 1995). In (9), some examples of the comprehension performance of these patients are presented, according to level of performance for the group (cf. Grodzinsky, et al., 1998, for discussion of this issue):

Construction type	Performance level
(9) a. The girl pushed the boy	*above chance*
b. The girl who pushed the boy was tall	*above chance*
c. Show me the girl who pushed the boy	*above chance*
d. It is the girl who pushed the boy	*above chance*
e. The boy was interested in the girl	*above chance*
f. The woman was uninspired by the man	*above chance*

(10) a. The boy was pushed by the girl	*chance*
b. The boy who the girl pushed was tall	*chance*
c. Show me the boy who the girl pushed	*chance*
d. It is the boy who the girl pushed	*chance*
e. The woman was unmasked by the man	*chance*

These experimental results (pooled from a large body of studies) speak against the "asyntactic comprehension" account. They suggest, rather, that while a syntactic deficit exists, it is partial. For details, see Grodzinsky (1995). Here, just a summary statement will be presented: given that the constructions in (10) are derived by a movement rule, the following account has been proposed (a revision of the trace-deletion hypothesis, TDH, Grodzinsky, 1986, 1990):

(11) Trace Based Account (TBA, Grodzinsky, 1995):
a. *Trace deletion:* Traces in θ-positions are deleted from agrammatic representation.
b. *R(eferential)-strategy:* Assign a referential NP a role by its linear position if it has no θ-role.

This proposal is corroborated by several types of results. Consider, first, comparisons with scores obtained from Broca's aphasics in a language with a different phrasal geometry. If the account would hold there, its generality would be significantly greater. Japanese is one such test case, as it has a different basic word order when compared to English (SOV vs. SVO). Further, its interaction with transformational movement is orthogonal to the active/passive distinction: it has two types of active sentences and two types of passives—each with a movement-derived version [nonscrambled for active (12a), direct for passive (13a)], and a version that is not [scrambled (12b) for active and indirect (13b) for passive]. Hagiwara (Hagiwara, 1993; Hagiwara and Caplan, 1990) has documented the comprehension skills of these patients systematically, and showed that movement is the decisive factor determining their comprehension (cf. Grodzinsky, 1998, for analysis). The Japanese data are summarized in (12)–(13):

(12) Japanese Active:
a. *Nonscrambled (basic):*
Taro-ga Hanako-ni   nagutta   *above chance*
-NOM -ACC hit
Taro hit Hanako
b. *scrambled (movement-derived):*
Hanako$_i$-o Taro -ga t_i nagutta   *chance*

(13) Japanese Passive:
a. *Direct (movement-derived):*
Taro$_i$-ga Hanako-ni t_i nagu-rare-ta   *chance*
-NOM   -ACC   hit-PASS-PAST
Taro was hit by Hanako

b. *Indirect (not derived):*
Okaasan-ga   musuku-ni kaze-o   hik-*are*-ta   *above chance*
mother-NOM a son-by   a cold-ACC catch-PASS-PAST
Mother had (her) son catch a cold on her

These results provide an important cross-linguistic angle to the account, and strengthen it significantly.

Next, our cross-linguistic account is further fortified with evidence that shows its intertask generality: in Grodzinsky and Finkel (1998) we tested some predictions of the TBA to grammaticality judgment. The leading idea of this study was that, if traces of movement are deleted from syntactic representations, then any task that critically relies on these constructs will reveal the deficit. Thus, we presented the patients with judgments such as those in (14)–(15). In order to be able to see that the strings in (14) are ungrammatical, a subject must know that the relationship between the (bolded) antecedent and the trace(*t*) is illicit. But for that, the trace must be represented. Our patients failed at this task. By contrast, they were successful in detecting ungrammaticality in other, analogous cases, in which traces were not involved, such as those in (15).

(14)   a. *__John__ seems that it is likely *t* to win
       b. *__Which woman__ did David think that *t* saw John?
       c. *I don't know __what__ who saw *t*

(15)   a. *Who did John see Joe?
       b. *Who John saw Joe?
       c. *The children sang the football over the fence
       d. *The children threw

These results provide an important angle on the TBA, corroborating the claim that trace deletion is a proper characterization of Broca's receptive skills through a study of grammaticality judgment. Next, a real-time perspective is in order. It is by now well established that normal language users demonstrate trace-antecedent relations in real-time tasks (e.g., Stowe, 1986; Swinney, Ford, Frauenfelder, & Bresnan, 1988; Bever & McElree, 1988; McDonald, 1989; Swinney & Zurif, 1995). The typical experiment exploits priming effects to uncover antecedent reactivation. The leading idea is that the link between a trace and its antecedent causes antecedent reactivation at the trace in the course of comprehension. Thus in (16), *the drink* will be active when heard (namely, at point *1*), will then decay (2), but will get reactivated following the verb (3), due to its link to the trace.

(16) The priest enjoyed **the drink**[1] that the caterer was[2] serving t[3]
to the guests

This is precisely what on-line experiments on normal language users have discovered. Experiments typically take *the drink* as prime, and while the sentence unfolds auditorily, a target is flashed on a screen at points (1)–(3). The expected finding, then, is that if a target word, say, *juice,* is presented visually to subjects at points (1), (2), and (3) when they are listening to the sentence, and the subjects have to make a lexical decision on it, priming effects would be documented at (1) and (3), but not at (2). This is found: priming effects are obtained only in (1) and (3).

Consider, now, the TBA and the expected real-time behavior of Broca's aphasics in such tasks. Deleted traces mean no reactivation at the trace. This means that only in point (1) would a priming effect be obtained. Decay would explain the lack of an effect in (2), and the correlate to trace-deletion would be a lack of priming in (3). Conducting such experiments is quite difficult, yet this is precisely the result of a series of carefully controlled studies of of both subject and object relative clauses (Zurif et al., 1993; Swinney & Zurif, 1995). Importantly, Broca's aphasics do prime, even if not in a fully normal fashion (e.g., Swinney, Zurif, & Nicol, 1989; Shapiro & Levine, 1990; Shapiro, Gordon, Hack, & Killackey, 1993). Yet, when faced with a task that involves priming within a movement-derived construction, they are seriously impaired. Finally, this failure is not characteristic of all aphasics, nor is it necessarily related to general comprehension skills: Wernicke's aphasics with posterior perisylvian lesions perform normally on this task, even though their comprehension abilities are severely compromised.

In sum, then, the claim that trace deletion characterizes the comprehension deficit in Broca's aphasia is reasonably corroborated by the empirical record. The next step in an assessment of OAA is to compare the linguistic accounts of receptive and productive skills in Broca's aphasia. If they are equivalent, the OAA will be supported; otherwise, its validity will, at the very least, be in serious doubt.

OVERARCHING AGRAMMATISM EXAMINED

We must now compare the two accounts, that are repeated below.

(17) PRODUCTION

Tree-Pruning Hypothesis (TPH, Friedmann & Grodzinsky, 1997, *simplified*): Broca's aphasics cannot represent T; higher branches of the tree are pruned.

(18) RECEPTION

Trace Based Account (TBA, Grodzinsky, 1995):
a. *Trace deletion*: Traces in θ-positions are deleted from agrammatic representation.
b. *R(eferential)-strategy*: Assign a referential NP a role by its linear position if it has no θ-role.

The question is whether the TPH is derivable from the TBA, or vice versa, or whether we can generalize over both. It is unclear how the pruning of subtrees can be made to follow from trace deletion; thus, (18) does not seem to follow from (17). The opposite, however, is not an impossibility. In fact, it has been proposed by Friedmann (1998), who seeks to derive the receptive deficit from its productive counterpart. The intuition behind her proposal is that in all cases for which there are comprehension results, the moved antecedents of the deleted traces are in subject positions which, by the TPH, are pruned off. If this account will hold, then OAA is vindicated. The notion is that any node beyond T cannot be constructed, and as a result, a constituent that is moved to such a position has no place on the tree, hence no thematic role. Since movement is to subject position, the aphasics' failure stems from the fact that moved constituents have no position, hence, presumably, no thematic role, and their comprehension failure follows. Technical details aside, for the data above, this idea may work. Yet there are data that remain problematic for such an account, at least as stated. These are comprehension asymmetries, as well as direct contrasts between production and reception of language, mostly in the domain of verb movement.

Consider the data in (19), obtained in a comprehension experiment by Hickok and Avrutin (1995), and (20) from Saddy (1995) and Balogh and Grodzinsky (1996):

(19) a. Who did the girl push *t*?   *above chance*
      b. Who pushed the girl?   *above chance*
      c. Which boy did the girl push *t*?   *chance*
      d. Which boy pushed the girl?   *above chance*

(20) a. The man is pushed by the boy   *chance*
      b. Every man is pushed by a boy   *above chance*

It is clear that just position on the tree constituent cannot determine the outcome. The contrast between (19a) and (19c) — a *who* object question and a *which* object question — demonstrated that. Both question expressions are in the same position, and still, a comprehension contrast is documented. Similarly, the contrast between the quantified and referential subjects in (20) determines comprehension, although they are clearly at the same syntactic position. So, it would appear that for OAA to hold here, more must be put in the account. Moreover, one would like to demonstrate a direct prediction of OAA, Friedmann style: that movement into lower positions in the tree is intact.

Finally, it seems that there is a direct comprehension/production contrast, in the domain of verb movement. While the production of moved verbs is severely impaired, as Friedmann has shown, all available data suggest that this is not the case for comprehension (cf. Grodzinsky & Finkel, 1998, for discussion).

If these problems are resolved, then overarching agrammatism will be vindicated. Zurif's original idea — that a supramodal account of the deficit is possible, and that as a consequence, Broca's area is home for certain syntactic abilities for all modalities — will, potentially, be correct, with the necessary refinements.

A TRIBUTE TO EDGAR ZURIF

A good friend of mine, Gedon Medini, once told a story of Duke Ellington who, in a TV interview with him late in his life, "was asked what he would like to say about the influences and events that shaped his starry life. He said something like this: 'Ya know what it's like runnin' around life, like a maze, and you comes to a corner and ya don't know which way to go, and then some guy is standing there and you asks him, "Which way?" and he points and says, "That way," and ya run and run until you come to another fellow and you ask him, and he points and says, "That way," and ya run and run until you come to another fellow and you ask him, and he points and says, "That way" — What I want to do today . . . is to thank all those guys who was standin' on these corners at the right time and pointed me off in the right way.'" (Medini, 1988).

Edgar's role in the international quest for understanding brain/language relations has been, in the past three decades, very central. As is clearly apparent from most contributions to this volume, and as an even cursory look at the current neuropsychological literature will reveal, he has been to many (certainly to me) that guy around the corner; and he did, it seems, point us off in the right way.

ACKNOWLEDGMENTS

    The preparation of this paper was made possible by NIH Grant 00081 and DC 02984 to the Aphasia Research Center, Boston University School of Medicine, and Israel–U.S. Bi-national Science Foundation Grant 97–00451 to Tel Aviv University.

REFERENCES

Balogh, J. & Grodzinsky, Y. (1996). *Varieties of passive in agrammatism.* Paper presented at the Academy of Aphasia, London.

Bastiaanse, R., & Van Zonnenfeld, R. (1998). On the relation between verb position in Dutch agrammatic aphasics. *Brain and Language* 64, 165–181.

Bever, T. G., & McElree, B. (1988). Empty categories access their antecedents during comprehension. *Linguistis Inquiry* **19(1),** 35–45.

Bradley, D. C., Garrett, M. F., & Zurif, E. B. (1980). Syntactic deficits in Broca's aphasia. In D. Caplan (Ed.), *Biological studies of mental processes.* Cambridge, MA: MIT Press.

Caramazza, A. (1986). On drawing inferences about the structure of normal cognitive processes from patterns of impaired performance: The case for single-patient studies. *Brain and Cognition, 5,* 41–66.

Caramazza, A. & Zurif, E. B. (1976). Dissociation of algorithmic and heuristic processes in sentence comprehension: Evidence from aphasia. *Brain and Language, 3,* 572–582.

Friedmann, N. (1994). *Tense and agreement in an agrammatic patient.* Masters thesis, Tel Aviv University.

Friedmann, N. (1998). *Functional categories in agrammatism.* Doctoral dissertation, Tel Aviv University.

Friedmann, N., & Grodzinsky, Y. (1997). Tense and agreement in agrammatic production: Pruning the syntactic tree. *Brain and Language, 56,* 397–425.

Friedmann, N., & Grodzinsky, Y. (1999). Neurolinguistic evidence for split inflection. In M. A. Friedmann & L. Rizzi, (Eds.) *The acquisition of syntax.* London: Blackwell.

Geschwind, N. (1970). The organization of language and the brain. *Science, 170,* 940–944.

Goodglass, H. (1976). Agrammatism. In H. Whitaker & H. H. Whitaker (Eds.), *Studies in neurolinguistics,* Vol. 2. New York: Academic Press.

Goodglass, H., & Kaplan, E. (1972). *The assessment of aphasia and related disorders.* Philadelphia, PA: Lea & Febiger.

Grodzinsky, Y. (1986). Language deficits and the theory of syntax. *Brain and Language, 27,* 135–159.

Grodzinsky, Y. (1990). *Theoretical perspectives on language deficits.* Cambridge, MA: MIT Press.

Grodzinsky, Y. (1995). A restrictive theory of trace deletion in agrammatism. *Brain and Language, 51,* 26–51.

Grodzinsky, Y. (1998). Comparative aphasiology: Some preliminary notes. In R. Bastiaanse & E. Visch-Brink (Eds.,) *Levels of representation in aphasia.* San Diego: Singular Press.

Grodzinsky, Y., & Finkel, L. (1998). The neurology of empty categories: Aphasics' failure to detect ungrammaticality. *Journal of Cognitive Neuroscience, 10,* 281–292.

Grodzinsky, Y., Pinango, M. M., Zurif, E., & Drai, D. (1999). The critical role of group studies in neuropsychology: Comprehension regularities in Broca's aphasia. *Brain and Language,* **67,** 134–147.

Hagiwara, H. (1993). The breakdown of Japanese passives and θ-role assignment principle by Broca's aphasics. *Brain and Language, 45,* 318–339.

Hagiwara, H. & Caplan, D. (1990). Syntactic comprehension in Japanese aphasics: Effects of category and thematic role order. *Brain and Language, 38,* 159–170.

Hickok, G., & Avrutin, S. (1995). Comprehension of Wh-questions by two agrammatic Broca' aphasics. *Brain and Language, 51,* 10–26.

Kolk, H., van Grunsven, M. (1985). On parallelism in agrammatism. In M.-L. Kean (Ed.), *Agrammatism.* New York: Academic Press.

McDonald, M. C. (1989). Priming effects from gaps to antecedents. *Language and Cognitive Processes* **4(1),** 35–56.

Medini, G. (1988). Clinical psychology in Israel: Identity and directions. *Israeli Journal of Psychiatry, 25,* 157–166.

Miceli, G., Mazzucchi, A., Menn, L., & Goodglass, H. (1983). Contrasting cases of English and Italian agrammatic aphasics. *Brain and Language, 19,* 65–97.

Miceli, G., Silveri, M., Romani, C., & Caramazza, A. (1989). Variation in the pattern of omissions and substitutions of grammatical morphemes in the spontaneous speech of socalled agrammatic patients. *Brain and Language, 36,* 447–492.

Nespoulous, J.-L., Dordain, M., Perron, Ska, B., Bub, D., Caplan, D., Mehler, J., & Lecours, A. R. (1988). Agrammatism in sentence production without comprehension deficits: Reduced availability of syntactic structures and/or of grammatical morphemes? A case study. *Brain and Language, 33,* 273–295.

Pollock, J.-Y. (1989). Verb movement, universal grammar and the structure of IP. *Linguistic Inquiry, 20,* 365–424.

Saddy, D. (1995). Variables and events in the syntax of agrammatic speech. *Brain and Language, 50,* 135–150.

Saffran, E., Schwartz, M., & Marin, O. (1980). The word-order problem in agrammatism: II. Production. *Brain and Language, 10,* 263–280.

Shapiro, L. P., Gordon, B., Hack, N., & Killackey, J. (1993). Verb–argument structure processing in complex sentences in Broca's and Wernicke's aphasia. *Brain and Language, 45,* 423–447.

Shapiro, L. P., & Levin, B. A. (1990). Verb processing during sentence comprehension in aphasia. *Brain and Language, 38,* 21–47.

Stowe, L. A. (1986). Parsing WH-constructions: Evidence for on-line gap location. *Language and Cognitive Processes, 1,* 227–245.

Swinney, D., Ford, M., Fraunfelder, U., & Bresnan, J. (1988). On the temporal course of gapfilling and antecedent assignment during sentence comprehension. In B. Grosz, R. Kaplan, M. Macken, & I. Sag (Eds.), *Language structure and processing,* Stanford, CA: CSLI.

Swinney, D. & Zurif, E. (1995). Syntactic processing in aphasia. *Brain and Language, 50,* 225–239.

Swinney, D., Zurif, E. B., & Nicol, J. (1989). The effects of focal brain damage on sentence processing. An examination of the neurological organization of a mental module. *Journal of Cognitive Neuroscience, 1,* 25–37.

Zurif, E. B. (1978). Language and the brain. In M. Halle, J. Bresnan, & G. Miller (Eds.), *Linguistic theory and psychological reality.* Cambridge, MA: MIT Press.

Zurif, E. B. (1980). Language mechanisms: A neuropsychological perspective. *American Scientist,* May.

Zurif, E. B. (1996). Grammatical theory and the study of sentence comprehension in aphasia: Comments on Druks and Marshall (1995). *Cognition, 58,* 271–279.

Zuriff, E. B., & Caramazza, A. (1976). Linguistic structures in aphasia: Studies in syntax and semantics. In H. Whitaker & H. H. Whitaker (Eds.), *Studies in neurolinguistics* (Vol. 2). New York: Academic Press.

Zurif, E. B., Caramazza, A. & Myerson, R. (1972). Grammatical judgments of agrammatic aphasics. *Neuropsychologia, 10,* 405–417.

Zurif, E. B., Caramazza, Myerson, R., & Galvin, J. (1974). Semantic feature representations in normal and aphasic language. *Brain and Language, 1,* 167–187.

Zurif, E. B., Swinney, D., Prather, P., Solomon, J., & Bushell, C. (1993). An on-line analysis of syntactic processing in Broca's and Wernicke's aphasia. *Brain and Language, 45,* 448–464.

Chapter 4

Speech Perception, Conduction Aphasia, and the Functional Neuroanatomy of Language

Gregory Hickok

INTRODUCTION

The classic functional–anatomic model of language holds that Broca's and Wernicke's aphasia are the only syndromes that result from damage to an actual language processing "center." All the rest result from a *disconnection* of one computational system from another. In the case of conduction aphasia, a central focus of this chapter, the disconnection supposedly involves the pathway between the two primary language centers themselves, Broca's area and Wernicke's area. In this chapter, I will argue that at least one type of conduction aphasia is not a disconnection syndrome at all, but a central language disorder in its own right, one which impairs phonological systems that normally take part not only in speech production, as has been claimed previously, but also in speech perception. Because Wernicke's model is frequently misunderstood, it's worth starting by reviewing his original 1874 proposal.

The Classic Model of the Functional Neuroanatomy of Language

Wernicke (1874/1977) proposed that language processing is supported by two centers, one in auditory cortex which houses sound-based representation of words, and the other in motor cortex which houses motor-based representations of the articulatory gestures required to produce words. According to Wernicke, these two language centers are connected to one another directly, and also to a highly distributed network involved

---

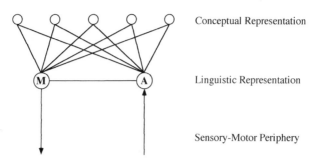

Figure 1   The present author's representation of Wernicke's model of the functional neuroanatomy of language. Directional arrows indicate sensory and motor input/output to the system. Nodes A and M are centers for representing the sensory and motor traces of linquistic events: A, center for auditory word representation; M, center for motor word representation. The top row of unlabeled nodes denotes a distributed cortical network for conceptual knowledge representation.

in the representation of conceptual knowledge. The connections between the language centers and the distributed conceptual representation system were assumed to be *bidirectional,* at least for the connection between auditory cortex and conceptual representation. Figure 1 summarizes Wernicke's model graphically. This representation of the model more accurately reflects Wernicke's ideas than does the oft used Lichtheim (1885) diagram, which is misleading with its unidirectional connections.[1]

Wernicke assumed that in normal language comprehension acoustic input activated stored auditory representations associated with the sound pattern of words, these auditory word representations then activated their associated conceptual representations. Volitional production, according to Wernicke, started with the activation of conceptual representations which in turn activated *both* their associated auditory *and* motor representations *in parallel.* The activation of auditory word representations served to constrain the selection of the appropriate (i.e., intended) motor pattern via the direct auditory–motor pathway:

> . . . the actual sensory image [concept] of an object is . . . able to activate the motor image directly . . . Observations of daily

[1]This is no fault of Lichtheim's. The diagram from Lichtheim's paper (1885) which is so often used to represent the Wernicke–Lichtheim model was not Lichtheim's conception of how the system works, but rather a hypothesis which he later rejects. Although not diagramming it fully, the version he adopts is one in which the connection between the auditory word center and the conceptual "center" is bidirectional, as Wernicke proposed.

speech usage and the process of speech development indicates the presence of an unconscious, repeated activation and simultaneous mental reverberation of the acoustic image which exercises a continuous monitoring of the motor images. (p. 106)

Therefore, the sum total of [the object concept and the acoustic word image] always functions in harmony with the appropriate intensity necessary for correct selection of the word. (p. 107)

Aphasic syndromes could be accounted for within this framework. Damage to the auditory word center leads to impaired comprehension because the sound pattern associated with the individual words can not be activated; production is fluent because motor memories are preserved and because they can be activated via the direct concept-to-motor pathway, but speech errors (paraphasias) are evident because the modulatory influence of auditory word representations on motor selection is lost. Damage to the motor word center yields impaired (i.e., nonfluent) production while leaving comprehension intact. And damage to the direct connection between auditory and motor systems leads to paraphasic output similar to that found with damage to the auditory word center because the lesion interrupts the pathway by which sensory–motor interaction takes place, but with spared comprehension because the auditory word center is intact. These symptom patterns correspond to Wernicke's, Broca's and conduction aphasia, respectively. Lichtheim later elaborated on the predictions of the model showing how the transcortical aphasias follow from damage to the connections between the language centers and (distributed) conceptual representations.

A Hypothesis

What I would like to suggest here is that Wernicke was essentially correct in hypothesizing (i) that auditory cortex participates in speech production and (ii) that the production deficit in conduction aphasia can be explained in terms of a loss of the modulatory influence of auditory-based representations on articulatory planning. Wernicke was wrong, however, in assuming that conduction aphasia is a disconnection syndrome. Based on a range of evidence I will argue that at least one type of conduction aphasia results from damage to phonological processing systems in auditory cortex which participate both in speech perception and in speech production. I will argue further that the asymmetry in conduction aphasia between production (impaired) and comprehension (spared) can be explained in terms of different degrees of lateralization in the computational systems that support (or can support) these two functions.

The hypothesis put forth here is motivated primarily by two observations. The first is that there is mounting evidence that auditory cortex in the posterior supratemporal plane (pSTP; see Figure 2), is the primary substrate for speech perception (Hickok & Poeppel, to appear).[2] The second observation is that conduction aphasia can result from damage to exactly this cortical region in the left hemisphere (Damasio & Damasio, 1980).[3] These observations lead to an apparent paradox: how is it that damage to speech perception systems can be associated with a syndrome in which auditory language comprehension is preserved and in which speech production is impaired? This paradox can be resolved given the following two assumptions: (i) that speech perception is mediated by the pSTP *bilaterally* (Boatman et al., 1998; Hickok & Poeppel, to appear), and (ii) that auditory cortex in the left pSTP participates in speech *production*, as Wernicke originally claimed. On these assumptions, one can explain the relatively spared auditory comprehension ability in conduction aphasia in terms of the right hemisphere's capacity for speech perception, and the impaired production in terms of damage to those left auditory cortex systems that play an important role in speech production. Given the post hoc nature of these two assumptions, it is important to determine if there is any additional evidence in support of these claims. We turn to that evidence now.

EVIDENCE FOR BILATERAL ORGANIZATION OF SPEECH PERCEPTION SYSTEMS

Profound Deficits in Auditory Comprehension Are Associated with Bilateral Posterior Supratemporal Plane Lesions

If it is the case that relatively preserved auditory comprehension in conduction aphasia can be attributed to the speech perception abilities of the

---

[2]I will follow Hickok and Poeppel's (to appear) definition of speech perception, which is "the process by which acoustic input is coded into neural representations suitable for making contact with the mental lexicon." This definition refers explicitly to those processes involved in normal language understanding, and not necessarily to those processes involved in performing laboratory speech-sound identification and discrimination tasks.

[3] Conduction aphasia is known to result from two lesion patterns. The most well-known is that which involves the supramarginal gyrus and the underlying arcuate fasciculus. But very clear cases of conduction aphasia have also been identified with lesions involving auditory cortex in the left supratemporal plane with complete sparing of the supramarginal gyrus and the arcuate fasciculus. Unless otherwise indicated, the term "conduction aphasia" is used here to refer to this latter STP-lesioned form. It will be important in future research to tease apart the symptom complex of these two forms of conduction aphasia.

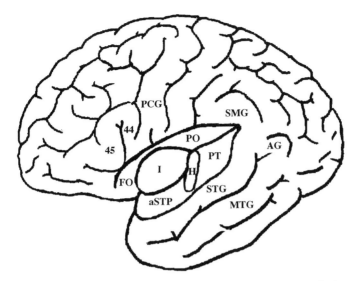

Figure 2 Lateral view of the left hemisphere with structures inside the sylvian fossa exposed. H, Transverse temporal gyrus of Heschl (which houses primary auditory cortex); PT, planum temporale; aSTP, anterior supratemporal plane; STG, superior temporal gyrus, note that the STG includes the STP; MTG, middle temporal gyrus; AG, angular gyrus; SMG, supramarginal gyrus; 44 and 45 refer to Brodmann's designations and together comprise Broca's area; PCG, precentral gyrus (primary motor cortex); FO, frontal operculum; PO, parietal operculum; I, insula. The term pSTP is used in this chapter to refer to the combination of Heschl's gyrus and the PT.

right pSTP, then it should be the case that if the pSTP were damaged *bilaterally*, a profound auditory comprehension deficit should result. This is exactly the most common etiology of word deafness (WD) an acquired syndrome which is characterized by a profound speech comprehension deficit (Buchman, Garron, Trost-Cardamone, Wichter, & Schwartz, 1986). The classic functional–anatomic interpretation of WD is that of a disconnection syndrome in which Wernicke's area is isolated from auditory input (Geschwind, 1965). An alternative interpretation suggested here is that WD results from damage to cortical speech perception systems (Hickok & Poeppel, to appear). On this latter view, WD should be considered a form of aphasia, rather than a form of auditory agnosia peripheral to the aphasias.

It is worth pointing out in this context that WD is the only aphasic syndrome dominated by a profound deficit in speech perception. To put it another way, none of the left unilateral-lesion-based aphasic syndromes have a speech perception deficit as a major component of the syndrome, which in turn further supports the view that speech perception is mediated bilaterally. This is not to say that speech perception deficits (as measured by syllable identification and discrimination) never occur in the unilateral aphasias. On the contrary, abnormal performance on such tests have been found in association with a range of aphasic types, but such deficits are not predictive of auditory comprehension performance (Blumstein, 1995; Blumstein, Baker, & Goodglass, 1977), suggesting that speech perception processes are functioning sufficiently well to support some degree of access to phonological information. This is true even for Wernicke's aphasics: Blumstein et al. (1977) showed that the comprehension deficit in Wernicke's aphasia is not predominantly phonological in nature, as one would expect if a speech perception deficit was the source of their comprehension problems, but rather predominantly semantic in nature. For this reason it has been argued that the comprehension deficit in Wernicke's aphasia represents a disorder somewhere in the mapping between phonological representations and the meanings with which they are associated (Geschwind, 1965). This in turn suggests that while speech perception processes are bilaterally organized, higher levels of language are more asymmetrically processed in the left hemisphere.

The Isolated Right Hemisphere Has Speech Perception Capacities

Evidence from split brain studies and intracarotid amobarbital studies suggests that the isolated right hemisphere has the capacity to both discriminate speech sounds (Boatman et al., 1998), and to understand syntactically simple speech (McGlone, 1984: Wada & Rasmussen, 1960; Zaidel, 1985). These findings are consistent with the view that speech perception systems are bilaterally organized.

Bilateral Activation in the Physiological Response to Speech

Intraoperative recordings from single units in awake patients undergoing surgical treatment for epilepsy have suggested the existence of cells responsive to different aspects of the speech signal such as a particular class of phonemic clusters, mono- versus multisyllabic words, task-relevant versus task-irrelevant speech, and natural versus distorted or backward speech (Creutzfeldt et al., 1989). The vast majority of speech responsive cells sere found in the middle portion of the superior temporal gyrus (STG) (recordings from more posterior sites were not made); very few sites in anterior STG or middle or inferior temporal gyrus yielded de-

tectable responses. Furthermore these units were found in equal distribution in the left and right hemispheres. Bilateral activation of pSTG is also
a consistent finding of positron emission tomography (PET) (Mazoyer et
al., 1993; Petersen, Fox, Posner, Mintun, & Raichle, 1988; Price et al., 1996;
Zatorre, Evans, Meyer, & Gjedde, 1992) functional magnetic resonance
imaging (fMRI)(Binder et al., 1994; Millen, Haughton, & Yetkin, 1995),
and magnetoencephalography (MEG) (Gage, Poeppel, Roberts, & Hickok,
1998; Poeppel et al., 1996) studies of passively presented speech stimuli.
Some studies have reported that the left hemisphere activation is slightly
more extensive; this asymmetry may reflect higher levels of language processing which *do* seem to be more strongly lateralized.

   Thus, it seems that there is good evidence in favor of the view that speech
perception systems are organized bilaterally in pSTP. There is also evidence
suggesting that the left and right hemisphere make nonidentical contributions to the speech perception process. This evidence has been reviewed
elsewhere (Hickok & Poeppel, to appear) and will not be detailed here.

EVIDENCE FOR LEFT POSTERIOR SUPRATEMPORAL PLANE PARTICIPATION IN SPEECH PRODUCTION

   The observation that conduction aphasia is associated with damage to
the pSTP is one source of evidence that this region participates in speech
production. There are several additional lines of evidence which also support this view.

Cortical Stimulation of the Left Superior Temporal Gyrus Results in Speech Production Errors

   Intraoperative cortical stimulation of left pSTG has been shown to produce speech production errors characterized by "distortion and repetition of words and syllables" (Penfield & Roberts, 1959).

Functional Imaging Studies of Speech Production Implicate Left Posterior Supratemporal Plane

   A magnetic source imaging (MSI) study of speech production during
object naming has identified the left posterior superior temporal region
as the source for a signal that is produced just prior to speech articulation
(Levelt, Praamstra, Meyer, Helenius, & Salmelin, 1998); the authors write
that the left pSTG is, "a favorite site for phonological encoding in word
production" (p. 562). And a recent fMRI study has provided direct

evidence that auditory cortex in the left supratemporal plane participates in speech production (Hickok et al., 1999). In this study subjects were asked to name (subvocally) visually presented objects. Despite the fact that there was no auditory stimulus, activation was noted in nonprimary unimodal auditory cortex in the pSTP. No activation was noted in right auditory cortex. These findings confirm and refine the MSI localization.

Production Deficits in Word Deafness

If we are correct in hypothesizing that (i) conduction aphasia is the result of damage to speech perception systems in the left hemisphere, (ii) that these same systems in pSTP participate in speech production, and (iii) that word deafness is the result of damage to speech perception systems in pSTP bilaterally, then we are lead to the following prediction: the output of word deaf patients should resemble the output of conduction aphasics. A common textbook assumption regarding word deafness is that production is perfectly intact, but in fact this is not typically the case. In a review of 37 cases of word deafness, Buchman et al. (1986) report that more than 70% (22/31) of the cases for which there was sufficient information, presented with paraphasic errors consistent with the predicted effect.

Behavioral Evidence for a Relation between Speech Perception and Production

The evidence above makes a reasonably strong case for the view that systems in the left pSTP participate not only in perception, but also in production. Are the very same pSTP cortical networks involved in both processes? Or are there separate systems within auditory cortex, one involved with speech perception, the other with speech production? There is some behavioral evidence which speaks to the question. Mackay, Wulf, Yin, and Abrams (1993) studied the effect of concurrent speech production on the verbal transformation effect (Warren, 1968), that is, the tendency to misperceive phonemes with repeated and prolonged presentation of a single word. In a series of experiments, they found that this tendency was reduced during concurrent speech production, even when production was subvocal. They argue that these findings support a processing model in which speech production and speech perception systems share processing units. Based on this evidence, we might then hypothesize that the same neural networks in left pSTP participate both in perception and production.

RELATION BETWEEN PHONOLOGICAL ENCODING, REPETITION, AND NAMING DEFICITS IN CONDUCTION APHASIA

So far we have considered evidence which suggests (i) that the preserved comprehension ability in conduction aphasia is due to the speech perception capacity of the right hemisphere, and (ii) that the phonemic paraphasias often present in the speech output of conduction aphasics can be accounted for in terms of damage to phonological processing systems in the left pSTP which participate both in speech perception and speech production. What about other aspects of the symptom complex of conduction aphasia, specifically the repetition deficit and the naming difficulties? I will propose that both of these symptoms might be reducible to difficulties in phonological encoding, that stage in language production where the phonological segments associated with selected lexical items are assembled (e.g., Levelt, 1989). The idea that a deficit in phonological encoding is the source of the production deficit in conduction aphasia is not new (Buckingham, 1992; Kohn, 1984; Shallice & Warrington, 1977), and so these issues will be discussed only briefly.

Repetition Deficit

The difficulty with verbatim repetition of speech is the aspect of conduction aphasia which is commonly considered to be the defining feature of the disorder. In fact conduction aphasia was first identified by Wernicke on the basis of paraphasias is speech production, not repetition ability. Based on Wernicke's assertion that (i) the conduction aphasics' paraphasias resulted from an interruption of the direct link between sensory and motor language systems and (ii) this pathway was critical for repetition of speech, Lichtheim proposed repetition as a simple diagnostic test of the integrity of this pathway. Repetition, then, was originally viewed simply as a diagnostic test which specifically targeted the functional component thought to underlie the speech production deficit in conduction aphasia. It was not viewed as an independent symptom. This is roughly the view taken by modern researchers (Buckingham, 1992; Shallice & Warrington, 1977)—at least for one type of conduction aphasia, referred to as reproduction conduction aphasia—and the view that is adopted here.

Naming Difficulties

One common feature of conduction aphasia is naming difficulty (Benson et al., 1973; Goodglass, 1993). While virtually every aphasic has word finding problems, it is interesting that conduction aphasics tend to make naming errors that are phonologically related to the target (Kohn, 1984), and tend to respond to phonemic but not semantic cueing (Li & Williams, 1990). This has suggested to some that the naming deficit in conduction aphasia stems from the proposed phonological encoding disorder. An experiment by Vigliocco, Antonini, & Garrett (1998) is enlightening in this respect. These authors examined the tip-of-the-tongue (TOT) phenomenon in Italian speaking subjects. The TOT phenomenon is interesting in the present context because it represents a state in which the speaker has accessed conceptual/semantic information but cannot access the phonological shape of the associated word. The motivation for studying Italian speaking subjects was that the grammatical gender-marking system in Italian provided a means for determining at what level of representation (e.g., lexical/lemma level or phonological encoding level) the difficulty arose in the TOT state. Their study showed that Italian speakers have access to grammatical gender information in the TOT state. Since grammatical gender information is typically assumed to be represented at the lemma level (Garrett, 1992; Levelt, 1989), it is reasonable to conclude that the locus of processing difficulty is at the level of phonological encoding.

The implications of this finding for conduction aphasia are as follows. The TOT state is a form of naming failure which arises from difficulties in phonological encoding. Conduction aphasia, which has been characterized as a deficit in phonological encoding , is associated with naming deficits. The left pSTP is implicated both in the etiology of conduction aphasia, and in the phonological encoding stage of speech production based on functional imaging studies of object naming (Hickok et al., 1999; Levelt et al., 1998). This constitutes rather strong circumstantial evidence suggesting that the naming deficit in conduction aphasia stems from difficulties in phonological encoding. The observation that naming difficulties in conduction aphasia often resemble a TOT state is further evidence supporting this view (Goodglass, Kaplan, Weintraub, & Ackerman, 1976).

OTHER AREAS PREVIOUSLY IMPLICATED IN SPEECH PERCEPTION MAY REFLECT A NETWORK SUPPORTING AUDITORY–MOTOR INTERACTION

The claim put forth here is that the pSTP, bilaterally, is the primary substrate for speech perception. How does this hypothesis relate to previous claims that Broca's area and/or the supramarginal gyrus is/are important for speech perception? Hickok and Poeppel (to appear) suggested that Broca's area and the SMG are involved in speech perception only indirectly through their role in phonological working memory which may be recruited during the performance of certain speech perception tasks. Evidence for this claim includes the observation that both of these regions are active during the performance of phonological working memory tasks as measured by hemodynamic-based functional imaging studies (Awh *et al.*, 1996; Paulesu, Frith, & Frackowiak, 1993), and the observation that they are not reliably activated during passive listening to speech sounds—a task that certainly involves speech perception.

Hickok and Poeppel (to appear) go on to suggest that the pSTP, SMG, and Broca's area serve as a network for auditory–motor interaction. Specifically, they argue that the pSTP is important for generating sound-based representations of speech which interface with lexical–conceptual systems on the one hand, and with speech-related motor–articulatory systems, such as Broca's area on the other. In this scheme, the SMG serves as an interface between speech-related auditory and motor systems, and together this circuit comprises an important substrate for phonological working memory (Aboitiz & García, 1997). This hypothesis was motivated by analogy to work in the visual domain which seems to indicate that the parietal lobe is important for visual–motor integration (Rizzolatti, Fogassi, & Gallese, 1997).

IMPLICATIONS FOR ANATOMICAL MODELS OF LANGUAGE

The present view of conduction aphasia is rather different from the classic view, which as noted at the outset, explains the disorder as a disconnection syndrome. How does this proposal fit into a more general model of the neuroanatomy of the aphasias? One possible formulation of a more general model is summarized in diagram form in Figure 3.

Toward a Model of the Functional Neuroanatomy of Language

According to this model, the pSTP (bilaterally) is the primary location of a network supporting sound-based computation of speech. This system supports both speech perception and aspects of speech production. This sound-based system interfaces with widely distributed conceptual knowledge systems (Damasio, Grabowski, Tranel, Hichwa, & Damasio, 1996) via auditory–conceptual interface systems in cortex located primarily at the junction of the *left* temporal, occipital, and parietal lobes. Damage to this region is associated with impaired comprehension, but

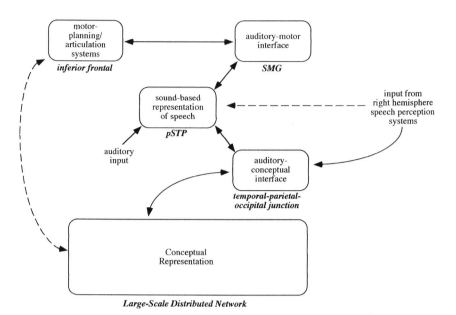

Figure 3   A rough model of the functional neuroanatomy of language.

spared repetition (Damasio, 1992). The idea that there exists networks responsible for binding together representations of different sorts (in this
case phonological and semantic) is not new. Damasio (1989) and Mesulam (1990, 1998) have been arguing for such "interface zones" (or "convergence zones" in Damasio's terminology), for more than a decade. And
Geschwind (1965) suggested that Wernicke's area "functions importantly
as the 'storehouse' of auditory associations. . . . It is probably thus that
Wernicke's area attains its essential importance in 'comprehension,' i.e.
the arousal of associations" (p. 286). This notion is also consistent with
psycholinguistic models which postulate an intermediate representational level (the "lemma" level) between sound- and meaning-based representations (Dell, Schwartz, Martin, Saffran, & Gagnon, 1997; Garrett,
1992; Levelt, 1989; Vigliocco et al., 1998).

The present model assumes that the right hemisphere systems supporting speech perception can provide input to this left hemisphere auditory–
conceptual interface systems. This assumption is driven by the observation that damage to the left pSTP does not significantly impair language

comprehension. There may also be a projection between the left and right pSTP (Damasio & Damasio, 1979).

The sound-based system interfaces not only with the conceptual knowledge system, but also with frontal motor systems via an auditory–motor interface system in the inferior parietal lobe. This circuit is the primary substrate for phonological working memory (Awh et al., 1996; Paulesu et al., 1993), but also probably plays a role in volitional speech production. In the present framework, this auditory cortex–SMG–Broca's area circuit replaces the notion of a direct sensory–motor link via the arcuate fasciculus. Connectivity studies in nonhuman primates is consistent with the claim that there is not a direct (i.e., one synapse) connection between auditory cortex and the ventral posterior frontal lobe, and with the claim that the parietal lobe is an important interface between these regions (Aboitiz & García, 1997; Romanski, Bates, & Goldman-Rakic, 1999).[4]

Following the lead of several authors (Friedrich, Glenn, & Marin, 1984; McCarthy & Warrington, 1984; Wernicke, 1874/1977) the present model also hypothesizes a link between conceptual representations and frontal lobe systems. On the assumption that conceptual representations are highly distributed, this "link" likely involves the convergence of many inputs onto interface systems in frontal cortex (Damasio, 1989; Mesulam, 1998). An example of one such input comes from (i) the observation that regions in the left inferior temporal lobe are important for accessing object-based lexical/conceptual knowledge for production (Damasio et al., 1996), and (ii) connectivity data in nonhuman primates showing projections from inferior temporal lobe to frontal cortex (Bullier, Schall, & Morel, 1996). Together, these findings suggest the possibility that a network involving projections from the inferior temporal lobe (and likely other structures) to frontal systems play a role in speech production. The present hypothesis is that this is (one part of) the previously proposed concept-to-motor route for speech production.

---

[4]There is an alternative formulation of the respective roles of the auditory cortex and SMG in speech production which is suggested by the monkey connectivity data. As mentioned, auditory cortex does not project to the homologue of Broca's area in the macaque, but it does project to the parietal lobe which in turn projects to "Broca's area." Auditory cortex has additional projections to the frontal lobe just anterior and superior to the Broca's area homologue (Romanski et al., 1999). Perhaps the auditory–parietal–Broca's area circuit is used for conscious access to phonological representations as when one is actively rehearsing speech, while an auditory-anterior/superior frontal–Broca's area circuit is used for natural speech production where access to sound based information proceeds in a relatively automatic and unconscious fashion. This hypothesis predicts that conduction aphasia which results from auditory cortex lesions versus SMG lesions should yield different patterns of production deficits that cleave along an automatic versus controlled process line.

Relation to Aphasia Syndromes

This rough sketch of a model can be used to interpret the clinical features of the fluent aphasias.

Conduction aphasia

One form of conduction aphasia results from damage to sound-based representations of speech in the left pSTG, which are used both for comprehension and production. Comprehension is relatively spared because the right pSTP can support speech perception operations sufficient for comprehension tasks. Production contains phonemic paraphasias because the left (but not right) pSTP is involved in "phonological encoding" for speech production. Repetition is disrupted for the same reason. Conduction aphasia which results from damage to the left SMG yields a roughly similar symptom complex because the lesion lies at another point along the cortical circuit important for auditory–motor interaction (i.e., one pathway important for speech production). We might predict subtle differences between pSTG and SMG type conduction aphasias (see footnote 4). Perhaps the distinction drawn between "reproduction" and "repetition" conduction aphasia (Shallice & Warrington, 1977) is relevant in this respect.

Transcortical sensory aphasia

Transcortical sensory aphasia is characterized by impaired comprehension, fluent but paraphasic production with semantic paraphasias dominating, and spared repetition (A. R. Damasio, 1991; Goodglass, 1993). This syndrome might reasonably be viewed as a disruption at the level of the auditory–conceptual interface system. On this view, the comprehension deficit follows from a failure to perform an appropriate mapping from phonological to conceptual representations. Likewise production might be affected because conceptual knowledge would not always be appropriately mapped onto phonological representations, but once a phonological representation of some sort is activated it would be produced appropriately. The ability to repeat heard speech is intact, because semantic processing is not necessarily required for verbatim repetition, and because phonological processing systems are intact along with the auditory–motor interface circuit. Note that this interpretation does not differ substantially from the classic view except in that here we assume that the damage involves a computational system, rather than a white matter pathway. The lesion most often associated with transcortical sensory aphasia is in multimodal cortex near the temporal–parietal–occulpital junction, areas 37 and 39, sparing most of Wernicke's area (posterior third of the superior temporal gyrus) (Damasio, 1992; H. Damasio, 1991). So let us hypothesize, tentatively, that the temporal–parietal–occipital junction area is, roughly, the location for the proposed interface systems, and that a pure form of the disorder associated with damage to this system is something like transcortical sensory aphasia.

Wernicke's aphasia

Wernicke's aphasia might be viewed, in part, as a hybrid syndrome. Many of the symptoms of Wernicke's aphasia are essentially a compound of those associated with both conduction aphasia and transcortical sensory aphasia: impaired auditory comprehension, production that contains both phonemic and semantic paraphasias, and impaired repetition (A. R. Damasio, 1991; Damasio, 1992; Goodglass, 1993). The distribution of lesions associated with Wernicke's aphasia is consistent with its hybrid status, overlapping partially with the lesions associated with both conduction aphasia and transcortical sensory aphasia (Damasio, 1992; H. Damasio, 1991). One difference between Wernicke's aphasics on the one hand, and conduction and transcortical aphasics on the other is that Wernicke's aphasics are more likely to present with paragrammatic production (Goodglass, 1993). It's possible that the extension of the lesion inferiorly into the middle temporal gyrus (Damasio, 1992; H. Damasio, 1991)—a region not typically involved in either conduction aphasia or transcortical sensory aphasia—could account for this effect.

Word deafness

Word deafness, according to the present account, is a primary aphasia resulting from damage to speech perception systems in the pSTP bilaterally (Hickok & Poeppel, to appear). Auditory comprehension is profoundly impaired for obvious reasons, speech production contains phonemic paraphasias because of damaged phonological encoding systems in the left pSTP, and of course, repetition ability is nil.

SUMMARY

The central ideas put forth in this chapter are that (i) speech perception systems are organized bilaterally in the posterior supratemporal plane (Hickok & Poeppel, to appear), (ii) these systems participate not only in speech perception, but in the left hemisphere, also in speech production, (iii) conduction aphasia can be viewed as a syndrome resulting from damage to these systems in the left hemisphere, and (iv) other regions previously implicated in speech perception ability such as the SMG and Broca's area reflect instead a network important for auditory–motor interaction (Aboitiz & García, 1997; Hickok & Poeppel, to appear).

REFERENCES

Aboitiz, F., & García V. R. (1997). The evolutionary origin of language areas in the human brain. A neuroanatomical perspective. *Brain Research Reviews, 25,* 381–396.

Awh, E., Jonides, J., Smith, E. E., Schumacher, E. H., Koeppe, R. A., & Katz, S. (1996). Dissociation of storage and rehersal in working memory: PET evidence. *Psychological Science, 7,* 25–31.

Benson, D. F., Sheremata, W. A., Bouchard, R., Segarra, J. M., Price, D., & Geschwind, M. (1973). Conduction aphasia: A clincopathological study. *Archives of Neurology, 28,* 339–346.

Binder, J. R., Rao, S. M., Hammeke, T. A., Yetkin, F. Z., Jesmanowicz, A., Bandettini, P. A., Wong, E. C., Estkowski, L. D., Goldstein, M. D., Haughton, V. M., & Hyde, J. S. (1994). Functional magnetic resonance imaging of human auditory cortex. *Annals of Neurology, 35,* 662–672.

Blumstein, S. (1995). The neurobiology of the sound structure of language. In M. S. Gazzaniga (Ed.), *The cognitive neurosciences* (pp. 913–929). Cambridge, MA: MIT Press.

Blumstein, S. E., Baker, E., & Goodglass, H. (1977). Phonological factors in auditory comprehension in aphasia. *Neuropsychologia, 15,* 19–30.

Boatman, D., Hart, J. J., Lesser, R. P., Honeycutt, N., Anderson, N. B., Miglioretti, D., & Gordon, B. (1998). Right hemisphere speech perception revealed by amobarbital injection and electrical interference. *Neurology, 51,* 458–464.

Buchman, A. S., Garron, D. C., Trost-Cardamone, J. E., Wichter, M. D., & Schwartz, M. (1986). Word deafness: One hundred years later. *Journal of Neurology, Neurosurgury, and Psychiatry, 49,* 489–499.

Buckingham, H. W. (1992). Phonological production deficits in conduction aphasia. In S. E. Kohn (Ed.), *Conduction aphasia,* (pp. 77–116). Hillsdale, NJ: Erlbaum.

Bullier, J., Schall, J. D., & Morel, A. (1996). Functional streams in occipito-frontal connections in the monkey. *Behavioral Brain Research, 76,* 89–97.

Creutzfeldt, O., Ojemann, G., & Lettich, E. (1989). Neuronal activity in the human lateral temporal lobe: I. Responses to speech. *Experimental Brain Research, 77,* 451–475.

Damasio, A. R. (1989). The brain binds entities and events by multiregional activation from convergence zones. *Neural Computation, 1,* 123–132.

Damasio, A. R. (1991). Signs of aphasia. In M. T. Sarno (Ed.), *Acquired aphasia* (2nd ed., pp. 27–43). San Diego: Academic Press.

Damasio, A. R. (1992). Aphasia. *New England Journal of Medicine, 326,* 531–539.

Damasio, H. (1991). Neuroanatomical correlates of the aphasias, *Acquired aphasia* (2nd ed., pp. 45–71). San Diego: Academic Press.

Damasio, H., & Damasio, A. (1979). "Paradoxic" ear extinction in dichotic listening: Possible anatomic significance. *Neurology, 29,* 644–653.

Damasio, H. & Damasio, A. R. (1980). The anatomical basis of conduction aphasia. *Brain, 103,* 337–350.

Damasio, H., Grabowski, T. J., Tranel, D., Hichwa, R. D., & Damasio, A. R. (1996). A neural basis for lexical retrieval. *Nature (London), 380,* 499–505.

Dell, G. S., Schwartz, M. F., Martin, N., Saffran, E. M., & Gagnon, D. A. (1997). Lexical access in aphasic and nonaphasic speakers. *Psychological Review, 104,* 801–838.

Friedrich, F. J. Glenn, C. G., & Marin, O. S. (1984). Interruption of phonological coding in conduction aphasia. *Brain and Language, 22,* 266–291.

Gage, N., Poeppel, D., Roberts, T. P. L., & Hickok, G. (1998). Auditory evoked M100 reflects onset acoustics of speech sounds. *Brain Research, 814,* 236–239.

Garrett, M. F. (1992). Disorders of lexical selection. *Cognition, 42,* 143–180.

Geschwind, N. (1965). Disconnexion syndromes in animals and man. *Brain, 88*, 237–294, and 585–644.

Goodglass, H. (1993). *Understanding aphasia.* San Diego: Academic Press.

Goodglass, H., Kaplan, E., Weintraub, S., & Ackerman, N. (1976). The 'tip-of-the-tongue' phenomenon in aphasia. *Cortex, 12*, 145–153.

Hickok, G., Erhard, P., Kassubek, J., Helms-Tillery, A. K., Naeve-Velguth, S., Strupp, J. P., Strick, P. L., & Ugurbil, K. (1999). Auditory cortex participates in speech production. *Cognitive Neuroscience Society Abstracts, 1999*, 97.

Hickok, G., & Poeppel, D. (to appear). The functional neuroanatomy of speech perception. *TICS.*

Kohn, S. E. (1984). The nature of the phonological disorder in conduction aphasia. *Brain and Language, 23*, 97–115.

Levelt, W. J. M. (1989). *Speaking: From intention to articulation.* Cambridge, MA: MIT Press.

Levelt, W. J. M., Praamstra, P., Meyer, A. S., Helenius, P., & Salmelin, R. (1998). An MEG study of picture naming. *Journal of Cognitive Neuroscience, 10*, 553–567.

Li, E. C., & Williams, S. E. (1990). The effects of grammatic class and cue type on cueing responsiveness in aphasia. *Brain and Language, 38*, 48–60.

Lichtheim, L. (1885). On aphasia. *Brain, 7*, 433–484.

MacKay, D. G., Wulf, G., Yin, C., & Abrams, L. (1993). Relations between word perception and production: New theory and data on the verbal transformation effect. *Journal of Memory and Language, 32*, 624–646.

Mazoyer, B. M., Tzourio, N., Frak, V., Syrota, A., Murayama, N., Levrier, O., Salamon, G., Dehaene, S., Cohen, L., & Mehler, J. (1993). The cortical representation of speech. *Journal of Cognitive Neuroscience, 5*, 467–479.

McCarthy, R., & Warrington, E. K. (1984). A two-route model of speech production. Evidence from aphasia. *Brain, 107*, 463–485.

McGlone, J. (1984). Speech comprehension after unilateral injection of sodium amytal. *Brain and Language. 22*, 150–157.

Mesulam, M.-M. (1990). Large-scale neurocognitive networks and distributed processing for attention, language, and memory. *Annals of Neurology, 28*, 597–613.

Mesulam M.-M. (1998). From sensation to cognition. *Brain, 121*, 1013–1052.

Millen, S. J., Haughton, V. M., & Yetkin, Z. (1995). Functional magnetic resonance imaging of the central auditory pathway following speech and pure-tone stimuli. *Laryngoscope, 105*, 1305–1310.

Paulesu, E., Frith, C. D., & Frackowiak, R. S. J. (1993). The neural correlates of the verbal component of working memory. *Nature (London), 362*, 342–345.

Penfield, W., & Roberts, L. (1959). *Speech and brain-mechanisms.* Princeton, NJ: Princeton University Press.

Petersen, S. E., Fox, P. T., Posner, M. I., Mintun, M., & Raichle, M. E. (1988). Positron emission tomographic studies of the cortical anatomy of single-word processing. *Nature (London), 331*, 585–589.

Poeppel, D., Yellin, E., Phillips, C., Roberts, T. P. L., Rowley, H., Wexler, K., & Marantz, A. (1996). Task-induced asymmetry of the auditory evoked M100 neuromagnetic field elicited by speech sounds. *Cognitive Brain Research, 4*, 231–242.

Price, C. J., Wise, R. J. S., Warburton, E. A., Moore, C. J., Howard, D., Patterson, K., Frackowiak, R. S. J., & Friston, K. J. (1996). Hearing and saying: The functional neuro-anatomy of auditory word processing. *Brain, 119*, 919–931.

Rizzolatti, G., Fogassi, L., & Gallese, V. (1997). Parietal cortex: From sight to action. *Current Opinion in Neurobiology, 7*, 562–567.

Romanski, L. M., Bates, J. F., & Goldman-Rakic, P. S. (1999). Auditory belt and parabelt projections to the prefrontal cortex in the Rhesus monkey. *Journal of Comparative Neurology, 403,* 141–157.

Shallice, T., & Warrington, E. (1977). Auditory–verbal short-term memory impairment and conduction aphasia. *Brain and Language, 4,* 479–491.

Vigliocco, G., Antonini, T., & Garrett, M. F. (1998). Grammatical gender is on the tip of Italian tongues. *Psychological Science, 8,* 314–317.

Wada, J., & Rasmussen, T. (1960). Intracarotid injection of sodium amytal for the lateralization of cerebral speech dominance. *Journal of Neurosurgery, 17,* 266–282.

Warren, R. M. (1968). Verbal transformation effect and auditory perceptual mechanisms. *Psychological Bulletin, 70,* 261–270.

Wernicke, C. (1874/1977). *Der aphasische symptomencomplex: Eine psychologische studie auf anatomischer basis.* In G. H. Eggert (Ed.), *Wernicke's works on aphasia: A sourcebook and review.* The Hague: Mouton.

Zaidel, E. (1985). Language in the right hemisphere. In D. F. Benson & E. Zaidel (Eds.), *The dual brain: Hemispheric specialization in humans* (pp. 205–231). New York: Guilford Press.

Zatorre, R. J., Evans, A. C., Meyer, E., & Gjedde, A. (1992). Lateralization of phonetic and pitch discrimination in speech processing. *Science, 256,* 846–849.

Chapter **5**

Overarching Agrammatism: When Comprehension Involves Production

Janet L. Nicol* and Tracy Love

INTRODUCTION

Perhaps the most striking feature of nonfluent (e.g., Broca's) aphasia is the telegraphic nature of the speech output: Sentences contain primarily content words (such as nouns and verbs); frequently omitted are function words (such as *the, of, is, that, who, by*) and other *closed class* elements (such as inflectional endings like past tense *-ed*). Superficially, comprehension of sentences by nonfluent aphasics is quite good. However, detailed investigation of their comprehension with sentences whose meaning depends critically on syntactic aspects of the sentence (such as functional morphemes and word order) suggests that comprehension is also impaired (Caramazza & Zurif, 1976).

Caramazza and Zurif (1976) used a sentence–picture matching task [the participant hears a sentence and points] to one picture (of several) which depicts the meaning of the sentence] to test comprehension of relative clause sentences. They found that Broca's aphasic subjects performed relatively well when a plausible meaning of a sentence could be derived simply on the basis of lexical semantics. For instance, it would be possible to understand the predicate–argument structure of a sentence like, "The apple that the boy is eating is red" based purely on an understanding of "apple," "boy," "eating" and "red" *and* an understanding of real-world probabilities and possibilities—boys can eat

---

*Author to whom correspondence should be addressed.

things but apples cannot, apples are typically red, etc. . . . However, these subjects performed close to chance level when lexical semantics did not limit the interpretation of the sentence—that is, when the subjects had to "decode" the syntax of the sentence in order to compute the correct meaning, as for sentences like, "The cow that the monkey is scaring is yellow." In principle, either a cow or monkey could be the agent (or recipient) of "scaring" and neither is more likely than the other to be yellow, hence, the structure of the sentence must be computed in order to derive the correct meaning. Based on results of this type, Caramazza and Zurif suggested that Broca's aphasics were "agrammatic" both in production and comprehension.

Since that time, a number of different accounts of the comprehension deficit in Broca's aphasia have been proposed. There are two families of explanation: one focuses on knowledge representations, the other on processing mechanisms. We review these briefly here.

Sentence representations are impaired. According to one variant of this, the representations contain no functional elements (Grodzinsky, 1984; Swinney, Zurif, & Cutler, 1980), possibly because such elements are unstressed (Kean, 1977). Another variant holds that sentence representations are missing the so-called *traces* that appear in sentences in which a constituent has been fronted (Hickok, Zurif, & Conseco-Gonzales, 1993; Grodzinsky, 1986; Mauner, Fromkin, & Cornell, 1993). For example, in English, in both passive sentences such as "The monkey was chased by the cow" and relative clause constructions like "The monkey that the cow chased was yellow," the object of the verb does not appear in its typical immediately postverbal position, but rather in sentence-initial position. One formal analysis of such constructions is that the object is moved leftward from its canonical position, and a *trace* of the object—an unpronounced "place-holder"—is left behind (Chomsky, 1981). The moved constituent and its trace are "linked" so that the former may still be interpretable as the object of the verb. Clearly, a disruption to a sentence representation that targeted traces would affect the interpretation of such sentences; the normal mechanisms for understanding predicate–argument relations (i.e., who did what to whom) would be impaired.

Sentence processing is impaired. There are many models which implicate sentence processing routines rather than sentence representations per se as the locus of the deficit. Several theories point to inefficient lexical retrieval of function words (e.g., Bradley, Garrett, & Zurif, 1980; Friederici, 1983; Haarman & Kolk, 1991); others implicate content words (e.g., Prather, Zurif, Love, & Brownell, 1997; Swinney, Zurif, & Nicol, 1989; Zurif & Swinney, 1994a, b; Zurif, Swinney, Prather, & Love, 1994; Zurif, Swinney, & Garrett, 1990). Both result in sentence interpretation failure.

One theory, proposed by Frazier and Friederici (1991), argues that a limitation in the "computational capacity" of Broca's aphasics gives rise to comprehension impairment for computationally demanding sentence constructions—those involving "longer inferential chains" (p. 55). Another, initially proposed by Linebarger, Schwartz, and Saffran (1983) assumes that sentence comprehension involves two major stages: first, the *computation* of phrase structure, and second, the *interpretation* of phrase structure. In other words, the first stage computes a hierarchically organized structure, the second works out what the sentence *means*. They point out that Broca's aphasic subjects are able to make accurate grammaticality judgments on sentence constructions that are typically problematic in comprehension tasks. That is, they can identify as grammatical or ungrammatical sentences whose grammaticality depends on the use of function words, such as "Was the girl enjoy the show?," and "The policeman was talking a woman." Linebarger et al. argue that this pattern—spared ability to make grammaticality judgments, impaired ability to perform sentence–picture matching tasks—suggests that the first stage, the computation of phrase structure, is intact, and that the comprehension impairment is due to a failure at the second stage, in which sentence meaning is computed. They characterize this problem as a problem in the *mapping* from a syntactic representation to a semantic one.

Below, we present data that support a different a view—and that is that the deficit is primarily due to a **maintenance problem**. According to this view, sentence–processing operations are broadly intact such that during comprehension, a relatively normal representation of a sentence is computed and interpreted. But such representations are fragile and subject to fast decay (see Haarman & Kolk, 1991, for a similar suggestion), and whereas unimpaired listeners are able to regenerate sentence representations (Potter & Lombardi, 1998), Broca's aphasics—who, after all, have notorious difficulty generating sentences—are unable to do so. Tasks that tap into comprehension relatively early in the process (such as grammaticality or acceptability judgments) will therefore show superior performance than tasks which do not (or cannot) elicit an immediate response (such as tasks that require the assessment of pictures or the selection and manipulation of objects). This scenario was explored in two sets of experiments described below.

EXPERIMENT 1

In this first experiment, the ability of Broca's aphasics to make acceptability judgments to active and passive sentences is compared to their ability to match spoken sentences to pictures. We assume that the former task cuts closer (in time) to sentence comprehension processes than the latter, and so performance should be better on the acceptability judgment task.

Participants

Nine nonfluent aphasic subjects were tested. Table I contains a brief description of each, with respect to age, sex, handedness, education, site and onset of lesion, and presence and degree of hemiparesis.

Materials and procedure

Two tests were administered: An acceptability judgment test and a sentence–picture matching test. Both tests included active and passive sentences, although they differed in content across the two types of tasks.

Acceptability Judgment

Materials

Ten sentence quadruplets were created. Each quadruplet consisted of two active sentences and two passive sentences; of each pair of active and passive sentences, one was plausible and one implausible, as shown in (1). The sentences were recorded on a cassette tape to ensure the identical presentation (intonation, stress, etc.) of stimuli to all subjects.

(1) a. Active–acceptable: Susan cooked the vegetables.
    b. Passive–acceptable: The vegetables were cooked by Susan.
    c. Active–unacceptable: The vegetables cooked Susan.
    d. Passive–unacceptable: Susan was cooked by the vegetables.

It is important to note that the sentences here differ from those used by Linebarger et al. (1983)—they are all grammatical in form, but vary in plausibility. In other words, accurate acceptability judgments to these stimuli require both accurate phrase structure parsing *and* accurate mapping from the syntactic representation to an interpretation.

Procedure

Participants listened to each sentence and simply indicated whether or not the sentence was "a good sentence" on a scale from 1 to 5 where 1 represented a "bad sentence" and 5 represented a "good sentence." Because these subjects have various expressive deficits, measures were taken to ensure that the subjects' responses were a true representation of their choice and not a basic production error. This was accomplished by providing a response sheet that visually displayed the numbers 1 through 5 vertically with the word "bad" printed next to the number "1" along with a frowning face "☹,"

Table I Characteristics of Participants in Experiment 1

Participant	Sex	Age	Date of stroke	Hemiparesis	Hand	Education	Lesion site
RB	M	52	06/30/84	R/wheelchair	R	MD	L frontoparietal
NB	F	62	11/22/94	R/wheelchair	R	MA	L basal ganglia, peri-insular
JS1	M	72	08/29/84	R weakness, cane	R	Tenth grade	L frontoparietal
GT	F	39	02/10/92	R weakness, cane	R	HS	L posterior frontal involving deep basal ganglia and periventricular white matter
JQ	M	72	04/19/79	R weakness, cane	R	BA	L MCA infarct—frontoparietal & anterior portions of the temporal cortex sparing W's area (BA 22)
JS2	F	46	06/09/95	R weakness, cane	R	HS	L MCA infarct—no temporal involvement
DW	M	55	11/22/88	R weakness	R	HS	L periventricular region, adjacent to lateral ventricle; involvement of the insular region extending into the basal ganglia
PS	M	80	06/03/94	R weakness	R	MA	Subacute L posterior frontal region
LR	M	52	12/22/93	R weakness, cane	R	BA	Large L MCA infarct involving parietal and temporal lobe sparing (Wernicke's area)

the word "O.K." and an indifferent face next to the number 3, and finally the word "good" and a smiling face "☺" next to the number 5 (note the numbers 2 and 4 were provided with no words or pictures). Subjects simply needed to point to their choice, no verbal response was required.

Participants came to the laboratory for individual 1-hour testing sessions. They sat in a quiet room with the experimenter and were instructed that they would be auditorily presented with tape-recorded sentences and that they were to decide if what they were hearing was a good English sentence, or a bad English sentence. They were then shown the response sheet and instructed on how to use the rating scale. Once the experimenter determined that participants were using the scale correctly, the experiment began. Participants were instructed that the sentence would be played for them once and that they would have plenty of time to respond, but that the sentence could not be repeated. The experimenter recorded the participants' response on an answer sheet. Breaks were taken as needed.

Scoring

To control for possible response bias, the numbers of correct responses for both acceptable and unacceptable sentences were summed for all active sentences and for all passive sentences. Hence, if a participant indicated that all the active sentences were acceptable, this participant would receive a score of 50% for the set of active sentences. If a participant indicated that half the acceptable active sentences and half the unacceptable active sentences were correct, then this participant also received a score of 50%.

Sentence–Picture Matching

Materials

Ten sentence pairs were created. Each pair consisted of an active sentence and passive sentence, as shown in (2). Each sentence was paired with a set of three pictures: a correct picture, a picture in which the predicate–argument relations were reversed, and an unrelated picture. Sentences were presented auditorily in a random order. The picture triplets were presented in a vertical array and the correct picture was balanced with respect to its position in the array (e.g., the correct picture appeared at the top, in the middle, and at the bottom equal numbers of times). There were five practice sentences.

(2) a. Active: The man pushed the boy.
    b. Passive: The boy was pushed by the man.

Procedure

In a separate testing session from the judgment task (described above), participants were instructed that they would be shown a set of three pictures, that the characters in each picture would be identified ("this is the man, this is the boy," etc.), and that they would then hear a sentence (each sentence was presented twice). Their job was to point to the picture that correctly depicted the sentence that they had just heard.

Again, as described above, participants were tested in individual 1-hour testing sessions in a quiet room with the experimenter. The subjects were presented with the pictures and then auditorily presented with a sentence. Again, no verbal response was required; the participants responded by simply pointing to the picture of their choice. The participants' choice was recorded on an answer sheet by the experimenter for scoring at a later time. The order of presentation between the two tasks was counterbalanced across participants.

Scoring

The type of response (correct, incorrect–related, incorrect–unrelated) was recorded for each sentence and summed over sentence types.

Results

The proportion of correct responses for both tasks appears in Table II. Overall, performance was better on active sentences than passive sentences [$F(1,8) = 20.95$; $p = .002$], and was better on the judgment task than on the sentence–picture matching task [nearly significant at $F(1,8) = 4.26$; $p = .073$]. Performance on passive sentences was better in the judgment task than the sentence–picture matching task (the interaction of the two factors was nearly significant; $F(1,8) = 3.886, p . < 084$).

Hence, as a group, the Broca's aphasics show the worst performance on passive sentences as tested in the sentence–picture matching task. It is important to point out, however, that not all nine participants in the study show the group pattern: Two participants actually show *better* performance on passives in the sentence–picture matching task than in the judgment task. Why this should be is not clear without further testing. Ultimately, it may simply be the case—and this possibility does not alarm us—that any explanation of the impairment in Broca's aphasia will typically only capture the data for some portion of the participants.

The individual data are shown in Table III.

Most of the participants show a clear decrement in performance on the sentence–picture matching task for passive sentences. This is to be expected

Table II Percent Correct Responses for Active versus Passive
Sentences in Two Tasks

	Task	
Sentence type	Judgment	Sentence–picture matching
Active	85	80
Passive	74	51

if the representation of sentences steadily decays over time. Passive sentences are likely to suffer more than active sentences because they rely more greatly on the presence of functional morphemes. If these morphemes are especially vulnerable to decay (or cannot readily be regenerated), then such sentence types should be more difficult when there is a lag between the utterance and the response, as is typically the case in sentence–picture matching tasks and other tasks which require the evaluation of a scenario. Whether the participant chooses a picture at random (the 50% correct cases), or based on so-called canonical word-order (the less-than-chance cases) is difficult to predict, and may depend on the extent of the participant's metalinguistic awareness (i.e., whether she knows that some sentences involve an inversion of the usual agent-before-patient ordering) or other factors.

Although we have been assuming that function words are particularly at risk in the maintenance of sentence representations, this first experiment did not explicitly test function words. The results of another study, however, did expressly examine memory for function words.

EXPERIMENT 2

This second experiment was reported by Nicol and Rapcsak (1994). This study contrasted performance on plausibility judgments with performance on an object manipulation task. In addition, a word probe task was conducted.

Participants

Participant 1 was a right-handed male who was 45 years old at the time of testing. Five years prior to testing, he had suffered a subarachnoid hemorrhage, complicated by vasospasm and extensive left fronto-temporo-parietal infarction. Results of the Western Aphasia Battery (WAB) showed a profile consistent with Broca's aphasia.

Table III Individual Scores

Subject[a]	Judgment (% correct)		S-P matching (% correct)	
	A	P	A	P
*RB	90	65	90	80
NB	100	95	90	20
JS1	95	85	80	70
GT	80	80	70	50
DW	75	65	100	40
LR	90	90	100	90
*JS2	75	50	70	60
JQ	75	75	70	50
PS	85	60	50	0

[a]Asterisks indicate subjects whose performance on passive sentences was better on Sentence–Picture Matching than on the Judgment task.

Participant 2 was also a right-handed male who was 63 at testing. Fifteen years prior to testing, he had suffered a massive left hemisphere stroke that resulted in global aphasia and right hemiplegia. At the time of testing, his profile on the WAB was consistent with Broca's aphasia. A recent magnetic resonance imaging (MRI) scan revealed a massive old infarction involving the distribution of all three major cerebral arteries supplying the left hemisphere. The lesion resulted in virtually complete destruction of the cortex and white matter of all four cerebral lobes in the left hemisphere.

Materials and tasks

Materials differed slightly for the two participants, however, the examples used below are representative of the structures tested. Our focus was on active and passive sentences; these sentences were embedded in a larger set of filler sentences which varied in structure. Both sentence types appeared either with two noun phrase (NP) arguments (e.g., The boy ate the apple, The apple was eaten by the boy) or with only one argument (e.g., *The boy ate quickly, The apple was eaten quickly*). In a sense, these provide a stronger test of the participants' ability to use morphology to compute predicate–argument structure because they cannot use partial information (i.e., they cannot simply look for the presence of the by-phrase).

1. Object manipulation. In this task, participants were asked to act out the sentences spoken by the examiner. Labeled cutouts of sentence participants were used (e.g., "Ken" appeared with a picture of a male character, "Ann" appeared with a picture of a female character), along with an instrument associated with the verb (e.g., for the verb *photograph*, a drawing of a camera was used).

2. Acceptability judgment. Participants were asked to indicate whether or not a spoken sentence was a "good sentence" of English. The sentences of interest are all syntactically well formed; however, half are implausible.

3. Probe recognition. Subjects were presented with a spoken sentence followed by a spoken word, and asked to indicate whether or not the word had occurred in the sentence. The spoken word was presented after a delay of 5 s, the minimum amount of time taken to perform the act-out task.

Results

Below, representative sentences and results from the two participants are shown. All percentages represent correct answers.

1. Object manipulation. The results are shown in Table IV. Both participants had difficulty with this task, although the patterns of performance are quite different: One participant performed well on active sentences and well below chance on passives; the other showed near-chance performance on both. It is possible that Participant 1 employs a heuristic whereby the first noun phrase is interpreted as the subject of the sentence, producing above chance performance on active sentences and below chance performance on passive sentence. Subject 2 simply shows near chance performance in both conditions. [Note that informal testing was also conducted with common objects such as pencils and paper clips (e.g., "the paper clip hit the pencil"); results were similar.]

2. Sentence acceptability judgment. Results of this task are presented in Table V. This pattern of performance suggests that both participants

Table IV   Performance on the Picture–Manipulation Task

Type	Example	Participant 1 (% correct)	Participant 2 (% correct)
Active	Ken photographed Sue	83%	62%
Passive	Ken was photographed by Sue	8%	54%
Average		*46%*	*58%*

are able to compute the proper syntactic analysis of these two sentence types and to assign the proper interpretation; that is, the surface subject of the passive sentence is understood to be the object of the verb. This result is consistent with the results of Experiment 1 and with findings reported by Schwartz, Linebarger, and Pate (1987), who tested comparable sentences. Although their Broca's aphasics showed worse performance on passive sentences and other complex structures than on active sentences, three of their six subjects showed good performance (better than 70% accuracy) on the set of complex sentences (including passives).

3. Probe recognition. Results appear in Table VI. This pattern of performance—more than 90% correct recognition of content words versus 60% correct recognition function words—suggests that these subjects are able to remember the content words better than the function words in these sentences (and other sentences in the test set; this pattern is representative of the overall performance pattern for a variety of sentence types). (Note that the two subjects do differ in the performance on function words: Participant 1 fairly consistently responds "No," whereas Participant 2 appears to be guessing. However, both average around 60% correct.) These results are consistent with findings by Caramazza, Zurif, and Gardner (1978), who also found poor performance on function words using a probe recognition task.

GENERAL DISCUSSION

The patterns of performance observed in our two studies suggest the following scenario: (At least some) Broca's aphasics comprehend even passive sentences relatively normally, in real time. To be able to make plausibility judgments as accurately as they do, they must be able to process function words, represent traces, *and* semantically interpret phrase structures. However, when the task demands a comparison of a scenario described by a sentence with an actual scene (either a set of depictions or the subject's own created scene), the task requires much more than mere sentence comprehension; the task also requires that sentences by maintained in memory in some format (or multiple formats).

A reasonable question about this process is why the Broca's aphasic individual does not maintain the semantic representation that has been computed, and then simply compare the semantic representation to the pictures or use the semantic representation to do the act-out task. In other words, if the participant is able to compute the correct meaning of a sentence like "The girl was chased by the boy," even if the participant can-

Table V Performance on the Judgment Task

Sentence type		Example		Participant 1 (% correct)	Participant 2 (% correct)
Active	Plausible	The boy ate the apple		100	95
		The boy ate quickly		75	89
			Average	**88**	**92**
	Implausible	The apple ate the boy		90	95
		The apple ate quickly		100	79
			Average	**95**	**87**
Passive	Plausible	The apple was eaten by the boy		92	75
		The apple was eaten quickly		92	75
			Average	**92**	**75**
	Implausible	The boy was eaten by the apple		100	95
		The boy was eaten quickly		92	100
			Average	**96**	**98**

Table VI Results of Probe Task[a]

Probe type	Participant 1 (%)	Participant 2 (%)
Content word probes		
Positive (Ken, photographed, Sue)	100	96
Negative (Tom, washed, Jane)	88	88
Average	**94**	**92**
Function word probes		
Positive (A: has; P: was, by)	13	67
Negative (A: was, had; P: has, of)	100	58
Average	**57**	**63**

[a]Given sentence examples *Ken has photographed Sue; Ken was photographed by Sue.*

not rehearse the sentence, she or he could presumably keep the *meaning* of the sentence active, and use this semantic representation for the act-out or picture matching task. But maintaining a semantic representation of a sentence may be hard to do *without* using language. One reason is that a semantic representation could be easily contaminated by the presence of related pictures and objects. If a surface form of the sentence were available in memory, it would be straightforward to double-check the semantic representation by replaying the sentence—unless one can't. This hypothesis—that people rely on a verbatim form of a sentence in memory to perform matching tasks—has been tested informally by asking unimpaired subjects to count backward from 100 (either aloud or silently) while performing the act-out task (they initiate counting once the target sentence is uttered); they do not perform as poorly as Broca's aphasic subjects, but they do make errors, particularly on passive and other "movement" constructions. More importantly, these findings have been supported in the field in more formal testing environments.

This analysis of the comprehension failure in Broca's aphasia is consistent with some recently reported research on the brain sites involved in verbal working memory (in unimpaired individuals). For example, Awh et al. (1996) performed a positron emission tomography (PET) imaging study involving a probe recognition task. Participants were presented with four uppercase target letters simultaneously and had to remember these during the subsequent 3-second blank period. Following the delay, subjects were presented with a lowercase letter and had to indicate (via yes/no response) whether or not the lowercase letter was identical in name to one of the earlier targets (e.g., A/a). This requires the subject to maintain the identity of the target letters in verbal memory. Broca's area (Brodmann 44) was one area that demonstrated significant levels of activation, implying reliance on implicit speech during this type of task. These results are consistent with PET findings reported by Paulesu, Frith, and Frackowiak (1993) who also used an item-recognition task. Again, Broca's area was reported to show significant levels of activation. Paulesu and colleagues also investigated whether frontal speech areas mediate rehearsal of phonological information. This task was a rhyming task in which subjects were presented with single letters and for each letter, they had to decide if it rhymed with the name of a previously given target letter. Again, activation in Broca's area was prominent, leading the authors to conclude that Broca's area mediates phonological processes, including rhyming judgment and subvocal rehearsal. Other findings by Smith, Jonides, Marshuetz, and Koeppe (1998), who used functional MRI (fMRI) to investigate similar questions, suggest that working memory involves distinct components, one of which is a phonological rehearsal component that is primarily mediated by left hemisphere frontal speech regions (including Broca's area) (see also Jonides et al., 1996).

This research suggests that Broca's area is necessary for the rehearsal of verbal material. If so, then impairment to Broca's area will disrupt rehearsal. If rehearsal is disrupted, then the tasks which implicitly require it, will induce poor performance. We believe that this is precisely why some Broca's aphasics fail on the matching and object-manipulation tasks.

It is not a giant leap to speculate that rehearsal of verbal material requires the same mechanisms as those which generate language. It makes sense that an impairment of language production would coincide with an impairment of language rehearsal. The comprehension impairment apparent in Broca's aphasia is therefore linked directly to the production impairment: There is "overarching agrammatism," but it is rooted in production.[1]

ACKNOWLEDGMENT

This work was supported, in part, by National Multipurpose Research and Training Center Grant DC-01409 from the National Institute on Deafness and Other Communication Disorders, in part by the Cognitive Science Program, University of Arizona, and in part by the National Institute of Health, DC-02984.

---

[1]The analysis given here applies to cases in which performance is worse on "long-lag" tasks such as sentence–picture matching than on "short-lag" tasks such as acceptability

REFERENCES

Awh, E., Jonides, J., Smith, E. E., Schumacher, E. H., Koeppe, R. A., & Katz, S. (1996). Disso-
ciation of storage and rehearsal in verbal working memory: Evidence from positron emis-
sion tomography. *Psychological Science, 7*, 25–31.
Bradley, C., Garrett, M. F., & Zurif, E. B. (1980). Syntactic deficits in Broca's aphasia. In D.
Caplan (Ed.), *Biological studies of mental processes.* (pp. 269–286). Cambridge, MA: MIT
Press.
Caramazza, A., & Zurif, E. B. (1976). Dissociation of algorithmic and heuristic processes in
language comprehension: Evidence from aphasia. *Brain and Language, 3*, 572–582.
Caramazza, A., Zurif, E. B., & Gardner, H. (1978). Sentence memory in aphasia. *Neuropsy-
chologia, 16*, 661–669.
Chomsky, N. (1981). *Lectures on government and binding.* Dordrecht: Foris.
Frazier, L., & Friederici, A. D. (1991). On deriving properties of agrammatic comprehension.
Brain and Language, 40, 51–66.
Friederici, A. D. (1983). Aphasics' perception of words in sentential context: Some real-time
processing evidence. *Neuropsychologia, 21*, 351–358.
Grodzinsky, Y. (1984). The syntactic characterization of agrammatism. *Cognition, 16*, 99–120.
Grodzinsky, Y. (1986). Language deficits and the theory of syntax. *Brain and Language, 27*,
135–159.
Haarmann, H. J., & Kolk, H. H. J. (1991). A computer model of the temporal course of agram-
matic sentence understanding: The effects of variation in severity and sentence complexity.
Cognitive Science, 15, 49–87.
Hickok, G., Zurif, E., & Conseco-Gonzales, E. (1993). Structural description of agrammatic
comprehension. *Special Issue: Grammatical Investigations of aphasia. Brain and Language, 45*,
371–395.
Jonides, J., Reuter-Lorenz, P., Smith, E. E., Awh, E., Barnes, L., Drain, M., Glass, J., Lauber,
E., Patalano, A., & Schumacher, E. (1996). Verbal and spatial working memory in humans.
In D. Medin (Ed.) *The psychology of learning and motivation* (pp. 43–88). New York: Acade-
mic Press.
Kean, M.-L. (1977). The linguistic interpretation of aphasic syndromes: Agrammatism in
Broca's aphasia, an example. *Cognition, 5*, 9–46.
Linebarger, M.C., Schwartz, M. F., & Saffran, E. M. (1983). Sensitivity to grammatical struc-
ture in so-called agrammatic aphasics. *Cognition, 13*, 361–392.
Mauner, G., Fromkin, V., & Cornell, T. (1993). Comprehension and acceptability judgments
in agrammatism: Disruptions in the syntax of referential dependency. *Special Issue: Grammatical Investigations of Aphasia. Brain and Language, 45*, 340–370.

judgment. However, it is likely that there other real comprehension problems that have
nothing to do with ability to rehearse. There are a number of sentence types which are problematic for Broca's aphasics, even in the acceptability judgment task. Sometimes the impairment involves long-distance matching, as in tag questions (Linebarger et al., 1983), which
may require that both a verb and pronoun match a previously mentioned verb and subject
NP. But similar problems may be seen for short-distance matching. Our own testing of these
individuals suggests that they have difficulty detecting feature mismatches involving number and gender, for example, reflexive–antecedent matching (e.g., John admires
himself/*herself) and subject–verb agreement (e.g., the goats are/*is crossing the stream).
Feature-matching of this type appears to be truly problematic, whatever the task.

Nicol, J. L. & Rapcsak, S. Z. (1994). *The closed class account revisited: Impaired memory for function words in Broca's aphasia.* Poster presentation. Theoretical and experimental neuropsychology (TENNET) Meeting, Montréal, Québec, May.

Paulesu, E., Frith, C., and Frackowiak, R. (1993). The neural correlates of the verbal component of working memory. *Nature. (London) 362,* 342–344.

Potter, M. C., & Lombardi, L. (1998). Syntactic priming in immediate recall of sentences. *Journal of Memory and Language, 38,* 265–282.

Prather, P. A., Zurif, E., Love, T., & Brownell, H. (1997). Speed of lexical activation in nonfluent Broca's aphasia and fluent Wernicke's aphasia. *Brain and Language, 59,* 391–411.

Schwartz, M., Linebarger, M., & Pate, D. (1987). Syntactic transparency and sentence interpretation in aphasia. *Language and Cognitive Processes, 2,* 85–113.

Smith, E., Jonides, J., Marshuetz, C., and Koeppe, R. (1998). Components of verbal working memory: Evidence form neuroimaging. *Proceedings from the National Academy of Science, United States of America 95,* 876–882.

Swinney, D., Zurif, E., & Cutler, A. (1980). The effects of sentential stress and word class upon comprehension in Broca's aphasics. *Brain and Language, 10,* 132–144.

Swinney, D., Zurif, E., & Nicol, J. (1989). The effects of focal brain damage on sentence processing: An examination of the neurological organization of a mental module. *Journal of Cognitive Neuroscience, 1,* 25–37.

Zurif, E., & Swinney, D. (1994a) Modularity need not imply locality; damaged modules can have non-local effects. An accompanying reply to Farah, M. J. Neuropsychological inference with an interactive brain: A critique of the "locality assumption." *Behavioral and Brain Science, 17,* 89–90.

Zurif, E., & Swinney, D. (1994b) The neuropsychology of language. In M.A. Gernsbacher, (Ed.), *Handbook of psycholinguistics* (pp. 1055–1074). Orlando, Florida: Academic Press.

Zurif, E., Swinney, D., & Garrett, M. (1990). Lexical processes in service of syntactic function. In A. Caramazza, (Ed.), *Cognitive, neuropsychology and neurolinguistics: Advances in models of cognitive function and impairment* (pp. 123–136). New York: Erlbaum.

Zurif, E., Swinney, D., Prather, P., & Love, T. (1994). Functional localization in the brian with respect to syntactic processing. *Journal of Psycholinguistic Research, 23,* 487–498.

Part III

The Memory–Language Interface

Chapter 6

Verbal Working Memory and Its Connections to Language Processing

Edward E. Smith and Anat Geva

INTRODUCTION

Working memory is the cognitive mechanism that allows us to keep active a limited amount of information (roughly, 5–7 items) for a brief period of time (roughly, a few seconds). It is not the case that there is a single general-purpose working memory; rather, research indicates that there are different kinds of working memories for different kinds of information. In particular, behavioral, neuropsychological, and neuroimaging evidence converge in indicating that there are separate systems for verbal and spatial information (see, e.g., Jonides et al., 1997, for a review). Given that this book is concerned with language, in this chapter we focus on verbal working memory and its neural implementation. Henceforth, unless otherwise noted, when we talk about "working memory" (or WM) we mean verbal working memory, where "verbal" often stands for "phonological."

Sometimes we use verbal WM to keep information active solely for storage purposes, as when we maintain a just-looked-up phone number until we can dial it. But perhaps the major function of WM is to temporarily store the outcome of intermediate computations when solving some sort of problem, and to perform further computations on these temporarily stored outcomes (e.g., Baddeley, 1986). For example, when we mentally multiply two digit numbers such as 29 × 19, we may first compute the partial product 9 × 9 = 81, hold this partial product in phonological

form in WM, later use it in further computations, and subsequently drop
it when it is no longer needed.

What does all this have to do with language processing? Several things.
First, there is evidence that components of the language system are recruited for assistance in verbal WM. For instance, neuroimaging studies
of WM report activation of Broca's area, a region that has been implicated
in speech and the comprehension of syntax (e.g., Caramazza & Zurif,
1976). Second, there are a couple of ways that a WM holding phonological information may be used in language processing. It is essential when
one has to learn the phonological component of a language, as phonological information is by nature spread over time. Moreover, there appear to
be some cases of sentence comprehension in which it is advantageous to
hold sentential information in phonological form until sentence processing is complete, and in such cases WM would be critical. Third, a discussion of the roles of a phonological WM will make clear the need for
another kind of linguistic WM, a syntactic or semantic one.

In light of the above, we will proceed as follows. In the next, or second
section we will review some of the major findings that have emerged in
neuroimaging studies of WM, which have used either positron emission
tomography (PET) or functional magnetic resonance imaging (fMRI).
These studies will highlight the role that Broca's area plays in maintaining phonological information for brief periods of time. In the third section we will turn to the issue of the role of WM in language learning and
understanding. Here, we first review evidence that WM plays a role in
learning phonological aspects of the language, and then consider cases in
which WM is used in the service of sentence comprehension. In the fourth
and final section, we will consider WM systems that hold linguistic information that is more abstract than phonological forms.

NEUROIMAGING STUDIES OF WORKING MEMORY

The neuroimaging studies that our laboratory has conducted have
taken as a starting point a view of WM that was derived from cognitive-
behavioral studies from the mid-1960s through the early 1990s. One influential summary of that literature was Baddeley's (e.g., 1986, 1992)
proposed architecture of WM. It consisted of two storage devices, corresponding to what we call verbal and spatial WM, and a "central execu-
tive" that regulated the operation of the storage devices. Baddeley further
maintained that verbal WM could be decomposed into a "phonological
buffer" that allows for the short-term maintenance of phonological information, and a rehearsal process that refreshes the contents of the buffer.

Our first neuroimaging experiment with verbal materials produced results in line with Baddeley's proposal, and suggested that the rehearsal process is implemented by left-hemisphere regions in prefrontal cortex that are known to be involved in speech. (This experiment, like all others described in this section, involved visual presentation.)

In the experiment (Awh et al., 1996), subjects were PET-imaged while they performed an item-recognition task (Sternberg, 1966). On each of a series of discrete trials: four letters were presented simultaneously for 200 ms, followed by a 3000-ms blank delay period (during which subjects had to remember the letters), followed by a probe letter presented for 1500 ms. Subjects had to respond "yes" or "no" to the probe (by pressing one of two buttons) indicating whether or not it was identical in name to one of the four target letters. Thus, this task necessitates verbal storage, but it includes other processes as well—for example, perception of the letters and execution of a response—and consequently the PET image acquired during performance of the task will include activations caused by the additional processes as well as activations due to WM. To eliminate the unwanted activations, subjects also participated in a control task, which presumably contained the unwanted processes but not the WM ones. The task was similar to the memory task except that the probe was presented immediately after the target letters (there was no delay), and the latter remained in view along with the probe. Hence, no memory was needed to accomplish the control task.

When the image acquired during the control task was subtracted from that acquired during the memory task, there were several sites of activation, mostly in the left hemisphere. These included: left posterior parietal cortex (Brodmann area, or BA 40), Broca's area (BA 44), left premoter area (BA 6), and left supplementary motor area (BA 6). Given that the latter three areas are known to be involved in the planning and production of speech (e.g., Fuster, 1995), and given that subjects routinely reported silently rehearsing the target letters during the delay period, we tentatively identified the three frontal areas in question as mediating a subvocal rehearsal process; the posterior parietal area was thought to underlie a storage process.

There is stronger evidence for a dissociation between rehearsal and storage processes in another PET experiment reported in Awh et al. (1996). This study used a "2-back" paradigm (e.g., Cohen et al., 1994). Subjects viewed a continuous stream of letters, each presented for 500 ms, with a 2500-ms interval between successive letters. For each letter, subjects had to decide whether it was identical in name to the letter two back in the sequence. Two different control conditions were used. One was a search task: Subjects saw the same kind of sequence of letters as in the memory condition, but now simply decided whether each letter matched a single target letter specified at the beginning of the experiment. It was hypothesized that this control would involve perceptual and response processes identical to those in the 2-back condition but no WM processes, and so subtracting the control from the 2-back condition would yield activations in the areas responsible for WM that are similar to those obtained in the item-recognition task. This was the case, as the subtraction image showed activations in the frontal speech regions, including Broca's area, and posterior parietal cortex.

The second control condition was intended to subtract out rehearsal processes in addition to perceptual and response processes. In this rehearsal control, subjects pressed a button when a new letter appeared, silently rehearsed it until the next letter appeared, pressed a button and rehearsed the new letter, and so on. It was expected that subtracting this control from the 2-back memory condition would remove much of the rehearsal circuit. Indeed, in this subtraction image, neither Broca's area nor the premoter area was significantly active. The results provide evidence that a rehearsal component can be isolated from the rest of the neural circuitry for verbal WM.

Our next source of evidence for a dissociation between rehearsal and storage comes from a somewhat different kind of experiment (Cohen et al., 1997). There were two major changes from the prior 2-back study. First, rather than relying on a comparison of a memory and a control condition, we varied memory load incrementally across a set of conditions. We used the *n*-back task—though with the interval between successive letters increased to 10,000 ms—and we varied whether subjects had to respond to memory matches 0-, 1-, 2-, or 3-back from the current item. In the 0-back task, subjects had to decide whether each letter matched a fixed target letter specified at the beginning of the letter sequence (the search task of our previous experiment); in the 1-back task, subjects had to decide whether each letter matched the one 1-back in the sequence; and so on for 2- and 3-back. If a neural area is involved in WM, its activation should increase monotonically with memory load. The second major change from the previous study was that we used fMRI rather that PET as the imaging modality. Using echoplanar imaging, we were able to scan subjects performing the tasks at four time periods during the 10-s delay period: 0–2.5 s, 2.5–5.0 s, 5.0–7.5 s, and 7.5–10.0 s. This allowed us to determine the temporal dynamics of areas that were sensitive to WM load, so that we could see if the temporal pattern of activation differs for the posterior parietal area that presumably mediates storage, versus an area that presumably meditates rehearsal (for this purpose, we focused on Broca's area).

The relevant data are presented in Figure 1, and they provide new evidence for a dissociation between Broca's area and the posterior parietal area. In Figure 1a, we have plotted activation as a function of WM load (0, 1, 2, or 3 items), separately for the posterior parietal area and Broca's area; temporal interval (scan 1–4) is the parameter. Note that the increase in activation with memory load is more linear and steeper for the parietal area than for Broca's area. Indeed, it seems that Broca-based rehearsal plays a minimal role in maintaining a memory load of one item. In Figure 1b, we have plotted changes in activation as a function of temporal interval, separately for the posterior parietal area and Broca's area; now memory load is the parameter. The point to notice is that activation is better sustained across the delay period for the parietal area than for Broca's area, especially for higher memory loads, which is consistent with the idea that the parietal area mediates a storage function. In sum, Broca's area differs from the posterior parietal area with respect to both its sensitivity to memory load and its temporal dynamics. These findings support the claim that Broca's area and the posterior parietal area mediate different cognitive functions, where presumably the function of Broca's area is subvocal rehearsal and the role of the posterior parietal area is short-term storage.

A comment is in order about our interpretation of the left-hemisphere posterior parietal area as mediating short-term storage. In making this interpretation, initially we were influenced by neuropsychological findings reported by Shallice (1988). He described a group of patients whose major deficit was in short-term memory for verbal material (particularly when presented auditorally), and whose most frequent lesion site was in the left-hemisphere posterior parietal area, usually including the supramarginal gyrus. Because there was something of a 1:1 correspondence between lesion and deficit, it seemed plausible to us to interpret the region as housing phonological storage. However, there is evidence that the supramarginal region may be involved in phonological processing in general (e.g., Cohen, 1992; Friedman, 1996). This raises the possibility that (1) the posterior parietal area becomes involved in these studies because of its role in naming the letters during their encoding; (2) the area then remains active for a few seconds, where this activity constitutes the pure storage component of WM; and (3) the activity can be reinstated by subvocal rehearsal (see Smith & Jonides, 1998).

In sum, the architecture of verbal WM has at least two components, a pure storage component and a subvocal rehearsal process. The storage component appears to be mediated by posterior parietal areas, whereas the rehearsal process is mediated by frontal speech areas, including Broca's area, and these two components can be neurologically dissociated. We turn now to the uses of this WM system in language processing.

a   **Posterior Parietal Area**

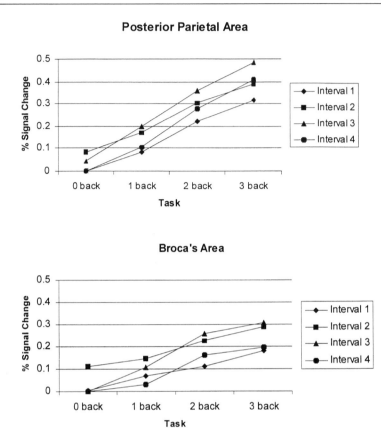

Broca's Area

Figure 1   (a) Percentage of MRI signal change in activation as a function of
WM load, with temporal interval as the parameter. (b) Percentage of MRI signal change in activation as a function of temporal interval, with WM load as the
parameter. (Adapted from Cohen et al., 1997, with permission from *Nature*.)

VERBAL WORKING MEMORY AND LANGUAGE PROCESSING

We are concerned here with two different ways in which WM may be
used in language processing. First, the WM system described above
would be expected to play a substantial role in the acquisition of phonological forms, given that the system represents phonological information.
Second, verbal WM might play a role in sentence understanding by serving as a backup record for situations in which linguistic processing demands become too great for the usual on-line syntactic and semantic
processes to operate effectively.

b

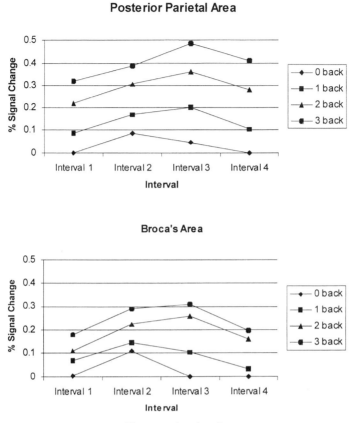

Figure 1 *(continued)*.

Acquiring New Phonological Forms

When acquiring a new phonological form, corresponding to new vocabulary item, one has to temporarily store the novel form while attaching semantic information to it. In addition, one may need to keep the phonological form active briefly while a long-term representation of it is developed. For these reasons, Baddeley and colleagues (e.g., Baddeley, Gathercole, & Papagno, 1998; Gathercole & Baddeley, 1989) have claimed that WM is essential for vocabulary acquisition. Indeed, these authors have gone so far as to claim that vocabulary acquisition is *the* primary function of verbal WM, with short-term storage and manipulation of verbal information being secondary functions. Empirical support for the Baddeley and Gathercole proposal comes from three sources: studies of initial vocabulary acquisition in children, studies of second-language learning in children and adults, and studies of word learning in certain neurological patients.

Studies on vocabulary acquisition in children show that digit span and pseudoword repetition scores—both standard WM measures—are strongly associated with vocabulary knowledge, even when controlling for general intelligence (e.g., Gathercole & Adams, 1994; Gathercole, Willis, & Baddeley, 1991). Thus, pseudoword repetition at age four is strongly correlated with vocabulary knowledge, and furthermore is a strong predictor of vocabulary development 1 year later (Gathercole & Baddeley, 1989). In fact, at age five, pseudoword repetition remains strongly associated with vocabulary knowledge even after vocabulary at age four is partialed out. These results suggest that the predictive value of the pseudoword-repetition measure is not merely a by-product of the vocabulary ability 1 year earlier. Further experiments suggest even more strongly that increased WM *causes* increased vocabulary development. Using a cross-lagged correlational analysis, Gathercole and colleagues (Gathercole, Willis, Emslie, & Baddeley, 1992) showed that pseudoword-repetition scores at age four appear to be more closely associated with vocabulary knowledge 1 year later than early vocabulary acquisition is associated with later pseudoword repetition ability.

There have also been studies examining the impact of WM on second-language learning in children (Service, 1992; Cheung, 1996). In a longitudinal study, Service (1992) administered phonological WM tasks such as pseudoword repetition to 9- and 10-year-old Finnish children who were about to start learning English. Repetition accuracy was strongly correlated with English vocabulary scores 2 1/2 years later. Again the findings imply that the ability to maintain novel phonological material in WM is closely related to the acquisition of vocabulary.

If WM is necessary for vocabulary acquisition, then factors known to interfere with WM should also interfere with learning new vocabulary. Word length and phonological similarity are two factors known to diminish the capacity of WM, and Papagno and Vallar (1992) have shown that these two factors also retard the acquisition of novel vocabulary in adults. When participants learned paired associates in their native language, phonological similarity had little effect on learning; but when they learned paired associates in a foreign language, phonological similarity had a disruptive effect. Apparently, participants were forced to rely more on phonological representation for the foreign-language words than for the familiar native-language ones, and consequently WM played a more critical role in learning the foreign-language pairs. Likewise, word length had a disruptive effect on learning phonologically novel forms (of Russian), but not on the acquisition of items in the participants' native language.

Neuropsychological research provides additional evidence that WM supports the learning of new phonological forms. The evidence comes from a patient with a verbal short-term memory deficit. Patient P.V. is unable to repeat pseudowords or learn new phonological sequences in her native language. Papagno, Valentine, and Baddeley (1991) compared P.V.'s memory for word pairs constructed either from her native language (Italian) or from a foreign language (Russian). As predicted, her ability to associate pairs in her native language was normal, but she was severely impaired in learning Russian word pairs. The case of P.V. therefore provides further evidence that WM is involved in vocabulary acquisition.

Understanding Sentences

When understanding a sentence, we rarely seem to maintain much information in phonological form, that is, in verbal WM. This observation fits with the evidence that our semantic and syntactic processes operate on each constituent as soon as possible (e.g., Just & Carpenter, 1992), thereby obviating an extensive need for a backup phonological representation. However, there are cases in which normal syntactic–semantic routines appear to break down—as when trying to understand doubly embedded sentences—and in such cases we may rely on a backup phonological representation of the thus-far presented sentence. The point, then, is that verbal WM might play a role in sentence comprehension only when sentences are sufficiently complex (Chomsky, 1957; Gibson, 1998; see Gathercole and Baddeley, 1993, for a review).

Perhaps the best evidence that WM contributes to sentence comprehension comes from studies of neurological patients with severe short-term memory deficits (patients like the one we considered in the previous section). These patients typically present with short-term recall spans of one to three items, and, in contrast to neurologically intact adults, have a smaller span for auditorily than visually presented material (Basso, Spinnler, Vallar, & Zanobio, 1982; Vallar & Baddeley, 1984a,b: Warrington and Shallice, 1969). Such patients are also less sensitive to word-length or phonological similarity effects, which is consistent with their having impaired WMs. Informal testing suggests these patients have fairly well preserved language comprehension. However, since phonological WM may become involved in language comprehension when sentences are syntactically or semantically complex, the linguistic consequences of an impaired verbal WM should become apparent with more complex sentences. There is mixed support for this claim.

Saffran and Marin (1975) studied patient I.L., a conduction aphasic with an auditory digit span of three items. I.L. Is characterized by a profound inability to repeat verbal information despite a relatively preserved capacity to comprehend and spontaneously produce language (I.L. could also be classified as a short-term memory patient). In a sentence-repetition task in which sentences varied in length and complexity, I.L.'s verbatim recall decreased as sentence length increased, particularly for lengths of six or greater. However, even for those sentences he could not repeat verbatim, I.L. demonstrated good retention of the semantic information. For example, the sentence "The old man sank gratefully into the yellow chair" was paraphrased as "The old man was tired. He wanted to sit in the chair." But, and this is the critical point, in contrast to his good understanding of simple, active sentences, I.L. frequently produced semantically incorrect paraphrases for passive constructions (e.g., "The soldier was watched by the man in the car") and center-embedded sentences (e.g., "The man the child hit carried the box"). Paraphrase errors in these cases involved reversing the subject and object terms. These results suggest that: (1) understanding passive and embedded constructions sometimes requires the use of a backup phonological representation stored in WM, and (2) because I.L. has an impaired WM, he has poor comprehension of such complex sentences (Saffran & Marin, 1975).

Subsequent research by Vallar and Baddeley (1984a,b) with patient P.V. showed the importance of another aspect of linguistic complexity. Following damage to the left hemisphere, P.V. also demonstrated an impaired WM and possessed a span of but two items (Basso et al., 1982; Vallar & Baddeley, 1984a). Nonetheless, P.V.'s comprehension of simple active sentences was intact, as demonstrated by her performance on a sentence–picture matching task. Unlike I.L., however, P.V. proved capable of comprehending passive and semantically reversible sentences. But she did show impaired performance on the token test, a task that requires participants to read a sentence conveying an instruction and then execute that instruction. Although P.V. succeeded in responding correctly to simple instructions, such as "Touch the black square," she often failed to cope with longer and more complex instructions, such as "If there is a black circle then pick up the red square." Based on these findings, Vallar and Baddeley (1984a) suggested that WM is necessary for the comprehension of complex syntactic structures that contain more semantic information than normal on-line semantic processes can assimilate.

The two patients considered thus far show deficits in comprehension as the sentences become more complex, but there are differences in the kind of complexity involved. Complexity for I.L. was varied syntactically, as he had problems with reversible sentences, while complexity for P.V. was varied at least partly semantically, as she had troubles only when sentences contained substantial semantic content. The picture becomes even more varied when we consider Baddeley and Wilson's (1998) study of patient T.B., who had an immediate verbal memory span of two items, and whose sentence-comprehension ability was assessed by a sentence–picture matching task. Syntactic structure that T.B. was capable of comprehending at a high level were increased in length from a mean of 6 to 10 words by adding redundant adverbial and adjectival material. For example, "The girl chases the horse" became "The little girl vigorously chases the poor old horse." Despite T.B.'s almost perfect score on the short sentences, his performance on syntactically identical but extended sentences was extremely poor. Thus for T.B., unlike the previous two patients, length per se seems to contribute to complexity.

Lastly, we note that there is at least one report of a patient who shows no evidence of a deficit in sentence understanding despite a substantial deficit in WM. This is patient B.O. (Waters, Caplan, & Hildenbrandt, 1987, 1991). Despite having a verbal span of two or three items, B.O. demonstrated intact comprehension for sentences requiring complex syntactic processing. She performed as well as normals in comprehending garden-path sentences and showed no difficulty in making sentence acceptability judgments of complex syntactic forms.

What can we conclude from these neuropsychological results? First, the studies generally show that a deficit in WM leads to a deficit in language understanding only when the sentences are complex in some respect. What differs among the studies is how the sentences are made complex—syntactically, semantically, or just by sheer lengthening. The relatively preserved performance of short-term memory patients on short, syntactically simple, sentences indicates that in the course of comprehending such sentences, linguistic analysis is performed as soon as sufficient information has accumulated and does not require phonological working-memory capacities. However, verbal WM is required when the information comes in at a rate that exceeds the handling capacity of the on-line mechanisms. Factors that determine whether this capacity is exceeded include syntactic complexity, subject–object order, semantic density, and sentence length.

OTHER KINDS OF WORKING MEMORIES FOR LANGUAGE UNDERSTANDING

The preceding studies concur that patients with deficits in WM are normal in understanding relatively short, simple, sentences. But even short simple, sentences, require some kind of short-term storage. For example, to understand "The girl chases the horse," one must store the initial noun phrase (perhaps semantically interpreted) while processing the verb phrase. The patient data indicate that the storage system involved is not verbal WM. Indeed, the kind of storage system needed to store syntactic structures, or semantically interpreted syntactic structures cannot in principle be a phonological WM because syntactic or semantic information cannot be reduced to phonology. Hence, there are compelling reasons to posit that other WMs are involved in language understanding.

This is hardly news. Computational analyses of language understanding routinely postulate syntactic/semantic WMs (e.g., Gibson, 1998; Lewis, 1996). Without such meaning-based WMs (as opposed to sound-based ones), it is not clear how symbolic computational models could ever do language understanding. Also, psycholinguists have argued for years that the working-memory system that underlies sentence understanding must involve more than phonological representations. One prominent example is the work of Just and Carpenter (e.g., 1992; Just, Carpenter, & Keller, 1996). They have extensively studied the relation between sentence understanding and a WM that is measured by people's ability to process and store material simultaneously; and they have explicitly assumed that this WM is *not* phonological, that is, not the WM system that we have emphasized in this chapter. As another prominent example of this position, Caplan and Waters (e.g., 1996; in press) have similarly argued that the WM system involved in assigning the syntactic structure of a sentence and subsequently determining the sentence's meaning is not phonological WM. (This negative claim seems to be the one point of agreement between the two research groups just referenced.)

Most of the behavioral evidence for the existence of a syntactic or semantic WM involves null findings; for example, patients with defective phonological WM do not necessarily have defective language understanding, therefore a nonphonological WM must be operative in sentence understanding. What about positive evidence for such a WM? There is such evidence for a semantic WM, some of which involves the effects of lexical status on memory-span. It has long been known that the span for familiar words exceeds that for pseudowords (Brener, 1940). The greater span for words than nonwords may result from the fact that only words have a semantic representation, in addition to a phonological one. Further support for this view has come from Hulme, Maughan, and Brown (1991) who demonstrated that span for Italian words increased for English-speaking individuals after the meaning of these words had been learned.

Perhaps the strongest evidence for a separate semantic WM has been advance by Martin, Shelton, and Yaffee (1994) who studied the WM capacities of two patients, E.A. and A.B. Although both patients presented with similar reductions in verbal span, the specific patterns of their WM deficit differed. Patient E.A., like other short-term memory patients, showed a lack of a phonological-similarity effect for visually presented words, a lack of word-length effect, and performed better with visually than auditorally presented material. Patient A.B., on the other hand, showed the pattern of phonological effects normally associated with neurologically intact individuals and superior performance for items presented auditorally. E.A., but not A.B., has a classic deficit in verbal or phonological WM. In contrast, E.A. showed a normal lexical–semantic effect for short-term list recall (i.e., significantly better recall of words over pseudowords) while A.B. did not. Thus, while E.A. has a deficit in phonological WM, A.B. has a deficit in semantic WM.

As a more direct contrast between phonological versus semantic WM, Martin et al. (1994) had E.A. and A.B., as well as a group of normal controls, perform two different WM tasks. In the phonological task, subjects were presented a varying number of target words (list length varied from one to seven items), followed by a 2-s delay, followed by a probe word; the subjects task was to determine whether or not the probe rhymed with any of the targets. The semantic WM task was the same except that now the subjects' task was to determine whether or not the probe was drawn from the same superordinate category as any of the probes. In both cases span length was measured by the list length at which the subject would score 75% correct. As expected, patient E.A. had a smaller phonological span than A.B. (2.65 vs. 4.62, whereas the normal control span was 7.02); in contrast, A.B. has a smaller semantic span than E.A. (2.19 vs. 2.82, whereas the normal control span was 5.38).

Subsequent testing addressed the issue of whether the nature of the difference found in E.A.'s and A.B.'s WM deficit would be observed in these patients' sentence processing abilities. On a test of syntactic comprehension, both patients performed well on simple reversible active and passive sentences (Martin et al., 1994). Yet, on syntactically simple structures involving a heavy semantic load, E. A. scored better than A.B. For instance, in answering a simple attribute question, such as "Which is quiet, a library or a concert?," E.A. was errorless, whereas A.B. had an accuracy rate of only 20%. These results are consistent with the view that A.B. has a deficit in semantic WM. In contrast, A.B.'s verbatim repetition of even syntactically complex sentences was superior to that of E.A. On lengthy sentences with adverbial and complement clauses, A.B. had an accuracy rate of 65%, compared to E.A.'s rate of 5%. These results are consistent with E.A. having a deficit in verbal or phonological WM. These two patients also differed in the types of errors they produced in sentence repetition. Patient A.B. tended to omit items completely, whereas E.A.'s errors consisted primarily of paraphrases and repetitions that were similar in meaning to the target.

Given the success of Martin et al.'s (1994) WM paradigms with neuro-logical patients, we have recently adapted these paradigms for use with normal subjects. However, we made a couple of changes. First, rather than using the tasks to determine spans, we employed a fixed number of target items (three) and measured the accuracy and latency of response. Second, and more importantly, we introduced a priming variation during the delay period; if the representation maintained during the delay in the semantic WM task is indeed semantic, then it should be affected by a semantic prime (and likewise for phonological representations in the phonological task). The tasks and the priming manipulations are illus-trated in Figure 2.

In both tasks: three target words are presented in lower case, followed by a 2.5-s delay during which a capitalized prime word is presented, fol-lowed by a probe word (which is flanked by asterisks). In each task, half the probes required positive responses, half required negative responses. In the semantic WM tasks, subjects had to decide whether the probe was in the same superordinate category as any of the targets, whereas in the phonological task subject had to decide whether the probe rhymed with any of the targets. In each task, the prime always "matched" one of the targets—a semantic match had the same superordinate as one of the tar-gets, a phonological match rhymed with one of the targets; half the time the matched target also matched the probe, resulting in a "primed posi-tive response," and half the time the matched target did not match the probe, resulting in a "primed negative response" (see Figure 2). Thus for each task, there are four kinds of trials, corresponding to primed or un-primed positive or negative decisions.

Latencies and accuracies for the four trial types are presented in Tables I and II. There are priming effects on positive responses in both the semantic and phonological tasks. Of particular interest is the semantic task. When a prime matched a target that would later match the probe (a primed posi-tive), the positive response was faster than when there was no prime. This positive priming effect fits with the hypothesis that the representation maintained during the delay of the semantic task was indeed semantic, which in turn supports the existence of a semantic WM. It is possible that the subjects initially stored the targets in phonological form, and only con-verted them to semantic representations when the prime was presented; but even if this was so, it is still the case that semantic representations were active during the delay, and hence there is still evidence for a semantic WM.

A potential difficulty with our interpretation stems from another find-ing evident in Tables I and II. In both tasks, when the prime matched a target other than the one that would be probed (a primed negative), the negative response was slowed compared to the no-prime condition. This suggests that part of the positive priming effect is due solely to the inter-

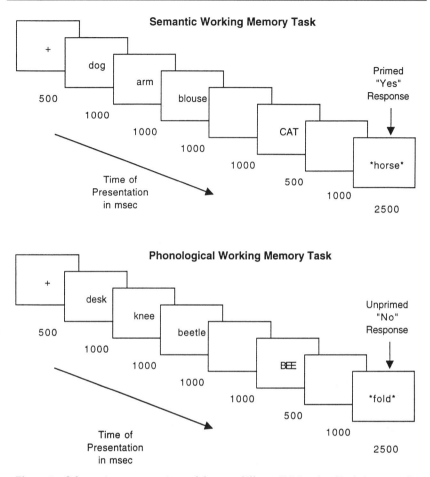

Figure 2 Schematic representations of the two different WM tasks. (Top) An example of the semantic WM task—a "primed positive" trial. (Bottom) An example of the phonological WM task—an "unprimed negative" trial.

action of the prime and probe; when they matched, participants were predisposed to respond positively, which facilitated positive responses but retarded negative responses. According to this suggestion, then, it is possible to explain part of the positive priming effect without assuming that the targets are maintained in a semantic code. But only *part*, for the negative priming effect in the semantic task is appreciably smaller than the positive priming effect, suggesting that part of the effect is indeed due to the representations being maintained in a semantic WM. Clearly the issue needs further work.

Table I   Reaction Time and Percent Correct in the Semantic Working Memory Task

	Primed				Unprimed			
	Percent correct		Reaction time (ms)		Percent correct		Reaction time (ms)	
Response	M	SD	M	SD	M	SD	M	SD
Yes	90	8.1	991	174	88	10.2	1091	180
No	88	10.6	1269	227	93	8.9	1221	195

SUMMARY

Neuroimaging experiments support the claim that verbal WM consists of a rehearsal process and a storage process. These studies further indicate that the rehearsal process is implemented by neural mechanisms involved in speech. Thus verbal WM clearly depends on language, or at least the phonological component of language. A kind of inverse question then arises: Do some aspects of language processing depend on verbal WM? Unsurprisingly, the answer seems to be "yes," when the language processing of interest is the learning of new phonological forms, as demonstrated by numerous studies of vocabulary acquisition. It is more controversial, though, whether verbal WM plays a substantial role in sentence comprehension. Studies of neurological patients who have defects in short-term storage suggest that verbal WM is sometimes used as backup, particularly when the syntactic or semantic complexity of the sentence outstrips the capacity of normal processing mechanisms. But the patient findings on this point are quite variable.

One thing that is clear from these patient studies, though, is that it is often possible to understand sentences normally with a deficient verbal WM. Since understanding virtually any kind of sentence requires some kind of short-term storage, there must be some form of syntactic–semantic

Table II   Reaction Time and Percent Correct in the Phonological Working Memory Task

	Primed				Unprimed			
	Percent correct		Reaction time (ms)		Percent correct		Reaction time (ms)	
Response	M	SD	M	SD	M	SD	M	SD
Yes	91	10	827	222	83	12	925	191
No	92	9.7	1072	259	95	7.8	931	225

WM. Computational accounts of language understanding routinely posit such linguistic WM systems, but empirical researchers are only beginning to obtain direct, experimental evidence about such systems. Already, though, studies with neurological patients provide some evidence for the existence of a semantic WM, and the paradigms used in these patient studies appear to be extendable for research with neurologically intact subjects.

REFERENCES

Awh, E., Jonides, J., Smith, E. E., Schumacher, E. H., Koeppe, R. A., & Katz, S. (1996). Dissociation of storage and rehearsal in verbal working memory: Evidence from positron emission tomography. *Psychological Science, 7*, 25–31.

Baddeley, A. D. (1986). *Working memory.* Oxford: Oxford University Press.

Baddeley, A. (1992). Working memory. *Science, 255*, 556–559.

Baddeley, A. D., Gathercole, S. E., & Papagno, C. (1998). The phonological loop as a language learning device. *Psychological Review, 105*, 158–173.

Baddeley, A. D., & Wilson, B. (1988). Comprehension and working memory: A single neuropsychological study. *Journal of Memory and Language, 27*, 479–498.

Basso, A., Spinnler, H., Vallar, G., & Zanobio, E. (1982). Left hemisphere damage and selective impairment of auditory-verbal short-term memory: A case study. *Neuropsychologia, 20*, 263–274.

Brener, R. (1940). An experimental investigation of memory span. *Journal of Experimental Psychology, 26*, 467–482.

Caplan, D., & Waters, G. (1996). Syntactic processing in sentence comprehension under dual-task conditions in aphasic patients. *Language and Cognitive Processes, 11*, 524–551.

Caplan, D., & Waters, G. (1999). Verbal working memory and sentence comprehension. *Behavior and Brain Sciences, 22*, 77–126.

Caramazza, A., & Zurif, E. B. (1976). Dissociation of algorithmic and heuristic processes in language comprehension: Evidence from aphasia. *Brain and Language, 3*, 572–582.

Cheung, H. (1996). Nonword span as a unique predictor of second-language vocabulary learning. *Developmental Psychology, 32*, 867–873.

Chomsky, N. (1957). *Syntactic structures.* The Hague: Mouton.

Cohen, J. D., Forman, S. D., Braver, T. S., Casey, B. J., Servan-Schreiber, D., & Noll, D. C. (1994). Activation of the prefrontal cortex in a nonspatial working memory task with functional MRI. *Human Brain Mapping, 1*, 293–304.

Cohen, J. D., Perlstein, W. M., Braver, T. S., Nystrom, L. E., Noll, D. C., Jonides, J., & Smith, E. E. (1997). Temporal dynamics of brain activation during a working memory task. *Nature (London) 386*, 604–608.

Cohen, S. (1992). *Conduction aphasia.* Hillsdale, NJ: Erlbaum.

Friedman, R. B. (1996). Phonological text alexia: Poor pseudoword reading plus difficulty reading functors and affixes in text. *Cognitive Neuropsychology, 13*, 869–885.

Fuster, J. M. (1995). *Memory in the cerebral cortex.* Cambridge, MA: MIT Press.

Gathercole, S. E., & Adams, A. (1994). Children's phonological working memory: Contributions of long-term knowledge and rehearsal. *Journal of Memory and Language, 33*, 672–688.

Gathercole, S. E., & Baddeley, A. D. (1989). Evaluation of the role of phonological STM in the development of vocabulary in children: A longitudinal study. *Journal of Memory and Language, 28*, 200–213.

Gathercole, S. E., & Baddeley, A. D. (1993). *Working memory and language.* Hillsdale, NJ: Erlbaum.

Gathercole, S. E., Willis, C., Emslie, H., & Baddeley, A. (1992). Phonological memory and vocabulary development during the early school years: A longitudinal study. *Developmental Psychology, 28,* 887–898.

Gathercole, S. E., Willis, C., & Baddeley, A. D. (1991). Differentiating phonological memory and awareness of rhyme: Reading and vocabulary development in children. *British Journal of Psychology, 82,* 387–406.

Gibson, E. (1998). Syntactic complexity: Locality of syntactic dependencies. *Cognition, 68,* 1–76.

Hulme, C., Maughan, S., & Brown, G. D. A. (1991). Memory for familiar and unfamiliar words: Evidence for a long-term memory contribution to short-term memory span. *Journal of Memory and Language, 30,* 685–701.

Jonides, J., Schumacher, E. H., Smith, E. E., Lauber, E. J., Awh, E., Minoshima, S., & Koeppe, R. A. (1997). Verbal working memory load affects regional brain activation as measured by PET. *Journal of Cognitive Neuroscience, 9,* 462–475.

Just, M. A., & Carpenter, P. A. (1992). A capacity theory of comprehension: Individual differences in working memory. *Psychological Review, 99,* 122–149.

Just, M. A., Carpenter, P. A., & Keller, T. A. (1996). The capacity theory of comprehension: New frontiers of evidence and arguments. *Psychological Review, 103,* 773–780.

Lewis, R. (1996). A theory of grammatical but unacceptable embeddings. *Journal of Psycholinguistic Research, 25,* 93–116.

Martin, R. C., Shelton, J. R., & Yaffee, L. S. (1994). Language processing and working memory: Neuropsychological evidence for separate phonological and semantic capacities. *Journal of Memory and Language, 33,* 83–111.

Papagno, C., Valentine, T., & Baddeley, A. D. (1991). Phonological short-term memory and foreign language vocabulary learning. *Journal of Memory and Language, 30,* 331–354.

Papagno, C., & Vallar, G. (1992). Phonological short-term memory and the learning of novel words: The effects of phonological similarity and item length. *Quarterly Journal of Experimental Psychology, 44A,* 47–67.

Saffran, E. M., & Marin, O. S. M. (1975). Immediate memory for word lists and sentences in a patient with deficient auditory short-term memory. *Brain and Language, 2,* 420–433.

Service, E. (1992). Phonology, working memory, and foreign-language learning. *Quarterly Journal of Experimental Psychology, 45A,* 21–50.

Shallice, T. (1988). *From neuropsychology to mental structure.* Cambridge: Cambridge University Press.

Smith, E. E., & Jonides, J. (1998). Neuroimaging analyses of human working memory. *Proceedings of the National Academy of Science of the United States of America, 95,* 12061–12068.

Sternberg, S. (1966). High-speed scanning in human memory. *Science, 153,* 652–654.

Vallar, G., & Baddeley, A. D. (1984a). Fractionation of working memory: Neuropsychological evidence for a short-term store. *Journal of Verbal Learning and Verbal Behavior, 23,* 151–161.

Vallar, G., & Baddeley, A. D. (1984b). Phonological short-term store, phonological processing, and sentence comprehension: A neuropsychological case study. *Cognitive Neuropsychology, 1,* 121–141.

Waters, G. S., Caplan, D., & Hildebrandt, N. (1987). Working memory and written sentence comprehension. In M. Coltheart (Ed.), *Attention and performance XII: The psychology of reading* (pp. 521–555). Hillsdale, NJ: Erlbaum.

Waters, G. S., Caplan, D., & Hildebrandt, N. (1991). On the structure of verbal STM and its functional role in sentence comprehension: Evidence from neuropsychology. *Cognitive Neuropsychology, 8,* 81–126.

Warrington E. K., & Shallice, T. (1969). The selective impairment of auditory–verbal short-term memory tasks. *Brain, 92,* 885–896.

Chapter 7

Sentence Memory in Amnesia

Laird S. Cermak

INTRODUCTION

The correspondence between language "utilization" and verbal memory ability has been a topic of concern to investigators of the amnesic syndrome for some time now. Zangwill (1969) was among the first to call for an investigation of the manner in which patients with memory disorders "abstract" information from incoming verbal input in order to store the material for later recall. Subsequently, Cermak, Butters, and Moreines (1974; Cermak, 1978) supported this call and found that amnesic Korsakoff patients exhibit deficits in their ability to abstract semantic features of a verbal stimuli. Using a, now-classic, version of the "release from PI" paradigm, they showed that Korsakoff patients do not improve their retrieval ability when information from a category different from all that which preceded is presented. This paradigm is designed to demonstrate a subject's ability to "utilize" specific features of words to both store and retrieve that information.

It has been demonstrated that whenever a subject becomes overwhelmed with similarly analyzed material, search for any one specific item from among these similarly represented items becomes increasingly impaired. When material from a new category is introduced the subject is provided with the opportunity to store this material on the basis of that new feature. These words then become more easily retrievable since their representation is no longer saturated at the time of retrieval. Since the only paradigmatic change that occurs takes place during item presentation, and involves the nature of the words' categorical representation, the only aspect of the paradigm that could produce a change in behavior is that which occurs at the time of encoding. Since our amnesic patients did not demonstrate an increase in performance, we felt that an encoding deficit, akin to Zangwill's abstracting deficit, had been demonstrated.

ENCODING DEFICITS

Encoding-deficits theory of amnesia was originally conceived of as a type of storage theory, one with far greater emphasis on input than on output. Much of the early emphasis in research stimulated by this theory was on the abstraction, analysis, and manipulation of the perceptual and semantic features of information prior to their storage, but it has always been the ability to retain and "utilize" this encoding that came under question in amnesia. Amnesic patients were shown to have difficulty utilizing feature representation, most notably semantic feature representation, to guide their search for the desired stimulus item because they had lost the ability to utilize features which promote normal storage, differentiation, and retrieval. Thus, a kind a language deficit, perhaps quite different from the language deficits generally considered by readers of this text, comes into play. Our amnesic patients have no trouble understanding semantic features or in using these features off-line for tasks such as category sorting of words. The patient does have difficulty when he has to use these features for differential storage on-line, at least on-line as it pertains to memory.

Gabrieli, Keane, and Stebbins (1993) have provided an excellent example of this ability of amnesics to use language while still showing a deficiency in the retention of that very material they so capably manipulated off-line. Once again, remember that by off-line we mean here, in this chapter, off-line with respect to being outside the information processing system needed to store the features of the verbal material. Gabrieli et al. adapted a paradigm originally introduced by Danneman and Carpenter (1980) in which subjects answer questions about auditorily presented sentences while simultaneously trying to remember the final word of each sentence for a later recall test. The subjects begin with one sentence and then recall the final word. Then, they proceed with increasingly larger numbers of sentences (two, three, four, etc.) before recalling the final word of each sentence and they continue to progress until they fail two of three trials for a given number of sentences. Gabrieli et al. found that amnesic patients could answer all the questions about each sentence correctly immediately following the reading of each sentence (so they understood them perfectly) but that they had a memory span for the final word of each sentence that averaged only 1.3 sentences. This span was about half of that accomplished by control subjects (2.3 sentences) who were matched for age and socioeconomic status. Thus, while the amnesic patient could process the linguistic features of the sentence appropriately (off-line as far as memory utilization is concerned), he could not utilize these features to aid his storage of the specific words for later recall nearly as well as do normals.

Now, one could conclude that this deficit was probably just a result of decreased word span capacity for amnesic patients. It seems logical that amnesic patients would have a decreased working memory span and that this would be reflected in any task in which they had to remember a string of items. However, when single words, or digits, are presented to amnesic patients in the usual memory span test they are presented as isolated single units and the patient is able to demonstrate an average span for this type of material. It is a well documented fact that amnesic patients' digit span on the Wechsler Intelligence and Memory Scales is consistently within normal limits. It was only when the patient was asked to incorporate the word within a sentence for its meaning, then to answer a question about the meaning prior to the memory test, that an impairment in memory span becomes apparent. When the patient had to analyze the word within the context of a sentence in order to understand and respond to the meaning of the sentence, he seemed less able to rehearse the word within working memory. The use of the word in context was antithetical to the rehearsal of the word as a phonetic unit. It is much like being distracted from the answer to a riddle by a mass of irrelevant information within the story line of the riddle. As one tries to keep track of the entire context of the riddle one forgets that specific information was given at the start of the riddle and when this information is then queried at the end of the riddle, we find we have forgotten it. The amnesic patient understands the last word of each sentence in the context of the sentence and he can use that meaning to answer the question, but he does not simultaneously have the ability to also use the specific features of that word to retain it as a single unit apart from the sentence.

RETRIEVAL OF STORED MATERIAL

Thus far in this chapter we have emphasized the encoding aspect of amnesic patients' information processing deficit, but there has always also been an equally likely contributor to the memory problems of these patients and that comes in the form of their ability, or inability, to retrieve stored material. Warrington and Weiskrantz (1970, 1974) have always favored the notion that amnesic patients are perfectly capable of encoding, or taking in, verbal material, but have an inordinate amount of difficulty retrieving that material. This controversy has been described in detail elsewhere (e.g., Verfaellie & Cermak, 1991) and it does impact on one aspect of the issue under discussion; namely, could it be the case that the amnesic patients retain the individual items in a sentence perfectly well, as evidenced by their ability to answer questions, but just fail in their ability to reconstruct the sentence verbatim? It may be that their strategy of recall is sufficiently impaired that they cannot, on demand, devise a means to search for and find the word that was the last one presented in the two or three sentences still in their memory. Evidence against this suggestion comes from a study reported by Naus, Cermak, and DeLuca (1977).

Naus et al. (1977) used the Sternberg (1966) paradigm to investigate the retrieval strategy used by amnesic patients. In a nutshell, these authors found that the patients' "search strategy" was perfectly normal, as was the set size from which the patients could retrieve information, but it was their search "rate" that was deficient. These investigators showed that amnesic patients could perform an exhaustive search of a learned set of items up to the normal span of six and that the length of time expended in this search increased directly as a function of the set size in a manner parallel to that seen for normal subjects. What was deviant with respect to the amnesic patients' retrieval was the speed of their interitem scan. In other words, they took more time to consider each item in memory but still progressed at a rate whose slope directly paralleled the slope of the normal subjects' retrieval. Thus, the notion that an impaired search process through working memory might explain these patients' inability to retain the last word in several sentences in a row seems unlikely. We have to come back to the possibility that it is the retention of the single item, displaced from the context of the sentence that is disturbed. The patient cannot retain all the features of the single word, but can retain the feature of the word that allows him to place that word in context as the sentence is being analyzed long enough to understand the gist of the sentence.

SENTENCE COMPREHENSION

This theory of single item, single feature, on-line, processing led us to wonder as well whether the amnesic patient's inability to retain all the features of a single item might also put him at a disadvantage when retention of more than one of these features becomes necessary to understand a sentence. In other words, we turned the thesis around and asked whether there might not be instances in which a person would have to retain more than one possible meaning of a word throughout a sentence in order to fully understand the sentence at completion. If so, then we had to suspect that amnesics might be impaired in this ability. In order to investigate the inverse comprehension/memory question, we (Shapiro, Mc-Namara, Zurif, Lanzoni, & Cermak, 1992) constructed sentences of varying complexities involving the necessity to keep more than a single feature of a word in memory till the end of the sentence in order to understand the meaning of the sentence and be able to repeat it back to the investigator. We felt that if the patient could not retain certain features of individual words long enough to place them in context of a complex sentence then he would become confused in his ability to reconstruct the sentence. On the other hand, when the construction was straightforward and the meaning flowed undirectionally, the patient would have little trouble repeating the sentence regardless of length (up to a point, of course).

In the experiment, patients were asked to repeat one of four types of sentences back to the examiner a few seconds after its presentation. Actually the patient had to count backward from ten to one (a relatively easy and automatic task not meant to interfere with retention so much as delay it) before reciting the sentence. The four types of sentences used were (1) active sentences, "The girl hit the boy," (2) passive sentences, "The boy was hit by the girl," (3) subject clefts in which the subject is left until the end of the sentence, "It was the girl that hit the boy," and (4) object clefts in which the action is left until the end of the sentence, "It was the boy that the girl hit." The first two sentences differ in complexity of direction of the action, but the latter two sentences had the additional complexity that the patient had to remember the slot into which to place the word held to the end of the sentence in order to comprehend what had happened. Of course, the latter two sentences are also longer than the first two so they could be harder to repeat simply by dint of exceeding working memory. So, in order to compensate for this length, padding was also introduced to

Table I   Percentage of Words Correctly Recalled across Sentences

Sentence type	No padding	Adjective padding
Control subjects		
Actives	99	96
Passives	97	96
Subject clefts	95	96
Object clefts	95	91
Amnesic subjects		
Actives	97	85
Passives	94	90
Subject clefts	88	76
Object clefts	76	72

make the first two types of sentence as long as the latter. For example, one such sentence would be, "The scared young girl hit the tall angry boy."

The results were that both amnesic patients and controls subjects were affected by sentence complexity and adjective padding. However, as can be seen in Table I, the amnesic patients were differentially affected by these two variables. Padding caused a depression of repetition ability across all conditions and this depression for amnesics was on a par with that seen for controls. However, the complexity of the sentence interacted with the group results in such a way that the amnesic patients performed significantly below normal controls in their repetition of subject and object cleft sentences. When the amnesic patients had to retain a portion of the sentence so as to fit a later word into the correct slot in order to comprehend the sentence, then the patient had difficulty repeating or comprehending the sentence. Comprehension was determined by assigning thematic roles to sentences in which an error occurred. The question was whether or not, even though the sentence was repeated incorrectly, the patient could at least assign the correct thematic roles to the participants in his response. The amnesic patients not only missed in their repetition of the sentence, but reversed thematic roles in these error-filled sentences to a significantly greater extent than normal controls.

These results were next extended in a second experiment using a different set of sentences. In this experiment, repetition ability was investigated using two types of verbs in the sentences: transitives (as in the prior experiment) and datives. Dative verbs are characterized by the fact that they require a third argument, an indirect phrase, so the listener knows at the time of the presentation of the verb that an indirect object is going to occur and that the relationship of the noun to this indirect object is going to be in the forward direction. For instance, the dative verb "to send" requires that the object be sent to the indirect object as in, "John sent the letter to Mary." Thus, dative verbs inject less complexity into a sentence than do pure transitive verbs in which the entire sentence must be retained online before the relationship of the participants in the sentence can be comprehended. The relationship of the principals involved in a dative sentence are established at the time of the presentation of the verb, while this is not the case for pure transitive verbs. The dative case being less complex might demand less on-line retention than the pure transitive and this should result in easier repetition and comprehension of the dative for amnesic patients. The procedure was exactly the same as the prior task except that the complexity of the verb varied. There was no inclusion of subject or object cleft relatives in this experiment, but padding was once again included for half the sentences, adding a second element of complexity to the verb type.

Table II   Percentage of Words Recalled across Sentences

	Control subjects		Amnesic subjects	
Verb type	No padding	Padding	No padding	Padding
Transitive	99	95	92	76
Dative	99	96	94	88
Average	99	96	93	82

As can be seen in Table II, the proportion of sentences correctly re-peated by the control subjects was significantly better than that by the amnesics overall, and there was the added effect of verb type since sentences containing dative verbs were repeated better than those containing transitive verbs. The effect of padding was again evident since sentences with no padding yielded significantly better performance than sentences with padding. Most importantly of all though, for our purposes, there was a significant group by verb interaction.

For the control subjects, there was no effect of verb type indicating that the amnesic patients must have contributed more to the overall effect of dative sentences being easier to remember and repeat. For amnesic patients the dative verb sentences resulted in significantly better performance than sentences with pure transitives (.92 vs. .83) when performance across padded and unpadded sentences was collapsed. Corresponding performance for the control subjects was .98 versus .97 when datives were compared to transitives across padding conditions.

Padding actually contributed in a comparable fashion to each group's performance which declined as a function of increased padding; both groups showing the same ratio of decline from unpadded to padded. Thus, the amount of material that had to be retained affected memory performance equivalently for amnesic patients and control subjects, but the complexity of the material to be retained had a very different effect on each group. As in the first experiment, the complexity, determined here by the difference in direction between dative and transitive verbs embedded in sentences, had a more detrimental effect on amnesics' performance than on controls.

The upshot of these two experiments is that amnesic patients' on-line processing deficit does seem to have an effect on their ability to follow the flow of complex sentences. The patients' difficulty manipulating the features of single words seems to generalize to the patients' inability to manipulate features of an entire sentence. The length of the sentence had an effect on amnesics' performance, but this effect was entirely in line with that expected by the effect that length of sentence has on normals.

However, the complexity of the sentence, determined by the extent to which the individual words had to be held in memory in order to make sense of the entire sentence did play a prominent role in amnesic patients' ability to retain and repeat those sentences. Furthermore, the patients also showed a deficit in their ability to understand the "theme" of these complex sentences as well as they had been able to understand the "theme" of straightforward, active sentences of equal length.

A report by MacKay, Stewart, and Burke (1998) substantiates this result we found with our amnesic patients on the well-known patient, H.M. The data they report had originally been collected on H.M. over a quarter century ago when his general cognitive capacities were much greater than they are today. Both Corkin (1984—but reported in Mackay et al., 1998) and Lackner (1974) asked this classic bitemporal amnesic patient to indicate when a sentence might have more than one meaning (due to its ambiguous nature) and then to try to explain those two alternative meanings. Lackner found that H.M. reported that two meanings existed in 34% of the instances of ambiguity, whereas controls, studied by MacKay et al. (1998) using the same sentences, detected 81%. In Corkin's study, H.M. was able to explain the second meaning of ambiguous sentences in only 37% of the cases, while controls (again MacKay) explained the second meaning 77% of the time. In this case, H.M. was told explicitly that there were two meanings and he was asked to try to explain both; in Lackner's study he had to detect sentences that had two meanings. But in both cases, the results were essentially the same, H.M. was significantly impaired in his ability to analyze the complex content of a sentence in order to answer questions concerning ambiguity of the content. He was perfectly all right understanding the question as it was being delivered, but as soon as he had to "think back" on the content of the message and to reflect on how it could, or could not, have two meanings, he demonstrated that he had been analyzing the meaning along only one level. This unidimensional analysis was sufficient for direct and immediate responding but it did not allow for contemplation, or reflection, back on other possible meanings of the sentence.

MacKay et al. (1998) interpreted this outcome in a manner which missed, I believe, the essence of an amnesic's disorder. I feel that the amnesic patient has the ability to analyze and understand a sentence on-line and that they can respond to that initial linguistic analysis, but they cannot reflect back on the sentence, even as they are hearing it, to detect possible ambiguity and/or complexity (our prior reported studies). MacKay et al., on the other hand felt that H.M.'s difficulty lay in a more basic deficit in language comprehension per se. These authors felt that H.M.'s memory storage and language comprehension could not be considered to be autonomous, sequentially ordered, processing stages in which ability to perform one could affect performance on the other. Instead, they felt that the deficit involved semantic-level binding processes that are inherent to both language comprehension and memory and therefore both deficits were occurring in parallel. I am suggesting that these theorists miss the fact that individuals are going to process just one meaning initially and that only after the sentence is completed will the person reflect on the fact that two meanings could have been drawn. For normals such reflection is often reflexive, but for amnesics such reflection is surely impeded by the fact that the sentence is no longer before them. Even when they are allowed to see the sentence over and over, the first meaning is going to always occur as the sentence is represented and the second meaning is going to take reflection. The fact that the patient is given chance after chance and still fails is not necessarily evidence for the notion that the two deficits are part and parcel of the same underlying disorder especially since each and every prior repetition is forgotten by the patient and essentially plays no role in the current presentation of the sentence. Instead the interpretation that the inability to look back at that which has just been analyzed in order to resolve complexity and/or ambiguity seems more likely to be the deficit underlying the impaired performance of the amnesic patients on this sentence ambiguity task.

CONCLUSIONS

In conclusion, it may well be the case that MacKay et al. (1998) are correct in proposing that memory and language processing processes occur in parallel, but where they may miss the point is when they assume that the memory processes are the same as language processes and fail to realize that memory processes can also interact with comprehension. In terms of the thesis of the present chapter, analysis for language and for memory can occur in parallel but they are quite different processes.

Linguistic processing is largely engaged for the use of on-line understanding of what is being conveyed to the subject and is based, perhaps, on the lexical and semantic features of the verbal information. Memory processes abstract features of the information that will permit storage in combination with similarly derived concepts and retrieval routes for eventual recall. Memory processes prepare the information for later retrieval and are simultaneously comparing and contrasting present information with knowledge from the past, while language processes are already comparing the present information with the reply that the individual is going to make to that material. The subject is already formulating an answer to the query as he is taking it in, and he is not attempting to actually store the information so much as use it. When complexity or ambiguity enter the picture, the subject must compare the answer already prepared on-line with his memory of the actual question itself. If he has amnesia, he has forgotten the actual question and has to rely on the answer already formulated. Since the answer was based on the first interpretation of the sentence, the amnesic patient would assume that no ambiguity was involved. Normal individuals check their initial reaction against the actual statement and acknowledge the presence of ambiguity or resolve the conflict inherent in the complexity of the sentence. Thus, sentence memory is deficient in the amnesic patient and this deficiency does affect his comprehension not because of any decrease in working memory capacity, or in any reduction in word span, but simply because loss of the actual wording of a sentence prevents looking-back on the sentence and evaluating the ambiguity between the original precept, now wrapped up in language of the reply, and the actual sentence itself. Repeating the sentence or even instructing the amnesic to prepare for ambiguity is not sufficient to overcome this problem with comparing and contrasting information held in working memory.

In summary, it has been shown that amnesic patients perform well below normal controls when asked to remember the last word in each sentence while simultaneously monitoring each sentence for meaning. Their ability to monitor the sentence is normal, but their ability to rehearse single words simultaneously is completely disrupted by any additional processing required for monitoring the rest of the completed sentence. Their digit span and performance on a Sternberg retrieval task is normal; therefore, a working memory deficit is not a good explanation for their sentence memory deficit. Instead, it appears that the complexity of the sentence that has to be processed determines the extent of their memory deficit. This hypothesis is further supported by the results of the series of sentence repetition tasks performed by amnesic patients. On these tasks it was demonstrated that the patients' repetition ability was normally affected by the length of the sentence, but was more than normally affected by increases in linguistic complexity. The amnesic patients performed worse than the control subjects when the sentence length was increased by the addition of adjuncts of the verb, when the verb selected more thematic frames, and when the sentences involved empty argument positions that had to be linked to antecedents across clausal boundaries. Thus, the amnesic deficit in sentence memory seems to be specific to certain representational types and/or processing routines resulting in an inability to reconstruct the specific words used in the sentence. Consequently, he can neither repeat the complex sentence nor reflect on it in order to gauge the presence of possible ambiguity.

REFERENCES

Cermak, L. S. (1978). The development and demise of verbal memory. In A. Caramazza & E. Zurif (Eds.) *Language acquisition and language breakdown: Parallels and divergencies* (pp. 277–289) Baltimore, MD: The Johns Hopkins University Press.

Cermak, L. S., Butters, N., & Moreines, J. (1974). Some analyses of the verbal encoding deficit of alcoholic Korsakoff patients. *Brain and Language, 1,* 141–150.

Corkin, S. (1984). Lasting consequences of bilateral medial temporal lobectomy: Clinical course and experimental findings in H.M. *Seminars in Neurology, 4,* 249–259.

Danneman, M., & Carpenter, P. A. (1980). Individual differences in working memory and reading. *Journal of Verbal Learning and Verbal Behavior, 19,* 450–466.

Gabrieli, J. D. E., Keane, M. M., & Stebbins, G. T. (1993). Reduced working memory capacity in patients with global amnesia: Evidence for a limbic/diencephalic contribution to working memory performance. *Society for Neuroscience Abstracts, 19,* 1002.

Lackner, J. R. (1974). Observations on the speech processing capabilities of an amnesic patient: Several aspects of H.M.'s language function. *Neuropsychologia, 12,* 199–207.

MacKay, D. G., Stewart, R., & Burke, D. M. (1998). H.M. revisited: Relations between language comprehension, memory, and the hippocampal system. *Journal of Cognitive Neuroscience, 10,* 377–394.

Naus, M., J., Cermak, L. S., & DeLuca, D. (1977). Retrieval processes in alcoholic Korsakoff patients. *Neuropsychologia, 15,* 737–742.

Shapiro, L. P., McNamara, P., Zurif, E., Lanzoni, S., & Cermak, L. S. (1992). Processing complexity and sentence memory: Evidence from amnesia. *Brain and Language, 42,* 431–453.

Sternberg, S. (1966). High speed scanning human memory. *Science, 153,* 652–654.

Verfaellie, M., & Cermak, L. S. (1991). Neuropsychological issues in amnesia. In J. L. Martinez & R. P. Kesner (Eds.), *Learning and memory: A biological view* (pp. 467–497). (revised ed.). New York: Academic Press.

Warrington, E. K., & Weiskrantz, L. (1970). Amnesic syndrome: Consolidation or retrieval? *Nature (London), 228,* 628–630.

Warrington, E. K., & Weiskrantz, L. (1974). The effect of prior learning on subsequent retention in amnesic patients. *Neuropsychologia, 12,* 419–428.

Zangwill, O. L. (1969). Neuropsychological models of memory. In G. A. Talland, & N. C. Waugh, (Eds.), *The pathology of memory* (pp. 161–166). New York: Academic Press.

Part IV

The Lexical–Structural Interface

Chapter 8

Toward a Neurochemistry
of Naming and Anomia

Martin L. Albert

Clearly, it is premature to attempt a detailed analysis of chemico-cognitive correlates of language; the cognitive systems involved in the processes of language have not, themselves, been fully detailed. Nevertheless, just as we can talk about principal functions of language (e.g., naming, comprehension, verbal production, etc.), and their different phases (e.g., for the category of "naming to confrontation," these may include object recognition, lexical semantics, and phonological output), we may not be premature in talking about gross chemico-linguistic correlates. The goal at this early stage is simply to correlate major pharmacosystems with the principal functions of language.

In this light, the goal of this chapter is to describe the likely neurochemical substrates for lexical semantics and phonological output in the process of naming. A disclaimer or warning label is perhaps warranted: it should be understood that no single neurotransmitter is likely to underlie any complex cognitive process. Most such processes probably depend on the dynamic interplay of many neuromodulators, some perhaps not even identified as yet. Thus any attempt to correlate single pharmacosystems with single functions or processes of language must be understood as representing schematic simplifications and preliminary efforts to understand the neurobiology of language from a new perspective.

The argument proposed in this chapter is that lexical semantics is dependent, in part, on the cholinergic pharmacosystem and that phonological output and verbal articulation are dependent, in part, on the dopaminergic pharmacosystem. Evidence to support this argument derives primarily, although not exclusively, from studies of anomia and verbal fluency impairments in aphasia, Alzheimer's disease, and Parkinson's Disease.

NEUROCHEMISTRY OF OUTPUT ANOMIA

Output Anomia

For the purpose of this chapter I refer to the naming deficits down-stream to lexical semantics as "output anomias."

"Simple failure to come up with a spoken response is the most common form of word-finding failure in aphasia. . . . Most theorists agree that re-trieval of word phonology begins after some level of semantic specifica-tion of the item to be named has been attained" (Goodglass & Wingfield, 1997, p. 10). With regard to failures of articulation "the classical anatomical model suggests that many patients should fail to emit the names of objects purely on the basis that they cannot generate or implement the articula-tory plan (p. 13)," as seen in the anterior aphasias. "It is difficult, however, to be convinced that a patient's failure lies only in the articulatory plan-ning when he or she cannot initiate a response at all or begins with a to-tally extraneous sound" (Goodglass & Wingfield, 1997, p. 13).

These citations from Goodglass and Wingfield in their 1997 book *Anomia: Neuroanatomical and cognitive correlates* suggest at least the possi-bility of overlap in the neural and cognitive systems beyond (downstream to) lexical semantics in the process of producing a spoken name. Naming in this postsemantic stage requires, *inter alia*, specification of metrical structure, combination of phonemic segments into syllables, and instruc-tion of motor systems of the lips, jaw, tongue, pharynx, larynx, and respi-ratory systems to orchestrate the actual production of speech sounds (Gordon, 1997). Failures or disruptions of any of these stages can produce an output anomia.

Impaired initiation of motor or motor planning activity and *impaired maintenance* of rhythm, speed, or force are among the principal neurologi-cal phenomena that can interfere with phonologicial output and verbal articulation, resulting in output anomia. The dopaminergic pharmacosys-tem is the primary neurotransmitter system underlying initiation and maintenance of complex motor activity.

Dopaminergic System and Language

Clinical evidence

Parkinson's disease is the best known of the clinical syndromes in which impairment of initiation or maintenance of motor or motor plan-ning activity is linked to reduced levels of dopamine. Speech and lan-guage problems in Parkinson's disease include abnormalities of speech volume and timing, impaired verbal fluency, reduced phrasal and syntactic constructions, word-finding difficulties, paraphasias, and impaired verbal abstraction (Mimura, Albert, & McNamara, 1995; Critchley, 1981; Illes, Metter, Hanson, & Iritani, 1988; Ruberg & Agid, 1988; Cummings, Darkins, Mendez, Hill, & Benson, 1988; Rosenberger, 1980). Verbal fluency in Parkinson's disease improves with dopamine therapy, whereas other cognitive impairments do not (Gotham, Brown, & Marsden, 1988).

Akinetic mutism (Ross & Stewart, 1981; Barett, 1991), post-traumatic dysarthria (Liebson, Walsh, Jankowiak, & Albert, 1994), and stuttering (Rosenberger, 1980; Fisher, Kerbeshian, & Burd, 1986; Rastatter and Harr, 1988) are additional clinical syndromes with impaired verbal fluency which have been shown, in experimental studies, to respond to dopaminergic therapy.

Dopaminergic projections

In addition to the better known midbrain dopaminergic projections to the nigrostriatal system, there is also an important dopaminergic pathway from brainstem to medial frontal areas (meso-cortical system) (Moore, 1982). The supplementary motor area (SMA) in the medial frontal region, together with the anterior cingulate area, form a link with midbrain dopaminergic centers.

The SMA and its mesocortical dopaminergic links play a major role in mediating production of sequential, voluntary motor activity. The SMA is the principal cortical structure in the neural network associated with initiation of speech (Mimura et al., 1995; Goldberg, 1985). Damage to the mesocortical dopaminergic system, particularly the SMA, produces impaired initiation of speech and decreased verbal fluency, and, in its most severe form, transcortical motor aphasia (Alexander & Schmitt, 1980; Freedman, Alexander, & Naeser, 1984).

Dopaminergic therapy for output deficits in aphasia

Catecholamine levels, including dopaminergic metabolites, decrease in cerebrospinal fluid following atherothrombotic cerebral infarction (Meyer et al., 1973; Robinson, Shoemaker, Schlumpf, Valk, & Bloom, 1975). Because dopaminergic activity is known to influence output and verbal articulation in Parkinson's disease, and because dopamine levels drop following stroke, some years ago we attempted to treat the output deficits of a patient with a left frontal lesion and transcortical motor aphasia with the dopamine agonist bromocriptine (Albert, Bachman, Morgan, & Helm-Estabrooks, 1988) We documented unequivocal improvement in selected aspects of language production, including naming. Thus, an output anomia was successfully treated with a dopaminergic agent.

A critical feature of that study was the targeting of aphasic signs and symptoms. We focused on hesitancies and impaired initiation of speech, and hypothesized that the same deficiency of dopamine that provokes hesitancies and bradykinesia in Parkinson's disease could be causing the speech output impairments in this patient with transcortical motor aphasia. Since then, we and others have tried various dopaminergic regimens for treatment of nonfluent aphasias with mixed success (Bachman & Morgan, 1988; Sabe, Leiguarda, & Starkstein, 1992; Sabe, Salvarezza, Garcia-Cuerva, Leiguarda, & Starkstein, 1995). Dopamine-related drugs, such as amphetamines (Walker-Batson, 1998) and piracetam (Huber, Willmes, Poeck, Van Vleyman, & Deberdt, 1997), have also shown promise. In single case studies in which the same individuals served as their own controls, dramatic improvements have been recorded. In double-blind, cross-over group studies, however, less or no improvement has been ascertained. In his critical review of the topic Small (1994) cautiously concluded that dopaminergic pharmacotherapy appears to benefit aphasic patients somewhat, when used as an adjunct to regular speech therapy.

NEUROCHEMISTRY OF LEXICAL SEMANTIC ANOMIA

Lexical Semantic Anomia

The process of naming a seen object (confrontation naming) is often considered in cognitive science to depend on three stages, each with subcomponents: first, visual recognition of the object; second, the lexical semantic stage, in which meaning is attached to the percept; and third, phonological output, in which phonological forms are attached to lexical labels prior to preparation of the articulatory system for speech production. This section addresses the lexical semantic stage.

Goodglass and Wingfield (1997) argue that anomia in aphasia is essentially a retrieval deficit and that "the words the patient is unable to produce are not lost from memory (p.4)." They, and many others, contend that loss of meaning of words (i.e., a deficit of lexical semantics) is more likely to be found in the anomia of Alzheimer's disease than in the anomia of aphasia. Although in the main I agree with this well-defended and well-supported position, newer research from our own studies of language in normal aging makes me question its generality. We found evidence suggesting that in addition to impaired access to the phonological form of the word, there may be an erosion of semantic knowledge that contributes to naming failures in otherwise healthy normal elderly persons (Nicholas, Obler, Au, & Albert, 1996; Barresi, Nicholas, Obler,

Connor, & Albert, 1997). Applying this observation to naming and word-finding problems in aphasia leads me to suggest that aphasic anomias (especially in posterior, fluent aphasias with comprehension deficit) represent a combination of retrieval deficit and semantic deficit.

The argument put forth in this segment of the chapter is as follows: anomia in posterior, fluent aphasia is a consequence, in part, of lexical semantic deficit; the lexical semantic system is linked to verbal memory systems; verbal memory systems are dependent, in part, on cholinergic neurotransmission; consequently anomia in posterior, fluent aphasia is dependent, in part, on cholinergic neurotransmission.

Cholinergic System and Language

Clinical and experimental evidence

Since the studies by Drachman a quarter of a century ago we have known that cholinergic drugs influence verbal memory. Anticholinergic agents, such as scopolamine, interfere with verbal memory (Drachman & Leavitt, 1975; Drachman, 1977) and have been considered to produce models of the memory deficits of normal aging and dementia of the Alzheimer type (Mohs, Davis, & Darley, 1980; Christensen, Maltby, Jorm, Creasey, & Broc, 1992). Christensen et al. (1992), for example, compared patterns of language and memory performance in patients with Alzheimer's disease and young persons subjected to cholinergic blockage induced by scopolamine, finding similar patterns of performance on tests of semantic memory and verbal intelligence. Aarsland, Larsen, Reinvang, and Aasland (1994), focusing specifically on language, used cholinergic blockade with scopolamine to demonstrate language impairments in healthy young women which were similar to those seen in Alzheimer's disease. They concluded that, "cholinergic loss may be associated with the language impairments found in dementia of the Alzheimer type (p. 1377)."

Treatment of patients suffering from Alzheimer's disease with varying doses and types of cholinergic agents has shown some influence of these agents on language function. Raffaele et al. (1995) reported improved verbal ability with low doses of the muscarinic cholinergic agonist arecholine, and Raskind et al. (1997) described improvement on six language tests following treatment with the cholinesterase inhibitor tacrine.

Cholinergic projections

Acetylcholine is widespread throughout the nervous system. The nucleus basalis of Meynert and the substantia innominata have been identified as primary sources of central (cortical) cholinergic innervation

(Mesulam, 1988). In humans, choline acetyltransferase (a marker for cholinergic activity) was found to be significantly higher in the left hemisphere than in the right, specifically in the left superior temporal gyrus, suggesting a prominent role for acetylcholine in language functions (Amaducci, Sorbi, Albanese, & Gainotti, 1981).

Cholinergic therapy for lexical semantic deficits in aphasia

Luria, to my knowledge, was the first to recommend cholinergic agents for treatment of aphasia. He used a powerful anticholinesterase agent to obtain a "disinhibitory" effect on impaired speech functions following, mainly traumatic, brain injury (Luria, Naydin, Tsvetkova, & Vinarskaya, 1969).

Moscowitch, McNamara, and Albert (1991) reported that an anticholinesterase agent selectively improved language performance in semantic aphasia. Eight patients with semantic aphasia treated with this agent showed improvement in several language domains compared with 13 age- and severity-matched controls.

More recently, we studied four right-handed patients with fluent aphasia and anomia after unilateral left cerebral infarction (Tanaka, Miyazaki, & Albert, 1997). We treated two with a cholinergic agent and left two untreated. Naming and auditory comprehension improved dramatically within 1 week in the treated group, compared with little or no improvement in the untreated patients.

CONCLUSIONS

In earlier studies I suggested that dopaminergic agents may be helpful for speech output, initiation, and fluency in nonfluent aphasia, while cholinergic agents may be helpful for naming in fluent aphasia (Albert, 1988, 1990). The present chapter builds on that earlier work.

Cholinergic neurotransmission may be preferentially lateralized to the left temporal lobe, a region of the brain fundamental to the support of lexical semantics. Anomia, verbal memory deficits, and fluent aphasia result from damage to the left temporal lobe in most right-handers. Neurological syndromes other than aphasia, such as Alzheimer's disease, in which anomia, lexical semantic impairment, and verbal memory deficit can occur, and which are associated with temporal lobe disease, are correlated with deficiencies of cholinergic activity. Also, cholinergic blockade interferes with naming in healthy young people. Furthermore, cholinergic therapy improves naming performance in patients with fluent aphasia. Tying these threads together, I conclude that lexical semantic deficits in anomia result, in part, from deficiencies of cholinergic neurotransmission, and that normal cognitive processes of lexical semantics are dependent, in part, on normal levels of cholinergic activity. With regard to dopaminergic neurotransmission, we know that midbrain dopaminergic centers send important projections to medial frontal regions, particularly the supplementary motor area, which is prominently correlated with initiation of speech. Output anomias and transcortical motor aphasia can result from damage to the supplementary motor area or to white matter pathways underlying this region. Also, neurologic syndromes other than aphasia, in which disorders of verbal fluency can occur, such as akinetic mutism and stuttering, have been associated with lesions in or under the left supplementary motor cortex. Dopaminergic pharmacotherapy of patients with left frontal lesions with disorders of initiation of speech, verbal fluency, and naming have, in individual cases, resulted in improved fluency and naming. Tying these threads together, I conclude that phonological output and verbal articulatory deficits in anomia result, in part, from deficiencies of dopaminergic neurotransmission, and that normal cognitive processes of phonological output and preparation for verbal articulation are dependent, in part, on normal levels of dopaminergic activity.

ACKNOWLEDGMENTS

Edgar Zurif has been my colleague and friend for almost 30 years. It is an honor and pleasure to contribute to his *festschrift*.

I thank Drs. Lisa Connor and Michael Gottfried for critical reviews of earlier drafts of this paper.

This work was supported, in part, by the National Institutes of Health (NIDCD: DC 00081) and the Medical Research Service of the Department of Veterans Affairs.

REFERENCES

Aarsland, D., Larsen, J. P., Reinvang, I., & Aasland, A. M. (1994). Effects of cholinergic blockade on language in healthy young women. *Brain, 117*, 1377–1384.

Albert, M. L. (1988) Neurobiological aspects of aphasia therapy. *Aphasiology, 2*, 215–218.

Albert, M. L. (1990). The role of perseveration in language disorders. *Journal of Neurolinguistics, 4*, 347–364.

Albert, M. L., Bachman, D. L., Morgan, A., & Helm-Estabrooks, N. (1988). Pharmacotherapy for aphasia. *Neurology, 38*, 877–879.

Alexander, M. P., & Schmitt, M. A. (1980) The aphasia syndrome of stroke in the left anterior cerebral artery territory. *Archives of Neurology, 37*, 97–100.

Amaducci, L., Sorbi, S., Albanese, A., & Gainotti, G. (1981). Choline acetyltransferase (ChAT) activity differs in right and left human temporal lobes. *Neurology, 31*, 799–805.

Bachman, D. L., & Morgan, A. (1988). The role of pharmacotherapy in the treatment of aphasia: Preliminary results. *Aphasiology, 2*, 225–228.

Barett, K. (1991). Treating organic abulia with bromocriptine and lisuride: Four case studies. *Journal of Neurology, Neurosurgery, and Psychiatry, 54*, 718–721.

Barresi, B., Nicholas, M., Obler, L. K., Connor, L. T., & Albert, M. L. (1997). *Consistency of naming failures in normal aging*. Paper presented at Annual Meeting of American Speech Language Hearing Association, Boston, November 20.

Christensen, H., Maltby, N., Jorm, A. G., Creasey, H., & Broc, G. A. (1992). Cholinergic blockade as a model of the cognitive deficits in Alzheimer's disease. *Brain, 115*, 1681–1699.

Critchley, E. M. R. (1981). Speech disorders of Parkinsonism: A review. *Journal of Neurology, Neurosurgery, and Psychiatry, 44*, 751–758.

Cummings, J. L., Darkins, A., Mendez, M., Hill, M. A., & Benson, D. F., (1988). Alzheimer's disease and Parkinson's disease: Comparisons of speech and language alterations. *Neurology, 38*, 680–684.

Drachman, D. A. (1977). Memory and cognitive function in man: Does the cholinergic system have a specific role? *Neurology, 27*, 783–790.

Drachman, D. A., & Leavitt, J. (1974). Human memory and the cholinergic system. *Archives of Neurology, 30*, 113–121.

Fisher, W., Kerbeshian, J., & Burd, L. (1986). A treatable language disorder: Pharmacological treatment of pervasive developmental disorder. *Journal of Developmental and Behavioral Pediatrics, 7*, 73–76.

Freedman, M., Alexander, M. P., & Naeser, M. A. (1984). Anatomic basis of transcortical motor aphasia. *Neurology, 34*, 409–417.

Goldberg, G. (1985) Supplementary motor area structure and function: Review and hypothesis. *Behavior and Brain Science, 8*, 567–615.

Goodglass, H., & Wingfield, A. (1997). Word-finding deficits in aphasia: Brain-behavior relations and clinical symptomatology. In H. Goodglass & A. Wingfield (Eds.), *Anomia: Neuroanatomical and cognitive correlates* (pp. 3–30). San Diego: Academic Press.

Gordon, B. (1997). Models of naming. In H. Goodglass & A. Wingfield (Eds.). *Anomia: Neuroanatomical and cognitive correlates*. San Diego: Academic Press.

Gotham, A. M., Brown, R. G., & Marsden, C. D. (1988). Frontal cognitive function in patients with Parkinson's disease "on" and "off" levodopa. *Brain, 111*, 299–321.

Huber, W., Willmes, K., Poeck, K., Van Vleyman, B., & Deberdt, W. (1997). Piracetam as an adjuvant to language therapy for aphasia. *Archives of Physical Medicine and Rehabilitation, 78*, 245–250.

Illes, J., Metter, E. J., Hanson, W. R., & Iritani, S. (1988). Language production in Parkinson's disease: Acoustic and linguistic considerations. *Brain and Language, 33*, 146–160.

Liebson E., Walsh, M., Jankowiak, J., & Albert, M. L. (1994). Pharmacotherapy for posttraumatic dysarthria. *Neuropsychiatry, Neuropsychology, and Behavioral Neurology, 7*, 122–124.

Luria, A. R., Naydin, V. L., Tsvetkova, L. S. & Vinarskaya, E. N. (1969). Restoration of higher cortical function following local brain damage. In P. J. Vinkin & G. W. Bruyn (Eds.), *Handbook of clinical neurology: Vol 3. Disorders of higher nervous activity* (pp. 368–433). Amsterdam: North-Holland Publ.

Mesulam, M. M. (1988). Central cholinergic pathways: Neuroanatomy and some behavioral implications. In M. Anoli, T. A. Reader, R. W. Dykes, & P. Gloor (Eds.), *Neurotransmitters and cortical function* (pp. 237–260). New York: Plenum.

Meyer, J. S., Stoica, E., Pascu, I., Shimazu, K., & Hartman, A. (1973). Catecholamine concentrations in CSF and plasma of patients with cerebral infarction and haemorrhage. *Brain, 96*, 277–288.

Mimura, M., Albert, M. L., & McNamara, P. (1995). Toward a pharmacotherapy for aphasia. In H. Kirshner (Ed.), *Handbook of neurological speech and language disorders* (pp. 465–482). New York: Dekker.

Mohs, R. C., Davis, K. L., & Darley, C. (1980). Cholinergic drug effects on memory and cognition in humans. In L. W. Poon (Ed.), *Aging in the 1980s* (pp. 181–190). Washington, DC: American Psychological Association.

Moore, R. Y. (1982). Catecholamine neuron systems in brain. *Annals of Neurology, 12,* 321–327.

Moscowitch, L., McNamara, P., & Albert, M. L. (1991). Neurochemical correlates of aphasia. *Neurology, 41* (Suppl. 1), 410.

Nicholas, M., Obler, L. K., Au, R., & Albert, M. L. (1996). On the nature of naming errors in aging and dementia: A study of semantic relatedness. *Brain and Language, 54,* 184–195.

Raffaele, K. C., Asthana, S., Berardi, A., Haxby, J. V., Morris, P. P., Schapiro, M. B., & Soncrant, T. T. (1996). Differential response to the cholinergic agonist arecoline among different cognitive modalities in Alzheimer's disease. *Neuropsychopharmacology, 15,* 163–170.

Raskind, M. A., Sadowsky, C. H., Sigmund, W. R., Beitler, P. J. & Auster, S. B. (1997). Effect of tacrine on language, praxis, and noncognitive behavioral problems in Alzheimer disease. *Archives of Neurology, 54,* 836–840.

Rastattar, M. P.. & Harr, R. (1988). Measurements of plasma levels of adrenergic neurotransmitters and primary amino acids in five stuttering subjects: A preliminary report (biochemical aspects of stuttering). *Journal of Fluency Disorders, 13,* 127–139.

Robinson, R. G., Shoemaker, W. J., Schlumpf, M., Valk, T., & Bloom, F. E. (1975). Effect of experimental cerebral infarction in rat brain on catecholamines and behavior. *Nature (London), 255,* 332–334.

Rosenberger, P. B. (1980). Dopaminergic systems and speech fluency. *Journal of Fluency Disorders, 5,* 255–267.

Ross, E. D., & Stewart, R. M. (1981). Akinetic mutism from hypothalamic damage: Successful treatment with dopamine agonists. *Neurology, 31,* 1435–1439.

Ruberg, M., & Agid, Y. (1988). Dementia in Parkinson's disease. In L. I. Iversen, S. D. Iversen, & Snyder S. H. (Eds.), *Handbook of psychopharmacology* (Vol. 20). New York: Plenum.

Sabe, L., Leiguarda, R., & Starkstein, S. E. (1992). An open-label trial of bromocriptine in nonfluent aphasia. *Neurology, 42,* 1637–1638.

Sabe, L., Salvarezza, F., Garcia-Cuerva, A., Leiguarda, R., & Starkstein, S. (1995). A randomized, double-blind, placebo-controlled study of bromocriptine in nonfluent aphasia. *Neurology, 45,* 2272–2274.

Small, S. L. (1994). Pharmacotherapy of aphasia: A critical review. *Stroke, 25,* 1282-1289.

Tanaka, Y., Miyazaki, M., & Albert, M. L. (1997). Effects of increased cholinergic activity on naming in aphasia. *Lancet, 350,* 116–117.

Walker-Batson, D. (1998). Pharmacotherapy in the treatment of aphasia. In L. B. Goldstein (Ed.), *Restorative neurology: Advances in pharmacotherapy for recovery after stroke.* Armonk, New York: Futura.

Chapter **9**

Language Deficits in Broca's and Wernicke's Aphasia: A Singular Impairment

Sheila E. Blumstein and William P. Milberg

INTRODUCTION

It has long been recognized that aphasic patients display sentence comprehension deficits. Further analyses have indicated that these impairments are particularly apparent when correct comprehension rests on grammatical (syntactic and morphological) properties of language. Thus, patients have particular difficulty understanding sentences when their meaning cannot be derived from lexical/semantic and real world constraints. For example, subjects have greater difficulty understanding semantically reversible sentences such as *John kisses Mary* than sentences such as *John ate a hamburger*. Though nearly all aphasic patients show these impairments, most research has focused on so called grammatical comprehension in nonfluent aphasics or patients who have characteristics of the classic diagnosis of Broca's aphasia. Attention has focused on these patients largely because their grammatical comprehension difficulties may exceed their difficulties in comprehending semantically rich material.

Research over the past 25 years has aimed at understanding the basis for this syntactic impairment. The explanations have varied considerably. Some have argued that the impairment is specifically syntactic in nature, affecting the syntactic representations themselves (Grodzinsky, 1984, 1995; Pulvermuller, 1995), the parsing operations required to build up syntactic structures (Friederici & Kilborn, 1989; Haarman & Kolk, 1991), or the mapping of syntactic structure to semantic interpretations (Linebarger, Schwartz, & Saffran,1983; Saffran, Schwartz, & Linebarger,

1998). Others view the impairment as a resource limitation that is specifically limited to the processing of language (Blackwell & Bates, 1995; Caplan, 1995; Caplan & Waters, 1995; Martin & Romani, 1994) or is related to more general purpose working memory capacities (Miyake, Carpenter, & Just, 1994).

The focus on syntactic impairments in these patients is understandable, given the difficulties that the patients have in comprehending sentences, and also in the juxtaposition for some patients of impairments in the production of syntactically well-formed sentences with that of syntactic comprehension deficits (Caramazza & Zurif, 1976). And yet, it is the case that in these same patients, there are other impairments in language processing. Broca's aphasics, including agrammatic aphasics, not only have syntactic processing impairments, but they also typically have lexical as well as speech processing deficits. The question remains whether different mechanisms are impaired for each of these deficits, that is, one mechanism for the syntactic problem, one for the lexical processing problem, and one for the speech processing problem. What we would like to propose in this chapter is that the co-occurrence of a number of language impairments that appear to be related to different components of the linguistic grammar, and hence regarded by most researchers as isolable and distinct impairments, may have at their basis a common etiology. In our view, this common etiology has at its basis a deficit in lexical activation. Specifically, we will argue that many aphasic language symptoms can be attributed to alterations in the dynamics of lexical activation and the resulting spread of activation from one lexical representation to another rather than a deficit due to alterations in the representations themselves. Because lexical access processes are crucially involved in all aspects of language processing including identifying word candidates from sound structure, deriving the meanings of individual words as well as the syntactic roles they play, this impairment will have repercussions at all "levels" of the linguistic grammar.

This point of view most assuredly is controversial, and most details of this theory have yet to be worked out. However, we have decided to present this hypothesis in the current _Festschrift_ to acknowledge the influence that Edgar Zurif has played in the field of aphasiology and in particular in our understanding of syntactic deficits in aphasia. In 1972, Zurif and colleagues (Zurif, Caramazza, & Myerson, 1972) presented for the first time the hypothesis that Broca's aphasics had a central syntactic deficit, one that affected not only their language output but also their comprehension. This hypothesis shaped the research for the field in the following 25 years, and has served as the benchmark for studies of syntactic processing deficits in aphasia.

THEORETICAL FRAMEWORK

Before we elaborate the research results that have shaped our perspective, we will briefly review the theoretical framework on which our research is based. We take as our working framework current neural net or distributed models of language processing (McClelland and Rumelhart, 1986; Plaut, 1995; Masson, 1995). Several critical assumptions are made in these models. These include the following:

- There are separate representations for phonological, lexical, syntactic, and semantic information.
- Linguistic representations are considered as patterns of activation of either populations of units (e.g., Masson, 1995) or as individual nodes (Dell, 1986).
- Every node (or population of representational units) has a resting state, rate of activation, a maximal level of activation (or gain), and a decay function which is reached over some temporal domain until it resumes its original resting state.
- These nodes are organized within a networklike architecture such that the activation of a node may influence others through processes of spreading activation (and also through processes of inhibition).
- The dynamic properties of the activation spreading among representations (i.e., the rate and gain of activation) reflect the functional and conceptual relationships between and among those representations.
- The system is interactive allowing for spreading activation to occur not only within a level of representation (e.g., within the lexical network), but also among different "levels" of representation, that is, phonological, lexical, syntactic and semantic.
- The direction of information flow through spreading activation is bidirectional. That is, activation at lower levels of representation may influence higher levels, and higher levels may influence lower levels.

With respect to the lexical network, it is assumed that words that share, for example, properties of meaning or sound structure may influence each other through processes of spreading activation. Thus, the presentations of a particular word will not only activate its lexical representation but also words that are semantically related to it.

This framework can account for the semantic priming phenomenon in which lexical decision latencies are shorter for a target word when it is preceded by a semantically related word than when it is preceded by a semantically unrelated word or a nonword. Semantic priming presumably arises because the presentation of a word not only changes the activation level of the particular lexical node, but also affects the pattern of activation of those words that are semantically related to it. Hence, the more closely related one representation is to another, the higher will be its levels of activation, and possibly the more quickly it will be activated compared to more distantly related representations. Thus, the presentation of a word such as *cat* results in partial activation of the word *dog*. As a consequence, response latencies are shorter in a lexical decision task for *dog* when it is preceded by a semantically related word like *cat* compared to the response latencies for *dog* when it is preceded by a semantically unrelated word like *nose*, because the lexical node for *dog* has already received partial activation from the preceding semantically related word and thus is closer to its threshold of activation.

LEXICAL PROCESSING DEFICITS IN APHASIA

The hypothesis that language processing deficits in aphasic patients may be characterized by differences in the activation of lexical representations comes from a series of studies conducted in our laboratory beginning in the early 1980s. We conducted a series of lexical processing experiments exploring semantic priming in a lexical decision task in aphasic patients. The purpose of these studies was to determine the nature of the mechanisms contributing to normal auditory language comprehension, and to explore, in particular, whether comprehension deficits, particularly in Wernicke's aphasics, could be attributed to a deficit in the representations of lexical entries or in the lexical network. The paradigm utilized was lexical decision in which subjects are presented with word and nonword stimuli either in the auditory or visual modality. The subjects' task is to make a lexical decision on the stimulus target. In some experiments, subjects were given a list of words, for example, *shoe . . . pear . . . fruit . . . gluf*, and they had to make a lexical decision on every stimulus item (Milberg and Blumstein, 1981). In others, the subjects were given either stimulus pairs (Blumstein, Milberg, & Shrier, 1982; Milberg, Blumstein, Katz, Gershberg, & Brown, 1995), for example *pear–fruit*, or stimulus triplets (Milberg, Blumstein, & Dworetzky, 1987), for example, *river–bank–money*, and they had to make a lexical decision on the final stimulus target. Still other experiments conducted in other laboratories have utilized a cross–modal priming paradigm. In this task, subjects had to make a lexical decision to a visually presented target which was presented at specific times during the course of an auditorily presented sentence (Swinney, Zurif, & Nicol, 1989).

As we will review, the research results suggest that both Broca's and Wernicke's aphasics have a lexical processing deficit affecting the activation of lexical entries. The nature of the deficit, however, appears to be different between the two groups, and hence, has different consequences not only for the patterns of comprehension performance of these patients but also for the clinical characteristics that they display (cf. Blumstein, 1997).

Broca's Aphasics

Results of these studies exploring semantic priming in a lexical decision task showed that Broca's aphasics displayed priming under some experimental conditions and failed to show priming under other conditions. In particular, when the stimuli were paired and were highly predictable, these patients showed semantic priming. When the stimuli were presented as lists (for a lexical decision on every word) (Milberg & Blumstein, 1981; Prather, Zurif, Stern, & Rosen, 1992), as triplets (for a lexical decision on the third word of the series) (Milberg et al., 1987), or when the stimulus target could not be easily predicted based on the preceding pairings (Milberg et al., 1987), they failed to show semantic priming. Thus, in these on-line tasks, Broca's aphasics showed a lexical processing impairment. And yet, in off-line tasks, using the same stimuli (Milberg & Blumstein, 1981; Blumstein et al., 1982), Broca's aphasics performed very well. Namely, although they failed to show semantic priming, they nonetheless could accurately judge whether stimulus pairs were related or were not.

We interpreted the failure of Broca's aphasics to show semantic priming under all of the lexical priming conditions described above as a lexical processing impairment due to a reduction in the activation of lexical entries (Milberg et al., 1995). The consequences of a reduction in the peak level of activation of a lexical entry will have repercussions not only for the lexical entry itself, but also its lexical network. For example, although a reduction of the lexical activation for the word *pear* will still activate those lexical items that are a part of its network, it will activate them to a lesser degree than it does normally. Hence, a lowered activation of the stimulus *pear* may fail to activate sufficiently the lexical entry for *fruit* to influence its threshold of activation. As a result, *pear* may fail to semantically prime *fruit*. That the Broca's aphasics can make semantic judgments indicates that although the activation level of lexical entries may be lowered, the lexical entries are being accessed and the organization of the lexical network appears to be intact. As a consequence, patients can use heuristics or strategies in an off-line task to judge whether two words go together. These finding are consistent with the generally good auditory language comprehension of these patients.

Further evidence that Broca's aphasics have a reduction in lexical activation was provided by a study exploring the effects of stimulus degradation on semantic priming. Normal subjects who are presented with a semantically related prime that is either phonologically distorted or phonetically degraded show a reduction in the magnitude of semantic priming that appears to be proportional to the degree of distortion of the prime. For example, if a prime stimulus such as *cat* is phonologically distorted such that its initial consonant is either one phonetic feature away from [k], for example, *gat,* or several phonetic features away, for example, *wat,* normal subjects show a reduction in the magnitude of semantic priming to the target word, *dog* (Milberg, Blumstein, & Dworetzky, 1988a). These same effects emerge not only when there is a phonological change, that is, a change in the phonetic category, but also if the initial consonant is phonetically "degraded" by either reducing the initial voice-onset time of the initial [k] (Andruski, Blumstein, & Burton, 1994) or by increasing the initial voice-onset time of the initial [k] (Kessinger, 1998). In both cases of "phonetic degradation," the initial consonant is still a member of the phonetic category [k]. Subjects identify the initial consonant as [k] and they identify the stimulus prime as the word *"cat."* However, the phonetic manipulations render these stimuli as poorer exemplars of the phonetic category.

Of interest, the reduction in semantic priming emerges whether or not the prime stimulus has other voicing lexical competitors, for example, *pear* as a prime for *fruit,* has a voiced lexical competitor, *bear,* whereas *cat* as a prime for *dog* does not have a real word voice lexical competitor (cf. *gat*). These effects emerge not only for within category phonetic manipulations that are made in initial position, but also for changes made in word medial as well as word final position (Utman, 1999). The fact that the magnitude of semantic priming is reduced when the semantically related prime word has been phonologically or phonetically distorted has been interpreted to mean that the initial contact with the lexicon is influenced by the "goodness" of the stimulus input, and that activation levels in the lexicon are graded. As a consequence, poorer exemplars fail to activate a lexical entry to the same degree as a good one, and the initial reduction in activation influences the activation levels within the lexical network itself.

What would the effects of a deficit in lexical activation be in these experiments? If initial lexical activation is reduced, then a degraded prime stimulus may produce even less semantic priming than in normal subjects or may fail to show any semantic priming at all. The results of a series of experiments have indicated that indeed Broca's aphasics lose the semantic priming effect as soon as the phonological properties of the prime word are manipulated. Although these patients show priming for *cat–dog*, they fail to show any semantic priming for *gat–dog* (Milberg, Blumstein, & Dworetzky, 1998b). Further, they show either reduced semantic priming or a loss of semantic priming when within phonetic category manipulations are made to prime words which have a voiced lexical competitor (Aydelott & Blumstein, 1995; Utman, 1997). Thus, they show reduced priming when the subcategory manipulations render the stimulus further away from the voiced–voiceless phonetic category boundary, for example, *pear–fruit* with the initial voice-onset time increased by four-thirds, and hence further from the [b] phonetic category than the unaltered stimulus (Kessinger, 1998). They lose semantic priming when the subcategory manipulations render the stimulus closer to the voiced–voiceless phonetic category boundary, for example, *pear-fruit* with the initial voice-onset time decreased by two-thirds and hence closer to the [b] phonetic category (Aydelott & Blumstein, 1995; Utman, Blumstein, & Sullivan, 1999). Importantly, Broca's aphasics show a sensitivity to the phonological and the within phonetic category manipulations that were made to the prime words. Thus, their failure to show semantic priming cannot be attributed to a speech perception deficit.

That lexical competitor effects emerge for Broca's aphasics under such conditions of stimulus degradation is also consistent with the view that initial activation levels are reduced. Namely, a stimulus input activates not only its lexical entry and semantically related words via spreading activation, but it also inhibits the activation of potential lexical competitors. Thus, when a stimulus word such as *pear* is presented, the lexical processing system must activate *pear* and inhibit phonologically related competitor words such as *bear*. Given the low activation levels for word candidates in Broca's aphasics, a stimulus, which is a poor phonetic exemplar of the lexical candidate, may fail to inhibit the activation of lexical competitors. As a result, it may take longer for the lexical processing system to settle on the most compatible lexical candidate, in this case *pear*, resulting in the emergence of a competitor effect on the magnitude of semantic priming (cf. Utman et al., 1999).

Wernicke's Aphasia

In contrast to Broca's aphasics, Wernicke's aphasics show semantic priming in a lexical decision task under all of the priming conditions regardless of whether the stimuli are presented in lists, in pairs, in triplets, and whether or not a strategy can be invoked for determining the semantic relationship between the prime and the target (Milberg & Blumstein, 1981; Blumstein et al., 1982; Milberg et al., 1988b). However, in semantic judgment tasks, Wernicke's aphasics perform at chance levels. Thus, although they appear to be able to access lexical entries and to activate the lexical network as shown by semantic priming, they are unable to use this information in an off-line task. Thus, the language comprehension deficit of these patients seems to be due to an inability to use or manipulate semantic information, rather than a loss of the underlying semantic representations of words.

Nonetheless, further consideration of the patterns of semantic priming under conditions of phonological or phonetic degradation suggest that Wernicke's aphasics might also have a deficit in on-line lexical processing. In particular, unlike normal subjects who show a reduction in the magnitude of semantic priming when a semantically related prime is altered by one or more than one phonetic feature, for example, *cat–dog* versus *gat–dog* versus *wat–dog*, Wernicke's aphasics do not show a reduction in semantic priming (Milberg et al., 1988b). In fact, they show significant and equal amounts of semantic priming in all three conditions. Similarly, unlike normal subjects, they show no reduction in semantic priming when the initial voice-onset time of prime word stimuli is increased by four-thirds (Kessinger, 1998). Once again, they show a similar magnitude of semantic priming whether the prime stimulus is acoustically manipulated or not. Finally, unlike normal subjects, they show no effects of the lexical competitor. Nonetheless, Wernicke's aphasics show perceptual sensitivity to the phonological changes between, for example, *cat* and *gat*, and they also show perceptual sensitivity to the acoustic manipulations of the voice-onset time of the initial stop consonants. Thus, the "pathological" patterns of semantic priming cannot be due to impairments in speech perception.

Based on these results, we proposed that Wernicke's aphasics also have a deficit in the processing mechanisms contributing to lexical access. The nature of this deficit may be attributable to either a decreased threshold for the activation of lexical representations or an overall increase in the gain of activation. As such, Wernicke's aphasics appear to have an *overactivation* for all represented information in the lexicon. Thus, phonologically altered stimuli or phonetically manipulated stimuli that are poor exemplars nonetheless activate the lexical entry to the same extent as do good exemplar stimuli.

The pattern of results obtained for the Wernicke's aphasics may provide, at least in part, an explanation for the auditory comprehension deficit of these patients. At the heart of the deficit is an overactivation of the lexical system where specific meaning representations do not "win out" but are activated along with many other potential lexical candidates and accompanying meaning representations. A consequence of such a generalized increase of gain within the system would be to reduce the difference between strongly and weakly related representations as both representations exceed the threshold of the system. Moreover, if one assumes that the word production mechanism obeys the same conditions for lexical access, such a deficit could result in paraphasic errors since multiple entries are activated—semantically related lexical entries (resulting in *verbal paraphasias*) and phonologically related entries (resulting in *phonemic paraphasias*).

We have recently tested these hypotheses about the underlying deficits for both Broca's and Wernicke's aphasics by constructing a self-organizing connectionist model of how sound structure contacts the lexicon and then by simulating the patterns of performance that emerge from either an *underactivation* of the lexicon or an *overactivation* of the lexicon (McNellis & Blumstein, 1999). Simulations are consistent with the behavioral data obtained from normal subjects and from Broca's and Wernicke's aphasics. Critically, the theoretical framework elucidated there considers aphasic deficits as stemming from the degree to which sound structure elicits activation in the language system as a whole, rather than considering the deficits as lying in the representation of sound structure, in the mapping of sound structure to the lexicon, or in the integrity of the lexical network itself. It is this proposal to which we would now like to turn in consideration of the basis for syntactic processing deficits in Broca's and Wernicke's aphasics.

SYNTACTIC DEFICITS IN APHASIA: A PRELIMINARY PROPOSAL

Just as the proposal that a deficit in lexical activation appears to account not only for the patterns of semantic priming but also for what may appear to be speech processing impairments, it is possible that a deficit in lexical activation may account for what may appear to be syntactic processing impairments in Broca's and Wernicke's aphasics. The assumption that we are making is a simple one. Namely, there is a common mechanism for lexical activation that serves the entire vocabulary of the language. Thus, we do not make a formal distinction between what has been identified in the literature as *open* and *closed* class vocabularies. It is our view that any differences which emerge in the "behavior" of these lexical items results from the activation patterns which arise from the cognitive architecture of the language processing system, and architecture that derives from experience that the language user has with the lexical items in the processes of speaking and understanding. Thus, the distinction between open and closed class vocabularies, if there is one, is an emergent property and is not represented formally in the linguistic grammar as two distinct vocabularies.

The critical assumption made in our proposal about the cognitive architecture of the lexicon is that lexical entries are "represented" in terms of patterns of activation, and that words that are semantically related are organized within a networklike architecture. Thus, words that are semantically related will be part of a rich network, and activation of one word within the lexicon will influence the potential activation of a word that is semantically related to it. Open class words are typically rich in semantic associations. They not only have a rich semantic content themselves, but they are also related to a large semantic cohort. In contrast, closed class words typically have minimal semantic content themselves, and they are also not a part of a rich semantic network. The full meaning of the closed class vocabulary, including both free-standing grammatical words such as *the* and *of* and grammatical morphemes such as *-ed* and *-ing,* is derived from the context in which this vocabulary occurs, and in relation to the other words in the sentence. In this sense, the closed class vocabulary can not stand alone and the meaning of a closed class word builds up as the sentence unfolds in time.

Given this view, a deficit in lexical activation will have serious repercussions on syntactic processing (cf. also Bates & Wulfeck, 1989; Bates, Wulfeck, & MacWhinney, 1991). If the lexicon is underactivated, then those lexical items which have a sparse semantic network may be only weakly activated. In addition, because these words do not have a rich semantic network, the processes of spreading activation (and inhibition) not only within the lexical network but also between "levels" of representation, that is, phonological, syntactic, and semantic which influence the activation patterns of lexical entries, may also be compromised. As such, the closed class vocabulary will be particularly vulnerable to a lexical deficit characterized by underactivation.

Such an impairment can account for many of the patterns of syntactic processing deficits shown in agrammatic aphasics. While it is beyond the scope of this chapter to do a detailed analysis of the rich literature on this topic (cf. Berndt, 1998), a summary of some of the characteristic findings will be briefly reviewed. With respect to receptive agrammatism, these patients show greater understanding for those closed class items that have semantic content. Thus, studies of comprehension of propositions have shown differences in comprehension depending on whether the preposition has intrinsic semantic content or not (Friederici, 1981; Friederici, Schonle, & Garrett, 1982). In fact, Zurif and Caramazza (1976) showed that although agrammatic patients were similar to normals in the hierarchical clustering of *"to"* when it had a semantic role as a preposition in a sentence such as "Gifts were given *to* John," they showed an inability to normally cluster *"to"* when its role was part of an infinitive in a sentence like "She likes *to* eat candy."

Of importance, cross-linguistic studies of agrammatism show that the syntactic impairments that emerge may vary as a function of the language, and the extent to which the morphology plays a "rich" semantic role in the language. In such cases, as in Italian and in German, subjects are less likely to fail to understand morphological markers in comprehension (Bates et al., 1991). Agrammatic aphasics also show an ability to judge the grammaticality of sentences, indicating that they have not "lost" the representations of these syntactic placeholders. On-line tasks exploring these patients' sensitivity to ungrammatical sentences indicate that they are similar to normals, showing a decrease in response time latencies as the location of the ungrammaticality appears later in the sentence. Thus, agrammatic aphasics are able to perform ongoing syntactic analyses, and use the information as it unfolds in the course of the sentence (Shankweiler, Crain, Gorrell, & Tuller, 1989; Wulfeck, 1987). Nonetheless, these patients do not perform such tasks normally, and often times show either an insensitivity to ungrammaticality in on-line tasks (Baum, 1988) or a delay in time in the processing of closed class morphology (Friederici & Kilborn, 1989).

A deficit in lexical activation should also have repercussions on the output side. Namely, if lexical entries are underactivated, they may be more vulnerable to omission or to incorrect usage. In fact, agrammatic patients have particular difficulty in producing free-standing grammatical words. Importantly, they are less likely to omit those functors that have an intrinsic semantic meaning. Thus, they may use locative prepositions such as *behind* or adverbials of time such as *yesterday* while failing to use an auxiliary such as *have*.

Similar to studies of comprehension, cross-linguistic studies show that the production of such words varies as a function of the semantic information they convey. That is, agrammatic aphasics are less likely to omit those syntactic markers that convey more semantic information. For example, in English the word *the* identifies the noun it modifies as "definite." In Italian, the definite article is also marked for both gender and number. And in German, it is marked for gender, number, and case. The less "semantic" information conveyed, the more likely the definite article will be omitted. Thus, in English, the definite article is omitted 70% of the time, in Italian, 25% of the time, and in German, only 15% of the time (Bates et al., 1991). Of importance, the omission of grammatical markers does not occur if the resulting output is a nonword in the language. Thus, in Hebrew and Arabic, tense is marked by infixing vowels on a verb stem. The patient never produces a verb stem without some marking for tense, even if it is the wrong tense (Grodzinsky, 1984). These results are consistent with the view that while there may be underactivation of the lexicon, the language processing system ultimately settles on an output that reflects the activation of the lexicon of the language.

Not only will underactivation of the lexicon impact on syntactic processing, but so will overactivation of the lexicon. If the lexical entries are overactivated, then auditory language comprehension deficits should also emerge, as they do for Wernicke's aphasics. The overactivation of the lexicon should result in failure of the lexical network and especially the open class vocabulary to consistently settle on the appropriate lexical entry, resulting in an increased likelihood for comprehension impairments. Overactivation of the closed class vocabulary may also negatively impact on sentence comprehension. Because sentence interpretation cannot be based on the closed class vocabulary as it can in the case of the open class vocabulary, overactivation of closed class words will at best fail to "assist" the patient in the processes of comprehension, and at worst, garden-path him/her by activating not only the particular closed class item, but also any cohort that it is related to, even if it is a restricted set. Thus, the wrong grammatical marker may reach threshold, resulting in failures that may appear to be syntactic in nature. Further, those closed class vocabulary items that do have a greater semantic network would also be likely to contribute to comprehension failures since the semantic network associated with that lexical entry would be activated as well. For example, in the case of directional prepositions, the full cohort may be activated resulting in the miscomprehension of the "directionality" of the lexical item. A preposition such as *down* may be understood as a direction but the patient may interpret it to mean *up*.

Similar to comprehension failures, overactivation of the lexicon should result in impairments in sentence production. In particular, output should be characterized by semantic paraphasias of open class vocabulary as well as *paragrammatism* or the incorrect usage of grammatical structures. Such patterns are typical of the language output of Wernicke's aphasics (cf. Goodglass, 1993).

One question, which remains, is how a deficit in lexical activation results in the patterns of auditory comprehension that emerge in Broca's aphasics. Most particularly, if Broca's aphasics have an underactivation of the lexicon that not only affects open class items but also renders closed class items below activation threshold, why do these patients generally show such good auditory language comprehension? The basic question is how can they glean meaning and act on it, when the system is broadly underactivated.

It may be useful to consider what other requirements are needed in addition to lexical activation, syntactic parsing, and mapping syntactic structures to meaning representations to ultimately understand sentences. Most particularly, there must be the integration of lexical, semantic, and syntactic information for auditory language comprehension to succeed. In other words, as lexical and syntactic information unfold in real time, the listener must be able to integrate this information to build up a complete semantic representation. It is possible that the integration of such information may still be possible in the face of underactivation of the lexicon. It is to this possibility that we now turn.

SEMANTIC INTEGRATION

Summation of activation is implicit in most characterizations of network and spreading activation models of lexical processing. And yet, it has been usually ignored as a process critical to understanding pathological changes imposed on those models. Even the earliest nodal and connectionist models were built around the ability of multiple sources of activation to converge on a single representation in some cases producing nonlinear summated output that exceeded input values of activation. Such nonlinear summation often serves the purpose of allowing one representation to "win out" over related representations when competing for response systems or attentional resources. Such summation processes are critical as the listener builds a semantic representation for a sentence based on the lexical items in a sentence and the syntactic role that they play. After all, open class words in a sentence are not necessarily and probably not typically semantic associates of each other, and yet the listener integrates the words in a sentence to interpret it as a whole. Put simply, the meaning of a sentence may be more than the sum of its parts.

Summation of activation is not at all straightforward and is dependent on the maintenance of activation over time (capacitance), the ability to compress or translate the range of input activation to be within the available range of the output, mechanisms for rejecting spurious or low level input signals, as well as the integrity of the actual input activation signals. The complexity and delicacy of the summation process make this a potentially vulnerable link in actual biological networks.

Given this view, lexical activation is a necessary but not sufficient condition for normal auditory language comprehension. Normal auditory language requires that semantic information be integrated over time and across lexical representations and syntactic structures that may be independent of each other. It is possible that despite initial lowered activation of lexical representations, Broca's aphasics have preserved internodal connections and summation processes, allowing them to integrate even weakly activated semantic information. In contrast, although Wernicke's aphasics appear to be able to initially activate lexical representations, their initial overactivation may result in an impairment in the summation of internodal activation, contributing to their auditory language comprehension failure.

We explored this question in a recent study (Milberg, Sullivan, & Blumstein, 1998) by investigating summation of semantic priming in an auditory lexical decision priming task. A set of triplets was designed in which the individual pairs of stimuli were conceptually but not associatively or semantically related, for example, *meal–morning–breakfast*. Three other conditions were created in which a nonword occurred in either the initial position of the triplet, for example, *jarm–morning–breakfast*, the second position of the triplet, for example, *meal–foncern–breakfast*, or two nonwords preceded the third word of the triplet, for example, *jarm–foncern–breakfast*. In each case, the first two words of each triplet served as a prime for the third word in the context of the lexical decision task. Of interest was whether the lexical decision latencies for the third word lexical decision target in the combined prime condition (e.g., *meal– morning–breakfast*) was equivalent to the sum of the priming effects in the word pairs (e.g., *jarm–morning–breakfast* and *meal–foncern–breakfast*). In this way, the individual items shared some relation to each other, but were not fully correlated with each other. This being the case, the amount of priming should be less between the individual pairs of lexical items, than it would be for the three lexical items combined. (If the test items were closely associated and hence their lexical network more closely correlated, semantic priming for a pair of words might be maximal or at least the combination of items would not produce greater priming than the amount of priming for the individual pairs.) At an interstimulus interval of 200 ms, normal subjects showed such a pattern of *additivity*. In contrast, Broca's aphasics showed a pattern of *overadditivity*. That is, the magnitude of priming in the combined prime condition was *greater* than the sum of the priming effects in the word pair stimuli. In fact, Broca's aphasics failed to show semantic priming in these latter two conditions at all, whereas they did show significant priming in the combined priming condition compared to the baseline (e.g., *jarm–foncern–breakfast*) condition. In contrast, Wernicke's aphasics showed a pattern of *underadditivity*. That is, the magnitude of priming in the combined priming condition was less than that of the sum of the word pair stimuli.

The pattern of results that emerged in this study is consistent with the view that Broca's aphasics are able to integrate semantic information despite the fact that the individual activation patterns are themselves weakened and hence below threshold. In contrast, Wernicke's aphasics fail to be able to integrate semantic information despite the fact that they show activation of lexical representations. Of interest and importance, the patterns of additivity that emerged for the aphasic groups correlated with both their auditory comprehension level as well their aphasia diagnosis. Thus, lexical activation appears to be a necessary but not sufficient condition for normal auditory language comprehension. Future work will need to explore how lexical and syntactic information integrate in sentence comprehension. However, the current results suggest that the basis for the auditory comprehension deficits of Broca's and Wernicke's aphasics may lie in the nature of lexical activation and the ultimate integration of semantic information both *intralexically* (i.e., at the level of single word processing) and *interlexically* (i.e., among the words within a sentence). This point of view also suggests that many of the deficits which have been interpreted as reflecting selective impairments to other components of the linguistic grammar, namely, phonological and syntactic, may be secondary to a lexical processing deficit.

ACKNOWLEDGMENTS

This research was supported by NIH Grant NIDCD00314 to Brown University and NIDCD0081 to the Boston University School of Medicine, and by a grant from the VA Merit Review Board.

REFERENCES

Andruski, J., Blumstein, S. E., & Burton, M. (1994). The effects of subphonetic differences on lexical access. *Cognition, 43*, 336–348.
Aydelott, J., & Blumstein, S. E. (1995). On the nature of lexical processing in Broca's aphasia: Effects of subphonetic acoustic differences on lexical access. *Brain and Language, 51*, 156–158.
Bates, E., & Wulfeck, B. (1989). Cross-linguistic studies of aphasia. In B. MacWhinney & E. Bates (Eds.), *The cross-linguistic study of sentence processing.* New York: Cambridge University Press.
Bates, E., & Wulfeck, B., & MacWhinney, B. (1991). Cross-linquistic research in aphasia: An overview. *Brain and Language, 41*, 123–148.
Baum, S. (1998). Syntactic processing in agrammatism: Evidence from lexical decision and grammaticality judgments tasks. *Aphasiology, 2*, 117–135.
Berndt, R. (1998). Sentence processing in aphasia. In M. T. Sarno (ed.), *Acquired aphasia* (3rd ed.), New York: Academic Press.

Blackwell, A., & Bates, E. (1995). Inducing agrammatic profiles in normals: Evidence for the selective vulnerability of morphology under cognitive resource limitation. *Journal of Cognitive Neuroscience, 7,* 228–257.

Blumstein, S. E. (1997). A perspective on the neurobiology of language. *Brain and Language, 60,* 335–346.

Blumstein, S. E., Milberg, W., & Shrier, R. (1982). Semantic processing in aphasia: Evidence from an auditory lexical decision task. *Brain and Language, 17,* 301–315.

Caplan, D. (1995). Issues arising in contemporary studies of disorders of syntactic processing in sentence comprehension in agrammatic patients. *Brian and Language, 50,* 325–338.

Caplan, D., & Waters, G. S. (1995). Aphasic disorders of syntactic comprehension and working memory capacity. *Cognitive Neuropsychology, 12,* 637–649.

Caramazza, A., & Zurif, E. B. (1976). Dissociation of algorithmic and heuristic processes in language comprehension: Evidence from aphasia. *Brain and Language, 3,* 572–582.

Dell, G. S. (1986). A spreading activation theory of retrieval in sentence production. *Psychological Review, 93,* 283–321.

Friederici, A. (1981). Production and comprehension of prepositions in aphasia. *Neuropsychologia, 19,* 191–199.

Friederici, A. D., & Kilborn, K. (1989). Temporal constraints on language processing: Syntactic priming in Broca's aphasia. *Journal of Cognitive Neuroscience, 1,* 262–272.

Friederici, A., Schonle, P. W., & Garrett, M. F. (1982). Syntactically and semantically based computations: Processing of prepositions in agrammatism. *Cortex, 18,* 525–534.

Goodglass, H. (1993). *Understanding aphasia.* New York: Academic Press.

Grodzinsky, Y. (1984). The syntactic characterization of agrammatism. *Cognition, 16,* 99–120.

Grodzinsky, Y. (1995). A restrictive theory of agrammatic comprehension. *Brain and Language, 50,* 27–51.

Haarman, H. J., & Kolk, H. H. (1991). Syntactic priming in Broca's aphasia: Evidence for slow activation. *Aphasiology, 5,* 247–263.

Kessinger, R. (1998). *The mapping from sound structure to the lexicon: A study of normal and aphasic subjects.* Unpublished doctoral dissertation, Brown University, Providence, RI.

Linebarger, M. C., Schwartz, M. F., & Saffran, E. M. (1983). Sensitivity to grammatical structure in so-called agrammatic aphasics. *Cognition, 13,* 361–392.

Martin, R. C., & Romani, C. (1994). Verbal working memory and sentence comprehension: A multiple-components view. *Neuropsychology, 8,* 506–523.

Masson, M. E. J. (1995). A distributed memory model of semantic priming. *Journal of Experimental Psychology: Learning, Memory, & Cognition, 21,* 3–23.

McClelland, J., & Rumelhart, D. (1986). *Parallel distributed processing: Explorations in the microstructure of cognition* (Vol. 2). Cambridge, MA: MIT Press.

McNellis, M., & Blumstein, S. E. (1999). *Self-organizing dynamics of lexical access in normals and aphasics.* Submitted.

Milberg, W., & Blumstein, S. E. (1981). Lexical decision and aphasia: Evidence for semantic processing. *Brain and Language, 14,* 371–385.

Milberg, W. P., Blumstein, S. E. & Dworetzky, B. (1987). Processing of lexical ambiguities in aphasia. *Brain and Language, 31,* 138–150.

Milberg, W., Blumstein, S. E., & Dworetzky, B. (1988a). Phonological factors in lexical access: Evidence from an auditory lexical decision task. *Bulletin of the Psychonomic Society, 26,* 305–308.

Milberg, W., Blumstein, S. E., & Dworetzky, B. (1988b). Phonological processing and lexical access in aphasia. *Brain and Language, 34,* 279–293.

Milberg, W., Blumstein, S. E., Katz, D., Gershberg, F., & Brown, T. (1995). Semantic facilitation in aphasia: Effects of time and expectancy. *Journal of Cognitive Neuroscience, 7,* 33–50.

Milberg, W., Sullivan, K. L., & Blumstein, S. E. (1998). Summation of semantic priming effects in aphasia: Deficits in the integration of activation are related to disorders of language. *Brain and Language, 65,* 76–78.

Miyake, A., Carpenter, P. A., & Just, M. A. (1994). A capacity approach to syntactic comprehension disorders: Making normal adults perform like aphasic patients. *Cognitive Neuropsychology, 11,* 671–717.

Plaut, D. (1995). Semantic and associative priming in a distributed attractor network. *Proceedings of the 17th Annual Conference of the Cognitive Science Society,* 37–42.

Prather, P., Zurif, E. B., Stern, C., & Rosen, J. T. (1992). Slowed lexical access in nonfluent aphasia: A case study. *Brain and Language, 42,* 336–348.

Pulvermuller, R. (1995). Agrammatism: Behavioral description and neurobiological explanation. *Journal of Cognitive Neuroscience, 7,* 165–181.

Saffran, E. M., Schwartz, M. F., & Linebarger, M. C. (1998). Semantic influences on thematic role assignment: Evidence from normals and aphasics. *Brain and Language, 62,* 255–207.

Shankweiler, D., Crain, S., Gorrell, P., & Tuller, B. (1989). Reception of language in Broca's aphasia. *Language and Cognitive Processes, 4,* 1–33.

Swinney, D., Zurif, E. B., & Nicol, J. (1989). The effects of focal brain damage in sentence processing: An examination of the neurobiological organization of a mental module. *Journal of Cognitive Neuroscience, 1,* 25–37.

Utman, J. A. (1997). *Effects of subphonetic acoustic differences on lexical access in neurologically intact adults and patients with Broca's aphasia.* Unpublished doctoral dissertation, Brown University, Providence, RI.

Utman, J. A. (1999). The role of phonetic exemplars in the mapping from sound to meaning. Submitted manuscript.

Utman, J. A., Blumstein, S. E., & Sullivan, K. (1999). Mapping from sounds to meaning: Reduced lexical activation in Broca's aphasics. *Brain and Language,* under editorial review.

Wulfeck, B. (1987). Grammaticality judgments and sentence comprehension in agrammatic aphasia. *Journal of Speech and Hearing Research, 31,* 72–81.

Zurif, E. B., & Caramazza, A. (1976). Psycholinguistic structure in aphasia: Studies in syntax and semantics. In H. Whitaker and H. A. Whitaker (Eds.), *Studies in Neurolinguistics* (Vol. I). New York: Academic Press.

Zurif, E. B., Caramazza, A., & Myerson, R. (1972). Grammatical judgments of agrammatic aphasics. *Neuropsychologia, 10,* 405–417.

Chapter **10**

Right Hemisphere Contributions to Understanding Lexical Connotation and Metaphor

Hiram Brownell

INTRODUCTION

The focus of this chapter is quite different from many others included in this volume. Most work on acquired language disorders explores the nature of phonology and syntax and the extent to which rules and representations at these levels of language description can be linked to structures in the left cerebral hemisphere (e.g., Caplan, 1987; Goodglass, 1993). In many ways, the right hemisphere's role in language comprehension appears to complement that of the left hemisphere. (See Beeman & Chiarello, 1998; Brownell, Gardner, Prather, & Martino, 1995; Joanette, Goulet, Hannequin, 1990; Myers, 1999; Tompkins, 1995, for reviews.) This chapter will consider how the right hemisphere—and different regions within the right hemisphere—contribute to the comprehension of metaphor and connotation.

The distinction between the denotative and connotative aspects of a word's meaning is a familiar one (e.g., Cairns & Cairns, 1976; Lyons, 1968); however, as will be shown, this distinction is not always easy to draw. The denotation of a word or concept is typically considered its literal or "dictionary" meaning, and the connotation, usually, its more broadly construed, often emotive aspects. One definition for the concept *tiger*, for example, includes both denotative and connotative components: a "large, fierce, flesh-eating animal (*Panthera tigris*) of the cat family, about the size of a lion, having a tawny coat striped with black: it is native to most of Asia" (*Webster's New World Dictionary of the American Language*,

2nd Edition, p. 1487). Of course, other versions of the definition of *tiger* are possible, and a person's mental representation of the tiger concept probably does not contain exactly the same information as this particular definition (e.g., Clark & Clark, 1977). A mental representation for *tiger* might contain other information, such as the shape of the head and body, that a person could use to identify a tiger from visual information. And, a mental representation for *tiger* might contain links to other representations, such as those for *mammal, animal,* or *predator* as a means of augmenting the details listed directly under *tiger* (e.g., Collins & Quillian, 1969; Smith & Medin, 1981).

The contrast between denotation and connotation can be expressed largely in terms of the degree of generality. The connotative meaning associated with *tiger* may evoke an emotional response but, in addition, includes other generally applicable elements such as strength, energy and, especially, ferocity. By "generally applicable," I mean elements of meaning that can apply within a wide variety of superordinate concepts from very different semantic domains. Graded variation along the connotative dimension of strength, for example, can carry distinctions within category concepts as different as *animal, vehicle, people,* and *sunlight.* In contrast, denotative features of meaning seem to serve much more restricted purposes within the lexicon: coding specific distinctions between concepts or between entire classes of concepts. The denotative *living–nonliving* distinction, for example, separates two extremely broad domains, but serves no other obvious purpose. The denotative distinction between having wings and not having wings separates the category bird from other living things, and separates airplanes and jets from other vehicles. Still, wingedness does not possess the nearly universal within-domain applicability of strength or ferocity. Accordingly, connotative meaning is defined here in terms of its generality. The affective aspect is less critical because connotative meaning elements can vary with respect to how affective they seem. For example, the active–passive dimension and the good–bad dimension discussed by Osgood, Suci, and Tannenbaum (1957) are both connotative, though the active–passive dimension seems to carry relatively little affective value. Specification of connotative meaning may even depend on context. The adjective concept *British* can be used denotatively to specify a place of origin; however, it can also be used to convey more general, that is, connotative, meaning such as high levels of formality. This connotation of *British* can apply to many semantic domains including social occasions, political attitudes, and a person's demeanor.

The classic work by Osgood and colleagues on the semantic differential (e.g., Osgood et al., 1957) exemplifies as well-known empirical approach to connotative meaning defined in terms of its generality. This work involved having participants judge disparate concepts' values along a number of rating scales defined by pairs of dimensional adjectives such as "happy ... sad" and "hard ... soft." Osgood et al. extracted three composite dimensions using factor analysis, *evaluation* (good–bad), *potency* (strong–weak), and *activity* (active–passive), all of which can be considered connotative because all of the original stimulus words could be assigned values along each of them. Indeed, the statistical analysis was designed to uncover generally applicable dimensions of meaning. Other researchers have used a mathematically related technique, multidimensional scaling, to achieve similar goals. Rips, Shoben, and Smith (1973; see also Caramazza, Hersh, & Torgerson, 1976) asked subjects to rate intuitive similarity for pairs of animals and birds, such as *lion–mouse, lion–robin, mouse–robin, mouse–eagle,* etc. Participants used denotative meaning to distinguish between the domains of birds and animals, and two connotative dimensions of *size* and *ferocity* to make distinctions within both the *bird* and the *animal* superordinate categories. Again, the broad applicability of relative values on size and ferocity dimensions within different domains underscores the connotative nature of these dimensions.

There are several issues bearing on how best to view connotative meaning. One is whether connotation is stored together with denotation as part of a unitary representation for a word or whether connotation is more appropriately viewed as something dissociable from other aspects of word meaning and, perhaps, linked to a person's episodic memories. The "correct" answer might vary across concepts, language communities, and even individual speakers. Thus, the fierceness of tigers may by now be so familiar to all speakers of English that this trait constitutes a major part of the definition of tiger and, as such, must be an integral part of a person's internal representation of the concept. This may be particularly true for American speakers of English who, by and large, do not know very much about tigers except that they are similar to lions, have stripes, and are fierce. In contrast, American speakers of English know a great deal about dogs. They are likely to have had personal experiences with dogs and may thus have idiosyncratic associations tied to the concept *dog*. These personal memories may or may not figure in mental representations of word meaning invoked during comprehension of metaphor or other aspects of language.

Connotative meaning has been implicated in metaphoric extensions of word meaning in a variety of ways (e.g., Aitchison, 1987; Brown, 1958; Miller, 1979). Metaphoric extensions based on connotation are so familiar that dictionary definitions sometimes include them: The third definition in *Webster's New World Dictionary* for tiger is "a) a very energetic or persevering person b) a fierce, belligerent person. . . " (p.1487). A concept's connotation must be an accessible part of its meaning to provide an effective basis for metaphor. The example "Microsoft Corporation is the tiger of the business world" rests on connotation in that it crosses semantic domains by linking a disparate *topic* (Microsoft Corporation) and a *vehicle* (tiger) on the basis of a shared *ground* (ferocity, tenacity) that is, by definition, connotative. According to the domains interaction approach (Hillson & Martin, 1994; Tourangeau & Sternberg, 1981), the communicative impact of a metaphor derives in large part from, first, the discrepancy between denotative domains and, second, the degree to which the topic and vehicle have similar values on the connotative dimension(s) common to both. Greater discrepancy between the semantic domains of a topic and vehicle results in a better metaphor. "Microsoft is the tiger of the business world" is more compelling than "the barracuda is the tiger of the fish world," or, worse yet, "the mountain lion is the tiger of North America." Once a discrepancy between topic and vehicle is noted, problem solving is used to identify the basis of similarity. A particularly apt metaphor is one that forces a listener to bridge two very dissimilar domains and, then, to appreciate an especially close equivalence between a topic and vehicle once that initial discrepancy is acknowledged. "IBM is the tiger of the business world" is not as good a metaphor as "Microsoft is the tiger of the business world" because Microsoft matches tiger more closely than does IBM on the relevant dimensions of ferocity and tenacity. (Note that the ground for a metaphor most often includes connotative meaning but need not be limited to connotation; denotative meaning elements can also contribute to a particularly apt metaphor.)

Frozen or dead metaphors provide a different perspective. A good metaphor can lose its appeal when it is repeated in the same way a good joke becomes tiresome on repetition; what was initially novel and noteworthy becomes familiar and boring. With sufficient repetition, a metaphor can "die" or "freeze" in the sense of being treated as a single lexical unit rather than analyzed as a string of words (e.g., Cruse, 1986), though it is hard to specify exactly how familiar or frequent in discourse a metaphor must be in order to be considered completely "dead" and part of the lexicon of most speakers. One expects the comprehension process to differ for novel and frozen metaphor. However, even if a frozen metaphor is in fact stored as a single lexical unit, there may be circumstances under which the literal meanings of the component parts can or must be retrieved. (See Clark & Clark, 1977, and Gibbs, 1986, for discussion of the same issue with respect to other forms of nonliteral language.)

NEUROPSYCHOLOGICAL INVESTIGATION OF CONNOTATION

A seminal study of Zurif and colleagues (Zurif, Caramazza, Myerson, & Galvin, 1974) nicely illustrates a separation of denotative from connotative components of meaning in a brain-damaged population. The stimuli used consisted of printed words that, as a set, represented variation along several semantic dimensions: *knight, cook, partner, mother, wife, husband, dog, tiger, shark, trout, turtle,* and *crocodile.* Some of the distinctions were literal and specifically concerned biological taxonomy involving species membership and, thus, were denotative. One dimension, degree of ferocity, was general in that it could apply equally well within several domains and, accordingly, was connotative. In addition to whether or not participants made distinctions among these terms' meanings on the basis of denotative and connotative dimensions, Zurif et al. addressed other issues such as whether or not there was a hierarchical organization to participants' mental representation and use of these category concepts.

The method used to evaluate the separability of meaning types was to test for selective changes in performance associated with unilateral brain damage due to stroke. Patients with damage due to stroke in the language areas of the left hemisphere (hereafter, LHD) are, of course, typically aphasic. The patients used in the Zurif et al. (1974) study presented with either of two broad types of aphasia associated, respectively, with lesion sites anterior and posterior to the Rolandic fissure. The anterior-lesioned patients were all diagnosed as having Broca's type aphasia, which is defined in part by relatively intact comprehension of language and naming ability (Goodglass & Kaplan, 1972). The posterior-lesioned patients were diagnosed, with one exception, as having Wernicke's aphasia, which is defined in part by impaired comprehension, poor naming, and a tendency to use indefinite terms ("thing") in place of more specific words ("chair"). The one exceptional posterior-lesioned patient had a level of comprehension that was better than the rest of the posterior-lesioned patients. In addition, non brain-damaged control participants were tested. One way to redescribe the distinction among groups of participants is in terms of severity of lexical–semantic impairment, ranging from none (the control group) to moderate (the anterior-lesioned, Broca's group) to severe (most of the posterior-lesioned group).

Although there is controversy regarding the homogeneity of functional deficits within groups of brain-damaged patients defined in terms of classic aphasic syndromes (cf. Caramazza, 1986; Zurif, Gardner, & Brownell, 1989), ordering the groups of patients in terms of severity of lexical impairment allows ready interpretation of the impairments. In addition, Zurif et al. (1974) took pains to assess the degree to which individual participants' data corresponded to the group results. The description of patterns was applicable to individuals with only one exception, the relatively mildly impaired posterior-lesioned patient whose data resembled more closely the results for the anterior-lesioned patients.

The authors used the method of triads as a means of obtaining similarities for all pairs of stimuli. A participant viewed all possible sets of three terms and, for each, selected the two terms that were the most similar in meaning. (Pretesting was carried out to ensure that all patients as well as control participants could read and understand the words.) Specifically, each of the 66 pairs of words co-occurred in 10 different triads; the measure of similarity for a pair was the number of times the two words were selected out of triads as being most similar. These "similarity scores" were then combined across participants within a group and subjected to hierarchical clustering (Johnson, 1967) and also multidimensional scaling (Schiffman, Reynolds, & Young, 1981; Torgerson, 1958). These statistical procedures are used to produce graphic displays of interstimulus similarity that illustrate which concepts participants consider most similar and which most dissimilar. With some caveats, the graphic displays (that is, the "solutions") provide maps of people's internal representation of the semantic concepts used in the study and provide clues about the meanings tied to specific concepts.

The results for the control group showed good appreciation of the fundamental distinction between human and nonhuman terms. There was also good indication of finer distinctions tied to biological taxonomy: *turtle* and *crocodile* were tightly linked as were *trout* and *shark*. In the multidimensional scaling analysis, the control group's average solution also reflected systematic attention to relative degrees of ferocity. Consideration of both taxonomic similarity, defined denotatively, and ferocity, defined in connotative terms, replicates results of other studies (Caramazza et al., 1976; Rips et al., 1973).

The aphasic patient groups performed quite differently. The anterior-lesioned group's average results represented denotative meaning distinctions less clearly than connotative and less constrained associations. The hierarchical clustering solution for the anterior-lesioned group showed a relatively clean discrimination between human and nonhuman terms except that the concept *dog* was not seen as belonging particularly well to either the human or the nonhuman cluster. Rather, *dog* was linked weakly to the human cluster, perhaps reflecting dogs' frequent association with human society. The other animal terms were grouped together; however, within the animal terms, the tightest grouping was in terms of ferocity rather than taxonomy: *shark* and *crocodile* were deemed highly similar, and *tiger* too was considered as part of the set of fierce animals; also, *trout* and *turtle* were grouped together. The posterior-lesioned group did not produce stable results; their greater degree of impairment may have rendered the task too difficult and, for that reason, the results not very informative. In sum, the relative emphasis paid to connotative meaning was increased for the anterior-lesioned patients over what was observed for the controls, and the emphasis paid to denotative meaning was decreased.

In contrast to the Zurif et al. (1974) report, a study by Gardner and Denes (1973) suggested the possibility of a selective reduction in sensitivity to connotative dimensions of meaning. Gardner and Denes offered a novel comparison: they examined related abilities in LHD patients, who were aphasic, and in a small group of right hemisphere brain-damaged (RHD) stroke patients who were not aphasic. The task involving matching connotative values across widely disparate domains, for example, matching a verbal concept like "wealth" with a drawing such as an arrow pointed up or down. The provocative result from this study, although preliminary in nature, was a surprising decrease in facility with connotative equivalence shown by many of the RHD patients, at least when appreciation of equivalence required translation across very different symbol systems.

NEUROPSYCHOLOGICAL INVESTIGATION OF METAPHOR

Winner and Gardner (1977) reported a related finding regarding phrasal metaphor. They tested comprehension of familiar, that is, frozen, metaphors such as "he has a heavy heart" using a multiple choice task in which participants chose the conventional interpretation from among four pictured alternatives. The alternatives were designed to illustrate the literal ("denotative") meaning of the entire phrase (a picture of a man staggering while lifting an oversized heart), the conventional metaphoric meaning (a crying man), or, in the case of the other two alternatives, different parts of the literal meaning (a picture of a heart, a picture of a large weight). Both LHD and RHD patients were tested. The most relevant result was that the RHD patients exhibited abnormality in comprehension of even overlearned, frozen metaphors. Their characteristic response was selecting the depiction of a stimulus phrase's literal meaning, even though one might expect that overlearned metaphors would be stored as a single lexical unit and, for that reason, would be easy to understand in figurative terms. RHD patients avoided common metaphoric interpretations and instead opted for literal meanings. Even in a language task, traditionally seen as an area of preserved ability in (nonaphasic) RHD patients, these patients showed marked abnormality.

A later study by Brownell, Potter, Michelow, and Gardner (1984; see also Brownell, Simpson, Potter, Bihrle, & Gardner, 1990) used the techniques refined by Zurif et al. (1974) to examine sensitivity to denotative and connotative meaning and metaphoric extensions in LHD and RHD patients. The stimulus set consisted of eight adjectives: *warm, cold, loving, hateful, deep, shallow, wise,* and *foolish.* The method of triads was again used: participants saw all possible triads and, for each, responded which two words went together best. Notice that these adjective concepts can be grouped in several different ways. One denotative dimension is human–nonhuman: half of the adjectives are personality descriptors whose dominant meanings apply primarily to people (*wise, foolish, loving, hateful*), and half are adjectives whose dominant meanings apply to attributes of the physical world (*warm, cold, deep, shallow*). Also, the tight associative and semantic links between antonyms (*warm–cold, deep–shallow, loving–hateful, wise–foolish*) represent a high degree of relatedness based on denotative meaning. Alternatively, these adjectives could be matched on the basis of metaphoric extensions of meaning: *deep–wise, shallow–foolish, warm–loving,* and *cold–hateful.* Finally, another connotative meaning dimension that can be used as a basis for judging relatedness is valence: words that are positive or unmarked in a linguistic sense (e.g., *warm, wise, loving, deep*) can be separated from words that are negative or marked (*cold, shallow, hateful, foolish*).[1]

For each triad, a participant had to make a choice concerning which type of relation was the most important. Hierarchical clustering analyses were performed on group data. One practical limitation of hierarchical clustering with this eight-adjective stimulus set is that the analyses reveal only the two most important grouping principles for each group of participants.

Results documented interpretable differences in LHD and RHD patients' treatment of denotative and connotative meaning. Clustering analyses revealed (1) non-brain-damaged controls grouped terms first on the basis of (denotative) antonymic association and secondarily on the basis of (connotative) metaphoric equivalence; (2) LHD patients grouped terms primarily on the basis of metaphoric equivalence and also on the basis of generally positive or negative cognitive valence; and (3) RHD patients grouped terms primarily on the basis of antonymic association and

---

[1]For dimensional adjectives such as deep and shallow, the unmarked member of the pair (deep) is the more general term that can apply to the entire range. One can ask, "How deep is the pool?" without prejudging the depth. In contrast, asking, "How shallow is the pool?" presupposes a value on the depth dimension toward one end of the continuum. A marked term carries an implicit negation (shallow means not deep) and is psychologically more complex in that marked terms take longer to understand, all else being equal (Clark & Chase, 1972). Languages may have an unmarked term without a marked term, as in French: "deep" can be translated into "profond," but shallow must be coded with an explicit negative "pas profond." However, languages will never have a marked term without also having an unmarked term for the same dimension (Clark, 1970, 1973).

secondarily on the basis of the (denotative) distinction between human (personality descriptors)–nonhuman (physical descriptors) terms.

Additional analyses based on more common inferential techniques (e.g., *t* tests) by and large underscored the reliability of these patterns. The 28 possible pairs constructed from the eight-adjective set were segregated by the type of semantic relation represented such that the members of a pair in each "condition" shared a very specific type of relation. The taxonomy used was exhaustive and mutually exclusive. Four pairs were placed in the antonym condition (e.g., *deep–shallow, wise–foolish*); four others in the metaphor condition (e.g., *deep–wise, shallow–foolish*); four others in the shared domain condition (e.g., *hateful–wise, cold–deep*); four in the polarity condition (e.g., *cold–foolish, warm–wise*); four in the domain *and* polarity condition (e.g., *loving–wise, cold–shallow*); and, finally, there were eight pairs in the no relation condition (e.g., *cold–wise, warm–hateful*). The dependent measure calculated (for individual participants) was the average similarity score collapsed across the word pairs in each condition. This breakdown into relation types allowed direct assessment of a participant's tendency to rely on a certain type of relation. These analyses confirmed the dissociability of denotative and connotative meaning. First, the RHD and control groups paid reliably more attention to antonymic links than did the LHD group. Second, the LHD patients paid reliably higher attention to polarity than the control participants, and more than the RHD patients, though the difference between the RHD and LHD averages was not significant. Third, the LHD patients and control groups paid reliably more attention to metaphoric relations than the RHD group. The LHD and control groups' greater preference for metaphoric relations was significant over and above any effect due to just shared polarity. The only effect suggested by the clustering analyses not borne out by the inferential analyses was the RHD group's reliance on domain of applicability (human personality descriptors versus physical descriptors), though the means were in the right direction.

Consistent with traditional description of aphasia (e.g., Goodglass, 1993), damage to the language areas of the left hemisphere of the brain renders a person's treatment of word meaning less tied to specific, literal, denotative content and, relatively more reliant on connotation. Right-sided damage, in contrast, leads to greater focus on the denotative elements. The Brownell et al. study used entirely verbal materials, which makes less likely accounts tied to problems crossing symbol systems (cf. Gardner & Denes, 1973) or responding appropriately to pictured alternatives (cf. Winner & Gardner, 1977).

A more recent study by Bottini et al. (1994) confirms the right hemisphere's role in metaphor processing. These authors used a very different paradigm, positron emission tomography (PET), and extended the investigation to include novel phrasal metaphors. Bottini et al. presented healthy young participants (21–35 years old) with three tasks in which they judged whether sentences were plausible or implausible at the literal level of analysis, and, in a different condition, whether sentences were plausible(interpretable) or implausible as metaphors, and, in a third condition, whether or not a nonword letter string occurred within a series of words. (Participants raised their left index finger on reading an implausible item.) The metaphor condition used items such as "The old man had a head full of dead leaves," which is plausible, and "The investors were trams" which is not plausible. The literal sentence condition used items such as "The boy used stones as paperweights" which is plausible, and "The lady has a bucket as a walking stick," which is not plausible. The items in the metaphor and literal conditions were also equated for length, syntactic complexity, and processing difficulty as measured by reaction times obtained in pilot testing. The measures of interest in PET are difference scores that reflect increased levels of metabolic activity associated with different experimental conditions.

As expected, comparison between literal sentence processing and single word processing showed heightened activation in extensive portions of the left hemisphere in the literal sentence condition. However, more relevant are comparisons between literal sentence processing and metaphoric sentence processing. These results identified several areas within the right hemisphere marked by increased activation during the metaphor condition: Brodmann's areas 46 (the dorsolateral prefrontal region), 21 (the middle temporal gyrus), and 31 (the precuneus, located in the medial parietal lobe).

In addition to providing important confirmation of conclusions based on earlier studies of brain-damaged patients, Bottini et al. (1994) extended the interpretation of the right hemisphere's role in important ways. Bottini et al. suggest that right posterior regions (specifically, the precuneus) and prefrontal regions reflect a contribution of episodic memory and imagery. (See also work by Fletcher, Shallice, Frith, Frackowiak, & Dolan, 1996, using PET to examine processing components for a cued recall task.) Metaphor comprehension may differ from literal sentence comprehension in that metaphors involve retrieving imageable experiences from episodic memory to support interpretation. Bottini et al. point out that these conjectures match the introspective reports of their participants. Calling on personal experiences and viewing images of those experiences might provide participants with the means to resolve the vagueness inherent in metaphor. Furthermore, Fletcher et al. (1996) suggest that increased activation in the right precuneus reflects conscious inspection of images and that greater activation in the prefrontal regions reflects the need to distinguish between alternative responses.

SUMMARY AND SOME UNRESOLVED ISSUES

I suggest that the intact right hemisphere plays a crucial role in processing metaphor, which is often based on connotative meaning. There are, however, several open questions. One such question is whether there is any useful distinction between connotation and metaphor with respect to the critical brain regions involved. Thus far in this chapter, I have treated processing of metaphor and connotation as identical for all intents and purposes. More generally, it is important to outline how problems understanding metaphor or processing connotation relate to other deficits associated with RHD.

A model outlined by Beeman (1998) provides a useful beginning for addressing these issues. In a series of papers, Beeman has suggested that the right hemisphere supports "coarse-grained" semantic processing while the left hemisphere supports "fine-grained" processing. (See Beeman, 1998, for a detailed review; see also, among others, Burgess & Simpson, 1988; and Chiarello, 1998, for reviews of closely related work.) The left hemisphere, according to Beeman's model, is best suited for literal language processing. On receipt of a word, the left hemisphere mediates focused activation of the limited subset of semantic content that is tied to the most frequent meaning or to the context at hand defined by preceding words or sentences. The activation concentrated on context-relevant content works to keep that meaning available for subsequent language comprehension. This processing characterization of the left hemisphere is not conducive to melding features from different semantic domains, as is required for most metaphors, even though it is efficient for understanding many other aspects of language. In contrast, on receipt of a word, the right hemisphere characteristically generates diffuse activation related to the word's semantic content, including even weakly associated connotative components. This diffuse activation of both closely and distantly associated concepts is one central claim of Beeman's model. In and of itself, the activation of a particular connotative association of a stimulus may not be strong enough to render that association available for conscious interpretation. However, the right hemisphere also appears good at maintaining the activation over a relatively long period of time, which is a second critical part of Beeman's model. On receipt of a potential metaphoric topic such as "Microsoft Corporation," weak activation spreads to many elements including connotations. On hearing a potential vehicle such as "tiger," some of the same (connotative) elements are activated. The activation summed over the topic and vehicle is sufficient to identify the metaphoric ground as a candidate for interpretation. A third aspect of Beeman's model is that the right hemisphere cannot select from among the many alternatives it generates; the selection is carried out by some other region. (I discuss this point below.) Thus, the right hemisphere is not all that useful for understanding most literal language at the level of words or sentences; nor is the right hemisphere able to finish the job of metaphor comprehension. It is, though, necessary for metaphor comprehension.

In his review, Beeman discusses how his notion of coarse coding can account for the deficits exhibited in RHD patients in understanding metaphor and connotation, and also many other problems in discourse comprehension associated with RHD (e.g., Joanette, et al., 1990; Myers, 1999; Tompkins, 1995). An appealing aspect of Beeman's notion of coarse coding is that it allows a merger of the traditional notions of connotation, such as the evaluative dimension as identified by Osgood et al. (1957), with other diffuse associations that can figure in apt metaphors. The processes are the same regardless of whether the ground of a potential metaphor is limited to the notion of a shared positive aura, or whether the ground is a combination of several features that can apply over some disparate semantic domains. The role of the right hemisphere is to sum weak associations: this highlights what—for the left hemisphere—is a nonobvious similarity between topic and vehicle. The nondirected, apparently effortless nature of spreading activation mediated by the right hemisphere fits with the inevitable ("automatic") nature of metaphoric processing: Glucksberg, Gildea, and Bookin (1982), for example, report that non-brain-damaged participants are unable to inhibit their appreciation of metaphoric meaning.

There are a couple of ways in which I think Beeman's model can usefully be amended. The most important point of departure from Beeman's model is adding specification of where any selection from among alternatives takes place. Left and right prefrontal regions, especially dorsolateral areas, are likely candidates for analysis of representations. Recall that Fletcher et al. (1996) report increased activation in the left and right prefrontal areas as demands for response selection increased in cued recall. Right prefrontal regions were linked to imageable materials, and left prefrontal regions to nonimageable materials. (See Brownell, Griffin, Winner, Friedman, & Happé, 1999, for additional discussion of how right prefrontal regions, together with their connections to other structures support aspects of discourse comprehension and social cognition, i.e., theory of mind.)

Work by Tompkins and colleagues provides additional perspective on the deficits associated with RHD that should be taken into account (e.g., Tompkins, 1990; Tompkins, Bloise, Timko, & Baumgaertner, 1994; and

Tompkins, Boada, & McGarry, 1992). One main finding of this program of research is that the deficits of RHD patients in metaphor comprehension are most notable in tasks requiring effortful or strategic processing. Tompkins (1990) used a lexical decision task in which a participant heard a first word (a prime) and then a target consisting of a second series of phonemes; the task was to decide as quickly as possible whether or not the target was a real word. On different trials, the prime word was related either to the metaphoric or to the literal meaning of (real) target words. The stimuli included terms such as the adjective concepts used by Brownell et al. (1984): *warm, loving*, etc. RHD patients showed apparently normal appreciation of metaphoric alternative meanings when the experimental context was designed to minimize any requirement for strategic planning or conscious effort by participants. Specifically, the time interval between the prime and target word was extremely short (500 ms), and participants did not have to consciously explore alternative meanings. However, RHD patients showed deficits in apprehending metaphoric alternative meanings when the task requirements were altered to maximized strategic requirements and the temporal interval was much longer (2 s). Additionally, Tompkins et al. (1994) has reported that working memory capacity assessed independently correlates positively with RHD patients' performance in discourse comprehension.

I think it is possible to reconcile the finding reported by Beeman's and Tompkins' laboratories by attributing different roles to the prefrontal regions and to the more posterior regions within the right hemisphere. The core functions supported by the posterior cortical regions within the right hemisphere are (1) unfocused, diffuse activation spread over many semantic associations, and (2) maintenance of that activation, that is, the absence of active dampening such as associated with left hemisphere processing (e.g., Beeman et al., 1994). The temporal durability of the activation allows summing of activation; this, in turn can account for how some distant associations can become sufficiently activated to be used in further analysis. The evaluation and selection per se of a particular activated representation from among two or more is a task most likely handled by prefrontal regions which are often identified as involved in working memory. (I view the construct of a working memory in terms of maintenance of activation of some type of representation rather than in terms of a durable repository of representations.) Lesions resulting from strokes affecting the middle cerebral artery distributions may serve to disrupt processing handled by the relatively posterior cortical regions of the right hemisphere or to disconnect them from prefrontal regions.

A final issue bears on how best to resolve differences between Beeman's account and that offered by Bottini et al. (1994) and Fletcher et al. (1996).

Beeman's account is based within the language system and does not invoke imagery or episodic memory. The discussion by Bottini et al. and Fletcher et al. argue for critical links among the maintenance and summation of activation, on the one hand, and the constructs of working memory and episodic memory on the other. One approach to resolution is to consider whether imagery and episodic memory are essential for metaphor comprehension or are simply coincident. The phrasal metaphors used in the studies I am aware of are all imageable in that they rely on either an imageable vehicle, topic, or both. ("Imageable" is used here to indicate that a representation allows inspection by the mind's eye regardless of whether all speakers experience the same image or whether each speaker experiences an idiosyncratic image drawn from personal history, cf. Fletcher et al., 1996.) It will be important to ascertain whether a person *must* inspect an image or an episodic memory in order to understand a metaphor. If mandatory, these components of metaphor will have to be incorporated into a model of right hemisphere language processing. Also, their relation to other right hemisphere processing capabilities, such as summation of diffuse activation, will need to be specified. These different functions may be separable: the metaphoric extensions of the adjective concepts *warm, cold, deep,* and *shallow* used by Brownell et al. (1984) and in the work by Tompkins intuitively seem less likely to require imaginal mediation for comprehension.

Invoking an underspecified neurological framework for any cognitive task often results in a dangerously powerful account. In the present case, the framework lacks specificity but, nonetheless, makes falsifiable predictions. This proposal organizes many findings from work in language and other domains within cognition and also highlights a couple of relevant topics for future study. One question concerns the precise nature of the links among episodic memory, imagery, and metaphor comprehension. It should be straightforward to test whether Beeman's findings apply equally to spreading activation emanating from abstract, nonimageable as well as imageable concepts, and it should be possible to test whether imagery is a mandatory component of metaphor processing. I predict that the imaginal components of metaphor processing can dissociate from summation of diffuse activation. A second question is whether working memory, presumably mediated by dorsolateral prefrontal structures, can be dissociated from the tasks of summing of activation, which involves participation of more posterior cortical regions. I expect so. Two remaining questions, which are not addressed in this chapter, concern the role of other structures. One is how orbital prefrontal–limbic structures should be incorporated into a model of metaphor comprehension. The second is how, in neurological as well as functional terms, the products of right hemisphere language processing are combined with the results of more constrained, algorithmic operations assigned to regions within the left hemisphere to support normal comprehension.

ACKNOWLEDGMENTS

I owe a great deal to Rick Griffin and Andy Stringfellow for comments on an earlier draft and for several extremely useful discussions on the content of this chapter. Preparation of this chapter was supported by Grants R01 NS 27894 and P01 DC00102.

REFERENCES

Aitchison, J. (1987). *Words in the mind.* Oxford: Basil Blackwell.
Beeman, M. (1998). Coarse semantic coding and discourse comprehension. In M. Beeman & C. Chiarello (Eds.), *Right hemisphere language comprehension. Perspectives from cognitive neuroscience* (pp. 255–284). Mahwah, NJ: Erlbaum.
Beeman, M., & Chiarello, C. (Eds.). (1998). *Right hemisphere language comprehension. Perspectives from cognitive neuroscience.* Mahwah, NJ: Erlbaum.
Beeman, M., Friedman, R., Grafman, J., Perez, E., Diamond, S., & Lindsay, M. (1994). Summation priming and coarse semantic coding in the right hemisphere. *Journal of Cognitive Neuroscience, 6,* 26–45.
Bottini, G., Corcoran, R., Sterzi, R., Paulesu, E., Schenone, P., Scarpa, P., Frackowiak, R. S. J., & Frith, C. D. (1994). The role of the right hemisphere in the interpretation of figurative aspects of language. A positron emission tomography activation study. *Brain, 117,* 1241–1253.
Brown, R. (1958). *Words and things.* Glencoe, IL: Free Press.
Brownell, H. H., Gardner, H., Prather, P., & Martino, G. (1995). Language, communication, and the right hemisphere. In H. S. Kirshner (Ed.), *Handbook of neurological speech and language disorders* (pp. 325–349). New York: Dekker.
Brownell, H., Griffin, R., Winner, E., Friedman, O., & Happé, F. (1999). Cerebral lateralization and theory of mind. To appear in S. Baron-Cohen, H. Tager-Flusberg, & D. Cohen (Eds.), *Understanding other minds: Perspectives from autism and development cognitive neuroscience* (2nd ed., pp. 311–338). Oxford: Oxford University Press.
Brownell, H. H., Potter, H. H., Michelow, D., & Gardner, H. (1984). Sensitivity to lexical denotation and connotation in brain damaged patients: A double dissociation? *Brain and Language, 22,* 253–265.
Brownell, H. H., Simpson, T. L., Bihrle, A. M., Potter, H. H., & Gardner, H. (1990). Appreciation of metaphoric alternative word meaning by left and right brain-damaged patients. *Neuropsychologia, 28,* 375–383.
Burgess, C., & Simpson, G. B. (1988). Cerebral hemispheric mechanisms in the retrieval of ambiguous word meanings. *Brain and Language, 33,* 86–103.
Cairns, H. S., & Cairns, C. E. (1976). *Psycholinguistics.* New York: Holt, Rinehart, & Winston.
Caplan, D. (1987). *Neurolinguistics and linguistic aphasiology.* Cambridge: Cambridge University Press.

Caramazza, A. (1986). On drawing inferences about the structure of normal cognitive systems from the analysis of patterns of impaired performance: The case for single-patient studies. *Brain and Cognition, 5,* 41–46.

Caramazza, A., Hersh, H. M., & Torgerson, W. S. (1976). Subjective structures and operations in semantic memory. *Journal of Verbal Learning and Verbal Behavior, 15,* 103–118.

Chiarello, C. (1998). On codes of meaning and the meaning of codes: Semantic access and retrieval with and between hemispheres. In M. Beeman & C. Chiarello (Eds.), *Right hemisphere language comprehension. Perspectives from cognitive neuroscience* (pp. 141–160). Mahwah, NJ: Erlbaum.

Clark, H. H. (1970). Word associations and linguistic theory. In J. Lyons (Ed.), *New horizons in linguistics* (pp. 271–286). Baltimore, MD: Penguin Books.

Clark, H. H. (1973). Space, time, semantics, and the child. In T. E. Moore (Ed.), *Cognitive development and the acquisition of language* (pp. 28–63). New York: Academic Press.

Clark, H. H., & Chase, W. G. (1972). On the process of comparing sentences against pictures. *Cognitive Psychology, 3,* 472–517.

Clark, H. H., & Clark, E. V. (1977). *Psychology and language.* New York: Harcourt Brace Jovanovich.

Collins, A. M., & Quillian, R. (1969). Retrieval time from semantic memory. *Journal of Verbal Leaning and Verbal Behavior, 8,* 240–247.

Cruse, D. A. (1986). *Lexical semantics.* Cambridge: Cambridge University Press.

Fletcher, P. C., Shallice, T., Frith, C. D. Frackowiak, R. S. J., & Dolan, R. J. (1996). Brain activity during memory retrieval: The influence of imagery and semantic cueing. *Brain, 119,* 1587–1596.

Gardner, H., & Denes, G. (1973). Connotative judgments by aphasic patients on a pictorial adaptation of the semantic differential. *Cortex, 9,* 183–196.

Gibbs, R. W. (1986). What makes some speech acts conventional? *Journal of Memory and Language, 25,* 181–196.

Glucksberg, S., Gildea, P., & Bookin, H. A. (1982). On understanding nonliteral speech: Can people ignore metaphors? *Journal of Verbal Learning and Verbal Behavior, 21,* 85–98.

Goodglass, H. (1993). *Understanding aphasia.* San Diego: Academic Press.

Goodglass, H., & Kaplan, E. (1972). *The assessment of aphasia and related disorders.* Philadelphia, PA: Lea & Febiger.

Hillson, T. R., & Martin, R. A. (1994). What's so funny about that?: The domains-interaction approach as a model of incongruity and resolution in humor. *Motivation and Emotion, 18,* 1–29.

Joanette, Y., Goulet, P., & Hannequin, D. (1990). *Right hemisphere and verbal communication.* New York: Springer-Verlag.

Johnson, S. C. (1967). Hierarchical clustering schemes. *Psychometrika, 32,* 241–254.

Lyons, J. (1968). *Introduction to theoretical linguistics.* Cambridge: Cambridge University Press.

Miller, G. A. (1979). Images and models, similes and metaphors. In A. Ortony (Ed.), *Metaphor and thought* (pp. 202–250). New York: Cambridge University Press.

Myers, P. S. (1999). *Right hemisphere damage: Disorders of communication and cognition.* San Diego: Singular Publishing Group.

Osgood, C. E., Suci, G. J., & Tannenbaum, P. H. (1957). *The measurement of meaning.* Urbana, IL: University of Illinois Press.

Rips, L. J., Shoben, E. J., & Smith, E. E., (1973). Semantic distance and the verification of semantic relations. *Journal of Verbal Learning and Verbal Behavior, 12,* 1–20.

Schiffman, S. S., Reynolds, M. L., & Young, F. W. (1981). *Introduction to multidimensional scaling.* New York: Academic Press.

Smith, E. E., & Medin, D. L. (1981). *Categories and concepts.* Cambridge, MA: Harvard University Press.

Tompkins, C. A. (1990). Knowledge and strategies for processing lexical metaphor after right or left hemisphere brain damage. *Journal of Speech and Hearing Research, 33,* 307–316.

Tompkins, C. A. (1995). *Right hemisphere communication disorders: Theory and management.* San Diego: Singular Publishing Group.

Tompkins, C. A., Boada, R., & McGarry, K. (1992). The access and processing of familiar idioms by brain-damaged and normally aging adults. *Journal of Speech and Hearing Research, 35,* 626–637.

Tompkins, C. A., Bloise, C. G. R., Timbo, M. L., & Baumgaertner, H. (1994). Working memory and inference revision in brain-damaged and normally aging adults. *Journal of Speech and Hearing Research, 37,* 896–912.

Torgerson, W. S. (1958). *Theory and methods of scaling.* New York: Wiley.

Tourangeau, R., & Sternberg, R. J. (1981). Aptness in metaphor. *Cognitive Psychology, 13,* 27–55.

Winner, E., & Gardner, H. (1977). The comprehension of metaphor in brain-damaged patients. *Brain, 100,* 719–727.

Zurif, E. B., Caramazza, A., Myerson, R., & Galvin, J. (1974). Semantic feature representations for normal and aphasic language. *Brain and Language 1,* 167–187.

Zurif, E. B., Gardner, H., & Brownell, H. H. (1989). The case against the case against group studies. *Brain and Cognition, 10,* 237–255.

Chapter 11

Aspects of Lexical Access: Evidence from Aphasia

Alfonso Caramazza

The study of aphasia has made significant contributions to our understanding of the organization of the lexicon. The contributions have come in several forms and have concerned many aspects of the lexical processing system. At the most general level, the selective deficit or sparing of the semantic, the grammatical, or the phonological (or orthographic) properties of words have been used to inform theories of the architecture of the lexical system. For example, there is ample evidence that the semantic component can be damaged selectively. Patients with focal lesions (e.g., Hillis, Rapp, Romani, & Caramazza, 1990) or diffuse brain damage (e.g., Hodges, Patterson, Oxbury, & Funnell, 1992) have been described who make semantic errors in all comprehension and production tasks but who produce grammatically and morphologically appropriate forms. There is equally clear evidence that access to lexical forms can be damaged selectively. Patients have been reported who comprehend words normally but can't retrieve them in naming or in spontaneous speech (e.g., Kay & Ellis, 1987). These contrasting patterns of lexical processing deficits invite the inference that the semantic and the lexical-form components of the lexicon constitute functionally and neurally distinct subsystems.

The analysis of aphasic language patterns has also been used to support more specific claims about the processing structure and the organization of the lexical system. For example, the distributions of naming error types have been used to argue for the interactivity assumption in lexical access—that is, for the claim that activation flows in both directions between levels of representation (e.g., Dell, 1986; Mackay, 1987; Stemberger 1985). And the patterns of semantic category-specific deficits have been used to make fairly specific claims about the organization of the conceptual knowledge that underlies lexical processing (see Caramazza, 1998, for a brief review).

Here I explore the implications of a particular type of disorder—modality-specific lexical processing deficits—for several aspects of the structure of lexical access mechanisms. I will consider two issues. First I will discuss the implications of these deficits for the general architecture of the lexical system with particular attention to whether we must assume that there are two or three lexical layers between the semantic and the segmental content of words. Along the way I will briefly discuss whether orthographic lexical access is phonologically mediated and the implications of this issue for claims about lexical access of morphologically complex forms. Second, I will discuss the implications of modality-specific lexical deficits for claims about lexical access in aphasia and for the types of inferences that can legitimately be drawn from impaired naming performance for normal processing.

MODALITY-SPECIFIC DEFICITS

Brain damage does not usually result in highly selective, discrete deficits. The typical brain-damaged patient we see in the clinic presents with a complex set of difficulties, involving different cognitive, perceptual, and motor functions. Thus, for example, aphasic patients usually have difficulties in comprehending and producing sentences, and in naming, reading, and writing single words. This is not surprising. Brain damage, either as the result of cerebrovascular accident (CVA), degenerative disease, surgical intervention, or trauma, typically involves fairly large areas of the brain, cutting across functionally important distinctions. For example, the distribution of the types of damage that result from CVAs is determined by the vascularization of the brain and not by its functional organization.

Despite the vagaries of the distribution of brain damage, it occasionally affects one cognitive system much more than any other, resulting in clear dissociations of symptoms. For example, some patients present with severe difficulty in reading in the context of a normal ability to write (pure alexia: E.G., Friedman & Alexander, 1984). Others seem to be totally incapable of understanding spoken language but show no difficulty with written language or language production tasks (word deafness; e.g., Kohn & Friedman. 1986). Others still seem to have much greater difficulty producing nouns than verbs, or vice versa (different subtypes of anomia; e.g., Damasio & Tranel, 1993; De Renzi & di Pellegrino, 1995; McCarthy & Warrington, 1985; Miceli, Silveri, Villa, & Caramazza, 1984; Zingeser & Berndt, 1988). These dissociations seem to involve either a modality distinction (e.g., auditory vs. visual) or a functional distinction (e.g., different grammatical classes). Although far less frequent, there are also cases in which the dissociation involves the intersection of a modality with a particular cognitive function. For example, there are patients who are impaired specifically in lexical processing, but only in the oral modality. Dissociations of this type are particularly interesting because, as we shall see, they allow (relatively) unambiguous attribution of the locus of the functional damage responsible for particular aspects of patients' performance.

Consider a simple picture-naming task. The patient is shown a pictured object (or event) and is asked to produce its name. Success in this task is only possible if all of the various mechanisms that support naming performance are intact. At the most general level of description of the naming process this includes visual object recognition mechanisms, the conceptual system, and speech mechanisms (see Figure 1). Damage to any of these mechanisms will result in some form of naming difficulty. For example, damage to visual perceptual mechanisms is expected to result in the misperception of objects and consequent failure to produce the correct name. In this case, the patient might incorrectly say "penny" in response to a picture of a *button*. Similarly, damage to the speech production component is expected to result in phonological errors. Here the expectation is that the patient might say "putton" or "butter" in response to a picture of a *button*. And damage to the conceptual/semantic system is expected to result in semantic substitution errors—the patient might produce "needle" in response to a picture of a *button*. These examples illustrate that the types of errors produced by patients provide helpful clues about the locus of damage to the cognitive system. In general, visual errors are associated with damage to visual processes, semantic errors with damage to the semantic system, and phonological errors with damage to the speech production system. However, this generalization is only a rough first approximation. Other facts besides the types of errors in a task must be considered in determining the locus of damage to a complex system.

Consider again a simple naming task. We could ask a patient to name a visually or a tactilely presented object. If the patient were to make naming errors in only one of the two tasks we could confidently ascribe the locus of damage to a modality-specific processing system. One of the best known of the modality-specific language deficits—optic aphasia (Lhermitte & Beauvois, 1973)—is a disorder characterized by selective difficulty in naming visually presented objects despite normal low-level visual processing and even "normal" ability to recognize visual objects (as indicated by the patients' surprisingly good ability to mime the actions of unnamed objects). These patients' naming (and recognition) errors consist of a mixture of visually and semantically related responses.

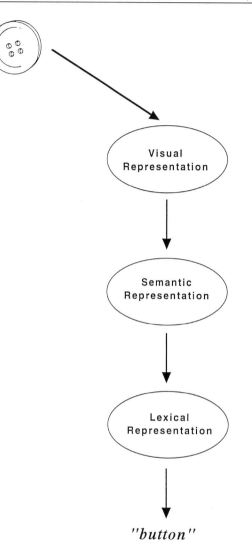

"button"

Figure 1   A simple model of the principal stages of picture naming.

Although the exact interpretation of the mechanisms responsible for the various features of this disorder remains controversial (see Hillis & Caramazza, 1995a) there is no doubt that the semantic system can be intact in some cases despite the presence of semantic errors in the visual naming task. This conclusion is based on the observation that (at least some of) these patients have entirely normal abilities in spontaneous language production, tactile naming, and naming in response to aurally presented definitions. Normal performance in these tasks would not be possible if the semantic system were damaged.

The case of optic aphasia illustrates two points relevant to our discussion here. First, if we were to rely only on error types in order to infer the locus of functional damage responsible for the naming deficit we could reach the wrong conclusion. The presence of semantic errors does not necessarily imply damage to the semantic system. Second, the comparison of task performance (e.g., naming) across modalities (e.g., visual vs. tactile) provides strong converging evidence about the relative integrity of the components of a complex process. In this example, the modality specific nature of the naming deficit can be used to infer the integrity of the semantic system. More generally, the joint consideration of modality effects and error types provides not only a powerful method for inferring the locus of functional damage to a complex cognitive process, but also provides important clues about the nature of representations involved in the process.

The Facts: Modality Effects in Lexical Access

Modality-specific naming deficits have also been observed for output modalities. There are many reports of patients who are more impaired in producing the spoken than the written name of an object or vice versa (Basso, Taborelli, & Vignolo, 1978; Bub & Kertesz, 1982; Friederici, Schoenle, & Goodglass, 1981; Hier & Mohr, 1977; Patterson & Shewell, 1987). By themselves, such dissociations are not particularly useful for constraining claims about the structure of lexical processing. Such dissociations could merely reflect differential damage to peripheral output processes, beyond the stage of lexical access. For example, a patient may have severe difficulties retrieving letter shape information, resulting in the production of unrecognizable graphemic paragraphias. However, there are also modality-specific naming deficits where the cause of the impairment can confidently be ascribed to a component of the lexical access process. These cases are of special interest because, as we shall see below, they set important constraints for models of lexical access.

Consider the picture-naming performance of the fluent aphasic patient RGB (Caramazza & Hillis, 1990). In an oral naming task, RGB produced 68% correct responses. The remaining responses consisted of semantic errors, either semantic substitutions or descriptions. RGB's naming difficulties are not the result of an input deficit (as is the case for optic aphasia) because he was similarly impaired in naming in response to tactilely presented objects and in response to aurally presented definitions. In these tasks, and in other oral production tasks such as oral reading and spontaneous speech, RGB made many semantic errors. The presence of exclusively semantic errors in these language production tasks would seem to suggest a pure semantic deficit. However, this is not the case for RGB. We know this because he performed at a very high level of accuracy and never produced semantic errors in written naming tasks. Further-more, he performed flawlessly in all word comprehension tasks. Thus, RGB's semantic system must be assumed to be intact. This conclusion is well supported by the fact that he clearly understood the meaning of the words he failed to read correctly and to which he made semantic errors. For example, in attempting to read *dollar* he said "money" but went on to define the stimulus as "A bill. . . . A hundred cents," and in reading *volcano* he said "lava" but went on to define the stimulus as "Fire comes out of it . . . a big thing . . . a mountain." In these examples it is clear that the semantic representation driving the activation of lexical forms is that of the stimulus and not that of the response. Finally, we know that his im-pairment in oral naming is not the result of damage to peripheral output processes because the errors he produced consisted of failures of lexical access: He produced semantic substitutions or descriptions and not phonological distortions of the target response.

The reverse pattern of dissociation to that shown by RGB has also been observed (patient SJD: Caramazza & Hillis, 1991; patient RCM: Hillis, Rapp, & Caramazza, submitted). Consider the performance of RCM in a written naming task. He correctly wrote the names of 53% of the pictures. His errors were distributed as follows: 42% semantic paragraphias (e.g., harp ⟶ violin), 3% visual errors (barn ⟶ lunch box), and 3% neol-ogisms (zebra ⟶ jephrys). However, he named all the pictures cor-rectly in an oral naming task and he made no errors in comprehension tasks. Normal performance in the latter tasks establishes that RCM has an intact semantic system. The fact that his naming errors in writing con-sisted almost entirely of semantic substitutions rules out a peripheral or-thographic processing deficit. Therefore, like RGB, the locus of deficit responsible for RMC's naming impairment is at a level of processing where modality-specific lexical forms are accessed.

Figure 2 summarizes the contrasting patterns of naming performance in oral and written output of four patients with modality-specific naming deficits.[1] There are several conclusions that follow from the empirical facts summarized in this figure.

---

[1]There are other compelling reasons for excluding a peripheral output deficit as the basis for the observed naming impairment in some of the patients with modality-specific naming def-icits. The modality-specific naming deficits in patients SJD and HW were further modulated

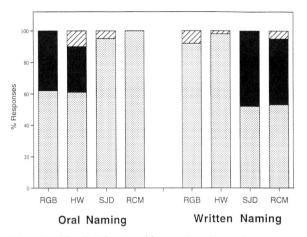

Figure 2 The distribution of four patients' correct responses (dots), semantic substitution errors (black), and other errors (striped) in spoken and written picture naming. (The four patients are reported in Caramazza & Hillis, 1990, 1991; and Hillis et al., submitted.)

One obvious conclusion is that the presence of semantic errors—even when they represent the only type of error produced by a patient—does not necessarily imply damage to the semantic system but, instead, can indicate damage at the level of modality-specific lexical representations.[2] But how can damage at the level of modality-specific lexical representations result in semantic errors? What is the nature of the relationship between semantic and modality-specific lexical representations such that damage in accessing lexical forms can result in semantic errors? One possibility is that the semantic system activates in parallel all semantically related lexical nodes in proportion to their similarity to the target response,

---

by a grammatical class effect. Thus, for example, in oral naming SJD produced the noun and verb forms of homonyms (the watch/to watch) without difficulty. However, in writing she was only able to produce correctly the noun form of the homonyms (Caramazza & Hillis, 1991; and see Hillis & Caramazza, 1995b; Rapp & Caramazza, 1997, for related cases). Such results clearly indicate that the patients' difficulties in naming are not the result of a peripheral output deficit for otherwise both forms of homonym pairs would be equally affected.

[2]In some cases the presence of semantic errors does indicate damage to the semantic system. Thus, patient KE (Hillis et al., 1990) made virtually exclusively semantic errors in all oral production tasks. However, this patient also made semantic errors in all other lexical production and comprehension tasks, as would be expected if damage were at the level of a common semantic system that is accessed in all lexical processing tasks.

and the node with the highest activation level is selected for production. For example, the semantic representation CAR activates the lexical nodes car, bus, transportation, garage, wheel, etc., but the lexical node car receives much more activation than the others and is selected for production. The crucial point here is that the cohort of lexical nodes with the highest activation levels consists of words that are semantically related to the target response. Consequently, any perturbation in the lexical access process that results in the incorrect selection of a lexical node would tend to favor the production of semantically related responses.

Another implication that follows from the modality-specific lexical deficits reviewed here is that the semantic system activates lexical orthographic nodes directly and not through lexical phonological representations. The fact that patient RGB did not produce semantic errors in written naming despite producing such errors in oral naming indicates that lexical phonological representations do not mediate access of lexical orthographic representations, for otherwise the patient should have produced semantic errors in both tasks. Similarly, the facts that patient RCM made no semantic errors in oral naming tasks but produced semantic paragraphias in written naming tasks indicates that lexical phonological representations do not mediate lexical access, for otherwise there should not have been semantic errors in the writing task.

The patterns of lexical production performance reviewed here provide a powerful set of constraints for models of lexical access and the ways in which this process is affected by brain damage. In what follows, I use the empirical phenomena of modality-specific lexical access deficits to evaluate current proposals about the organization of the lexical system and the lexical access process.

THE ORGANIZATION OF THE LEXICAL SYSTEM: MUST WE POSTULATE MODALITY-NEUTRAL LEXICAL NODES?

One of the most clearly articulated models of lexical access interposes two lexical layers between the semantic level and the segmental content of words (Levelt, Roelofs, & Meyer, 1999). The first layer (sometime referred to as the syntactic or lemma stratum) consists of modality-neutral lexical nodes or lemmas that act as pointers to syntactic nodes such as "noun," "feminine," "count," and "plural." The second layer (sometime referred to as the form stratum) consists of modality-specific lexical nodes or lexemes. Lemma nodes are activated by semantic representations. The most active lemma node is selected and it sends activation to its associated lexeme (or lexemes in the case of morphologically complex words). The lexeme, in turn, sends activation to the nodes that specify its segmental content and

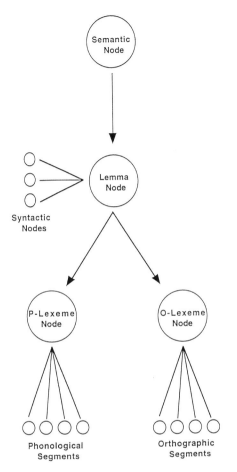

Figure 3 Schematic representation of Levelt et al.'s (1999) model of lexical access.

metric structure[3] (see Figure 3). This architecture of the lexical system is intended to capture the fact that semantic, grammatical, and phonological representations represent independent types of lexical information.

---

[3]In this model, information flows unidirectionally and discretely between stages. That is, activation flow from one layer to another only begins when a node has been selected and it flows from one layer to another and not beyond that. Thus, this model differs from models that assume cascading activation flow (e.g., Humphreys, Riddoch, & Quinlan, 1988) and those that assume interactive activation (Dell, 1986; for discussion see Peterson & Savoy, 1998).

The distinction between lemma and lexeme nodes has gained much currency in the area of language production. However, despite the repeated assertion that there are all kinds of evidence in support of this distinction, close scrutiny of the putative evidence shows that it falls far short of being able to do the work with which it is credited. There is no dispute that the evidence from slips of the tongue, the tip-of-the-tongue phenomenon, anomia, and reaction time measures in naming experiments shows that semantic, grammatical, and phonological effects are each independent from the others. However, from this simple fact we are not compelled to draw the inference that there must be two lexical layers between the semantic level and the segmental content of words. The evidence is more parsimoniously explained by models that postulate a single layer of modality-specific lexical nodes. These lexical nodes have links to their syntactic features and mediate between the semantic and the segmental properties of words [see Figure 4; and see Caramazza (1997) and Caramazza & Miozzo (1997) for detailed discussion].

Can models that assume a modality-neutral representation between the semantic level and modality-specific lexical representations account for the fact that some patients make semantic substitution errors in only one modality of output? As argued above, semantic substitution errors can result from damage to the semantic level, the connections from the semantic level to the lexical nodes, or the lexical nodes themselves. However, damage to any of these three levels in models that assume modality-neutral lexical nodes will necessarily affect phonological and orthographic lexical representations equally (see Figure 3). This is because the lemma representation mediates access to both phonological and orthographic lexemes. If semantic errors can only result from the three forms of damage described above then we would have to reject those models that postulate modality-neutral lexical nodes between the semantic level and modality-specific lexical nodes.

In order to save the lemma assumption, Roelofs, Meyer, and Levelt (1998) proposed that semantic errors could arise from damage at the level of lexeme selection. They argued as follows:

In our view, however, substitution errors need not result from failures in lemma selection but may also result from failures of mapping lemmas onto modality-specific morphemic representations. Occasionally, access to the spoken form of a word from a lemma may be impossible while access to the written form is intact, or vice versa, access to the spoken form may be intact, while access to the written form is impossible. If form access fails, the speaker's wish to communicate verbally may lead to a random selection of an alternative lemma from the semantic cohort

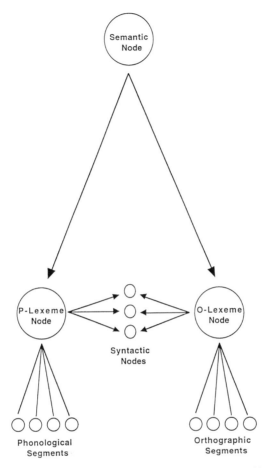

Figure 4   Schematic representation of Caramazza's (1997) model of lexical access.

established by the message concept and to subsequent access of the corresponding form (Levelt et al., 1991; Roelofs, 1992). Thus, substitution errors may differ between modalities and between trials, as empirically observed. (p. 224)

This ingenious attempt to save the lemma assumption does not work, however. Roelofs et al.'s (1998) proposal of how semantic errors might arise can be interpreted in one of two ways. One interpretation is that patients are aware of their difficulty in retrieving the intended target and adopt a strategy of producing semantically related words when they fail to retrieve the word they want to produce. The other interpretation is that the semantic errors are not the result of a "conscious" effort to fill a gap but the result of an "unconscious" repair process that blindly and mechanically completes the access process within the constraints of the available opportunities. Neither solution works.

The proposal that patients consciously produce semantic substitution errors in order to produce any response at all is inconsistent with several features of their behavior. Under this scenario it is not clear why someone with an intact semantic system would want to randomly select a semantically related word when unable to retrieve the intended target. Why would someone who is trying to produce *zebra* say "giraffe" instead? Why not produce a description of the concept whose name cannot be accessed? Or why not simply indicate failure to retrieve the target response? But leaving aside these obvious difficulties with the proposal, the behavior of patient RGB shows that he was not aware that he was making semantic errors until he heard himself produce the incorrect response. When RGB produced a semantic error he seemed surprised to hear himself make that response. Furthermore, his performance in oral reading indicates that whenever he produced semantic substitution errors he clearly was trying to produce the correct response. This is shown by the fact that when he was asked to both read aloud and define a set of words he produced the correct definition even when he made semantic substitution errors in reading a word (see above).

The more plausible version of the Roelofs et al. (1998) proposal is that the patients' production of semantic substitution errors reflects an unconscious repair of a failure to select the target response. However, it is not clear that the processing structure of the model of lexical access proposed by Levelt et al. (1999) can accommodate this proposed solution. Recall that lexical access in this model operates in several distinct stages. In stage 1, the semantic system activates a set of lemmas and selects the most active node. In stage 2, the selected node sends activation to its associated lexeme node. The node with the highest activation at this stage is selected for further processing. Roelofs et al. propose that the patients' naming failure occurs at stage 2. Presumably at this stage of the process none of the lexeme nodes is sufficiently activated for selection. If the lexical access system were to blindly try to produce a response by returning to the lemma level and selecting again a node for output, it would necessarily select the target lemma again since it is the most highly activated node. Thus, a mechanical repair process that operates at a stage that is different from the stage where the difficulty is encountered does not seem to work. It seems, then, that neither the "conscious" strategy nor the "unconscious" repair version of Roelofs et al.'s proposal is able to account for the facts of modality-specific lexical access deficits.

The evidence from modality-specific lexical deficits is highly problematic for models that postulate a lemma/lexeme distinction of the sort reviewed here. The empirical facts from aphasia are more naturally explained by assuming an organization of the lexicon in which the semantic component activates in parallel distinct lexical nodes for speech and writing (see Figure 4). The crucial feature of this organization of the lexical system is that orthographic lexical representations are activated directly by the semantic system and not through modality-neutral or phonological lexical nodes. This conclusion has implications for a more recent model of lexical access of morphologically complex words.

THE ORGANIZATION OF THE LEXICAL SYSTEM: MORPHOLOGY IN SPOKEN AND WRITTEN LANGUAGE

Marslen-Wilson, Zhou, and Ford (1996) proposed an organization of the lexical system that has the structure shown in Figure 5. The motivation for proposing this architecture stems from a set of results concerning the recognition of morphologically complex words. Using a lexical decision task, they found that the pattern of morphological priming effects obtained with auditory stimuli differed markedly from that found with visual stimuli. With auditory–auditory stimulus pairs, they found equally strong morphological priming effects for phonologically transparent pairs (e.g., friend/friendly) and phonologically opaque pairs (e.g., sane/sanity). However, with visual–visual pairs they found that the degree of orthographic/phonological transparency affected the magnitude of the priming effect: greater priming was obtained for transparent (e.g., pressure/press) than for opaque pairs (e.g., collision/collide). Table I shows an example of the contrasting patterns of priming effects reported by Marslen-Wilson et al.

Marslen-Wilson et al. (1996) argued that since the priming effect in the auditory–auditory condition was independent of the degree of phonological transparency it must mean that the two words access a common lexical node. These nodes represent the root form of words, which are underspecified for the feature dimension that varies in an allomorphic set (as in the example, sane/sanity). Furthermore, since access to this common representation was unaffected by allomorphic variation it must mean that the surface form of a word directly accesses its underlying morphologically decomposed form. However, allomorphic variation did affect performance in the visual–visual condition. Marslen-Wilson et al. interpret this result as

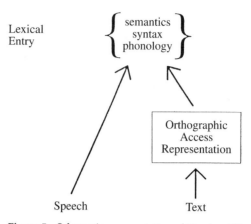

Figure 5 Schematic representation of Marslen-Wilson et al.'s (1996) model of lexical access.

demonstrating that lexical access in the visual modality is not direct but is mediated by orthographic access representations corresponding to the surface form of words.[4] Thus, there are three components to Marslen-Wilson et al.'s claim about the organization of the lexicon.

1. Lexical representations consist of triplets of semantic, syntactic, and phonological information.

2. Phonological input maps directly onto morphologically decomposed representations that specify the morphological cohort of a word. Assumptions 1 and 2 are schematically represented in Figure 6.

3. Orthographic inputs do not map directly onto central lexical representations but must go through orthographic representations of the surface forms of words (as shown in Figure 5).

Marslen-Wilson et al. (1996) claim that their model is able to account for a wide array of results concerning the recognition of morphologically complex words. Here I am not interested in evaluating the veracity of this claim. I have a narrower objective—to use the data from modality-specific lexical disorders to assess specific claims about the

---

[4]In a cross-modal, auditory–visual priming task Marslen-Wilson et al. (1996) obtained results similar to the auditory–auditory task. That is, they found equally strong morphological priming effects irrespective of variation in phonological transparency between root and derived word forms. They interpret these results as being consistent with the mediated access hypothesis. However, the logic underlying this conclusion is not transparent. Since the stimulus to which the lexical decision must be made is visual, why isn't access mediated by the orthographic form of the word?

Table I Morphological Priming Effect as a Function of the Degree of Phonological/Orthographic Transparency[a]

Stimulus	+m+p	+m–p	+m––p
Auditory–auditory	84	80	84
Visual–visual	47	27	12

[a] From Marslen-Wilson et al. (1996). Morphology, modality, and lexical architecture. In G. Booij & J. van Marle (Eds.), *Yearbook of Morphology*, with kind permission from Kluwer Academic Publishers. +m+p, morphologically and phonologically transparent pairs, e.g., "friendly"/"friend." +m–p, morphologically related and phonologically opaque, e.g., "elusive"/"elude." +m––p, morphologically related and phonologically opaque, where the phonological change involves the first vowel, e.g., "sanity"/"sane."

role of modality in lexical representation and access. And from this perspective it is immediately apparent that a core assumption of the model is false. The model's assumption that access to written words involves phonological mediation is inconsistent with the data and arguments from modality-specific lexical deficits. The data from modality-specific lexical deficits unambiguously show that orthographic lexical forms are accessed directly from semantic representations and not through phonological lexical nodes. Thus, any theory that assumes phonological mediation in orthographic lexical access cannot be correct.

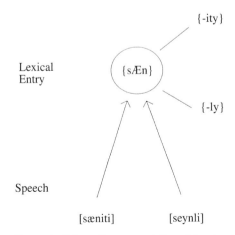

Figure 6 Schematic representation of the structure of lexical entries in Marslen-Wilson et al.'s (1996) model of lexical access.

It could be argued that the model of lexical organization proposed by Marslen-Wilson et al. (1996) concerns only word recognition and not production, and that the modality-specific lexical deficits reviewed here concern only word production. Thus, the data disconfirm a production version of the lexical access model proposed by Marslen-Wilson but not the original recognition version. This is a fair argument, but one would then be forced to conclude that there are radically different lexical architectures for word recognition and production. That is, we would have to conclude that the word recognition process has the structure shown in Figure 5 while the word production process is organized as in Figure 4. There is no independent support for such an inelegant solution to the challenge from modality-specific deficits. And, in any case, there are various results from aphasia that challenge the phonological mediation assumption in word recognition (e.g., Hanley & McDonnell, 1997; Shelton & Weinrich, 1997). There are also results from modality-specific word recognition deficits that undermine the phonological mediation assumption in the Marslen-Wilson et al. model.

Hillis and Caramazza (1995b) report the performance of a patient, EBA, who performed essentially flawlessly in all auditory word recognition and comprehension tasks. However, EBA was severely impaired in recognizing and comprehending verbs but not nouns (see Table II). If orthographic lexical access in recognition were to be phonologically mediated we would not expect a grammatical class effect restricted to one modality of input. Failure to access phonological lexical nodes would result in deficits for both written and spoken inputs. A deficit at the level of orthographic access representations would be expected to affect words of all grammatical classes equally since at this level of representation grammatical class is not specified (see Figure 5). In short, the empirical facts derived from modality-specific lexical deficits severely undermine the model of lexical access proposed by Marslen-Wilson et al. (1996).

Table II   EBA's Written and Spoken Word Comprehension Performance in a Picture–Word Verification Task[a]

	Performance (% correct) for word class	
Form of input	Noun	Verb
Aural	100	100
Visual	98	43

[a]From Hillis and Caramazza (1995). Representation of grammatical categories of words in the brain. *J. Cog. Neurosci.* 7 (3), 396–407. © 1995 by the Massachusetts Institute of Technology.

EVALUATING COMPUTATIONAL MODELS
OF LEXICAL ACCESS IN APHASIA

In the preceding sections I have shown that the lexical processing performance of brain damaged patients can be used to assess the adequacy of specific assumptions in models of normal lexical access. Dell, Schwartz, Martin, Saffran, and Gagnon (1997) have similarly argued that the analysis of naming errors produced by fluent aphasics can be used to test their computational model of lexical access. The model is a variant of a more general theory of lexical processing proposed by Dell (1986). It postulates three kinds of structures: nodes, links, and layers. Nodes are organized into three layers—semantic, lexical, and phonological—and they are linked to certain other nodes in other layers. Semantic nodes are linked to lexical nodes and lexical nodes are linked to phonological nodes[5] (see Figure 7). All links are bidirectional, thereby allowing both forward and backward activation. Activation from the semantic layer spreads forward to the lexical layer and then to the phonological layer, but because links are bidirectional activation also flows back from the lexical layer to the semantic layer and from the segmental layer to the lexical layer. Thus unlike models in which each layer passes activation (either discretely or in cascading form) to the next layer downstream, in the Dell model each layer is constantly interacting with adjacent layers (both downstream and upstream).

Dell and collaborators have used variants of the general model to account for a wide variety of speech production phenomena in normal speakers (Dell, 1986, 1988, 1990; Dell, Juliano, & Govindjee, 1993; Dell & O'Seaghda, 1991; Martin, Weisberg, & Saffran, 1989). More recently they extended the reach of the model to disorders of lexical access. They attempted to simulate the pattern of errors produced by fluent aphasic patients in a simple picture-naming task. They considered the following five error types: semantic, phonological, mixed (both semantically and phonologically related) and unrelated word substitutions, and neologisms. They reasoned that success in reproducing the error profiles observed in aphasic patients would constitute support for the core assumptions of the model used to reproduce the error patterns. And since the model consists of assumptions about the structure of the normal lexical access process and assumptions about the ways in which the process is altered by brain

---

[5]Note that this architecture of the lexical access process is similar to the model proposed by Caramazza (1997) and differs from the model proposed by Levelt et al. (1999). As pointed out above, Levelt et al.'s model postulates two lexical nodes intervening between semantic and segmental layers.

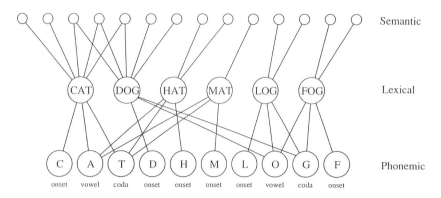

Figure 7   Schematic representation of Dell et al.'s (1997) model of lexical access.

damage, the success of the model in simulating patient performance would extend support to both sets of assumptions.

Dell et al. (1997) are especially interested in two assumptions: the *interactivity* and the *globality* assumptions. We have seen that the interactivity assumption is a fundamental component of the processing structure of Dell et al.'s model of normal lexical access. The *globality* assumption is the claim that the different patterns of naming errors produced by fluent aphasics can be explained by the assumption that brain damage affects all levels of lexical processing equally. This assumption is represented in the model by changing the value of the *decay* and the *connection strength* parameters at all levels of the network. The decay parameter affects the maintenance of activation and the connection strength parameter affects the flow of activation in the network. By varying the values of these two parameters, the distribution of errors produced by the model changes. Thus, the task becomes one of trying to determine whether there are values of these parameters such that the resulting distribution of errors matches the error profile of a given patient.

Dell et al. (1997) tested their model against the performance of 21 fluent aphasics and claimed that the model is able to fit these patients' profiles of naming errors. On the basis of these results they concluded as follows:

The good fit between the patient data and the model suggests [the following] conclusions. . . . [I]t extends support for the interactive two-step approach to naming. A model that successfully characterized normal performance could be applied to the range of performance that fluent aphasic individuals exhibit. Although only a restricted set of error patterns are (sic) allowed by the model, the patient's patterns appeared to fall within that set. [And] the fit supports the hypothesis that variation in patient error patterns can be associated with global lesions in activation transmission, representational integrity, or both. (p. 820)

We can evaluate these claims at three levels. We can ask whether the fits of the model to the patient data are as good as claimed. We can ask whether even if the fits of the model to the data were as good as claimed, they would compel us to accept the conclusions reached by Dell et al. (1997). And we can ask whether there are data other than those used by Dell et al. which undermine the model (see Ruml & Caramazza, in press, for detailed discussion).

HOW GOOD A FIT?

Dell et al. (1997) did not provide a direct measure of how well the model performed in fitting the patient data. Rather they interpreted the quality of their fits to patient data by comparing them to the fit of their model to ten sets of six random numbers. However, this comparison does not tell us how well the model does in fitting the patient data but how much worse it does at fitting the sets of random numbers. It is possible that both fits are poor.

Wheeler Ruml working in my laboratory has been able to show that the conclusions reached by Dell et al. (1997) are not empirically justified. He has shown by chi-square tests that 9 of 21 patients are fit very poorly by the model ($p < .01$). More importantly, he carried out an exhaustive investigation of the space of possible error patterns that could be generated by changing the *decay* and *connection strength* parameters in the model. The results show that a majority of the patients tested by Dell et al. produce error profiles that fall outside the range generated by the model. Figures 8, 9, and 10 show the relation between different error types that can be obtained using the Dell et al. two-parameter representation (dots) and the actual patient performance (circles). It is immediately apparent that the fits of the model to the patient data are poor. For example, the model cannot represent patients who make many semantic errors but few phonological errors or who make many phonological errors and few semantic errors (Figure 8). Similarly, the model cannot account for patients who make many mixed errors but few unrelated word errors (Figure 9) or few semantic errors and a moderate number of neologisms (Figure 10).

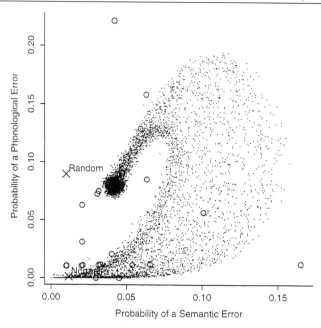

Figure 8   The relations between semantic errors and phonological errors that are obtained using Dell et al.'s (1997) two-parameter representation. Patients are plotted as circles.

AND IF THE FITS HAD BEEN GOOD?

But what if the fits had been good? Would we have been compelled to accept Dell et al.'s (1997) conclusion that the ability of the model to fit patient data provides support *specifically* for the *interactivity* and *globality* assumptions? Not necessarily. Consider the case where the model fails to fit the data. Could we use this result to reject the two assumptions in question? It should be immediately obvious that the only conclusion we can reach is that the model as a *whole* fails. The results do not allow a more specific attribution of blame. The model could have failed because the *interactivity* assumption is false, the *globality* assumption is false, both are false, or because some other assumption(s) in the implemented model is (are) false. But if we cannot conclude that the model's failure would have allowed the rejection of a specific assumption within the model, can one claim that empirical success would have provided support for this assumption? Here, too, the answer must be that the results would only have allowed the conclusion that the model as a *whole* is consistent with the

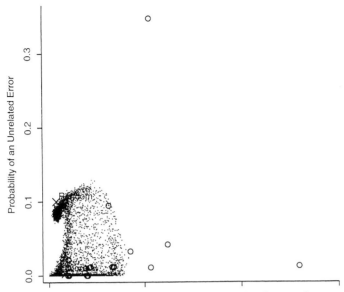

Figure 9 The relations between mixed and unrelated errors that are obtained using Dell et al.'s (1997) two-parameter representation. Patients are plotted as circles.

data but we do not know whether any one of the specific assumptions of interest is necessary to the success of the model.

To reach more specific conclusions one would have had to have systematically manipulated the assumptions of interest and shown that it is precisely those assumptions that guarantee the empirical success of the model. This was not done in Dell et al.'s (1997) paper and therefore the only secure conclusions would have concerned the model as a whole and not any specific assumption, including the *interactivity* and *globality* assumptions.[6] In order to conclude that the simulation results support the *globality* assumption, for example, Dell et al. would have had to shown that failure to implement the assumption (e.g., by testing different parameter values for different layers of the model) would have resulted in poorer fits to the data. This manipulation was not carried out and, therefore, no strong inference can be made about the *globality* assumption.

[6]Of course, in attributing credit or blame to the various aspects of a model we are not limited to considering only the data from a specific project. We can rely on other results in the field to help us decide which of the various assumptions are likely to be the ones carrying the burden in the work under consideration.

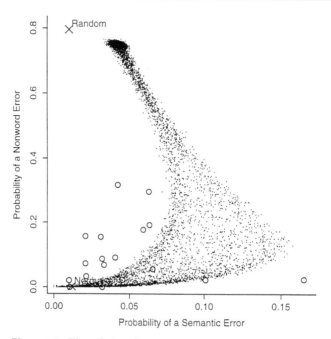

Figure 10   The relations between semantic errors and nonword errors that are obtained using Dell et al.'s (1997) two-parameter representation. Patients are plotted as circles.

Thus, Dell et al.'s claim that the putative success of their model to fit the patient data would have extended support to the *interactivity* and the *globality* assumptions in naming deficits would be unjustified even if the fits had not been as poor as has been demonstrated.

THE GLOBALITY ASSUMPTION AND THE DATA FROM MODALITY-SPECIFIC LEXICAL DEFICITS

However there are strong empirical reasons for rejecting the *globality* assumption. This assumption would be shown to be false if there exist (fluent) aphasic patients whose naming deficit result from damage to just one level of the lexical access process. Such patients exist. They are the patients with modality-specific naming deficits—such as the ones described above. These patients make exclusively (or disproportionately) semantic errors in only one modality of output. I have shown that their

semantic errors must arise from damage at some level other than the semantic system. This is because they do not make semantic errors in one
modality of output and can comprehend words normally. I have further
argued that the damage in these patients must be at the level where lexical nodes are activated/selected since their errors consist only of lexical
substitutions. Thus, there is independent evidence that the globality assumption is false: there are fluent aphasics whose naming deficit is
demonstrably due to a nonglobal lesion to the lexical access system.

It should be noted that these patients' error profiles—almost exclusively
semantic paraphasias (or paragraphias)—fall outside the range of error patterns that could be generated by the two-parameter changes in Dell et al.'s
(1997) model (see, e.g., Figure 8). Don't they, then, provide a further reason
for rejecting the globality assumption. Not necessarily. As I argued above,
the failure of the model to fit any particular error profile need not indicate
failure of the specific assumption of interest to us. That is, the reason the
model might fail to account for RGB's pattern of errors, for example, may
have nothing to do with the veracity of the globality assumption. This assumption could be true and the reason for the model's failure to fit the data
might be because of some other incorrect assumption in the model. Thus,
no strong inference is possible from patient data on a single task, no matter
how sophisticated the computational model that exploits it.

There is a methodological moral that follows from this analysis of the
kinds of inferences that we can legitimately draw from the success or failure of Dell et al.'s (1997) model to simulate error profiles. The analysis
illustrates a fundamental weakness in research that focuses on performance on a single task across different patients. These studies do not provide the sorts of data that could be used to unambiguously establish
which of the various mechanisms in a complex process might be damaged. For the latter purpose we must turn to the methods of cognitive
neuropsychology. This approach relies on the convergence of performance on various tasks and the detailed analysis of error performance
across tasks in order to infer a possible locus of damage to a cognitive
system. By focusing on the single task of oral naming, Dell et al. excluded
from consideration just the performance that would have shown that
their globality assumption is false.

CONCLUSION

In this chapter I have used a specific phenomenon from the performance of brain-damaged patients to shed light on several issues of current interest in lexical processing. Brain damage can result in a language

production (or comprehension) deficit restricted to one modality of output. The discreteness of the deficit immediately sets precise constraints on the possible forms of the organization of the lexical system. One inescapable implication is that orthographic lexical access is not mediated by access to lexical phonological representations. This evidence undermines the model of lexical access of morphologically complex words proposed by Marslen-Wilson et al. (1996). Another implication follows from the fact that patients with such deficits produce semantic substitution errors in only one modality of output. This fact is inconsistent with models that interpose a modality-neutral lexical node between the semantic component and modality-specific lexical nodes (e.g., the model proposed by Levelt et al., 1999). And finally, since modality-specific naming deficits unambiguously allow the inference that the semantic system in these patients is intact, we can conclusively reject the claim that the naming profiles of fluent aphasics result from global lesions that equally affect all levels of the lexical system (Dell et al., 1997).

ACKNOWLEDGMENTS

The work reported here was supported in part in NIH Grant NS22201. I thank my colleagues Argye Hillis, Michele Miozzo, Brenda Rapp, and Wheeler Ruml for sharing with me their insights on matters of lexical access. A version of this chapter was presented at the Seventeenth European Workshop on Cognitive Neuropsychology, Bressanone, Italy, 24–29 January 1999.

REFERENCES

Basso, A., Taborelli, A., & Vignolo, L. A. (1978). Dissociated disorders of speaking and writing in aphasia. *Journal of Neurology, Neurosurgery and Psychiatry, 41*, 556–563.
Bub, D., & Kertesz, A. (1982). Evidence for lexicographic processing in a patient with preserved written over oral single word naming. *Brain, 105*, 697–717.
Caramazza, A. (1997). How many levels of processing are there in lexical access? *Cognitive Neuropsychology, 14*, 177–208.
Caramazza, A. (1998). The interpretation of semantic category-specific deficits: What do they reveal about the organization of conceptual knowledge in the brain? *Neurocase, 4*, 265–272.
Caramazza, A., & Hillis, A. E. (1990). Where do semantic errors come from? *Cortex, 26*, 95–122.
Caramazza, A., & Hillis, A. E. (1991). Lexical organization of nouns and verbs in the brain. *Nature (London), 349*, 788–790.
Caramazza, A., & Miozzo, M. (1997). The relation between syntactic and phonological knowledge in lexical access: Evidence from the "tip-of-the-tongue" phenomenon. *Cognition, 64*, 309–343.

Damasio, A. R., & Tranel, D. (1993). Nouns and verbs are retrieved with differently distributed neural systems. *Proceedings of the National Academy of Sciences of the United States of America, 90,* 4857–4960.

Dell, G. S. (1986). A spreading-activation theory of retrieval in sentence production. *Psychological Review, 93,* 283–321.

Dell, G. S. (1988). The retrieval of phonological forms in production: Tests of predictions from a connectionist model. *Journal of Memory and Language, 27,* 124–142.

Dell, G. S. (1990). Effects of frequency and vocabulary type on phonological speech errors. *Language and Cognitive Processes, 4,* 313–349.

Dell, G. S., & O'Seaghda, P. G. (1991). Mediated and convergent lexical priming in language production: A comment on Levelt et al. (1991). *Psychological Review, 98,* 604–614.

Dell, G. S., Juliano, C., & Govindjee, A. (1993). Structure and content in language production. A theory of frame constraints in phonological speech errors. *Cognitive Science, 17,* 149–195.

Dell, G., Schwartz, M. F., Martin, N., Saffran, E. M., & Gagnon, D. A. (1997). Lexical access in aphasic and nonaphasic speakers. *Psychological Review, 104,* 801–838.

De Renzi, E., & di Pellegrino, G. (1995). Sparing of verbs and preserved but ineffectual reading in patient with impaired word production. *Cortex, 31,* 619–636.

Friederici, A. D., Schoenle, P. W., & Goodglass, H. (1981). Mechanisms underlying writing and speech in aphasia. *Brain and Language, 13,* 212–222.

Friedman, R. B., & Alexander, M. P. (1984). Pictures, images, and pure alexia: A case study. *Cognitive Neuropsychology, 1,* 9–23.

Hanley, J. R., & McDonnell, V. (1997). Are reading and spelling phonologically mediated? Evidence from a patient with a speech production impairment. *Cognitive Neuropsychology, 14,* 3–33.

Hier, D. B., & Mohr, J. P. (1977). Incongruous oral and written naming. *Brain and Language, 4,* 115–126.

Hillis, A. E., & Caramazza, A. (1995a). Cognitive and neural mechanisms underlying visual and semantic processing: Implications from "optic aphasia." *Journal of Cognitive Neuroscience, 7,* 457–478.

Hillis, A. E., & Caramazza, A. (1995b). Representation of grammatical categories of words in the brain. *Journal of Cognitive Neuroscience, 7,* 396–407.

Hillis, A. E., Rapp, B., & Caramazza, A. (1999). When a rose is a rose in speech but a tulip in writing. *Cortex, 35,* 337–356.

Hillis, A. E., Rapp, B., Romani, C., & Caramazza, A. (1990). Selective impairments of semantics in lexical processing. *Cognitive Neuropsychology, 7,* 191–243.

Hodges, J. R., Patterson, K., Oxbury, S., & Funnell, E. (1992). Semantic dementia: Progressive fluent aphasia with temporal lobe atrophy. *Brain, 115,* 1783–1806.

Humphreys, G. W., Riddoch, M. J., & Quinlan, P. T. (1988). Cascade processes in picture identification. *Cognitive Neuropsychology, 5,* 67–103.

Levelt, W. J. M., Roelofs, A., & Meyer, A. S. (1999). A theory of lexical access in speech production. *Behavioral and Brain Sciences, 22,* 1–75.

Kay, J., & Ellis, A. W. (1987). A cognitive neuropsychological case study of anomia: Implications for psychological models of word retrieval. *Brain, 110,* 613–629.

Kohn, S., & Friedman, R. (1986). Word-meaning deafness: A phonological-semantic dissociation. *Cognitive Neuropsychology, 3,* 291–308.

Levelt, W. J. M., Schriefers, H., Vorberg, D., Meyer, A. S., Pechmann, T., & Havinga, J. (1991). The time course of lexical access in speech production: A study of picture naming. *Psychological Review, 98,* 122–142.

Lhermitte, F., & Beauvois, M.-F. (1973). A visual-speech disconnection syndrome: Report of a case with optic-aphasia, agnosic alexia and colour agnosia. *Brain, 96,* 695–714.

Alfonso Caramazza

Mackay, D. G. (1987). *The organization of perception and action. A thoery for language and other cognitive skills.* New York: Springer-Velag.

Marslen-Wilson, W., Zhou, X., & Ford, M. (1996). Morphology, modality, and lexical architecture. In G. Booij & J. van Marle (Eds.), *Yearbook of morphology, 1996* (pp. 117–134). Dordrecht: Kluwer.

Martin, N., Weisberg, R. W., & Saffran, E. M. (1989). Variables influencing the occurrence of naming errors: Implications for models of lexical retrieval. *Journal of Memory and Language, 28,* 462–485.

McCarthy, R., & Warrington, E. W. (1985). Category-specificity in an agrammatic patient: The relative impairment of verb retrieval and comprehension. *Neuropsychologia, 23,* 709–727.

Miceli, G., Silveri, M. C., Villa, G., & Caramazza, A. (1984). On the basis for the agrammatic's difficulty in producing main verbs. *Cortex, 20,* 207–220.

Patterson, K., & Shewell, C. (1987). Speak and spell: Dissociation and word-class effects. In M. Coltheart, G. Sartori, & R. Job (Eds.), *The cognitive neuropsychology of language* (pp. 273–294). London: Erlbaum.

Peterson, R. R., & Savoy, P. (1998). Lexical selection and phonological encoding during language production: Evidence for cascaded processing. *Journal of Experimental Psychology: Learning, Memory, and Cognition, 24,* 539–557.

Rapp, B., & Caramazza, A. (1997). The modality-specific organization of grammatical categories: Evidence from impaired spoken and written production. *Brain and Language, 56,* 248–286.

Roelofs, A. (1992). A spreading-activation theory of lemma retrieval in speaking. *Cognition, 42,* 107–142.

Roelofs, A., Meyer, A. S., & Levelt, W. J. M. (1998). A case for the lemma/lexeme distinction in models of speaking: Comment on Caramazza and Miozzo (1997). *Cognition 69,* 219–230.

Ruml, W., & Caramazza, A. (2000). An evaluation of a computational model of lexical access. Comments on Dell et al. (1997). *Psychological Review,* in press.

Shelton, J. R., & Weinrich, M. (1997). Further evidence of a dissociation between output phonological and orthographic lexicons: A case study. *Cognitive Neuropsychology, 14,* 105–129.

Stemberger, J. P. (1985). An interactive activation model of language production. In A. W. Ellis (Ed.), *Progress in the psychology of language* (Vol. 1, pp. 143–186). Hillsdale, NJ: Erlbaum.

Zingeser, L. B., & Berndt, R. S. (1988). Retrieval of nouns and verbs in agrammatism and anomia. *Brain and Language, 39,* 14–32.

Chapter 12

Using the Recording of Event-Related Brain Potentials in the Study of Sentence Processing

Enriqueta Canseco-Gonzalez

INTRODUCTION

Communication is essential to humans. We communicate our emotions, thoughts, and intentions through several types of nonverbal mechanisms like facial expressions, gestures, body language, signals, etc. However, it is through oral or written verbal communication that we manage to transcend the limits of time and space. In the absence of any neurological deficit, every child acquires language in her first years and continues to use it productively all through her life.

It is due to the generality of this phenomenon and its apparent simplicity, that we tend to take language for granted. However, as soon as we try to explain the processes by which we are able to acquire language in such a short period of time, or to explain how it is possible for one to read and understand these lines in such an effective and rapid manner, we find ourselves discovering that language is a symbolic system with a very complex structure. Consequently, we are required to carry out very demanding and rapid computational processes in order to produce and understand language in real time. This complexity becomes evident with the apparent current failure of technology to develop "speaking and listening" machines capable of carrying out even the simplest linguistic interactions.

Furthermore, language is a complex system formed by various types of information. Linguists have proposed that the well-formedness of a sentence is determined by constraints applied at various levels of representation (e.g., phonological, syntactic, semantic, etc.; Chomsky, 1981). These levels have been proposed based on the analysis of linguistic intuitions obtained from native speakers of a language. While the existence of these levels is widely accepted as a formal description of a language, it is unclear whether they are equally honored by the processing system. If they do, language comprehension may require a rapid and effective computation and combination of information provided at each of these levels.

There are two main positions in this regard. One group of researchers proposes a direct relation between the representational levels formulated by linguistic theory, and those involved during on-line comprehension processing (Clifton & Frazier, 1989; Fodor, 1978; Ford, Bresnan, & Kaplan, 1982). According to this position, distinct levels of mental representation are built on-line corresponding to each of the formal levels defined by linguistic theory. A second group of researchers proposes, for example, that the semantic interpretation of a sentence is constructed directly from the input, without the need for a syntactic representation (Elman, 1990; MacWhinney, Bates, & Kliegel, 1984).

Several attempts have been made to determine the characteristics of the language processing system through various methods and techniques (Ferreira & Clifton, 1986; Swinney, Zurif, Prather, & Love, 1996; Hickok, Canseco-Gonzalez, Zurif, & Grimshaw, 1992). One of these methods is the recording of event-related brain potentials (ERPs), which is the brain electrical activity time-locked to some external event. Usually the electrical changes associated with a specific event are of a considerably smaller amplitude in relation to the continuous background brain electrical activity (EEG). Therefore, a common strategy is to obtain the average of a large number of ERPs elicited by a specific type of event, with the intention of reducing the random background brain activity and enhancing the specific brain response time-locked to the event of interest. In general terms, the smaller the brain response to a specific event, the larger the number of times you need to present such event. This is known as increasing the signal-to-noise ratio.

In regard to the study of language, the use of the ERP technique rests on the assumption that different cognitive processes are mediated by differential patterns of brain activity. It is possible then to investigate separate linguistic representational levels as evidenced by distinct ERP patterns. In general these patterns are identified based on their functional identity, amplitude, latency, and distribution. Since the pioneering work of Kutas and Hillyard in the 1980s, a fruitful approach in the study of language has been the recording of brain electrical activity associated with

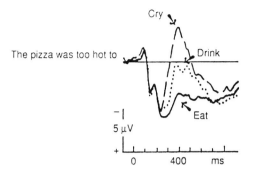

Figure 1 ERPs elicited by sentence-final words at a midline central site, showing the positivity (solid line) for a predictable word, N400 elicited by an incongruous word (dashed line). When the final word is semantically incongruent but related to the expected final word (dotted line), it elicits a smaller N400 than an unrelated incongruity. Sample endings are for illustrative purposes only, since the same sentence frames were never repeated in this experiment. Figure from Kutas and Van Petten (1994).

the detection and processing of a variety of linguistic "errors," intended to demand processing at various linguistic representational levels.[1] In the next section I briefly review the studies that have associated certain specific brain activity with semantic processing.

EVENT-RELATED BRAIN POTENTIALS AND SEMANTIC PROCESSING

The N400 component has been identified as a brain response associated with semantic processing. Kutas and Hillyard (1980) first observed that a negative component peaking at about 400 ms poststimulus was elicited by words violating semantic expectations (e.g., "The pizza was too hot to *cry*") (Figure 1).

---

[1]Unless specifically noted, in the rest of this chapter I will use the following conventions: (a) An asterisk on the left of words or sentences indicates an anomaly of various types. (b) The critical word, where we expect the ERP effects to appear, will be in italics. This may be the word which determines the point when a sentence becomes anomalous, where a garden path effect is triggered, at the word that resolves ambiguity in a sentence, etc., and the corresponding control words. (c) When the original material is in a language other than English, I will use the English gloss unless specifically noted.

Since then, it has been observed that most words elicit an N400 varying in amplitude and latency depending on several factors. In one extreme, a semantically anomalous open-class word produces the largest N400. On the other extreme, a wholly predictable word elicits a positive-going wave instead. Between these two extremes there is a whole range of N400 amplitudes determined by a number of factors such as word position in a sentence, first or repeated presentation of the word, mode of presentation (words in a list, in word pairs, or inside of sentences), etc. Therefore, rather than being elicited specifically by semantic anomalies, the N400 component is inversely related to the semantic expectation of a given word in relation to its context. It has been found in the auditory as well as in the visual modality and in several languages, including signed languages. The N400 effect is broadly distributed but is larger in posterior than in anterior sites, and larger in the right than in the left hemisphere (Kutas & Van Petten, 1988, 1994). It has also been proposed that the N400 is a language specific effect (but see Deacon, Breton, Ritter, & Vaughan, 1991, for the proposal that N400 is a longer-latency N2, a more general component independent of modality).

Although the N400 component has been used as the prototypical "semantic" ERP component, other types of semantic violations, such as negative polarity (e.g., *"Tina liked the movie at all") and hyponymy (e.g., *"Susie never eats dessert, so after dinner she always likes to have some cake") elicit ERP components different from the N400 (Shao & Neville, 1996). Based on their results, Shao and Neville conclude that the N400 is specifically associated with pragmatic violations and emphasize the dangers of using the N400 component as a general marker of semantic processing.

In what follows I focus on ERP studies of syntactic processing. I first describe the two main components associated with this level. I then present and discuss some of the conflicting interpretations of these components, providing evidence in favor and against each of them. I conclude by presenting a new line of research in the study of language processing that makes use of the recording of slow sentence-long potentials.

EVENT-RELATED BRAIN POTENTIALS
AND GRAMMATICAL PROCESSING

Two separate ERP components have been associated with syntactic processing. First, a left anterior negativity has been elicited by syntactic (e.g., phrase structure, subcategorization) and morphosyntactic (e.g., subject–verb agreement, pronoun case, and verb number) violations. This component has an anterior distribution, starting as early as 250 ms, and a larger amplitude in the left hemisphere. It has been elicited by visual and auditory stimuli, and it has been observed with word-pairs as well as with sentences (Neville, Nicol, Barss, Forster, & Garrett, 1991; Osterhout & Holcomb, 1992; Rosler, Friederici, Putz, & Hahne, 1993; Friederici, Pfeifer, & Hahne, 1993; Canseco-Gonzalez et al., 1997; Coulson, King, & Kutas, 1998; Münte, Matzke, & Johannes, 1997).

The second component associated with syntactic violations is a large positive wave termed P600 (Osterhout & Holcomb, 1992), or "syntactic positive shift" (SPS) (Hagoort, Brown, & Groothusen, 1993). It has been elicited by phrase structure, subcategorization, subject–verb agreement, and different kinds of pronoun–antecedent agreement violations. This component has a centroparietal distribution starting around 500 ms and lasting for several hundred milliseconds.

Interestingly, both types of effects, the late positivity and the anterior negativity can be produced by a single violation type (Neville et al., 1991; Osterhout & Holcomb, 1992, Coulson et al., 1998). Although it is clear that these two "syntax-related" components are different from the "semantics-related" N400 component in timing, scalp distribution, and eliciting stimuli, their specific contribution to syntactic processing and their possible interaction are still under investigation. In what follows I present and discuss the eliciting conditions and factors affecting each of these two components.

Anterior Negativity

In one of the first studies comparing semantic and syntactic violations, Kutas and Hillyard (1983) reported a left anterior negativity elicited by morphosyntactic violations embedded in sentences (e.g., *"Turtles will spit out things they *does* not like to eat"). Since then, several other studies have reported a negativity appearing in anterior areas of the scalp associated with various types of syntactic violations. However, there seems to be a difference in distribution and latency depending on the specific nature of the stimuli.

For example, Münte, Heinze, and Mangun (1993) found a frontal negativity elicited by the second word of a syntactic "mismatching" word–pair (e.g., *your–*write*, *you–*administration*). This negativity was maximum at 500–550 ms and at frontopolar sites, and different from an N400 elicited by "semantic" violations[2] (Figure 2).

---

[2]Their semantic anomalies were word–pairs containing two unrelated words in contrast with synonym pairs (e.g., *"Parliament–cube" vs. "gangster–robber").

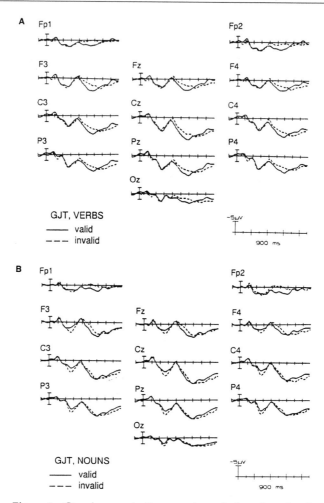

Figure 2   Grand means to the second words for selected scalp
sites from the syntactic (grammaticality) judgment. Both verbs (A)
and nouns (B) preceded by incongruent primes are associated with
a more negative ERP in the 300- to 600-ms range (dashed line). This
effect is largest for anterior scalp sites. GJT, Grammaticality judgment task. Figure from Münte et al. (1993). *J. Cog. Neurosci.* © 1993
by the Massachusetts Institute of Technology.

Several other studies have replicated the observation of a broad anterior negativity associated with grammatical violations in word–pairs
(Münte & Heinze, 1994), as well as embedded in sentences (Friederici et
al., 1993) or in pseudoword sentences (Münte at al., 1997).

However, in response to various syntactic violations, an increasing number of ERP studies (Friederici et al., 1993; Rosler et al., 1993) have observed an early negativity in anterior areas of the brain that is clearly lateralized to the left hemisphere (left anterior negativity, or LAN). Furthermore, various researchers have found a biphasic ERP response, in the form of a left anterior negativity followed by a late centroparietal positivity, correlated with syntactic anomalies (Canseco-Gonzalez et al., 1997; Coulson et al., 1998; Kutas & Hillyard, 1983; Neville et al., 1991; Osterhout & Holcomb, 1992) (Figure 3).

Although the late positivity has received more attention in the literature, its specific role in syntactic processing has been questioned (see below).

In contrast, the left anterior negativity has been proposed as a component specifically associated with syntactic processing by several groups (but see below and Kluender & Kutas, 1993). The range of syntactic violations eliciting LAN is wide. It has been observed with word-category errors, and in violations of phrase structure, verb agreement, and verb subcategorization. It has also been suggested that some of the observed latency differences in LAN may be related to the particular modality and to the specific type of violation involved (Friederici & Mecklinger, 1996). Furthermore, LAN has been observed in association with syntactic anomalies contained in pseudowords sentences void of semantic information (Canseco-Gonzalez et al., 1997; Münte et al., 1997, but see Hagoort & Brown, 1994), and in grammatically anomalous word-pairs (Münte et al., 1993).

Nevertheless, the interpretation of LAN as a pure reflection of syntactic processing is questioned in an ERP study of filler-gap constructions (Kluender & Kutas, 1993). In these constructions a constituent of the sentence ("filler") moves to the front of the sentence leaving a "gap." For example, in the sentence, "Who did John hit____?," linguistic theory proposes that the word *who* starts out in its original direct object position following the verb (indicated by a ____ in our example) and then moves to the front of the sentence in the process of question formation leaving a gap after the verb. Nevertheless, we have no problem interpreting such filler as the direct object of the verb *hit*. When we hear or read a sentence like this, we must keep the filler in working memory until we find its corresponding gap and we are able to interpret the sentence. Kluender and Kutas investigated several filler-gap constructions and found a LAN associated with the storage of a filler in working memory and their subsequent retrieval on gap detection. More importantly, this effect was independent of grammaticality. Therefore, Kluender and Kutas propose that studies that have found a LAN in response to grammatical violations, may be reinterpreted as reflecting working memory load demands. However, at this time it is difficult to find a unifying working memory account for all the studies that have

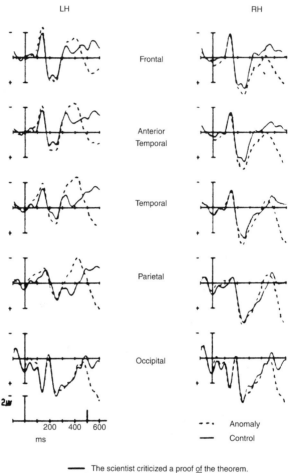

LH   RH

Frontal

Anterior
Temporal

Temporal

Parietal

Occipital

200   400   600   - - - Anomaly
ms   ——   Control

—— The scientist criticized a proof of the theorem.
- - - The scientist criticized Max's of proof the theorem.

Figure 3   ERPs averaged across 40 subjects from over several
homologous sites over the left (LH) and right (RH) hemispheres.
Responses in dashed lines were elicited by words (underlined) that
rendered the sentence grammatically deviant. ERPs in solid lines
were elicited by comparison words in grammatically acceptable sentences. Note that at 500 ms (darkened on time base) another word
was presented. Figure adapted from Neville et al. (1991). *J. Cog. Neurosci.* © 1991 by the Massachusetts Institute of Technology.

reported a LAN in response to syntactic violations. Further studies will be
needed to clarify the distinctiveness of these two apparent separate LAN

effects. We may in fact be observing the same underlying mechanism manifested in different constructions.

P600 or Syntactic Positive Shift

As we mentioned above, several studies have also reported the elicitation of a large late positivity termed P600 or SPS associated with a large number of syntactic violations (Osterhout & Holcomb, 1992; Hagoort, Brown, & Groothusen, 1993). For example, Osterhout and Mobley (1995) found a late positivity associated with subject–verb number violations and with reflexive–antecedent gender and number disagreements (Figure 4).

Subject–verb
The elected officials hope/*hopes to succeed.

Reflexive–antecedent (number)
The hungry guests helped *themselves/*himself* to the food.

Reflexive–antecedent (gender)
The successful woman congratulated *herself/*himself* on the promotion.

The P600 component is elicited not only by syntactic violations but also by syntactically disambiguating words that go against a favored syntactic analysis[3] (see below) (Osterhout, Holcomb, & Swinney, 1994; Mecklinger, Schriefers, Steinhauer, & Friederici, 1995). This suggests that, rather than being an index of the detection of an outright violation, the P600 is a reflection of the perceived syntactic well-formedness of a sentence.

However, more recent studies have questioned the linguistic specificity of P600 or its particular role in grammatical processing. Among other hypotheses, it has been suggested that this late positivity might be part of the P300 family elicited by several linguistic and nonlinguistic events (Coulson et al., 1998). It has also been suggested that the P600 is correlated with a second-pass parsing process (Friederici & Mecklinger, 1996; Friederici, Hahne, & Mecklinger, 1996) or that it is the reflection of a recomputation routine in an attempt to rescue the meaning of a sentence after encountering a grammatical violation (Münte et al., 1997; Canseco-Gonzalez et al., 1997). Different approaches have been used to investigate these possibilities. In what follows I present and discuss some of the evidence in favor and against each of these proposals.

---

[3]This is known as the garden path phenomenon. In constructions containing temporary syntactic ambiguities, the reader/listener typically follows a preferred syntactic analysis until she encounters a disambiguating word. This word makes evident that the nonpreferred analysis is appropriate, forcing a reinterpretation of the sentence (e.g., "The judge believed the defendant was lying").

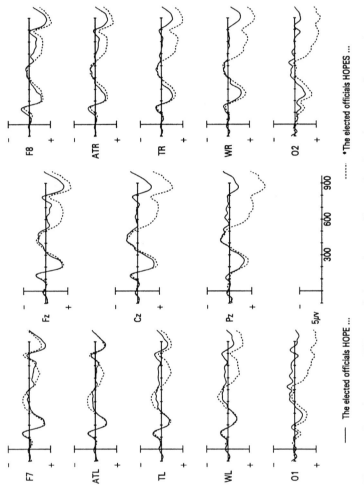

Figure 4 Grand average ERPs recorded over three midline and 10 lateral sites to subject–verb number violations and controls. Onset of the critical words in nonviolating (solid line) and agreement-violating (dashed line) conditions is indicated by the vertical bar. Each hash mark represents 100 ms. Figure from Osterhout and Mobley (1995).

Is the P600 a member of the P300 family?

The P300 component is typically elicited by attended stimuli which are task-relevant. However, rather than a single P300 component, investigators have described various positive components as part of the P300 family. One of them, the P3b has a centroparietal distribution, similar to that of the P600, with a variable onset depending on stimulus complexity. It is also affected by several other factors like salience, probability, and task relevance, which can modify both its latency and amplitude (Donchin, 1981; Hillyard & Picton, 1987, Johnson, 1986; Pritchard, 1981).

Osterhout et al. (Osterhout, McKinnon, Bersick, & Corey, 1996) suggest two different strategies to address the functional separability of the P300 and the P600 components. The first one is to carry out a systematic comparison between the characteristics of the late positivity (or P600) and the P300, for example, morphology, distribution, latency, etc. The second one is to investigate whether the manipulations that normally influence the P300 response do, in fact, have an effect on the P600, suggesting a functional relation between them. However, this research strategy has produced conflicting results.

In one study Coulson et al. (1998) presented two types of morphosyntactic violations to native speakers of English. A moderately salient violation of subject–verb number agreement (e.g., "Every Monday he *mow* the lawn"), and a more salient violation of overt case marking on pronouns (e.g., "The plane took *we* to paradise and back"). In addition, Coulson et al. manipulated the proportion of grammatical and ungrammatical sentences creating a grammaticality probable block (20 ungrammatical and 80 grammatical sentences) and a grammaticality improbable block (20 grammatical and 80 ungrammatical sentences). As mentioned above, these two manipulations, salience and probability, have been found to influence the amplitude of the P300 component.

Coulson et al. (1998) propose that if the P600 is a P3b type of response, then it should be similarly affected by these factors. More specifically, they predicted larger positivities for less salient and for improbable stimuli. Furthermore, the P600 should display a similar scalp distribution to that found for the P3b. Finally, the grammaticality and probability effects should interact if they are generated by the same neural substrate. This would predict a small probability effect on grammatical stimuli compared with a much larger effect on ungrammatical stimuli.

Coulson et al.'s (1998) findings supported their hypotheses. First, they found a grammaticality effect on the amplitude of the late positive response ratifying previous findings. However, they also found that this response was larger for improbable events, and especially larger at central and posterior scalp sites for ungrammatical improbable events (Figure 5). Finally, Coulson et al. (1998) found a larger effect for the more salient pronoun case marking violation. They interpret these findings as support for their claim that the late positivity elicited by ungrammatical events cannot be interpreted as a direct manifestation of syntactic processing, but rather that this is a member of the P300 family elicited by a rare linguistic event, namely, the ungrammatical event. Similar findings were reported by Gunter, Vos, and Mulder (1995).

These findings are in conflict with a study carried out by Osterhout et al. (1996). In a combination of three experiments, native English speakers were presented with three types of sentences, a subject–verb number agreement violation (e.g., *"The doctors *believes* the patient will recover"), a sentence containing a word in uppercase letters (e.g., "The doctors BELIEVE the patient will recover"), and a sentence containing a "doubly anomalous word," that is, an agreement violation elicited by a word in uppercase letters (*"The doctors *BELIEVES* the patient will recover"). In addition, the authors manipulated the probability of agreement violations in relation to the probability of uppercase sentences creating two different lists. List A contained 20% agreement–60% uppercase sentences, while list B contained the opposite ratio, 20% uppercase–60% agreement sentences. An identical number of control sentences was contained in each list. Finally, the authors manipulated task relevance by requiring a grammaticality judgment in one group of subjects, and a passive-reading task in a second group.

In previous studies, physically anomalous words had elicited a "P300" component (Kutas & Hillyard, 1980), and agreement violations had elicited a syntactic positive shift (Hagoort et al., 1993; Osterhout & Mobley, 1995). Therefore, and in line with the study mentioned above, Osterhout et al. (1996) predicted that if the P600 is independent from the P300 family of components, then the two types of sentences used in their study would elicit different ERP responses. Second, the ERPs elicited by the uppercase condition would be more sensitive to manipulations of probability and task relevance than those elicited by the agreement condition. Finally, they predicted that in the case of a doubly anomalous word, these two distinct ERP effects would be additive instead of interacting.

In contrast to Coulson et al. (1998), and in line with their predictions, Osterhout et al. (1996) found two distinct ERP patterns associated with each of these two types of anomalies. In general, the positivity elicited by uppercase anomalies had an earlier onset, especially in anterior sites, and was clearly larger than that produced by agreement violations. In addition, in the case of the sentence-acceptability judgment, the scalp distribution of these two effects was different at the 500–to–800–ms window. It was largest in posterior portions of the right hemisphere for uppercase

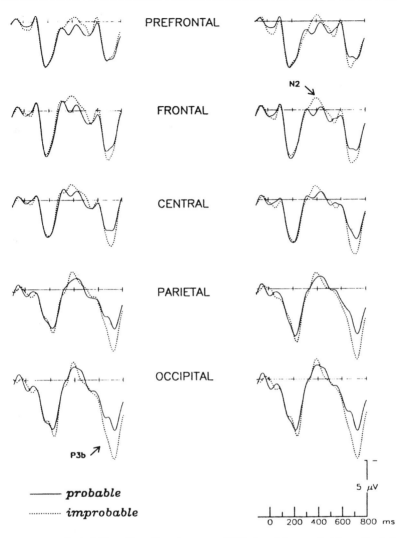

Figure 5 Probability effect. Grand average ERPs (n = 16) recorded from the left and right prefrontal, frontal, central, parietal, and occipital scalp sites. Compared with probable stimuli, ERPs to improbable stimuli displayed slightly enhanced negativity 300–500 ms, and enhanced positivity 500–800 ms, after word onset. Probable stimuli were grammatical in grammatical probable blocks, and ungrammatical in grammatical improbable blocks. Figure from Coulson, S., King, J., & Kutas, M. (1998). Expect the unexpected: Event-related brain response to morphosyntactic violations. Reprinted by permission of Psychology Press Limited, Hove, UK.

words, and over the left hemisphere for agreement violations. More importantly, Osterhout et al. found large effects of probability on the positivity elicited by a physical anomaly, but no effect on the ERPs elicited by subject–verb number agreement anomalies (Figure 6).

The effect of task was similar for both types of anomalies. The passive reading condition produced smaller effects than the sentence acceptability judgment. In contrast with the results from the sentence-acceptability task condition, in the passive reading condition the distribution and amplitude of ERPs to both types of violations did not differ reliably in the 500 to 800-ms window. Nevertheless, the effects of task were clearly larger for the uppercase words than for the agreement violations.

Finally, in the same 500 to 800—msec window, a doubly anomalous word elicited a large positive-going wave that was reliably larger than the effects elicited by either of the two anomaly types in isolation. In addition, the difference between the uppercase and the doubly anomalous conditions, and that between the agreement violation and control sentences both appeared at about 500 ms. Osterhout et al. (1996) interpret these results as supporting the independence of the two effects (Figure 7).

Furthermore, in an attempt to investigate the additivity of the uppercase and agreement anomalies, they also calculated algebraically a composite waveform created by adding the three factors that presumably contributed to the observed response to the doubly anomalous sentences: ERPs elicited by the nonviolating lowercase controls, plus the effects of uppercase words alone and the effects of agreement violation alone. A comparison between these composite waveforms and the observed response to doubly anomalous words, revealed that they did not differ reliably at the critical 500 to 900-ms window, although the authors acknowledge that the additivity of the two effects was not a simple linear summation, possibly due to other factors playing a role (Figure 8).

In summary, Coulson et al. (1998) find evidence suggesting that the P600 is a member of the P300 family. In contrast, Osterhout et al. (1996) conclude that the P600 is independent of the P300 effect. How can we reconcile these conflicting results? An obvious place to start is by looking at the methodological differences between the two studies. More specifically, if we limit our comparison to the verb agreement violation of Coulson et al. and the subject–verb agreement violation of Osterhout et al., which are presumably similar in salience, the best candidate to explain their different findings is the manipulation of probability. Coulson et al. contrasted 20 versus 80% probabilities. Osterhout et al. contrasted 20 versus 60% probabilities.

Osterhout et al. (1996) argue that this contrast in probability should be enough to modulate the amplitude of a P300 component. However Coulson et al. (1998) point to the different nature of stimuli typically used in oddball paradigms eliciting P300 responses, where participants develop experiment-specific expectations. In contrast, they argue, participants

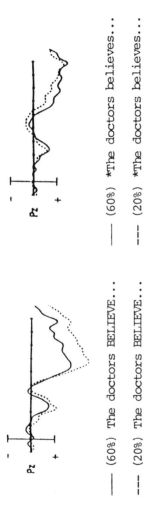

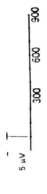

—— (60%) The doctors BELIEVE...

– – – (20%) The doctors BELIEVE...

—— (60%) *The doctors believes...

– – – (20%) *The doctors believes...

Figure 6 Grand average ERP's to uppercase words (left) and agreement violations (right) when they comprised 60% (solid line) and 20% (dashed line) of the trials. Figure adapted from Osterhout et al. (1996). *J. Cog. Neurosci.* © 1996 by the Massachusetts Institute of Technology.

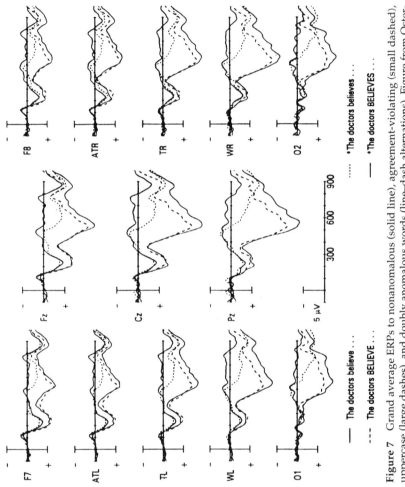

Figure 7 Grand average ERPs to nonanomalous (solid line), agreement-violating (small dashed), uppercase (large dashes), and doubly anomalous words (line–dash alternations). Figure from Osterhout et al. (1996). *J. Cog. Neurosci.* © 1996 by the Massachusetts Institute of Technology.

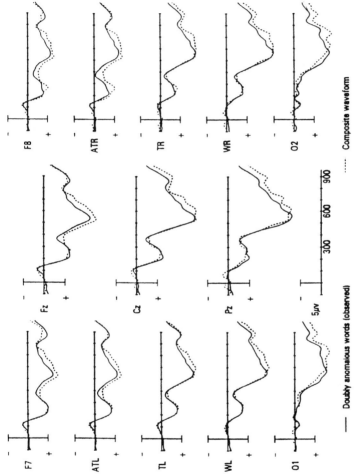

Figure 8 ERPs to doubly anomalous words (solid line) and a composite waveform (dashed line). Figure from Osterhout et al. (1996). *J. Cog. Neurosci.* © 1996 by the Massachusetts Institute of Technology.

Doubly anomalous words (observed)

Composite waveform

245

come to language studies with prior subjective probability expectations about natural language stimuli. Therefore, the subjective probabilities in the two types of studies may vary considerably. However, is this enough to explain the large differences in their findings?

Osterhout et al. (1996) also argue that there is no a priori reason to negate the possibility that probability may have an effect on a purely grammatically driven P600 and still be distinct from the P300 response in terms of their underlying neural and cognitive events. It may also be the case that the effect of probability is present in both cases, but it is different in magnitude. Coulson et al. (1998) respond to this argument by noticing an increment in the amplitude of the positivity elicited even by grammatical stimuli in grammatically improbable blocks. If the P600 is a reflection of syntactic reanalysis which is sensitive to probability, why should we find effects of probability even when no reanalysis is necessary, as in grammatical sentences? Otherwise, this effect can be explained if we assume that this is a sign of the participants' updating of their expectations, which is one of the cognitive factors proposed to elicit a P300 response.

But even if Coulson et al. (1998) have answers to some of Osterhout et al. (1996) arguments, there are still some findings which are difficult to reconcile between the two studies. For example, why did the composite waveform of a doubly anomalous word showed additive effects of a P600 and a P300 type? Why is the scalp distribution of the two effects different? On the other hand, Osterhout et al. need to explain why the differences in scalp distribution disappear in the passive reading condition, and why there is an effect of probability on the positivity elicited by grammatical sentences of Coulson et al. Clearly further studies are necessary to solve these apparent contradictions.

Isolating syntactic from semantic information

It has also been proposed that the P600 component might reflect a re-computation routine to rescue the meaning of the sentence once the reader/listener encounters a grammatical error. One strategy used to investigate this possibility involves getting rid of semantic information leaving intact the grammatical information. The rationale behind it is that in the absence of semantic information, there is no meaning "to be rescued." Consequently, if the P600 is a reflection of such semantically based recomputation processes, then it will decrease in amplitude or disappear under these conditions. Three studies have been carried out using this strategy.

In two experiments, Münte et al. (1997) investigated morphosyntactic (subject–verb number agreement) violations contained in real German word sentences or in pseudoword sentences.

Some teachers *punish* the students.
*Some teachers *punishes* the students.
Some globbies *higgle* the vlinch.
*Some globbies *higgles* in vlinch.

Using a memory task in their fist experiment, violations contained in pseudoword sentences elicited a widespread negativity, slightly larger in the left hemisphere, starting at 280 ms and extending to 600 ms (at Fz) and 800 ms (at Pz). In their second experiment, using a grammaticality judgment task, they found that violating pseudoword sentences elicited a shorter negative effect (280–500 ms) with a centroparietal maximum. Importantly, no late positivity was observed with pseudoword sentences. In contrast, grammatical violations contained in German sentences elicited a wide positivity similar to the syntactic positive shift or P600 but no negativity at all (Figure 9).

Münte et al. (1997) conclude that their findings support the hypothesis that the P600 reflects a recomputation mechanism necessary to construct a meaningful representation when we encounter an error during sentence processing. When there is no meaning to be recomputed, as in pseudoword sentences, no positivity arises. They also propose that the negativity observed in violations with pseudoword sentences may be a real reflection of syntactic processing. However, it is unclear why this negativity was not observed in their real word sentences.

With the same rationale, Canseco-Gonzalez et al. (1997) presented two types of phrase structure violations in English and their corresponding counterpart in "jabberwocky" sentences to native speakers of English. Jabberwocky sentences were created by replacing most content words with pronounceable pseudowords having the same number of syllables and similar length. The closed class words were left unmodified (similar to Münte et al., 1997) in order to keep the grammatical structure intact.

Phrase structure I
The actress resented Tom's comments *about* her looks and her cooking.
* The actress resented Tom's *about* comments her looks and her cooking.
The celtron resented Tom's malwars *about* her nabs and her cesting.
* The celtron resented Tom's *about* malwars her nabs and her cesting.

Phrase structure II
The broker persuaded to conceal the transaction *was* sent to jail.
* The broker planned to conceal the transaction *was* sent to jail.
The broder persuaded to conceal the tempkishin *was* sent to julp.
* The broder planned to conceal the tempkishin *was* sent to julp.

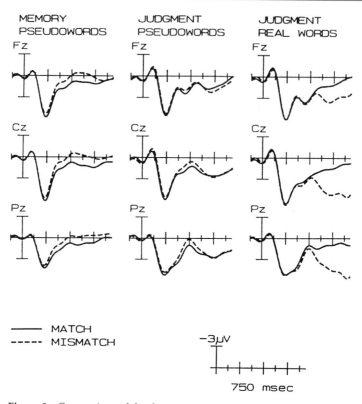

Figure 9   Comparison of the three experimental conditions. ERPs to the verb of the sentence are shown. While for the two pseudoword conditions an additional negativity is found for the mismatching verbs, the incongruent verbs of the real-word condition are associated with a positivity starting at 400 ms. Figure adapted from Münte et al. (1997). *J. Cog. Neurosci.* © 1997 by the Massachusetts Institute of Technology.

Canseco-Gonzalez et al.'s (1997) results replicate in part Münte et al.'s (1997) findings. Phrase structure violations in English elicited both a left anterior negativity and a broadly distributed late positivity, with a maximum in medial posterior areas of the right hemisphere. Grammatical violations contained in jabberwocky sentences elicited a larger and more broadly distributed left anterior negativity, but in contrast with English, one type of violation elicited a small and restricted late positivity, while the other failed to elicit any reliable positive effect (Figure 10).

The difference between these two studies is that in the second one a left anterior negativity was elicited by grammatical violations in English, as well as in jabberwocky sentences. This is expected if the negativity is directly related to syntactic processing, which is presumably taking place in both types of sentences. In contrast, Münte et al. (1997) observed a broad anterior negativity only in the case of violations contained in pseudoword sentences but no negative effect at all in English sentences. To account for this, they propose that their judgment task may have elicited an early positivity which masked a potential anterior negativity. This explanation is plausible considering that Canseco–Gonzalez et al. (1997) found a larger negativity in jabberwocky sentences. This could be due also to the fact that in the absence of a positive effect, the left anterior negativity is "released" and more easily observed. In addition, the differences in distribution may be due to the smaller number of recording sites in Münte et al., which may have obscured a clearer distributional pattern.

However, both of these findings stand in contrast with a third study using a similar strategy. Hagoort and Brown (1994) presented three types of violations contained in Dutch syntactic prose sentences to native Dutch speakers.

Agreement
The boiled watering-can *smokes* the telephone in the cat.
*The boiled watering-can *smoke* the telephone in the cat.

Subcategorization
The hair-line in the washed bread borrows the *root* of his newspaper.
*The hair-line in the washed bread boasts the *root* of his newspaper.

Phrase structure
The heel tripped over the rather inhabited *cat* on his pocket.
*The heel tripped over the inhabited rather *cat* on his pocket.

Syntactic prose sentences were derived from Dutch sentences used in a prior study (Hagoort et al., 1993), by replacing each word with another word of the same class. This manipulation made sentences semantically uninterpretable, while keeping the same constituent structure as their source (normal prose) sentences. Hagoort and Brown (1994) found an SPS (albeit smaller than in their original study using normal prose) elicited by syntactic prose sentences violating agreement and phrase structure rules (Figure 11).

In contrast, Hagoort and Brown (1994) failed to find an SPS in the case of subcategorization violations. Because this was true even in normal prose sentences, they argue that both, syntactic and semantic information, are contained in subcategorization frames. In summary, Hagoort and Brown conclude that the SPS (or P600) is a direct indicator of structural or syntactic analysis per se.

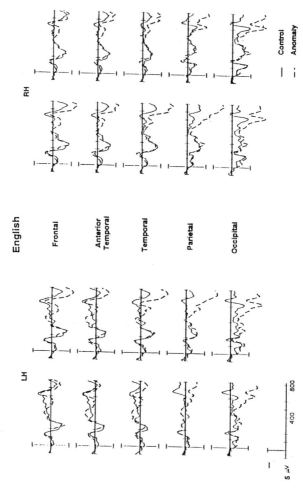

Phrase Structure I

English

RH

Frontal

Anterior Temporal

Temporal

Parietal

Occipital

LH

400 800

5 μV

Control
Anomaly

250

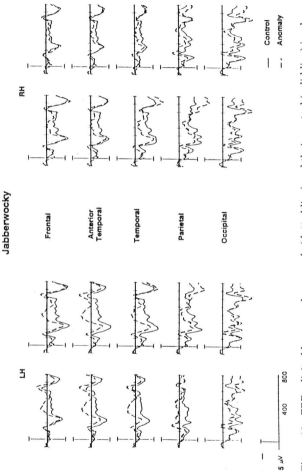

Figure 10 ERPs elicited by anomalous words (dotted line) and their control (solid line) in phrase structure violation type I, in English (top) and jabberwocky (bottom) sentences. Figure from Canseco-Gonzalez et al. (1997).

251

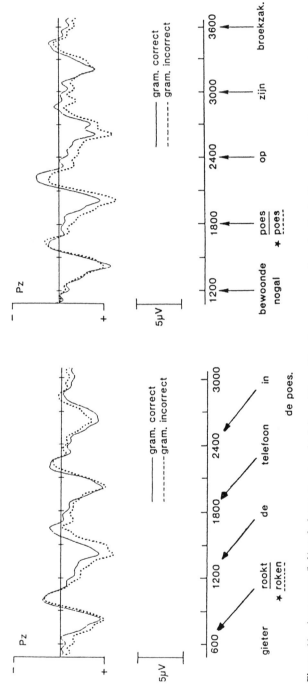

Figure 11 Agreement (left) and phrase structure (right) conditions. Grand average waveform for Pz, for the grammatically correct, and incorrect critical words. Figure adapted from Hagoort and Brown (1994).

In order to reconcile the findings of these three studies, we need to consider several factors: Manipulations to isolate syntactic from semantic information, grammatical violations used, language of study, task required, etc. The most promising explaining factor is the manipulation of semantic information. Münte et al (1997) and Canseco-Gonzalez et al. (1997) used a similar method. They left closed class words intact but replaced open class words with pseudowords. In contrast, Hagoort and Brown (1994) used real words replacing them with other words of the same category. Based on grammaticality judgments from all three studies, it seems that the authors managed to maintain structural or grammatical information intact. However, and more importantly for the interpretation of the role of P600 or SPS, it is unclear to what extent subjects still had access to semantic information of any kind across experiments. Hagoort and Brown had real words replacing the correct open class words. It may be that the presence of "incorrect" real words still provides subjects with enough semantic information to trigger a semantically based recomputational process, even if it ultimately fails. This interpretation seems plausible in view of the similarity between the two studies that used pseudowords. However, it is important to notice that Canseco-Gonzalez et al. left some open class words intact, which were necessary to maintain structural information. Could the presence of these few content words still trigger a recomputational mechanism? If so, what then accounts for the presence of an SPS in the case of Hagoort and Brown and its absence in the case of Canseco-Gonzalez et al.? In this regard, Münte et al. took advantage of the morphosyntactic features of German, and managed to avoid any open class words in their pseudoword sentences.

In regard to the types of grammatical violations studied, Hagoort and Brown (1994) and Canseco-Gonzalez et al. (1997) used one similar phrase structure violation. On the other hand, Hagoort and Brown and Münte et al. (1997) also used a similar agreement violation. Therefore, there doesn't seem to be a distributional pattern of violation types that could explain the corresponding pattern of results.

Except for the morphological features of German, it is unclear how the three languages studied, German, English, and Dutch can account for the observed pattern of results. Finally, in regard to the task used, Hagoort and Brown (1994) required the silent reading of sentences, Canseco-Gonzalez et al. (1997) used a grammaticality judgment, and Münte et al. (1997) used both a memory task and a sentence acceptability judgment. Both studies using grammaticality judgments failed to find a P600 using pseudowords. It is feasible that the presence of an SPS is linked to the passive reading of sentences, but this is unlikely given the multiple number of tasks used in studies eliciting P600.

Syntactic positive shift as a reflection of second pass parsing processes

Proposing a two-stage model of syntactic processing, Friederici et al. (1993, 1996; Friederici & Mecklinger, 1996) argue that the left anterior negativity and the late positivity or P600, reflect first-pass and second-pass parsing processes respectively. Based on a model initially proposed by Frazier and Fodor (1978), they assume that the first process consists of the identification of word category information and the building up of the simplest structure in line with the input. This first stage is highly automatic and independent of lexical semantic information. The second-pass parsing processes involve not only the interpretation of that initial structure (using case and θ-role assignment), but also the necessary reanalysis process of the initial structure if/when the initial assignments are impossible.

In a study using phrase structure violations, Friederici et al. (1993) find support for their claim that the left anterior negativity is a reflection of the first-pass parsing mechanism. Furthermore, they suggest that the LAN is elicited only by the detection of a violation of a **required** syntactic category, rather than a **preferred** category (Friederici et al., 1996).

On the other hand, in support of their claim that the late positivity is a reflection of a second-pass parsing process, Mecklinger et al. (1995) find a late centroparietal positivity correlated with syntactic ambiguity resolution, and in line with prior reports by Osterhout et al. (1994). They presented well-formed German sentences containing either a subject or an object relative clause. These sentences remain ambiguous (subject or object relative) until the appearance of the sentence final auxiliary, which is marked for number, thereby disambiguating the structure of the sentence. They also manipulated the main verb of the sentence (which preceded the auxiliary), by using verbs with a strong bias to assign one of the noun phrases as the subject or as the object of the action. For example,

These are the students that the professor examined has.
These are the professors that the student examined have.

It is more likely for professors to examine students than the other way around. Prior behavioral studies had demonstrated that the subject relative structure is preferred over the object relative. Consequently, Mecklinger et al. (1995) predicted larger positivities to be elicited by object relatives, due to the need for reanalysis. They also predicted that if syntactic processing is independent of semantic information, then the semantic information provided by the verb should have a null effect on this positivity. Their results supported both predictions. There was a larger P345 for object relatives, compared with subject relatives. In support for their second hypothesis, they also found that this positivity was unaffected by the semantic bias of the verb (Figure 12).

Mecklinger et al. (1995) conclude that the parsing system does not rely on lexical semantic information to resolve syntactic ambiguity. They also conclude that the amplitude of this component reflects the syntactic reanalysis process, and propose that its latency might be directly related to the complexity of the reanalysis of nonpreferred structures. In a later study, Friederici, Steinhauer, and Mecklinger (1995), specifically manipulate the complexity of the particular reanalysis involved and conclude, in line with Osterhout et al. (1994), that the amplitude of the late positivity reflects the cost of reprocessing produced by a garden path (see footnote 3), rather than the process of simply computing the required syntactic structure. Furthermore, they claim that the latency of this positivity is correlated with the number of computational steps involved in such reanalysis.

On the specificity of P600

Finally, one more strategy to investigate the cognitive processes underlying P600 is to study its specificity. That is, we can investigate if there are conditions, other than those involving syntactic processing, which elicit a P600. Conversely, we can also explore if there are conditions involving syntactic processing which fail to elicit a late positivity.

With this idea in mind, Münte, Heinze, Matzke, Wieringa, and Johannes (1998) carried out a study visually presenting three types of violations embedded in stories to German speakers. First, a morphosyntactic violation in the form of case inflection errors, which according to prior studies should elicit a late positivity. Second, they used a semantic violation which should elicit a typical N400 response. Third, they presented an orthographic violation in the form of misspelled words. An important methodological feature of this study is the fact that they used the same words, at the same positions within stories, to produce the three types of violations. For example,

Control
The witch used her *broom* to fly to the forest.

Case inflection error
*The witch used her *broom's* to fly to the forest.

Semantic anomaly
*The witch used her *dream* to fly to the forest.

Orthographic anomaly
*The witch used her *broome* to fly to the forest.

Münte et al. (1998) found a typical centroparietal N400 response elicited by semantic violations. In a similar time window, case inflection

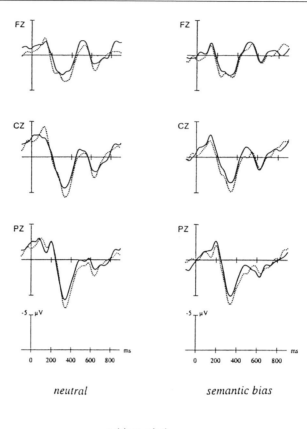

neutral   semantic bias

―― subject relative
······ object relative

Figure 12   Grand averages of ERPs obtained from the sentence-final auxiliary in the subject relative clause (solid lines) and the object relative clause (broken lines) in the semantically neutral condition (left panel) and in the semantically biased condition (right panel). Both panels present the midline electrodes. The vertical lines indicate the onset of the auxiliary. Figure from Friederici and Mecklinger (1996).

errors elicited a smaller and frontally distributed negativity. No negativity was observed for orthographic errors. However, beginning at approximately 500 ms, all three types of violations elicited a large positive-going wave which was similar in amplitude across conditions. The positivity to semantic violations had a more focal parietal distribution, while it was more evenly distributed in the syntactic and orthographic conditions (Figure 13).

Münte et al. (1998) conclude that the late positivity, previously associated with syntactic processing per se, can be elicited by different types of linguistic violations, including semantic and orthographic ones. Based on the different distributions observed, they also suggest that the late positivity may have multiple generators associated with different cognitive correlates. Therefore, an interpretation of this positivity as a reflection of syntactic reanalysis after encountering a syntactic violation or ambiguity (see above), needs to be extended to include reanalysis after any kind of linguistic error. Münte et al. point out that prior studies investigating semantic violations may have failed to observe a late positivity due to a low signal-to-noise ratio, or to the specific materials used. They argue that the use of coherent stories in their own study, may have forced the subjects to go back and recheck previous parts in order to make sense of the semantic violation. In addition, by using the exact same material to elicit all their anomalies, they created optimal conditions for their comparison. However, Münte at al., in line with other researchers, point out that even if the P600 is not a specific marker of syntactic processing, it can still be a valuable tool in the study of syntactic processing. It has been proposed that the amplitude, latency, and duration of P600 can serve as an index of reprocessing costs, or the timing of parsing processes (Osterhout et al., 1994; Friederici & Mecklinger, 1996; Friederici et al., 1995, 1996).

Using the opposite rationale, Hopf, Bayer, Bader, and Meng (1998) investigated syntactic violations involving a different kind of reanalysis. These authors recorded ERPs elicited by case-disambiguating verbs presented at the end of sentences containing case-ambiguous NPs (noun phrases). Their sentences were presented in German, which allows more freedom than English in terms of the order of syntactic constituents. Consequently, the specific syntactic role of an NP is determined in large part of its case morphology. However, German also has many situations where an NP is temporarily ambiguous in regard to its case. More specifically, the morphology of an NP can be ambiguous between dative or accusative case, until the clause final main verb resolves the ambiguity. Furthermore, Hopf et al. argue that, under these conditions, these NPs are initially assigned accusative case by default. If the final verb turns out to assign dative case instead, a garden path effect is triggered and reanalysis is necessary. An important point for their claim is the fact that the reanalysis carried out with these sentences does not have phrase structural consequences. Therefore, they name these as "pure case assignment ambiguities" (PCA).

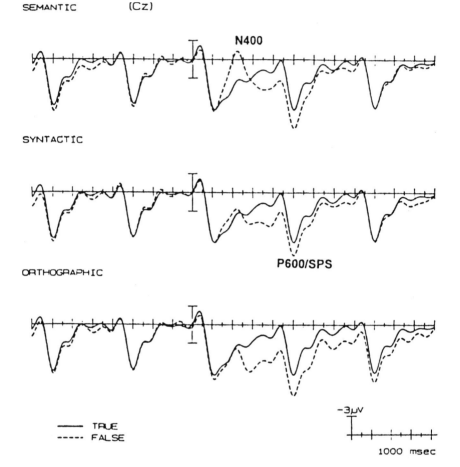

Figure 13   Grand average ERPs with an extended epoch including the effects of two words before and two words after the critical word for the CZ electrode. Reprinted from *Neuropsychologia* **36**; T. F. Munte, H. J. Heinze, M. Matzke, B. M. Wieringa, & S. Johannes; Brain potentials and syntactic violations revisited: No evidence for specificity of the syntactic positive shift, pp. 217–226. Copyright 1998, with permission from Elsevier Science.

Hopf et al. (1998) found a centroposterior pronounced negative shift after final dative disambiguating verbs, instead of a late positivity. They compared these ERPs to those elicited by accusative assigning verbs, or those appearing in unambiguous sentences (Figure 14).

This suggests that an ambiguous accusative/dative NP is initially assigned accusative case, but needs to be revised by the parser when the final dative assigning verb is encountered.

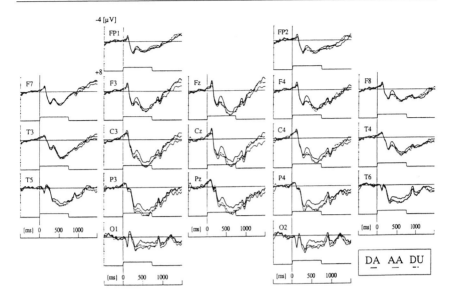

Figure 14   Average ERP waveforms evoked by the final verb of dative ambiguous (DA), dative unambiguous (DU), and accusative ambiguous (AA) sentences. The trace at the bottom of each diagram indicates the time window in which the word occurred on the video screen. At about 900 ms, a short biphasic potential (N1/P1) complex with a maximum at occipital electrodes is visible; it represents the offset potential to the disappearance of the final word. Figure from Hopf et al. (1998). *J. Cog. Neurosci.* © 1998 by the Massachusetts Institute of Technology.

As mentioned above, previous studies investigating garden path sentences requiring a structural reanalysis, or filler-gap ambiguities, have both elicited a P600 response (Osterhout et al., 1994; Friederici & Mecklinger, 1996; Friederici et al., 1995). Hopf et al. (1998) then suggest that in PCAs in contrast, the necessary reanalysis takes place at the level of the lexicon rather than at the parsing domain, and that it may be due to this that they find an enhanced N400-like response instead of a late positivity.

While it is clear that PCAs do not elicit a P600, Hopf et al. (1998) also propose that it is only in the case of phrase structure revisions that a late positivity is elicited. However, the large number of syntactic violations (and nonsyntactic violations, see above) eliciting a late positivity, make this proposal implausible. For example, some syntactic violations involving long-distance dependencies (Osterhout & Mobley, 1995; McKinnon & Osterhout, 1996), or morphosyntactic violations (Kutas & Hillyard, 1983; Coulson et al., 1998) also elicit a P600. In addition, particular types of violations have produced conflicting findings. In the case of subcategorization violations, which are also lexically based, Osterhout and Holcomb

(1992) report a P600. In contrast, Rosler at al. (1993) found only a left anterior negativity, and Hagoort et al. (1993) failed to find any effect.

SLOW POTENTIALS IN THE STUDY OF LANGUAGE PROCESSING

One promising line of research is the study of sentence-long slow potentials that show systematic variations in time across the sentence, and in space across the scalp (Kutas, 1997). If these slow potentials vary systematically according to specific sentence types, we then have a useful electrophysiological tool to investigate language processing beyond the word level.

Kutas and collaborators have carried out a series of studies using this approach to investigate the role of working memory in language processing (King & Kutas, 1995, Kutas & King, 1996; Mueller, King, & Kutas, 1977). In one study (Kutas & King 1996), individuals read simple sentences presented one word at a time for comprehension (e.g., "The secretary answered the phone because . . ."). The brain activity recorded under these conditions was low-pass filtered, leaving only the slow activity. The authors correctly assume that the comprehension of these simple sentence require analysis at various linguistic levels and impose demands on working and long-term memory.

Analyzing the slow cross-clause averages, Kutas and King (1996) describe a sustained negativity in occipital regions, slightly larger over the left hemisphere. They hypothesize that this activity reflects the continuous processing of visual stimuli. They also found a positivity at more anterior and temporal sites starting at the main verb of the clause. They suggest that this positivity may be associated with thematic role assignment. Finally, they describe a large and slow positivity which develops bilaterally in frontal sites but larger on the left hemisphere. Based on previous findings, Kutas and King (1996) suggest that this activity may reflect working memory functions (Figure 15).

In another study, King and Kutas (1995) recorded word by word and cross-sentence potentials, while subjects read subject relative (e.g., "The reporter that harshly attacked the senator admitted the . . .") and object relative (e.g., "The reporter that the senator harshly attacked admitted the . . .") sentences. The latter ones are assumed to impose larger working memory demands on the listeners given that a constituent must be maintained longer in memory (e.g., "The reporter" must be kept a long time in memory before it can be assigned as the direct object of the verb "attacked"). In

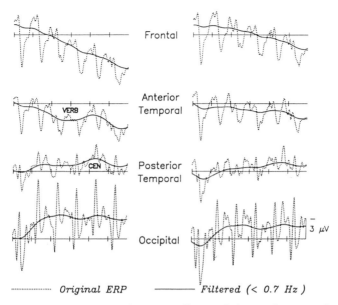

.... *Original ERP* ————— *Filtered (< 0.7 Hz)*

Figure 15 Superimposed are originally recorded cross-clause grand average ERPs and the slow activity only (low pass filtered at 0.7 Hz) for four pairs of sites going from front to back of the head over left and right hemispheres, separately. The CEN labels the clause-ending negativity. Figure from Kutas (1997). Reprinted with the permission of Cambridge University Press.

line with this proposal, reaction time studies have found longer reading times for object relative (OS) than for subject relative (SS) sentences.

The King and Kutas (1995) findings support this hypothesis. They found a larger left anterior negativity (LAN) elicited by the main verb for OS sentences compared with SS sentences. This is also in line with previous findings reporting in LAN effect associated with working memory demands in filler-gap constructions (see Kluender & Kutas, 1993 above) (Figure 16).

More importantly, they also found a sustained negativity over frontal and central sites for OS sentences much earlier, as soon as the two types diverge in their working memory demands (Figure 17). Furthermore, these effects were larger in good than in poorer comprehenders.[4]

In a later study, Müeller et al. (1997) replicated the main findings using auditory presented sentences. Although the scalp distributions were

[4]The authors carried out a median split of good (87%) versus poorer (60%) comprehenders based on their comprehension scores.

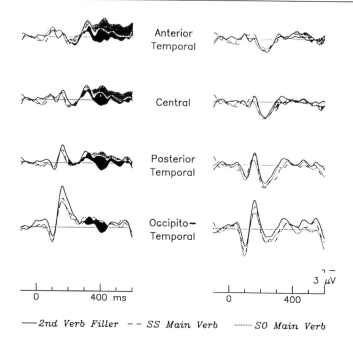

—— *2nd Verb Filler*   – – *SS Main Verb*   ·········· *SO Main Verb*

Figure 16   Grand average ERPs to main clause verbs from subject relative (SS) and object relative (SO) sentences contrasted with the ERPs to second verbs in multiclausal sentences without embeddings ("The psychologist completed the experiment because she really wanted to know the answer.") The shaded differences in relative negativity over the more anterior sites is known as the LAN effect. The electrode pairs go from the front to the back of the head. Figure from Kutas (1997). Reprinted with the permission of Cambridge University Press.

more widespread and larger over the right hemisphere for auditory stimuli (plus some additional modality-specific effects), the frontal effects of the relative clauses were very similar across modalities. This suggests that these effects reflect language processes independent of modality.

CONCLUSION

In closing this chapter I want to raise some of the many remaining questions and problems posed by the evidence reviewed. For example, it is unclear if the LAN associated with syntactic anomalies mentioned above is the same as a broad frontal negativity reported by Münte et al. in several

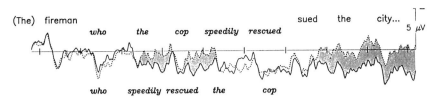

Figure 17 Comparison of the grand average cross-sentence ERPs elicited by subject relative (solid line) and object relative (dotted line) sentences recorded over a left anterior location. The two sentence types are equivalent both before and after the relative clause. The relative clause above the baseline is an example of an object relative and that below the baseline is an example of a subject relative. Words were presented one at a time every 0.5 s for a duration of 200 ms. The shading represents the area of where object relative sentences are reliably more negative than the subject relative sentences. Figure from Kutas (1997). Reprinted with the permission of Cambridge University Press.

studies (Münte & Ideinze, 1994; Münte et al., 1993, 1997). Investigating different types of syntactic anomaly, these authors fail to find hemispheric differences in the negative component elicited by the violations. The discrepancy could be due to the fact that Münte et al. have often used a smaller number of recording sites. This may have obscured an otherwise highly localized and left lateralized effect. An unlikely alternative explanation emerges when we consider that these authors have often used word-pairs as opposed to full sentences. The rationale is as follows. In our previous discussion about the late positivity (see Münte et al. in the section entitled Isolating Syntactic from Semantic Information), Münte et al. argue that under these conditions lacking a sentential context (word pairs or pseudoword sentences), there is no possibility of semantic reinterpretation. Consequently, the late positivity associated with such reinterpretation is absent. Following this line of thought, it could be that when syntactic violations are embedded in full sentences, the elicitation of a late positivity overlaps with an otherwise broad anterior negativity elicited by the syntactic violation. If this positivity is broad enough to affect anterior sites and tends to be larger on the right hemisphere, the net effect would be a larger negativity on the left hemisphere (LAN). Again, when there is no positivity, no overlap is produced, and a broad anterior negativity is observed. We find this explanation unlikely due to the fact that at least in one study using syntactic violations embedded in pseudoword "sentences," the negativity associated with violations showed a clear laterality effect in spite of the absence of a late positivity [see Canseco-Gonzalez et al. (1997) in the section entitled Isolating Syntactic from Semantic Information].

Other questions are: Is the late positivity a direct reflection of syntactic processing or a member of the P300 family elicited by unexpected events?

(See the section entitled Is the P600 a Member of the P300 Family?) If the latter is true, can we still make use of this component in the study of syntactic processing? We need to wait for further research before we can answer the first question. However, if eventually it turns out that the P600 is a member of the P300 family, or a sign of semantic reinterpretation (see the section entitled Isolating Syntactic from Semantic Information), there is no reason in principle why we could not use it to investigate syntactic processing. In fact, it would be exactly due to its properties, that we could design our studies carefully in such a way for this component to be a valuable tool in the study of syntactic or semantic processing.

What can we then conclude from all the evidence presented and discussed in this chapter? Certainly we have made great progress in language research in general, and in the study of language processing using electrophysiological evidence in particular. However, fortunately for all of us interested in the study of language, there are still many more questions than answers available. We also have new and promising paths to follow, and techniques to use.

REFERENCES

Canseco-Gonzalez, E., Love, T., Ahrens, K., Walenski, M., Swinney, D., & Neville, H. (1997, March). *Processing of grammatical information in jabberwocky sentences: An ERP study*. Poster presented at the Fourth Annual Meeting of the Cognitive Neuroscience Society. Boston.

Chomsky, N. (1981) *Lectures on government and binding*. Dortrecht: Foris.

Clifton, C., Jr., & Frazier, L. (1989). Comprehending sentences with long-distance dependencies. In G. N. Carlson & M. K. Tanenhaus (Eds.), *Linguistic structure in language processing* (pp. 273–317). Dordrecht: Kluwer.

Coulson, S., King, J., & Kutas, M. (1998). Expect the unexpected: Event-related brain response to morphosyntactic violations. *Language and Cognitive Processes, 13*, 21–58.

Deacon, D., Breton, F., Ritter, W., & Vaughan, H. G. (1991). The relationship between N2 and N400: Scalp distribution, stimulus probability, and task relevance. *Psychophysiology, 28*, 185–200.

Donchin, E. (1981). Surprise! . . . Surprise? *Psychophysiology, 18*, 493–513.

Elman, J. L. (1990). Representation and structure in connectionist models. In G. T. Altmann (Ed.), *Cognitive models of speech processing*. Cambridge, MA: MIT Press.

Ferreira, F., & Clifton, C. (1986). The independence of syntactic processing. *Journal of Memory and Language, 25*, 348–368.

Fodor, J. D. (1978). Parsing strategies and constraints on transformations. *Linguistic Inquiry, 9*, 427–473.

Ford, M., Bresnan, J., & Kaplan, R. (1982). A competence based theory of syntactic closure. In J. Bresnan (Ed.), *The mental representation of grammatical relations* (pp. 727–796). Cambridge, MA: MIT Press.

Frazier, L., & Fodor, J. D. (1978). The sausage machine: A new two-stage parsing model. *Cognition, 6*, 291–325.

Friederici, A. D., Hahne, A., & Mecklinger, A. (1996). Temporal structure of syntactic parsing: Early and late event-related brain potentials effects. *Journal of Experimental Psychology: Learning, Memory, and Cognition, 22,* 1219–1248.

Friederici, A. D., & Mecklinger, A. (1996). Syntactic parsing as revealed by brain responses: First-pass and second-pass parsing processes. *Journal of Psycholinguistic Research, 25,* 157–177.

Friederici, A. D., Pfeifer, E., & Hahne, A. (1993). Event-related brain potentials during natural speech processing: Effects of semantic, morphological and syntactic violations. *Cognitive Brain Research, 1,* 138–192.

Friederici, A. D., Steinhauer, K., & Mecklinger, A. (1995, March). *Syntactic complexity and latency of the late positivity.* Paper presented at the Second Annual Meeting of the Cognitive Neuroscience Society, San Francisco.

Gunter, T. C., Vos, S. J., & Mulder, G. (1995, March). *Syntactic violations and ERPs: P600 or P3b?* Poster presented at the Eight Annual CUNY Conference on Human Sentence Processing. Tuczon, AZ.

Hagoort, P., & Brown, C. M. (1994). Brain responses to lexical ambiguity resolution and parsing. In C. Clifton, L. Frazier, & K. Rayner (Eds.), *Perpectives on sentence processing* (pp. 45–80). Hillsdale, NJ: Erlbaum.

Hagoort, P., Brown, C., & Groothusen, J. (1993). The syntactic positive shift as an ERP measure of syntactic processing. *Language and Cognitive Processes, 8,* 439–484.

Hickok, G., Canseco-Gonzalez, E., Zurif, E., & Grimshaw, J. (1992). Modularity in locating wh-gaps. *Journal of Psycholinguistic Research, 21,* 547–563.

Hillyard, S. A., & Picton, T. (1987). Electrophysiology of cognition. In F. Plum (Ed.), *Handbook of physiology. Section 1: Neurophysiology.* New York: American Physiological Society.

Hopf, J.-M., Bayer, J., Bader, M., & Meng, M. (1998). Event-related brain potentials and case information in syntactic ambiguities. *Journal of Cognitive Neuroscience, 10,* 264–280.

Johnson, R., Jr. (1986). A triarchic model of P300 amplitude *Psychophysiology, 23,* 367–384.

King, J. W., & Kutas, M. (1995). Who did what and when? Using word- and clause-level ERPs to monitor working memory usage in reading. *Journal of Cognitive Neuroscience, 7,* 376–395.

Kluender, R., & Kutas, M. (1993). Bridging the gap: Evidence from ERPs on the processing of unbounded dependencies. *Journal of Cognitive Neuroscience, 5,* 196–214.

Kutas, M. (1997). Views on how the electrical activity that the brain generates reflects the functions of different language structures. Presidential Address, 1996. *Psychophysiology, 34,* 383–398.

Kutas, M., & Hillyard, S. A. (1980). Reading senseless sentences: Brain potentials reflect semantic anomaly. *Science, 207,* 203–205.

Kutas, M., & Hillyard, S. S., (1983). Event-related brain potentials to grammatical errors and semantic anomalies. *Memory and Cognition, 11,* 539–550.

Kutas, M., & King, J. W. (1996). The potentials for basic sentence processing: Differentiating integrative processes. In I. Ikeda & J. L. McClelland (Eds.), *Attention and performance* (Vol. 16, pp. 501–546). Cambridge, MA: MIT Press.

Kutas, M., & Van Petten, C. (1988). Event-related potential studies of language. In P. K. Ackles, J. R. Jennings, & M. G. H. Coles (Eds.), *Advances in psychophysiology.* Greenwich, CT: JAI Press.

Kutas, M., & Van Petten, C. (1994). Psycholinguistics electrified: Event-related brain potential investigations. IN M. Gernsbacher (Ed.), *Handbook of Psycholinguistics* (pp. 83–143). New York: Academic Press.

MacWhinney, B., Bates, E. S., & Kliegel, R. (1984). Cue validity and sentence interpretation in English, German, and Italian. *Journal of Verbal Learning and Verbal Behavior, 23,* 127–150.

McKinnon, R., & Osterhout, L. (1996). Constraints on movement phenomena in sentence processing: Evidence from event-related brain potentials. *Language and Cognitive Processes*.

Mecklinger, A., Schriefers, H., Steinhauer, K., & Friederici, A. D. (1995). Processing relative clauses varying on syntactic and semantic dimensions: An analysis with event-related potentials. *Memory and Cognition, 23*, 447–494.

Müeller, H. M., King, J. W., & Kutas, M. (1997). Event-related potentials to relative clause processing in spoken sentences. *Cognitive Brain Research, 5*, 193–203.

Münte, T. F., & Heinze, H. J. (1994). ERP negatives during syntactic processing of written words. In H. J. Heinze, T. F. Munte, & G. R. Mangun (Eds.), *Cognitive electrophysiology* (pp. 211–238). Boston: Birkhaeuser.

Münte, T. F., Heinze, H. J., & Mangun, G. R. (1993). Dissociation of brain activity related to syntactic and semantic aspects of language. *Journal of Cognitive Neuroscience, 3*, 335–344.

Münte, T. F., Heinze, H. J., Matzke, M., Wieringa, B. M., & Johannes, S. (1998). Brain potentials and syntactic violations revisited: No evidence for specificity of the syntactic positive shift. *Neuropsychologia, 36*, 217–226.

Münte, T. F., Matzke, M., & Johannes, S. (1997). Brain activity associated with syntactic incongruencies in words and pseudo-words. *Journal of Cognitive Neuroscience, 9*, 318–329.

Neville, H. J., Nicol, J. L., Barss, A., Forster, K. I., & Garret, M. F. (1991). Syntactically based sentence processing classes: Evidence from event-related brain potentials. *Journal of Cognitive Neuroscience, 3*, 151–165.

Osterhout, L., & Holcomb, P. J. (1992). Event-related brain potentials elicited by syntactic anomaly. *Journal of Memory and Language, 31*, 785–806.

Osterhout, L., Holcomb, P. J., & Swinney, D. (1994). Brain potentials elicited by garden-path sentences: Evidence of the application of verb information during parsing. *Journal of Experimental Psychology: Learning, Memory, and Cognition, 20*, 786–803.

Osterhout, L., McKinnon, R., Bersick, M., & Corey, V. (1996). On the language specificity of the brain response to syntactic anomalies: Is the syntactic positive shift a member of the P300 family? *Journal of Cognitive Neuroscience, 8*, 507–526.

Osterhout, L., & Mobley, L. A. (1995). Event-related brain potentials elicited by failure to agree. *Journal of Memory and Language, 34*, 739–773.

Pritchard, W. S. (1981). Psychophysiology of P300: A review. *Psychological Bulletin, 89*, 506–540.

Rosler, F., Friederici, A., Putz, P., Hahne, A. (1993). Event-related brain potentials while encountering semantic and syntactic constraint violations. *Journal of Cognitive Neuroscience, 5*, 345–362.

Shao, J., and Neville, H. J. (1996, March). *ERPs elicited by semantic anomalies: Beyond the N400.* Poster presented at the Third Annual Meeting of the Cognitive Neuroscience Society, San Francisco.

Swinney, D., Zurif, E., Prather, P., & Love, T. (1996). Neurological distribution of processing resources underlying language comprehension. *Journal of Cognitive Neuroscience, 8*, 174–184.

Chapter **13**

Grammatical Gender Is Not Always Syntactic

Harold Goodglass

An article by Badecker, Miozzo, and Zanuttini (1995) has brought into contention the significance of "grammatical gender" as a property of lexical items. Badecker et al. unquestioningly translate the term grammatical gender as signifying a *syntactic* property of words and, therefore a property which is part of the "lemma" of a word, according to Levelt's (1989) definition of the lemma. In this article it will be argued that the term grammatical gender is a misnomer, and that this property is more accurately referred to as "arbitrary gender assignment." However, for the sake of convention, we will continue to use the term grammatical gender in the discussion to follow.

Badecker et al. (1995) described the performance of an Italian-speaking anomic aphasic patient (Dante) who was almost invariably correct in indicating the gender of nouns whose names he could not retrieve. Dante was just as accurate on nouns that contained no phonological cues as to their gender as for those nouns that ended in -o or -a—the most common structural clues to masculine or feminine gender, respectively. The authors interpreted Dante's performance as indicating that he would access the syntax of the nouns, but not their phonology. If this were so, it could be taken as evidence favoring the lemma model of lexical access for production. In this model, lemma attainment includes accessing the syntactic properties of the target, but none of its phonology, although phonological retrieval cannot begin until the lemma has been specified.

The Badecker at al. (1995) finding gained support from a study by Vigliocco, Antonini, and Garrett (1997) in which the authors examined gender knowledge in normal Italian speakers during tip-of-the-tongue (TOT) states. They found that subjects could reliably access the gender of nouns for which they were unable to supply any phonology. A different result was obtained by Caramazza and Miozzo (1997), who also probed the latent lexical knowledge available to Italian speakers in a TOT state. Caramazza and Miozzo found that fragmentary phonological information and gender information were equally available when subjects could not retrieve the full phonology of a word, and that the availability of partial phonological information was unrelated to the availability of gender information.

In this discussion we do not address the lemma model of lexical retrieval, but only the claim that access to the gender of an object is equivalent to retrieving its syntactic properties. For a critique of the lemma model, see Caramazza and Miozzo (1997).

THE NATURE OF GRAMMATICAL GENDER

According to Corbett (1994) gender is recognized as existing in a language when there are families of nouns that have similar agreement patterns. In many cases the commonality among the nouns in such families is one of biological gender, that is, it is semantically based. Undoubtedly, the term "gender" was assigned to such noun groups because the sharing of gender is the prototypical basis for having a shared agreement pattern. However, gender is not the only feature around which noun families may form. In the Algonquin languages animacy, and not biological gender, is the basis for such shared patterns of agreement inflection (Corbett, 1994). Regardless of the particular semantic criterion that is used in any given language, the phenomenon is always referred to as gender.

Gender would present little problem theoretically if there were always a transparent basis for a noun's category membership. Because of the penchant for many languages to assign gender category membership arbitrarily, we have a phenomenon that is well known to anyone who speaks or has studied any of the European languages (except Hungarian). Namely, the class of words that have the masculine agreement pattern includes all nouns that denote males, whether human or not, as well as thousands of nouns that denote inanimate objects or abstract concepts for which maleness is irrelevant. Mutatis mutandis, the same applies to the feminine agreement class. Some languages (e.g., German, Russian) have a third or "neuter" agreement family.

Once the principle of agreement families for nouns becomes established in a language the criteria for belonging to a particular pattern may follow seemingly arbitrary and illogical rules. For example, Rumanian has a family of words that follows the feminine agreement pattern in both singular and plural as well as a family that is masculine in agreement in both singular and plural. There is, however, a third family that takes masculine forms in the singular and feminine forms in the plural. In Dutch, masculine and feminine nouns share the same agreement pattern (regardless of their biological masculinity or femininity), but there is a second inflectional family consisting almost entirely of nouns that have no semantic gender properties. Curiously, however, the word for "girl" is in the latter class.

The phenomenon of gender has been recognized as having a similarity to the classifier system of Chinese and other less well-known languages. Classifiers are particles that are required to precede a noun in certain contexts. The assignment of a classifier to a noun is somewhat predictable for the Chinese speaker, on the basis of the physical (i.e., semantic) properties of the object, but for many nouns it must simply be learned. The arbitrariness of classifier assignment is precisely analogous to arbitrary gender assignment. However, there is no agreement involved other than the selection of the appropriate classifier.

HOW DOES A SPEAKER KNOW A WORD'S GENDER?

This question has a built-in trap, because of the multiple meanings of the word "know": procedural and declarative knowledge. In one sense, the procedural, knowing a word's gender refers to the capacity for automatic, "on line" use of the appropriate agreement inflections in normal speech or even in experimentally elicited forms. In this type of usage, there is no basis for drawing a distinction between natural gender and arbitrary or "grammatical" gender.

The feature of gender appears in a variety of phenomena within a sentence. Among these are agreement of determiners with their nouns and agreement of adjectives with the nouns that they modify. Also included in some languages is the agreement of the verb with the gender of the subject. All of the foregoing, because they represent intrasentential relations, are truly syntactic.

The marking of pronouns for gender is semantic, rather than syntactic, because the choice of pronoun gender agrees with an object in the environment, which is not necessarily expressed in a sentence, although it is presupposed by speaker and listener. For example, "Look at her! She's ahead of them all!"

The status of pronouns for inanimate nouns is more problematic. Animacy in English is marked by the use of *he/she/him/her* versus *it*. This choice is clearly based on semantic and not syntactic influences. In French, however, while the pronouns *il* and *elle* may represent animate (naturally gendered) or inanimate objects, reference to an inanimate noun generally requires explicit prior mention of the presupposed referent. For example, "Regarde cette robe! Elle est tres jolie." [Look at that dress! It (fem) is very pretty.] Analogously with English, the selection of the pronoun *elle* is a semantic choice, based on the property of femininity which for the French speaker is intrinsic to the word *robe* (dress).

It could be argued that the pronoun is syntactically influenced, across sentence boundaries. However, it is not always necessary for the referent noun to have been mentioned for the gender-appropriate pronoun to be used in discourse. There is a telling example, available to any visitor to Montreal, that indicates that even the choice of article may be governed by semantic, rather than syntactic features. There is a large lighted sign over the Queen Elizabeth hotel that reads "LE REINE ELISABETH." This seems, for the user of high school French, to be a jarring error in gender agreement of the article preceding "Reine." But the reason for this choice of article is that the concept referred to is *hotel* (masculine). Even though the *hotel* does not appear in the title, the property of grammatical masculinity dominates the choice of article. It appears then that the property of masculinity of linguistic gender has become attached to the concept. We do not argue that grammatical gender identity is always attached to the concept of a noun. We do argue that it may be, for some words, as in the case of *hotel*. In any case, as Corbett (1994) and van Berkum (1997) hold gender is intrinsic to the word and must be acquired for each noun as it is learned.

The second, or declarative, sense of *knowing* is the metalinguistic one—the ability to consciously state a grammatical rule (or gender). In this sense *knowing* that a word is masculine or feminine is no different from knowing other, clearly nonsyntactic, facts about it. Among such metalinguistic facts are whether it is of Anglo-Saxon or Greco-Roman origin, whether it is long or short, whether it is a mass noun or a count noun, whether it has a funny spelling, whether it is a homonym of another word, or whether it is a singular or a plural (e.g., data). As an example of how far metalinguistic knowledge can go, I can cite an anomic patient whom I have on audio tape. Asked to recount how he would change a flat tire, he immediately blocked on the word *jack*. Finally, he said, "You know,—the two kids that went up the hill." In this way the patient revealed that his metaknowledge that the object *jack* is homophonous with the name *Jack* is independent of and more robust than his ability to access the phonology of either one of these words.

All of the foregoing may legitimately be considered to be part of the semantic baggage of the word. This does not deny the fact that some of these properties have syntactic consequences. So it is with gender. Badecker et al. (1995) tested gender knowledge in Dante through the metalinguistic approach and are open to the criticism that they may have been probing only his linguistic metaknowledge. It is conceivable that some individuals, when asked to supply the gender of a word metalinguistically, prompt themselves by producing it with its article, thus using their automatic syntactic processing as a crutch. However, we know that Dante was unable to use this route, since he could not tell which of the two alternate forms of the masculine singular article went with the targets that he could not name.

The fact that gender metaknowledge may be more easily accessible than word phonology should come as no surprise. There are a number of examples of the robustness of sensitivity to gender, at least in the domain of written word recognition. For example, Morton and Patterson (1980) report that their deep dyslexic P. W. had 11 of 12 correct judgments of the gender of personal pronouns, as opposed to 9 of 18 correct judgments of case and 15 out of 22 correct judgments of person. Goodglass, Lindfield, and Alexander (199) found that both of their pure alexic patients were almost error-free in judging names as belonging to boys or girls. This type of semantic decision was by far better preserved than any other category decisions, such as animal versus nonanimal.

CONCLUSIONS

In summary, I have assembled some evidence to argue against the assumption that the ability to identify the grammatical gender of a noun (in a gender language) is the same as accessing the syntactic feature of gender agreement. Metaknowledge of a word's gender assignment is analogous to other forms of metaknowledge about words and is semantic in nature. A number of examples were given as evidence that grammatical gender knowledge may be assimilated to the concept of the noun and become part of its semantics, thus sharing some of the properties of biological gender knowledge. Consequently, demonstration of metaknowledge about grammatical gender cannot be cited as evidence that the syntactic component of a lemma has been accessed.

ACKNOWLEDGMENTS

The preparation of this manuscript was supported in part by USPHS Grant DC 00018. I wish to acknowledge the critical comments of my colleagues in the Wednesday Naming Group: Art Wingfield, Errol Baker, Jean Berko Gleason, Mary R. Hyde, Kim Lindfield, Roberta F. Gallagher, and Susan E. Ward. However, any flaws in reasoning are purely my responsibility.

REFERENCES

Badecker, W., Miozzo, M., & Zannutini, R. (1995). The two stage model of lexical retrieval: Evidence from a case of anomia with selective preservation of grammatical gender. *Cognition, 57,* 193–213.

Caramazza, A., & Miozzo, M. (1997). The relation between linguistic and phonological knowledge in lexical access: Evidence from the tip-of-the-tongue phenomenon. *Cognition, 64,* 309–343.

Corbett, G. G. (1994). Gender and gender systems. In R. E. Asher & J. M. Y. Simpson (Eds.), *The encyclopedia of language and linguistics* (Vol. 3, pp. 1347–1353). Oxford: Pergamon.

Goodglass, H., Lindfield, K., & Alexander (1999). Limited semantic processing without word recognition in two patients with pure alexia. In press.

Levelt, W. J. M. (1989). *Speaking: From intention to articulation.* Cambridge, Massachusetts: MIT Press.

Morton, J., & Patterson, K. (1970). Little words—No! In M. Coltheart, K. Patterson, & J. Morton (Eds.), *Deep dyslexia* (pp. 279–285).

van Berkum, J. J. A. (1997). Syntactic processes in speech production: The retrieval of grammatical gender. *Cognition, 64,* 115–152.

Vigliocco, G., Antonini, T., & Garrett, M. F. (1997). Grammatical gender is on the tip of Italian tongues. *Psychological Science, 8,* 314–317.

Chapter 14

The Time-Course of Lexical Access and the Role of Context: Converging Evidence from Normal and Aphasic Processing

David Swinney, Penny Prather, and Tracy Love

PREFACE

The purpose of this chapter is to consolidate existing literature and intro-duce new evidence from both focal lesion and neurologically unimpaired populations which speak to the behavioral processes and neural substrates involved in lexical access and lexical ambiguity resolution during sentence comprehension. The chapter is dedicated to Edgar Zurif, and in many ways, writing it has brought each of its authors full circle. It was in the very initial years of dealing with issues of context effects, lexical access, and mental modularity in Boston that Edgar exerted his influence on work by the first author concerning the issues inherent in claims of contextually in-dependent mental processes and how such processes might play out in terms of brain organization. His influence in those early years was crucial, conceptually, central, and substantial (not to mention insistent). Soon there-after, the second author joined Edgar at the Veterans Administration in Boston, and new consideration of the work on "bugs, bugs, bugs" (as the lexical ambiguity issues were referred to in those environs) brought on a resurgence of (re)considerations of the role of lexical processes in agram-matic aphasia. The third author joined this team a few years later. None of the excitement nor effectiveness of the work in either of those eras could have occurred without Edgar's central role. Now, after quite a number of years working in other realms of language processing, we find ourselves returning to this fertile area of research, with some new localization-of-function evidence which allows a comprehensive and integrated view of the work. It leads, not surprisingly, to the story that Edgar has continually championed throughout his career working with each of the authors. His intuitions, like his research, have always been spot-on. Thus, it is with a sense of déjà vu that we present this story and link it, as it belongs, with our most happy associations and collaborations with Edgar.

INTRODUCTION

Investigations of the nature of access to lexical information during sentence comprehension have been a centerpiece or research in the language processing literature since the inception of the field of psycholinguistics. Questions concerning whether such access is fundamentally a form-directed process (or alternatively, whether it is directed from predictions based on world knowledge and/or sentential context), whether it is a serial (or alternatively, parallel) process, and whether it is an exhaustive (or alternatively, delimited) process all form central issues that are still under debate today. The goal of this chapter is to resolve some of the key conflicts in the vast literature on these critical issues. We argue that the key to such resolution lies in the consideration of three fundamental issues.

The first is recognition that lexical access is not a single, uniform process. Like language processing in general, lexical access can be seen to have (some) different properties in (some) different situations. The work in this chapter will focus on one such (albeit major) situation: lexical access as it takes place *during auditory language comprehension,* at normal speaking rates. Such a focus potentially differs, for example, from a focus concerned with how such access might take place in isolated single-word presentation conditions, or two-word contexts, or in reading (to name but a few).

The second issue is methodological. It is the (surprisingly elusive) point that research methodologies (even on-line research methodologies) are not all alike. The literature in this field divides greatly based on the research techniques utilized to examine lexical access. Put simply, some methodologies reveal more about the details of language processing than others, and some interfere and interact with the ongoing process being measured less than others. Only detailed analysis of the manner in which methodologies interact with the process they are intended to reveal will allow an understanding of what part of the evidence derived from each method truly reflects the nature of lexical access as it occurs during auditory language comprehension.

Third, a more thorough understanding of the lexical access can be found by simultaneously considering evidence from both brain-damaged and non-neurologically involved populations. There is a great deal of work on lexical processing which exists largely independently in two separate research domains: evidence from examinations of processing in non-neurologically involved populations, and evidence derived from processing in populations with language disruptive focal lesions—the aphasias. However, with a few notable exceptions, there has been only minimal integration of these literatures. This chapter will compare and contrast relevant evidence from both types of populations, demonstrating a converging, coherent story of lexical processing. In the same vein, this chapter will also examine the role of each of the cerebral hemispheres in lexical processing in both normal and brain-damaged populations.

THE BASIC EVIDENCE

The work we will examine focuses on the access of words with more than one meaning—lexical ambiguities (specifically, homophones). Such words (which have been one of the standard workhorses of the lexical processing literature) allow for separable examination of access and processing of individually addressable interpretations attached to the same word-form (sounds). This allows for precise examination of issues such as "modularity" of access (e.g., Fodor, 1983), form-driven versus meaning-driven access, the role of context in access, and serial versus parallel accounts of access to information associated with words.

Access of information associated with lexical ambiguities during ongoing auditory sentence comprehension has been demonstrated to be an exhaustive process, *ceritus paribus*. An enormous array of evidence has supported the view that in the absence of a biasing context all interpretations of a lexical ambiguity are activated and accessed. Further, and more critically, the same exhaustive activation effect has even been shown to hold in the presence of a strong prior biasing context. Overall then, access of the several meanings of the lexical ambiguity is momentarily achieved independent of world knowledge or prior biasing context. (This last evidence has come from a small set of tasks which have been demonstrated to reflect the access process, but to have minimal interaction with the lexical access process itself; more on this, below.) Moreover, these findings have reliably led to a model which holds that lexical access per se is a form-driven, autonomous, exhaustive process (see, e. g., Love & Swinney, 1996; Onifer & Swinney, 1981; Picoult & Johnson, 1992; Prather & Swinney, 1977; Seidenberg, Tanenhaus, Leiman, & Bienkowski, 1982; Simpson,

1981; Swinney, 1979; Swinney & Prather, 1989; Tanenhaus, Leiman, & Seidenberg, 1979, among others). Much of this same literature has demonstrated that a short time after access, only the contextually appropriate meaning of a lexical ambiguity encountered in a sentence remains active, an effect which may take place within 300 ms of initial activation (see, e.g., Swinney, 1979; Onifer & Swinney, 1981.) Thus, encountering the phonetic form of a word during ongoing auditory sentence comprehension appears to result in the immediate access to (and activation of) all meanings for that word. And, prior-occurring context has an effect only on the results of this access, acting to very rapidly determine the "appropriate" interpretation of the ambiguity from among the many activated.

This evidence stands in strong contrast to claims that lexical access is a contextually conditioned, predictive, highly interactive, process. Such claims (e.g., Liu, Bates, Powell, & Wulfeck, 1997; Tabossi, 1988) have resulted from several entangled lines of argument and data. We mention three here. First has been the confusion over claims concerning modularity of lexical access; some interactionist proponents have implied that evidence upholding modularity is effectively a denial of context effects on lexical processing. That, of course, is hyperbole—no one questions the fact that context has an effect on lexical processing. Rather, the issue is *when* and *where* such contextual effects take place during ongoing processing. (The answer to that question appears to be, based on the best empirical evidence, only following access but not before it.) Thus, while context may not be used predictively in lexical access, it does have an effect on the processing of information, once accessed. Second, the claim has also been made that modularity makes no sense due to the fact that efferent fibers run from "higher" cortical areas to "lower" areas providing a built-in neural basis for top-down control. However, two issues make this fact irrelevant to questions of mental modularity re lexical access. First, we have little enough evidence about the neurological organization of language in the broadest form, much less the neurological organization of word access. And, we certainly have no evidence that there is hard wiring from centers of higher-order knowledge (or whatever organization is desired to describe such neurological representation) to lexical access (not do we have evidence that even were such wiring present, that it might control/direct such access). More crucially, of course, this argument simply misses the essential distinction between claims of modularity of mind and modularity of brain. The claims and evidence about the autonomy of lexical access are concerned with functional facts—with modularity of mind—which, independently of any issue of afferent and efferent connections, is concerned with what is functionally used during access. Put more succinctly, even if it could be shown that there were such efferent connections between representations of higher order knowledge and lexical access, and that such connections could in principle be used to control the latter, whether they actually were used to "control" or direct access is an issue for functional, behavioral research only—it cannot be established any other way. Therefore, it is only an issue resolvable via behavioral evidence, however difficult that is to obtain. Which brings us to the third issue—data purporting to demonstrate interactivity of prior context and lexical access. This data tends to come from two types of studies—those involving processing of isolated lexical items (or pairs of items) and a few studies involving the processing of words in sentences. The first of these will not be discussed in this chapter, as the processing of isolated (or paired, etc.) lexical items involves considerations of a wide range of issues that are unrelated to lexical processing in sentences. However, in both cases (and particularly those involving sentences), careful consideration of the methodologies involved in these studies mandates the rejection of these data as relevant to the basic question. Thus, it is necessary to have a methodological discussion before we proceed further.

Methodological Considerations

Fundamentally, examination of the question of precisely when and where context has its effects on lexical processing requires a methodology that is both temporally fine grained and sensitive to unconscious perceptual processes (yet, does not interact with them). This means, first, that only "on-line" methodologies are capable of distinguishing between competing theories of lexical access. The "on line–off line" distinction represents a continuum of techniques, where on-line refers to measures of processing that are employed during on-going processing. It should be noted that the concept on-line is often inappropriately conflated with some of the empirical methods used to measure on-line processing, such as "reaction time" or even "fast reaction time"; on-line refers to a well-defined match of (not only temporal, but other) critical parameters of the comprehension-process-of-interest to a particular technique. Speed of response alone is absolutely no guarantee that the task will capture any of the critical on-line processing information that is being investigated (see, e.g., discussion of Liu et al. 1997, below).

What is requisite in any examination of comprehension is finding the best match of the technique to the question under investigation. In that regard there are at least three separate (but often interacting) issues to be concerned with: (1) sensitivity of the task to the process of interest, (2) ability of task to reflect the process-of-interest *independently* of other comprehension (or task) processes, and (3) timing of task as applied to (relative to) the time-course of the process-of-interest. We discuss each of these in turn.

Task sensitivity

First, there is the issue of whether any given task actually reflects (is sensitive to) the process under exploration. For example, using an on-line sentence grammaticality judgement task ("Is it a 'good' sentence in English?") may not be sensitive to experimentally induced perturbations in lexical access, although it may reflect other aspects of comprehension, such as the difficulty of integration of a lexical item into a sentence. Consider another example, the case of dual process interference tasks, such as phoneme monitoring (Foss, 1998), word monitoring (Foss, Starkey, & Bias, 1978), cross-modal lexical decision (Shapiro, Zurif, & Grimshaw, 1987), or Stroop technique (Stroop, 1935) tasks. These tasks all share the assumption of a "central processing bottleneck"; when subjects are both processing sentences and doing the secondary task (e.g., monitoring for a word), any increase in processing load in the former will be reflected in slowed reaction times in the second (caused by interference). These tasks are quite valuable as on-line reflections of processing *when* an interference/ processing load effect is found. A problem occurs, however, when no increased load "effect" is found. It may be that there *is* simply no effect to be found, or it may be that the particular interference task utilized is simply *insensitive* to the *level* of processing load actually present. It might be, for example, that the processing load increase caused by some variable is small and does not create sufficient interference to be reflected in a secondary "load" task. Or, it may be that the task load caused by (for example) phoneme monitoring is simply interfering with a response decision at a level of processing which is not involved in the level of processing being examined (e.g., inferencing at a discourse level). Unfortunately, it is very difficult to determine which of the various possibilities is actually true. In all, this first issue of task sensitivity can be an extremely difficult one to verify and establish (and, sadly, such effort is often omitted entirely), and yet it may be the easiest of the three concerns we have raised to meet adequately.

Task independence

Far more difficult to deal with is the second issue, which is concerned with how uniquely a task reflects *only* the subprocess of interest, and not *that subprocess along with several other processes* involved in comprehension. A large number of tasks are sensitive to several putative levels of processing, and, if these tasks are to be used effectively it is critical both to know precisely which levels the task is sensitive to, and to factor out those levels that are not of interest. Unfortunately, this too can be extremely difficult. Take, for example, the task of "lexical-repetition-during-sentence-comprehension," which has been taken by some investigators to be a measure of lexical activation and access (e.g., Liu et al., 1997). The mechanics of this task are as follows: First, subjects hear a stimulus sentence presented auditorily. At some point during the sentence a key word in the sentence is spoken in a voice (male/female) different from that of the rest of the sentence. Hearing this "difference voice" is the cue for a subject to repeat this word out loud (this "key" word is standardly the last word in the sentence or phrase which is heard; reaction time to repeat the word is measured, beginning with the onset of the key word). Resulting reaction times are often taken by researchers as a measure of lexical access alone. However, this task, while it involves aspects of lexical access, *also* standardly reflects the time taken to integrate the word into the prior sentential material. That is, the time to "consciously hear and repeat" the word spoken in the "other" voice not only includes the time involved in preparing the word to be produced (and perhaps, reaccessing aspects of the word for such production), but also the time involved in understanding the word in light of the sentential context in which it is being comprehended. Unfortunately, the two factors of access and integration are totally intertwined in their effect on response reaction time. This task is essentially identical to the class of tasks in psycholinguistics which can be termed "sentence continuation" (or sentence interruption) tasks, tasks which are standardly used to study the effect of integration of material into sentential contexts. These tasks are commonly used to demonstrate ease or difficulty of integrating lexical elements with certain types of characteristics into the prior sentential material (e.g., Ahrens & Swinney, 1995; Tyler & Marslen-Wilson, 1977, 1982; Wright & Garrett, 1984), and, in fact, have been shown to be quite sensitive to such "ease of integration" effects.

In general, there are at least two major, but related, types of confounds involved in sorting out the answer to any concern over whether a particular task reflects *only* the process of interest: *specificity confounds* and *task-induced confounds*. The above discussion of the "lexical repetition" task demonstrates an example of a *specificity confound*—the operating characteristics of the task cannot be isolated to the single process of interest (here, lexical access); the task necessarily reflects other processes in its operation. The other type of counfound, *task-induced confounds*, distribute themselves into several subclasses. One such class (the only one we will discuss here), can be termed metalinguistic confounds. These are confounds introduced when a task requires conscious reflection on a typical unconscious ongoing process (such as normal sentence comprehension). One example is the "gating" task (in which a subject is required to "guess" which words are still possible candidates from an auditory partial-word fragment, thus putatively providing a "uniqueness point" for word recognition (Grosjean, 1980). While this task most certainly does provide a consciously determinable uniqueness point, such a point may not relate in any direct way to lexical identification/access involved in standard fluent language comprehension, where conscious introspection concerning words is at a minimum. "Word-by-word reading" is another such task. The single-word-by-single-word aspect of the sentence presentation leads many subjects to treat each word as if it were the final one in the sentence (particularly in judgement/monitoring versions), hence encouraging "early closure" of sentences (for discussion, see, e. g., Ferreira, & Henderson, 1990). Thus, many uses of this technique force (encourage) conscious resolution of the sentence before the end of the sentence may occur (at each possible ending point). Examples of these types abound; the solution is to find, where possible, tasks that do not encourage such (metalinguistic or other) intrusions into the normal comprehension process.

Task timing

The third issue is that of the *timing* of the occurrence of the task in relation to the time-course of the process of interest. Most sentential processes are temporally evanescent. Reflecting such rapidly fading, brief, subtle, and momentary processing events is difficult for any task. Clearly, however, to be maximally useful, such a task must be one that can be equally applied *at any point during* sentence processing (i.e., not just at certain points—such as only after words, or at the beginning or ends of clauses, etc.). Rather than focusing on tasks that do not meet this criteria, we will focus on some tasks that best accomplish the needed timing and flexibility, while also not producing the problems associated with the first two issues raised above.

The set of such tasks is a small one, involving both electrophysiological and reaction time techniques. Electrophysiological techniques such as event-related brain potentials (ERP) or MEG have the virtue of being continuous-recording tasks (they can be gathered throughout the entire time-course of the sentence/discourse being examined). Such techniques hold the promise of ultimately becoming one of *the* methods of choice for real-time examination of language processing at some point in the future. Currently, however, with few exceptions, ERP examinations of language involve visual word-by-word presentation (reading) of language stimuli—typically with 500 ms or more occurring between successive words. This slow presentation changes the nature of the comprehension process (see task induced confounds, above) and does not reflect the form of language processing we will consider here (auditory comprehension; the nature of how reading related to auditory comprehension is still far from determined). Among reaction-time based behavioral techniques, one of the most temporally flexible and temporally relevant behavioral methods currently is use is cross-modal lexical priming. In what follows, we will briefly focus on how this task works, and on both appropriate and inappropriate uses of the task in measuring language processes.

Cross-modal priming techniques

While many on-line behavioral methodologies each have revealed important properties of language processing, cross-modal lexical priming (CMLP; Swinney, Onifer, Prather, & Hirshkowitz, 1979) has proven to be a particularly illuminative and sensitive measure of moment-by-moment sentence processing. CMLP comes in many varieties, but all involve the following conditions and properties: First, the sentential material under study is presented *auditorily* to subjects, who are told that their major job is to understand the sentence(s) or discourse they hear. (Subjects are standardly tested for comprehension throughout the experiment—to keep attention to the task of comprehension.) Second, subjects are told they have another task to perform: at some point while they are listening to the sentence(s) a visual item will appear on a screen in front of them and they will have to make a decision about that visual item. This visual item may be a letter string (to which subjects may be required to make a lexical decision, or a classifying decision, or a "naming" response) or it may be a picture (again to which some type of classifying response is made, such as "animal/nonanimal"). Work has shown that most two-choice classification responses work quite well in obtaining basic effects with this task.

Several aspects of this technique require specific mention: First, presentation of the auditory sentence is always continued throughout and beyond presentation of the visual item (and on to the end of the sentence). That is, the sentence is never ended with the visual probe; this prevents the probe from being integrated into the ongoing sentential material (provided, of course, that the sentential material is presented normally—see, e.g., Nicol, Swinney, Love, & Hald, 1997). Second, this "secondary" task never involves metalinguistic judgments about the sentential material (such as, "Was this word in the sentence?"). Third, at least up to the point of the visual target presentation, processing of the sentence is uninterrupted and "normal." In this regard, the task differs considerably from many other on-line techniques that require subjects to evaluate each word in a sentence as it appears, or to hold a target in mind while the sentence is being processed. Thus, this task is one of the least intrusive behavioral techniques we have for the on-line examination of the normal comprehension process. There is, of course, a planned relation between the two tasks the subject performs (auditory sentence comprehension and visual target classification) in CMLP. On experimental trials, the visual target is associatively semantically related to a critical word (or phrase) in the sentence. Following the principle of automatic semantic priming, occurrence of an auditory word (the prime) in the sentence just prior to processing of another item (the visual target word) that is associatively related to that auditory word results in speeded processing/classification of the target, a result that is generally known as priming (see, e.g., Meyer, Schvaneveldt, & Ruddy, 1974; Neely, 1991). The CMLP task uses the fact that such priming occurs to provide an indication of WHEN critical words in the sentence are active during processing. Thus, if a visual target is "primed" when presented at a certain point in the sentence, this is taken as evidence that, at that point, the meaning of the relevant (associatively related) word in the sentence is active. The fact that such priming has been demonstrated for interpretations of a lexical ambiguity (even following strong biasing context) has been the prime evidence of autonomous lexical access during sentence comprehension.[1] With the critically fundamental considerations of methodology now on the table, we return to the basic facts of lexical access during ongoing sentence comprehension.

---

[1]There is one additional methodological issue that deserves airing, even though not directly relevant to the issue of lexical ambiguity, and that relates to the difference between the use of CMLP in *interrupted versus noninterrupted sentential presentation procedures*. Following publication of a large array of CMLP studies demonstrating *reactivation* of "fronted" direct object NPs following the matrix verb in object-relative constructions (see e.g., Swinney, Ford, Frauenfelder, & Bresnan, 1987, as reported in Nicol & Swinney, 1989: Hickok, Canseco-Gonzalez, Zurif, & Grimshaw, 1992; Love & Swinney, 1996; Nagel, Shapiro, & Nawy, 1994; Nicol & Pickering, 1993; Swinney, Zurif, Prather, & Love, 1996, among others), McKoon and Ratcliff (1994) raised a particular objection to these findings. A model of priming effects supported by McKoon and Ratcliff—the compound cue model of priming (see, e.g., Ratcliff & McKoon, 1988)—has no principled mechanism to allow for priming during sentence processing when an overt-prime is not present. Hence the findings of reactivation as generated by structural processes was quite disturbing to this general approach. McKoon and Ratcliff took as a point of attack the materials in the first paper demonstrating such reactivation (research by Ford, Frauenfelder Bresnan, & Swinney, which motivated much of the later work—see, Swinney et al., 1987). They pointed out that there was a possible confound between the experimental and control probes used by Swinney et al., such that reaction time to the experimental probes may have been faster than that for the control probes not because of priming at the "empty" postverb position, but because the experimental probes

"fit" more easily into the ongoing sentence than did the control probes at that point. They then attempted to demonstrate experimentally that this potential confound could cause the incongruity reaction time (RT) effect they predicted. In this they used a subset of the sentences and target items originally employed by Swinney et al. (1987), altering the sentences so that the filler NP appeared *after* the probe point, as in the following example (compare to object-relative example, above): "The crowd at the party accused the boy." Here, what had been the head of the relative clause ("the boy") now appears after the verb, and the sentence no longer contains a filler-gap relation.

Now the critical point relevant to methodological concerns: McKoon and Ratcliff (1994), in attempting to replicate the "potential confound" in the Swinney et al. (1987) work, CHANGED THE TASK from the cross-modal lexical priming (CMLP) task used by Swinney et al. to a word-by-word visual presentation format study. In the latter, subjects see (rather than hear, as in CMLP) sentences presented visually, word by word, so that each new word in the sentence overwrites the preceding word. Further, in this task, target words also appear visually, offset to the right of the sentence presentation area, marked with asterisks, at one of two positions: immediately before and immediately after the verb. The targets, were either a semantic associate of the direct object (e.g., "girl") or a matched nonassociate (e.g., "body"). McKoon and Ratcliff found speeded response times to "girl" (relative to the control) after the verb "accused," but the reverse pattern before it. Their interpretation of this finding was that after the verb, the set of "related" target items (here "girl") simply fit better into the ongoing sentence than the controls. They then concluded (again, from results obtained with an entirely different task) that that the findings from the fluent, continuous-sentence presentation format of auditory CMLP were due to these differences in "congruence of the targets with the sentences."

The question is, of course, can such generalizations across sentence-presentation formats be validly made? First, however, we wish to interject at least a couple of points about the operation of CMLP. For one thing there has long been evidence, based on extensive experience with the CMLP task, that the visually presented probes are *not* typically integrated into the ongoing auditory sentence (and hence that the "fit" of visual targets with the sentence is not a factor with CMLP, when used standardly). This assumption has been backed by evidence, the major piece of which will be described immediately below. A second point is that the basic finding of Swinney et al. (1987) on gap-filling has been replicated a number of times with the CMLP Technique in studies that do *not* contain the potential confound of "probe fit" pointed to by McKoon and Ratcliff (1994). Most recently, for example, Love and Swinney (1996), in a study which used relative-clause constructions, explicitly controlled for equivalence of "fit" or "integratability" into the auditory sentence of both related and unrelated targets; their findings fully replicated (and extended) the earlier findings obtained by Swinney et al. (1987; reported in Nicol & Swinney, 1989). Thus, it is important to make clear at the outset that the effect demonstrating "reactivation" of fillers at gap sites with the CMLP technique is secure and replicable, *independent* of any *potential* confound in the original Swinney et al., 1987 materials, and the speculations by McKoon & Ratcliff, 1994).

To explore the question of whether inferences about sentence processing and methodology can be validly transferred across two very different types of sentence-presentation formats, Nicol et al. (1997) performed an experiment aimed precisely at comparing effects revealed by CMLP to those discoverable via the unimodal visual sentence interruption technique employed by McKoon and Ratcliff (1994). The particular focus here is on a technique in which subjects are presented with a fluent, uninterrupted, auditory sentence, and also make a judgment about a visually presented target word which appears *concurrently* with some portion of the auditory sentence (but before the end of that sentence), as compared to a technique in which the sentence is presented (visually) in such a fashion that the visually presented target interrupts the ongoing flow of the sentence being comprehended. The focal question was, will the targets integrate into the ongoing sentence in either case?, thus potentially distorting findings obtained with a priming task under either mode of sentence presentation (via differential responses to "good fit" targets compared with "bad fit" targets).

For this study, identical materials were created for use in two separate methodologies: (1), the CMLP continuous (uninterrupted) auditory sentence presentation approach and (2) the unimodal visual probe–sentence interruption paradigm employed by McKoon and Ratcliff (1994). Sentences were of the following structure: noun phrase, prepositional phrase, verb, noun phrase, prepositional phrase; as in example (1), below (probe/target point is indicated with an asterisk). Each (pair of) sentence(s) was paired with two target words, one of which was (and the other was not) "congruent" with the sentence fragment (although neither target was meant to be predictable from the prior context; congruence was tested in continuation-judgement prestudies). Members of each target pair were matched in length and frequency, and, most importantly, a priori lexical decision times (taken from a lexical decision test performed on the words presented in isolation) as well as for length and frequency. Thus, the word *apple* is more congruent with the sentence fragment than the word *agony* on the grounds that an apple may be pushed, but agony cannot.

> (1) *The cat at our house pushed* * *the old soccer ball from the neighbor's roof.*
> Congruent target: APPLE
> Incongruent target: AGONY

In addition, the target words were paired with a second sentence which provided a matched-sentence control case. As can be seen, the incongruent target for sentence (1) is the congruent target in sentence (2).

> (2) *The mother with the pony instilled* * *great happiness in her young daughter.*
> Congruent target: AGONY
> Incongruent target: APPLE

These materials were then presented to (different groups of) subjects under each of the two different sentence-presentation techniques. The data were unequivocal: In the unimodal sentence-interruption paradigm, there was *significant priming* for congruent targets compared to incongruent targets, fully replicating McKoon and Ratcliff (1994). However, in the CMLP study there was NO *priming* for congruent versus incongruent targets.

The CMLP results contrast sharply with those of the McKoon and Ratcliff (1994) task. The utter lack of a congruence effect in CMLP argues that the cross-modal continuous-sentence presentation, at least when used with normal fluent speech, effectively prevents integration and intrusion of visually presented target words.

The morals of this last set of methodological issues is clear. First, one cannot make assumptions about the mechanics of any one task based on data or properties of performance from another task. And, relatedly, McKoon & Ratcliff (1994) are simply wrong about their assumptions that priming in CMLP (when used normally, of course) is affected by congruence of the target words with the sentence; hence their model of priming is also likely wrong (or at least highly insufficient)—structural processing can cause priming without an overt NP present. Second, fluent, uninterruptable presentation of sentential material is crucial to the study of comprehension, as it resists intrusion of extraneous material (including visual targets) into the ongoing comprehension process. Finally, CMLP is extremely flexible, with reliable tasks, and is among the most sensitive measures of on-line sentence processing in the comprehension task inventory.

LEXICAL ACCESS AND CONTEXT EFFECTS: EVIDENCE FROM NEUROLOGICALLY INVOLVED AND NON-NEUROLOGICALLY INVOLVED POPULATIONS

Lexical Processing in Nonimpaired Populations

As stated earlier, an abundance of evidence from real-time processing studies of lexical ambiguities has demonstrated that access to the surface (phonetic) form of lexical ambiguities results in the immediate activation of all meanings for that word. These finding have been used to support the view that the initial access of meanings for lexical ambiguities in sentences involves modular, exhaustive, context-independent, encapsulated processing (e.g., Swinney, 1991). This phonetic, form-driven access provides a tool that allows us to gain leverage in questioning the underlying neural substrates of this level of language processing.

However, before turning to that evidence, we will briefly review a small portion of a comprehensive study which used lexical ambiguities as antecedent fillers in object-relative constructions, a study which will allow us to examine more details of the time-course of activation of the several meanings of an ambiguous word in biasing contexts than has previously been available in the literature (Love and Swinney, 1996). In this study, participants (non-neurologically involved college students) heard sentences such as:

The professor insisted that the exam be completed in ink, so Jimmy used the new pen[*1] that his mother-in-law[*2] recently purchased[*3] because the multiple colors allowed for more creativity.

Strong biasing contexts in these sentences were created according to criteria used by Tabossi (1988). In this study priming for each of two meanings of the antecedent filler "pen" (i.e., "pencil" and "jail") was examined at the offset of the ambiguous word via a CMLP technique. The results demonstrated significant priming for words related to both the primary (most frequent—"pencil") and the secondary (less frequent—"jail") meanings immediately following initial occurrence of the ambiguity in the sentence ([*1]). This study thus replicated a long established finding of context-independent, exhaustive access for lexical ambiguities, thus reiterating evidence supporting a model of lexical access as a modular, autonomous, and encapsulated process. At the second test (point ([*2]), only visual target words related to the contextually relevant interpretation of the ambiguity (pencil) were found to be primed, as was the case at test point ([*3]). Thus, context has a rapid effect in choosing the appropriate interpretation of the meaning of the ambiguous word, and that is maintained (and perhaps reactived) later in sentence processing. This pattern of exhaustive, form-driven access has also been demonstrated in pre-school-age children (Swinney and Prather, 1989; Love, Swinney, Bagdasaryan, & Prather, 1999), in studies involving cross-modal picture priming (the children tested were too young to make lexical decisions). Children as young as 3 years, 11 months demonstrate context-independent access for lexically ambiguous words.

Lexical Processing in Brain-Injured Populations

Work with focal lesion populations has provided an interesting and critical addition to the literature on lexical processing. This arena of research provides a vehicle via which certain aspects of intricately entwined cognitive subsystems can be disentangled. In one study that is central to the issues of this chapter, an attempt to examine the role of lexical processing in the disorder known as Broca's (agrammatic) aphasia, and in an attempt to discern the role of neural substrate(s) underlying Broca's aphasia, work studying the effects of semantic context on lexical access in nonfluent agrammatic (Broca's) and fluent aphasic (Wernicke's) patients was undertaken by Swinney, Zurif, and Nicol (1989). They presented agrammatic aphasics, fluent aphasics and nonimpaired control subjects with sentences biased toward the primary interpretation of a (already inherently biased) lexical ambiguity (e.g., SCALE: where the interpretation of "WEIGHT" is given 75% of the time in the absence of context). In replication of past findings, the nonimpaired control population demonstrated exhaustive access for both meanings of the ambiguous word (via CMLP priming) regardless of sentential bias. The fluent aphasic population also displayed the same pattern of effects (contextually independent access, as inferred from priming for visual target words related to each meaning of the ambiguity). In contrast to these two populations however, the agrammatic aphasics demonstrated a very different pattern of results: only the primary, most frequent interpretation of the ambiguous word was found to be primed immediately after the word was heard in a sentence. This result led to the conclusion that only the most frequent interpretation of ambiguous words is immediately available to Broca's aphasics, with other lexical meanings only available following a more temporally protracted (slower-than-normal "rise time") period.

Prather, Zurif, Love, and Brownell (1997) further examined the "slowed activation" hypothesis in Broca's and Wernicke's aphasia by studying the time course of lexical activation in two patients. Using a list-priming paradigm, temporal delays between successive words were manipulated—ranging from 300 to 2100 ms. In contrast to elderly subjects, who prime at relatively short interstimulus intervals (ISIs) beginning at 500 ms, the

Broca's aphasic subject showed reliable *automatic* priming *only* at a long ISI of 1500 ms. That is, this subject retained the ability to access lexical information automatically if allowed sufficient time to do so, a finding that may help explain disrupted comprehension of normally rapid conversational speech.

In further support of the notion of slowed access to (some aspects of) word meanings following damage to Broca's area, Swaab, Brown, and Hagoort (1997) studied whether spoken sentence comprehension deficits in Broca's aphasics result from their inability to access the subordinate meaning of ambiguous words or from a delay in their selection of the contextually appropriate meaning. They employed an ERP methodology. Broca's aphasics and unimpaired control subjects were asked to actively listen to the sentences presented auditorily. The status of "activation" of a sentence-final ambiguous word was inferred from the amplitude of the N400 to the targets at two interstimulus intervals (ISIs)- short and long. The ERP evidence demonstrated that Broca's aphasics, in contrast to elderly controls, were not successful at selecting the appropriate meaning of the ambiguity in the short ISI condition. But at the long ISI, the patients were able to successfully complete the contextual selection process.

Thus, overall, it appears that the (left-hemisphere) neural substrate underlying Broca's aphasia (Broca's area) is involved in the ability to have rapid/immediate access of multiple interpretations of a word and the resolution of those interpretations to a single meaning; damage to that cortical area appears to damage both the ability to initially have all interpretations of a word under consideration (only the most frequent appears to be in play initially) and to integrate context into consideration of the appropriate interpretation of an ambiguous word.

DIFFERENTIAL CEREBRAL HEMISPHERIC CONTRIBUTIONS TO LEXICAL ACCESS (AND CONTEXT EFFECTS)

Over the past few years there has been work on the role of the individual (independent) contributions of the left (LH) and right (RH) cerebral hemispheres in non-neurologically involved individuals to lexical processing, work which fits interestingly with the work on aphasia, as presented above. For instance, in studies of visual (isolated) word processing, Burgess and Simpson (1988) demonstrated, via a visual hemiretinal priming paradigm,[2] that the LH provides activation of multiple interpretations (primary and

[2]In this, ambiguous words are presented foveally, and visual targets associated to one or another meaning of the ambiguity are presented in only one or the other visual field (thus limiting each hemisphere's access to the information).

secondary meanings) of ambiguous words immediately on *viewing* the word. However, by 750 ms later, only the primary (more frequent) interpretation of the ambiguity is actively maintained (can be primed). In contrast, the RH appears to initially only have access to the more frequent interpretation of an ambiguous word, and "exhaustive" availability of both meanings of an ambiguous word (as measured via priming) are only found at longer temporal delays (750 ms) in the RH. Thus, from this visual, isolated word study, it would appear that the LH is involved in initially accessing all interpretations of lexical entry, and this same hemisphere also has the capacity to select and maintain activation for the most contextually relevant meaning of such words. In contrast, the RH appears to have the capacity to slowly develop and maintain activation for ancillary semantic information (e.g., secondary meanings) for words (see also Faust & Chiarello, 1998). A number of related papers tend to support this view of the role of the individual hemispheres in lexical processing. For example, Tompkins, Baumgaertner, Lehman, and Fossett (1997) conducted a study with RH damaged (RHD) individuals involving auditorily presented sentences with sentence-final lexical ambiguities. In this, an interference task involving presentation of visual targets 1 s after the end of the sentence was used. It was found that the RHD individuals (as opposed to nonimpaired control subjects) demonstrated difficulty in suppressing the contextually inappropriate meaning of the ambiguities. The authors argue that this lends support to the role of the right hemisphere in maintaining alternate (secondary) interpretations. Similarly, in a study involving non-brain-damaged subjects, Faust and Chiarello (1998) investigated hemisphere asymmetries in resolving lexical ambiguity within a sentence context. Sentences containing sentence-final ambiguous words (biased toward a single meaning) were presented, followed by a hemifield lateralized target word which was related to either the contextually relevant or contextually incongruent meaning of the ambiguous word. Right-visual-field-presented contextually congruent targets were facilitated, while RVF incongruent targets were not. In contrast, in the left visual field both congruent and noncongruent targets were facilitated, regardless of sentence context. This suggests that selecting the contextually appropriate word meaning requires the left hemisphere, and supports a right hemisphere role in maintaining alternate word senses. In a final related study, Titone (1998) also used an end-of-sentence-ambiguity hemifield-target paradigm and found evidence consistent with differential sensitivity to semantic relationships in the cerebral hemispheres. All of the above studies, however, employed end-of-sentence ambiguity targets, something that has been called into question due to end-of-sentence ambiguity targets, something that has been called into question due to end-of-sentence wrap-up effects in other studies of sentence processing (see, e.g., Balogh et al., 1998).

Hickok, Swinney, Bouck, and Hald (1998) conducted a study with 66 native English right-handers exploring the hemisphere asymmetries found in lexical ambiguity resolution by utilizing a CMLP experiment with divided field presentations. This study employed ambiguous words which were embedded *within* (not at the end of) a contextually biased auditorily presented sentence. Visual lexical decision targets related to the primary and secondary meanings of the ambiguity were presented to either the LH or RH only. Preliminary analysis of data from this study demonstrates clearly that priming for both interpretations of a lexical ambiguity is initially available in the LH, but only that for the contextually relevant interpretation is immediately available in the RH. With a short temporal delay, the LH shows priming ONLY for the contextually relevant interpretation, while the RH demonstrates priming for BOTH interpretations. This overall body of work thus supports a story that integrates well with data reported for both neurologically impaired lexical processing and normal sentence processing.

AN INTEGRATED VIEW OF LEXICAL ACCESS AND CONTEXT EFFECTS: CONVERGING EVIDENCE FROM NORMAL AND APHASIC POPULATIONS

The overall story that emerges is one in which the left and right hemispheres work *together* to produce the findings that have been gathered from the focal lesion literature and the general language-processing literature. The left hemisphere's role appears to be one that underlies initial form-driven exhaustive lexical access and rapid contextual postaccess choice during ongoing sentence comprehension. In this hemisphere, immediately on encountering an ambiguity, there is exhaustive access of all meanings of the ambiguity. Broca's aphasic patients, who have damage to a particular portion of the left hemisphere, do not demonstrate such immediate exhaustive access. Thus, it follows that anterior regions of the frontal lobe (Broca's area) appear to be responsible for the exhaustive, form-driven, fast-acting aspect of lexical access demonstrated in studies of normal processing involving lexical ambiguities. When this area is damaged, individuals (Broca's aphasic's) must rely on lexical activation from the RH, which, as shown by the CMLP hemifield studies, initially results in activation of only a single interpretation of an ambiguity. Other meanings of the ambiguity are made available in this hemisphere only with a considerable time delay—thus accounting for the apparent "slow rise time" of secondary meanings found for ambiguities in Broca's aphasics. This same LH area also appears critical for the ultimate selection of a single interpretation of the ambiguity to be used in later processing during normal fluent sentence comprehension. (This is evidenced in the hemi-field studies by the finding of priming for only a single contextually relevant interpretation of an ambiguity following a short delay.) The right hemisphere displays the opposite pattern of access/activation effects (only the contextually relevant meaning is active immediately, whereas at a delayed point in processing, all meanings of the ambiguity are active). However, this effect is not reflected in processing displayed in standard on-line studies of normal sentence processing. Thus, it appears that the right hemisphere, while active, has no critical contribution to first-pass analysis of language in STANDARD language processing conditions in non-brain-damaged individuals (although it appears to be critical to Broca's aphasics processing). Note in all of this that the fluent (Wernicke's) aphasics' processing is similar to that of non-neurologically involved subjects. Thus, it is specifically the anterior portions of the left hemisphere (Broca's area) that subserves the exhaustive, fast-acting process of lexical access found in normal processing. And, the fact that damage to this area results in lexical processing that demonstrates slowed access to secondary interpretations suggests that important aspects of Broca's (agrammatic) aphasics' processing relies on more "temporally forgiving" routines involved at a discourse level, and fits well with the evidence of reliance on right-hemisphere (lexical and other) processing in these patients. Just as Edgar would have it (see, e.g., Zurif and Swinney, 1994).

ACKNOWLEDGMENTS

The authors express their appreciation and gratitude to their friend and colleague Edgar Zurif, for his continual inspiration and central involvement in the work reported herein (and elsewhere). The authors also gratefully acknowledge the contributions of Vikki Bouck to the research and writing reported in this chapter and support from NIH Grants DC02984 and DC01409 for support of the research reported in, and the writing of, this chapter.

REFERENCES

Ahrens, K., & Swinney, D. (1995). Participant roles and the processing of verbs during sentence comprehension. *Journal of Psycholinguistic Research, 24*, 533–547.

Balogh, J., Zurif, E., Prather, P., Swinney, D., & Finkel, L. (1998). Gap-filling and end-of-sentence effects in real-time language processing: Implications for modeling sentence comprehension in aphasia. *Brain and Language, 6*, 169–182.

Burgess, C., & Simpson, G. (1988). Hemispheric processing of ambiguous words. *Brain and Language, 33*, 86–104.

Faust, M., & Chiarello, C. (1998). Sentence context and lexical ambiguity resolution by the two hemispheres. *Neuropsychologia, 36*, 827–835.

Ferreira, F., & Henderson, J. M. (1990). Use of verb information in syntactic parsing: Evidence from eye movements and word-by-word self-pacing reading. *Journal of Experimental Psychology: Learning, Memory, and Cognition, 16,* 555–568.

Fodor, J. A. (1983). *The modularity of mind.* Cambridge, MA: MIT Press.

Foss, D. J. (1998). Two strands of scholarship on language comprehension: Phoneme monitoring and discourse context. *Journal of Psycholinguistic Research, 27,* 191–201.

Foss, D. J., Starkey, P., & Bias, R. (1978). Sentence comprehension processes in the preschooler. In R. N. Campbell & P. T. Smith (Eds.), *Recent advances in the psychology of language: Formal and theoretical approaches.* New York: Plenum.

Grosjean, F. (1980). Spoken word recognition processes and the gating paradigm. *Perception and Psychophysics, 28,* 267–283.

Hickok, G., Canseco-Gonzalez, E., Zurif, E., & Grimshaw, J. (1992). Modularity in locating wh-gaps. *Journal of Psycholiguistic Research, 21,* 545–561.

Hickok, G., Swinney, D., Bouck, V., & Hald (1998). Hemispheric asymmetries in lexical ambiguity resolution. UCSD manuscript, In preparation.

Liu, H., Bates, E., Powell, T., & Wulfeck, B. (1997). Single-word shadowing and the study of lexical access. *Applied Psycholinguistics, 18,* 157–180.

Love, T., & Swinney, D. (1996). Conference processing and levels of analysis in object-relative constructions: Demonstration of antecedent reactivation with the cross-modal priming paradigm. *Journal of Psycholinguistic Research, 25,* 5–24.

Love T., Swinney, D., Bagdasaryan, S., & Prather, P. (1999). *Real-time processing of lexical ambiguities by pre-school children.* Poster presented at the 12th annual CUNY Conference on Human Sentence Processing: New York.

McKoon, G., & Ratcliff, R. (1994). Sentence context and on-line lexical decision. *Journal of Experimental Psychology: Memory, Language and Cognition, 20,* 1239–1244.

Meyer, D. E., Schvaneveldt, R. W., & Ruddy, M. (1974). Functions of graphemic and phonemic codes in visual word-recognition. *Memory and Cognition, 2,* 309–321.

Nagel, N., Shapiro, L., & Nawy, R. (1994). A matched-target replication where the effect cannot be a confound—it is shown to appear (and disappear) with structural prosody cues using the same matched targets. *Journal of Psycholinguistic Research, 23,* 473–487.

Neely, J. (1991). Semantic priming effects in visual word recognition: A selective review of current findings and theories. In D. Besner (Ed.), *Basic processes in reading: Visual word recognition.* Hillsdale, NJ: Erlbaum.

Nicol, J., & Pickering, M. (1993). Processing syntactically ambiguous sentences: Evidence from semantic priming. Special Issue: Sentence processing: III. *Journal of Psycholinguistic Research, 22,* 207–237.

Nicol, J., & Swinney, D. (1989). The role of structure in coreference assignment during sentence comprehension. *Special Issue on Sentence Processing, Journal of Psycholinguistics Research, 18,* 5–24.

Nicol, J., Swinney, D., Love, T., & Hald, L. (1997). Examination of sentence processing with continuous vs. interrupted presentation paradigms. *Center for Human Information Processing Technical Report 97–3.* San Diego: University of California.

Onifer, W., & Swinney, D., (1981). Accessing lexical ambiguities during sentence comprehension: Effects of frequency-of-meaning and contextual bias. *Memory and Cognition, 9,* 225–236.

Picoult, J., & Johnson, M. (1992). Controlling for homophone polarity and prime-target relatedness in the cross-modal lexical decision task. *Bulletin of the Psychonomic Society, 30,* 15–18.

Prather, P., & Swinney, D. (1977). *Some effects of syntactic context upon lexical access.* Presented at a meeting of the American Psychological Association, San Franciso, California, August 26.

Prather, P. A., Zurif, E., Love, T., & Brownell, H. (1997). Speed of lexical activation in nonfluent Broca's aphasia and fluent Wernicke's aphasia. *Brain and Language, 59,* 391–411.

Ratcliff, R., & McKoon, G. (1988). A retrieval theory of priming in memory. *Psychological Review, 95*, 385–408.

Seidenberg, M. S., Tanenhaus, M. K., Leiman, J. M., & Bienkowski, M. (1982). Automatic access of the meaning of ambiguous words in context: Some limitations to knowledge-based processing. *Cognitive Psychology, 14*, 489–537.

Shapiro, L., Zurif, E. B., & Grimshaw, J. (1987). Sentence processing and the mental representation of verbs. *Cognition, 27*, 219–246.

Simpson, G. B. (1981). Meaning dominance and semantic context in the processing of lexical ambiguity. *Journal of Verbal Learning and Verbal Behavior, 20*, 120–136.

Stroop, J. R. (1935). Studies of interference in serial verbal reactions. *Journal of Experimental Psychology, 18*, 643–662.

Swaab, T., Brown, C., & Hagoort, P. (1997). Spoken sentence comprehension in aphasia: Event-related potential evidence for a lexical integration deficit. *Journal of Cognitive Neuroscience, 9*, 39–66.

Swinney, D. (1979). Lexical access during sentence comprehension: (Re)consideration of context effects. *Journal of Verbal Learning and Verbal Behavior, 18*, 645–659.

Swinney, D. A. (1991). The resolution of interdeterminacy during language comprehension: Perspectives on modularity in lexical, structural and pragmatic process. In G. B. Simpson (Ed.), *Understanding word and sentence*. Amsterdam: North-Holland Publ.

Swinney, D., Ford, M., Frauenfelder, U., & Bresnan, J. (1987). On the temporal course of gap-filling and antecedent assignment during sentence comprehension. In B. Grosz, R. Kaplan, M. Macken, & I. Sag (Eds.), *Language structure and processing*. Stanford, CA: CSLI.

Swinney, D. A., Onifer, W., Prather, P., & Hirshkowitz, M. (1979). Semantic facilitation across sensory modalities in the processing of individual words and sentences. *Memory and Cognition, 7*, 159–165.

Swinney, D., & Prather, P. (1989). On the comprehension of lexical ambiguity by young children: Investigations into the development of mental modularity. In D. Gorfein (Ed.), *Resolving semantic ambiguity*. New York: Springer-Verlag.

Swinney, D., Zurif E., & Nicol, J. (1989). The effects of focal brain damage on sentence processing: An examination of the neurological organization of a mental module. *Journal of Cognitive Neuroscience, 1*, 25–37.

Swinney, D., Zurif, E., Prather, P., & Love, T. (1996). Neurological distribution of processing resources underlying language comprehension. *Journal of Cognitive Neuroscience, 8*, 174–184.

Tabossi, P. (1988). Accessing lexical ambiguity in different types of sentential contexts. *Journal of Memory and Language, 27*, 324–340.

Tanenhaus, M. K., Leiman, J. M., & Seidenberg, M. S. (1979). Evidence for multiple stages in the processing of ambiguous words in syntactic contexts. *Journal of Verbal Learning and Verbal Behavior, 18*, 427–440.

Titone, D. (1998). Hemispheric difference in context sensitivity during lexical ambiguity resolution. *Brain and Language, 65*, 361–394.

Tompkins, C., Baumgaertner, A., Lehman, M. T., & Fossett, T. (1997). Suppression and discourse comprehension in right brain-damaged adults: A preliminary report. *Aphasiology, 11*, 505–519.

Tyler, L., & Marslen-Wilson, W. (1977). The on-line effects of semantic context on syntactic processing. *Journal of Verbal Learning and Verbal Behavior, 16*, 683–692.

Tyler, L., & Marslen-Wilson, W. (1982). Speech comprehension processes. In J. E. Mehler, T. C. Walker, & M. Garrett (Eds.), *Perspectives on mental representations*. Hillsdale, NJ: Erlbaum.

Wright, B., & Garrett, M. (1984). Lexical decision in sentences: Effects of syntactic structure. *Memory and Cognition, 12*, 31–45.

Zurif, E., & Swinney, D. (1994). The neuropsychology of language. In M. A. Gernsbacher (Ed.), *Handbook of psycholinguistics*, pp. 89–90. Orlando, FL: Academic Press.

Part V

The Syntax–Discourse Interface

Chapter 15

Comprehension of Discourse-Linked and Non-Discourse-Linked Questions by Children and Broca's Aphasics

Sergey Avrutin

INTRODUCTION

Over the last two decades, a significant amount of research has been carried out in the fields of both language acquisition and language impairment. With regard to the former, a variety of experimental and theoretical projects attempted to investigate the degree to which young children have mastered their native language, what kind of errors children make at the initial stages of language acquisition, and how they eventually overcome these errors to become competent adult speakers. In the field of language impairment, researchers have attempted to characterize the speech production and comprehension capacity of patients with specific linguistic disorders (such as Broca's aphasia). The main goal of this research is to provide a picture of what part of the human language capacity is lost as a result of a specific brain damage, and the characterize the patients' linguistic knowledge in terms of a contemporary linguistic theory.

Needless to say, the similarities (at least superficial) between the linguistic performance of the two populations did not elude researchers (for more discussion, see Caramazza and Zurif, 1978, and references cited therein). The observations of similar speech patterns have given rise to several influential psycholinguistic theories, such as *Ribot's law*. According to this view (expressed as early as 1883, see Ribot, 1883), the order of language development is mirrored, in reverse, by the order of language loss. Put simply, the later a piece of linguistic knowledge is acquired, the more susceptible it will be to be lost in language impairment. In phonology, for example, a particular sound pattern that appears late in child speech is predicted to be more likely problematic for brain damaged patients (aphasics) than a sound pattern present in the speech of younger children. In syntax, structures more problematic for production and comprehension by older children should be missing from the speech of and difficult to comprehend by Broca's aphasics more often than structures present and comprehensible by younger children.

A somewhat similar, but more linguistically based approach is due to Roman Jakobson (e.g., Jakobson, 1941/1968), which is known as the regression hypothesis. The claim here is that the order of language dissolution is identical to, but yet opposite in direction, to the order of language development. In phonology, for example, if the child acquires certain phonological distinctions (e.g., [+labial]/[-labial] prior to other featural distinctions (e.g., [+voiced]/[-voiced]), it means that the order of dissolution of the linguistic system should be reversed: Aphasic patients should be more likely to first lose the [+/-voiced] distinction, while preserving (at this stage) the [+/-labial] distinction.

A more recent approach to the comparison between the two populations is due to Yosef Grodzinsky (Grodzinsky, 1990) and is based on the influential subset principle (e.g., Dell, 1981; Berwick, 1985; Wexler & Manzini, 1987). According to this theory, each stage in language development can be characterized by a particular grammar—a system that can generate all grammatical and no ungrammatical (at this stage) sentences. The linguistic system moves from one grammar to another as a result of changing parameter settings; moreover the development proceeds in such a way that the grammar that generates fewer possible structures ("a more restrictive grammar") necessarily precedes a "more permissible grammar" that can generate more acceptable structures. With regard to language loss Grodzinsky presents a formal model of the "reverse" development, that is the formal picture of what stages of linguistic dissolution should look like if the language loss, indeed, is identical to, yet opposite in direction from, the order of acquisition.

The following three observations are characteristic of the above views. First, no particular reason is given for the existence of the predicted reversal. In other words, there is no independent motivation for the claim that the later a piece of knowledge is acquired the more vulnerable it should be in language impairment. Nor is it clear why the hierarchy of, say, phonological feature acquisition should be reversed in aphasia, or why the parameters should be "re-set" in language breakdown in the order exactly opposite of the way they are set in language development. As these views are formulated, they are more descriptive generalizations (observed and/or predicted) than theoretical systems based on independent motivations.

Second, none of the above approaches make any connections to the psycholinguistic research with normal adult speakers. It is well known, however, that even for normal speakers certain linguistic constructions may present more difficulties in processing than the others. It would be fruitful, therefore, to establish whether there is any correlation between the comprehension pattern exhibited by normal adults, on the one hand, and children and aphasics, on the other. Indeed, if it turns out that those constructions that are more complicated for normal adults are also most vulnerable for children and aphasics, such an observation would be more consistent with the view that the actual reason for the errors observed in studies with these two populations have nothing to do with their knowledge of language but rather with their limited ability to implement this knowledge.

Finally, and related to the previous comment, it is important to remember that, as in any other science, psycholinguists deal with empirical observations, and then, based on these observations attempt to provide theoretical explanations for the collected data. But observations, that is experimental results, can be due to various factors. Linguistic errors in comprehension, for example, can be due to the lack of specific linguistic knowledge required for the correct interpretation of a given sentence, or they can be due to the inability to implement the knowledge which, by itself, is intact. All of the above approaches, however, unanimously vote to attribute the observed linguistic anomaly to the anomaly of the language faculty (that is to say that the knowledge is different from that of normal adult speakers in a particular way—either because of a hierarchical reversal, or because of a different parameter setting). While this view, of course, is legitimate, it is by no means the only possible one. Children and aphasics can demonstrate similar problems with some linguistic constructions in spite of the fact that their knowledge of language is no different from that of normal adults. If it were possible to provide independent evidence that certain constructions require more processing resources (and to explain why it should be so), the observed similarities in errors would have a different explanation.

A simple example may illustrate this point. Suppose we observe that my digital watch is showing a wrong time (we have independent evidence of what the correct time is.) In fact, suppose we know that there is a certain area inside of this watch such that when it is damaged, the watch will slow down. We know this by observing many watches with damages to this particular area. We might conclude that some chip, responsible for conducting time measuring operations, is broken, or even missing.

But is this conclusion necessarily correct? Not really. The putative area may contain a battery which, when damaged, will not be able to supply the *intact* mechanism with the necessary amount of power. The result, and our observations, will be the same: the watch is not showing the time showed by other, unimpaired watches. But our conclusions with regard to the function of the damaged area will be wrong.

In this article I present results of a recent experiment with children and compare the obtained results with those reported in the literature with regard to Broca's aphasics. The main point is to show that, for both populations, more "resource consuming" structures are more problematic. In particular, I argue that the integration of syntactic- and discourse-related knowledge requires more resources and, therefore, results in more errors. I also briefly discuss other evidence that supports this claim while referring the reader to Avrutin (1994) and Avrutin (1999) for more discussion. The main hypothesis (which, of course, requires further research) is that, in spite of the observed errors, children's and aphasics' knowledge of language is no different from that of normal adults, but the integration of different linguistic modules (e.g., syntax and discourse) turns out to require more resources than these speakers have.

BACKGROUND

The goal of the reported studies was to compare children's (and aphasics') comprehension of the D-linked and non-D-linked subject and object Wh-questions. These questions are exemplified in (1).

(1) a. Who chased the tiger?   Non-D-linked subject Wh-question.
    b. Who did the tiger chase?   Non-D-linked object Wh-question.
    c. Which lion chased the tiger?   D-linked subject Wh-question.
    d. Which lion did the tiger chase?   D-linked object Wh-question.

For simplicity, I will refer to (1a) as a Who-subject question, to (1b) as a Who-object question, to (1c) as a Which-subject-question, and to (1d) as a Which-object question.

The notion of D-linking (or *discourse-linking*) is originally due to Pesetsky (1987). Before turning to the syntactic characteristics of these questions, let me briefly discuss the notion of discourse linking. Even informally, there is a clear difference between the D-linked and non-D-linked questions with regard to *discourse presupposition*. Consider (2).

(2) a. What did you eat this morning   (non-D-linked)
   b. Which apple did you eat this morning?   (D-linked)

in (2a), there is no presupposition on the part of the speaker with regard to what the addressee could have eaten that morning—whether it was an apple, or an orange, or a plum. In (2b), on the other hand, there is a mutually understandable presupposition that there was a set of apples one of which was allegedly eaten by the addressee. Such a presupposition constitutes a common ground of conversation (Stalnaker, 1979), and is required to be available to all participants in the conversation in order for the discourse to be pragmatically felicitous. In other words, in addition to regular syntactic constraints on sentence well-formedness (as in 2a), (2b) has an additional, discourse-related constraint due to the presence of the D-linked Wh-word *which*.

As noted by many linguists (e.g., Pesetsky, 1987; Rizzi, 1990; Cinque, 1990; Dobrovie-Sorin, 1990; Frampton, 1991, among others), *Who-* and *Which*-questions (non-D-linked and D-linked) appear to exhibit different syntactic properties.[1] Pesetsky, for example, presents the following contrast:

(3) *a. Mary wants to know what who read.
   ?b. Mary wants to know *which* of the *books* which man read.

Pesetsky argues that only non-D-linked Wh-questions move at the level of *logical form* (LF), which results in the violation of the *empty category principle* (ECP). D-linked questions do not move at LF and no violation arises. Other examples of the distributional differences between D-linked and non-D-linked phrases are presented and analyzed in Cinque (1990) (see also Rizzi, 1990).

Although detailed discussion of the syntactic differences between D-linked and non-D-linked questions is beyond the scope of this work, it is worth noticing that the two questions differ in more than the *which*-questions simply containing one extra word. There are very specific, perhaps structurally defined differences in their distribution.

Having said that, however, let me return to the difference introduced above which is the main focus of the reported study. While the well-formedness of sentences containing *who*-questions is determined solely by syntactic constraints, *which*-questions impose additional requirements:

---

[1] Other authors, such as Comorovski (1989) and Kroch (1989), attribute the differences between the apparently syntactic differences in distribution of the two types of questions to pragmatic factors.

Being D-linked, they require the integration of the syntactic and discourse-related knowledge. From the syntactic point of view, the interpretation of (all) wh-questions requires speakers to establish a link (or, *a chain*, in linguistic terms) between the wh-phrase and its original position. This position is represented by a trace (*t*). Thus, the full syntactic representation of the sentences in (1) is given in (4) (irrelevant details omitted):

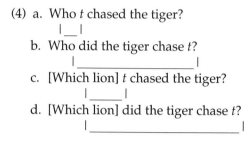

(4) a. Who *t* chased the tiger?

       | _ |

    b. Who did the tiger chase *t*?

       | _____ |

    c. [Which lion] *t* chased the tiger?

       | ____ |

    d. [Which lion] did the tiger chase *t*?

       | _____ |

The chain is necessary for the interpretation as it allows the speakers to correctly assign the thematic role to the wh-question, that is to correctly answer the question, "Who did what to whom?" In addition, and only in the case of D-linked questions (4c,d), speakers are required to introduce a set of presupposed objects (lions) to which *Which*-phrase could refer. Thus, the interpretation of (4a,b) is "purely syntactic": the Wh-phrase–trace relationship is interpreted as a logical operator–variable relationship, with no reference to the discourse. The interpretation of (4c,d) requires an additional operation of introducing a discourse referent (for more details see, e.g., Heim, 1982).

It seems reasonable that implementation of each linguistic operation is associated with spending a certain amount of resources. As in the case of anything else in the physical world, one might be tempted to use the notion of "energy": when a speaker is to process a certain linguistic structure, he/she is required to have available a certain amount of energy necessary for carrying out phonological, lexical, morphological, syntactic, and discourse-related operations. Processing structures that involve more operations will require then more energy. In this sense, the difference between D-linked and non-D-linked questions is straightforward: the former involve all of the operations involved in the latter, plus the discourse-related operations. In this sense, they are more "expensive."

Below I will attempt to show that the difference between "purely syntactic" and "syntax plus discourse" constructions in terms of the required resources explains, in a coherent way, some similarities observed in the performance of children and Broca's aphasics. I will focus, mostly, on their comprehension of Wh-questions, but will also discuss other studies, such as interpretation of pronominals, tense and agreement, lexical access, and comprehension of contrastive stress.

EXPERIMENTAL RESULTS

Comprehensive of Wh-Questions by Broca's Aphasics

Hickok and Avrutin (1995) report results of an experiment with agrammatic Broca's aphasics who were presented with four types of Wh-questions: Who-subject, Who-object, Which-subject, and Which-object questions [see (1) above]. The two subjects showed a similar performance: their comprehension of Which-object questions was at chance and significantly worse than the comprehension of the other three types of questions (the summary of these results is presented in Table I).

The analyses of the results presented by Hickok and Avrutin (1995) are based on the distinction between *government* and *binding* chains, as in Cinque (1990). According to Cinque, the mechanism connecting the Wh-phrase with its trace is qualitatively different for D-linked and non-D-linked questions. Only D-linked phrases can form the binding chain. The non-D-linked phrases form only government chains. Assuming this distinction, Hickok and Avrutin speculate that only binding chains are impaired in aphasia, while government chains are preserved. This explains why comprehension of (1a) and (1b) is significantly better: Who-questions are non-D-linked, therefore they form government chain, which is intact. The comprehension of Which-subject questions is also close to normal: the assignment of the PATIENT thematic role to the (unmoved) object noun phrase (NP) in (1c) is sufficient to figure out who is doing the chasing and whom is being chased. But in the case of (1d), the situation is different. Which-phrase is D-linked and, therefore, forms the binding chain with its trace. This chain, the claim goes, is broken. The moved Wh-phrase is not connected to its trace and cannot be assigned the thematic role PATIENT. In an attempt to interpret the sentence by some other, nonsyntactic means, the subjects may assign the role of AGENT to the first NP (the which-phrase).[2] But the following NP (the subject of the sentence) is also AGENT

---

[2]This is, of course, very similar to Grodzinsky's (1990) analyses of aphasics strategy in interpreting passive constructions.

(through a syntactic assignment). Having two AGENTS at hand, the subjects resolve to guessing, which results in their chance performance.[3]

Tait, Thompson, and Ballard (1995) disagree with the Hickok and Avrutin (1995) claim, both on empirical and theoretical grounds. They present results of an analogous study with four agrammatic Broca's aphasics and show that only two of them demonstrate the performance identical to that reported in the Hickok and Avrutin study. They conclude that "the comprehension profile described by Hickok and Avrutin is not characteristic of a majority of this population." (Tait et al., 1995, p. 78).

For those subjects who do demonstrate the described difference between different types of questions, the authors (Tait et al., 1995) mention two possible alternative explanations. One, based on Chomsky's bare phrase structure theory (Chomsky, 1994), relates the observed difference to the difference between full projections of *which*-questions and only X^0 (head) projections of *who*-questions. As the authors do no make their claim precise (they do not explain how the difference in the phrase structure results in the observed asymmetry) it is difficult to evaluate this claim.

The second proposal is based on the semantic representation of the four types of questions. The authors (Tait et al., 1995) argue that additional computations involved in processing *which*-questions are related to the presence of an additional predication relation, for example,

(5) *For WHICH X,* tiger(x) *AND chase-lion* (X)

In my view, the attempt to relate the relatively poor performance of some subjects to the processing complexity is on the right track, although, as discussed above and will be discussed again below, the difficulty is not semantic in nature but is related to the integration of the syntactic and discourse-related knowledge.

In Table I, I present a summary of the results reported in these two studies.[4]

As can be seen from Table I, the overall subjects' performance on *which*-object questions is significantly worse than their performance on all other three types of questions. The *t* test revealed a statistically significant

---

[3]It should be noted, however, that Hickok and Avrutin (1995) leave open a possibility of a "processing" account of the observed difference:

Referential NPs require interpretive links to discourse representations, and in situations in which referential presuppositions are not satisfied, appropriate discourse representations must be created. Nonreferential NPs do not require links to preestablished discourse referents; thus they may impose less processing demands leading to better performance. (p. 23).

[4]Both studies report percentage of correct responses. The results presented in Table I show percentage of errors, which was obtained by deducting the reported results from 100%.

Table I   Broca's Aphasics Comprehension Errors on Wh-Questions

Subject	Who-subject (% errors)	Who-object (% errors)	Which-subject (% errors)	Which-object (% errors)
RD[a]	20	13	13	53
FC[a]	7	13	13	53
MD[b]	24	16	24	24
CH[b]	40	20	44	36
DL[b]	4	16	16	48
FP[b]	16	28	28	52
Mean (%)	18.5	17.7	23.0	44.3

[a]Based on Hickok and Avrutin (1995).
[b]Based on Tait, Thompson, and Balard (1995).

difference between their performance on *which*-object and *who*-object questions [$t(5) = 5$, $p < .05$]. The difference between *which*-object and *which*-subject questions was also statistically significant [$t(5) = 2.5$, $p = .05$], whereas the subjects' performance on *which*-object questions was not significantly different from chance. No difference was observed between *who*-subject and *which*-subject questions, and no difference was found between *who*-subject and *who*-object questions, while the difference between subject and object questions exists in the case of D-linked (*which*) questions.

Comprehension of Wh-Questions by Children

While a significant amount of research addressed children's comprehension and production of Wh-questions (see, e.g., a special issue of *Language Acquisition*, 1995, vol. 4 on this topic, and also Thornton, 1990; Sarma, 1990; Stromswold, 1990; de Villiers, 1991, among others), researchers usually looked at more complex structures involving long-distance movement, strong crossover, inversion etc., but did not specifically address the differences between comprehension of different types of wh-subject and object questions. Nevertheless, it is interesting that a certain difference between D-linked and non-D-linked questions was observed in at least some of the studies. Thornton (1995), for example, found (in an elicited production study) that the certain errors in production of young English speaking children are characteristic of *which*-questions only. Although not directly relevant to the study reported here, these results are interesting because they show children's sensitivity to D-linking.

The experiment reported below specifically addressed the differences between children's comprehension of the four types of Wh-questions.[5]

[5]I thank Kerry Fisher for her assistance in conducting this study.

Subjects

Fifteen English speaking children (ages: from 3;5 to 5;2, mean age: 4;3) participated in the study. All children were monolingual native speakers of the English language. A signed permission of the parent/guardian was obtained prior to conducting the test.

Procedures

Toy figurines representing various animals were used in an object manipulation task. The study used nine verbs.[6] Each verb was used only once in any specific structure. Question forms evaluated were: *who*-subject (e.g., *who chased the tiger?*), *who*-object (e.g., *who did the tiger chase?*), *which*-subject (e.g., *which lion chased the tiger?*), and *which*-object (e.g., *which lion did the tiger chase?*). Lexical comprehension of the verbs and nouns used in the study was tested prior to the experiment. All children demonstrated 100% accuracy. Six normal adult speakers were also tested on all conditions (college students). In each condition they demonstrated 100% correct performance.

Children were told that they will participate in a game in which a puppet will watch together with them what is going on but will not always understand. The puppet therefore will ask the child to clarify what happened. The experimenter then placed three figurines on the table and explained what was happening. For example, one lion was placed between two tigers and the experimenter showed that the lion is chasing one of them, while the other tiger is chasing the lion. The puppet (operated by the experimenter) would ask then one of the target questions (e.g., *which tiger chased the lion?*). All sentences were plausibly semantically reversible (e.g., there were two tigers and, depending on whether the child understands the question or not, one of them could be selected as the answer). Fillers were also introduced in the test battery. All children showed 100% accuracy on fillers.

Results

Results of this study are summarized in Table II.

---

[6]Children RG and SN were so interested in continuing the "game" that they asked to be given another sentence type. Thus, for these children the total number of verbs used was 10 for each type of question. For the same reason, AY was given 10 verbs for all question types except who-subject, for which he also had 9 verbs. All other children were presented with total of 36 target sentences, AY with 39, and RG and SN with 40. Rather than excluding these extra data points I chose to report all data. The statistical results remain the same whether these extra verbs are excluded or included.

Table II Preschoolers Comprehension Errors on Wh-Questions

Child	Age (months)	Who-subject (% errors)	Who-object (% errors)	Which-subject (% errors)	Which-object (% errors)
RD	41	0	0	0	22
GD	43	22	44	22	67
GC	43	0	11	0	44
MH	45	11	67	0	100
KH	48	67	0	89	33
BH	48	89	0	89	0
SL	49	0	0	0	11
LF	50	22	11	11	44
MM	53	0	0	0	89
AL	53	11	0	0	67
RG	57.5	10	0	0	60
SN	59.5	10	0	0	30
RD	60	0	0	0	67
BV	60	11	0	11	78
AY	62	44	70	80	70
Mean	*51.4 months*	*19.8%*	*13.6%*	*20.1%*	*52.1%*

As can be seen from Table I, children's performance on *which*-object questions is significantly worse than their performance on all other three types of questions. The *t* test revealed a statistically significant difference between their performance on *which*-object and *who*-object questions $[t(14) = 5.44, p < .000]$. The difference between *which*-object and *which*-subject questions is also statistically significant $[t(14) = 2.41, p < .05]$, whereas the subjects' performance on *which*-object questions was not significantly different from chance. No difference was observed between *who*-subject and *which*-subject questions, and no difference was found between *who*-subject and *who*-object questions, while the difference between subject and object questions exists in the case of D-linked (which) questions.

Discussion

Table III presents a summary of the reported results with children and Broca's aphasics.

Both populations demonstrate chance performance on which-object questions, which is significantly worse than their performance on the other three types of questions. If we attempt to explain these results from a purely syntactic point of view, we may run into the problems discussed in the first section of this chapter. Consider, for example, a view advanced in Grodzinsky (1995) where he presents a version of his trace deletion hypothesis (Grodzinsky, 1990). According to this view, traces of

306

Sergey Avrutin

Table III Summary of Children's and Broca's Aphasics Comprehension Errors on Wh-Questions

Group	Who-subject (% errors)	Who-object (% errors)	Which-subject (% errors)	Which-object (% errors)
Children	19.8	13.6	20.1	*52.1*
Broca's aphasics	18.5	17.7	23	*44.3*

referential (and only referential) Wh-phrases are deleted in aphasia. If so, subject's comprehesion of which-object questions is predicted to be at chance because there is no possibility for the moved which-phrase to be connected to the place where it is assigned a thematic role. As discussed above, the sentence appears to have two AGENTS and subjects resolve to guessing.

But the questions remain the same: Why are referential, and only referential traces missing? Are they missing in children, too? Why such a curious similarity? Is there any connection between the missing referential traces in aphasia (and, allegedly, in children) and normal processing? Finally (and this is something I will discuss below), is there any connection between these findings and others reported in the literature on aphasia and language development? In other words, do we want to postulate a new theory for every new finding? Wouldn't it be more correct to attempt to provide a more or less unified explanation for all available findings?

Exactly the same can be said regarding the Hickok and Avrutin (1995) claim about the disruption of government chains. As these views stand now, they present only descriptive generalizations which attempt to necessarily relate the observed data to the deficiency of the *knowledge* of language while putting aside the possibility of the deficiency of the required resources.

From the processing point of view the observed similarities are not surprising if we make one (rather obvious) assumption: the processing resources in children and Broca's aphasics are limited. In children, because their brains are not yet fully mature, and in aphasics because their brains are damaged.[7]

Consider now the representation of the experimental sentences repeated in (6).

---

[7]According to Yakovlev and Lecours (1964), the dendritic density of Broca's area reaches its full development only at the age of 72 months.

(6) a. Who *t* chased the tiger?   above chance
   | __ |

  b. Who did the tiger chase *t*?   above chance
    | _____ |

  c. [Which lion] *t* chased the tiger?   above chance
    | ____ |

  d. [Which lion] did the tiger chase *t*?   chance
    | _____ |

As discussed in the section entitled Background, D-linked wh-phrases involve both syntactic and discourse-related operations and, therefore, require additional resources. Wh-phrases in (6a,b) are not D-linked, thus "less expensive," and we correctly predict overall above-chance performance. In (6c), the subjects need to carry out both syntactic operation of connecting *which*-phrase with its trace, and the discourse-related operation of satisfying the discourse presupposition (see Crain and Steedman, 1985, on this issue in normal sentence processing). Such integration of syntactic and discourse-related operations may require more resources than there are available to children and aphasics, and the correct thematic interpretation of *which*-question may not be achieved. This is not too crucial in this case, however, because, following Grodzinsky (1990), this phrase can be interpreted through some kind of a strategy that assigns the role of AGENT to the first NP. As the second NP [the tiger] is interpreted as PATIENT, no conflict arises between the two NPs and the sentence can be correctly interpreted. But the problem arises in (6d): if *which*-question remains thematically uninterpreted and is assigned the AGENT role, it will be in conflict with the syntactic assignment of AGENT to [the tiger]. Subjects (children and aphasics) will then have to guess, which will result in a chance performance.

The theoretical difference between *who*- and *which*-questions follows from independent, linguistic reasons. On the assumption that integration of different linguistic modules (syntax and discourse) requires more "energy," and that the amount of energy available to children and aphasics is limited, the obtained results receive a coherent explanation. The processing account is also in a better position to explain certain individual differences exhibited by children and aphasics. If the problem in comprehension were related to the lack of knowledge of a particular structure, or a missing part of the structure (e.g., a trace), one might expect a more or less uniform pattern of responses. But the deficiency in processing resources may well be gradual, depending on a number of factors. That is why the only possible way to obtain interpretable results is to conduct a group study: Data from an individual subject may be misleading.

Moreover, there is evidence that the requirement for more processing capacity in the case of *which*-questions is observed in real-time studies with normal adults. This evidence comes from processing of D-linked and non-D-linked *Wh*-questions by adult Italians (De Vincenzi, 1991) and from a priming study with normal adult English speakers (L. Shapiro, e-mail communication, February 1998). The obtained results are also consistent with other published studies, some of which will be briefly discussed below.

CONSISTENCY WITH OTHER FINDINGS

In this section I briefly discuss several studies that were conducted with both children and Broca's aphasics.

Interpretation of Pronominals

Grodzinsky and Reinhart (1993) provide analyses of similarities between children and aphasics with regard to their interpretation of pronouns and reflexives in English. Both populations exhibit the following pattern:

(7) a. Reflexives (syntactic operations only):
Father Bear washed himself. $\longrightarrow$ above chance
b. Pronouns bound by quantifier (syntactic operations only):
Every bear washed him. $\longrightarrow$ above chance
c. Pronouns bound by a referential NP (syntactic and discourse-related operations):
Father Bear washed him. $\longrightarrow$ chance

From the linguistic perspective, (7c) is different from (7a,b) in that it involves both syntactic and discourse-related operations. Grodzinsky and Reinhart also explain these results in terms of the lack of resources necessary to correctly interpret structures involving extrasyntactic operations.

Comprehension of Contrastive Stress

Children and Broca's aphasics demonstrate similar pattern of errors in switching reference for a stressed pronouns. Consider (8).

(8) a. John hit Bill and then Sarah hit him.
b. John hit Bill and then Sarah hit HIM.

The capitalized pronoun HIM indicates stress. In (8a), normal speakers interpret the pronoun as referring to the matrix object *Bill*. But when the pronoun is stressed, as in (8b), they switch reference and interpret HIM as referring to the matrix subject *John*. The stress signals that the default discourse referent of the pronoun has changed.

Maratsos (1973) reports that 5-year-old children sometimes interpret the stressed pronoun in (8b) as referring to *Bill*, that is they fail to correctly implement the requirement of switching reference. More recently, these finding were replicated with six Broca's aphasics (Avrutin, Lubarsky, & Greene, 2000). As the correct interpretation of the pronominal reference requires the integration of the syntactic (the structural position: subject vs. object) and discourse-related knowledge (identifying the default discourse referent), these findings are consistent with the above claim regarding the deficiency of processing resources necessary for the implementation of the syntactic and discourse operations.

Lexical Access

The deficiency of processing resources may manifest itself not only in the syntax–discourse interface, but in other domains as well. Based on their studies of lexical ambiguity resolution, Swinney, Nicol, and Zurif (1989) and Swinney and Prather (1989) argue that the lexical access in children and Broca's aphasics is slowed down.[8] This claim is based on their observation that both populations first access the most frequent meaning of an ambiguous word, independently of the context. It seems reasonable to suggest that the general slow down of the linguistic mechanism is due to the lack of processing resources required for fast and automatic linguistic operations.

Tense

In their linguistic development, children pass through the so-called optional infinitive stage (Wexler, 1995), that is a stage when they incorrectly produce untensed verbs in matrix clause, for example, (9).

(9) a. Mommy eat cookie
    b. Daddy sleep.

Similar pattern is reported for Broca's aphasics (e.g., Goodglass and Geschwind, 1976). In general, children make more errors with tense than

---

[8]A similar claim with regard to the slowing down of syntactic operations, for example, gap filling, is made in Zurif, Swinney, Prather, Solomon, and Bushell (1993).

with agreement (see Wexler, 1995, for discussion). More recently, a similar claim regarding Broca's aphasics was made by Friedmann and Grodzinsky (1998).

This similarity is also consistent with the proposed account. The crucial difference between the two systems (tense and agreement) is that agreement is a purely morphosyntactic system, with no discourse operations involved. It is part of the computational system. Tense, on the other hand, goes beyond the computational system itself and requires access to the discourse representation. The following example will illustrate the point. The sentence "In 1917, Lenin comes to power" is syntactically well-formed but pragmatically odd: Present tense cannot be used to refer to past events. However, in specific contexts, such as historical narration (presented in a specific historical context with a specific intonation), the sentence becomes acceptable. The discourse, in other words, is relevant for the acceptability of a particular tense form (see also Enç, 1991 for the notion of *Tense anchoring*). In the case of agreement, discourse is irrelevant. (10) is ungrammatical independently of the context, intonation, and other factors:

(10) *In 1917, Lenin come to power.

For more discussion of the syntax–discourse interface and interpretation of tense the reader is referred to Avrutin (1999). The point of this example is quite simple: tense, but not agreement, requires integration of syntactic and discourse-related knowledge, and, therefore, as predicted, both children and aphasics make more errors in this system.

Other Similarities

There may be other similarities between the two populations that could be explained in terms of a lack of processing resources. These may include null (phonologically empty) subjects in child and aphasic speech, their abnormal use of definite determiners, abnormal quantification, and perhaps some phonological anomalies.[9] A full discussion of these topics is far beyond the scope of this chapter and will be left for future research.

---

[9]According to Kunt (1998), fricatives are acquired later by children and are first to be lost in aphasia. Interestingly, these are precisely the elements that require most precise motor control. Whether most precise motor control requires more resources remains to be seen.

CONCLUSIONS

Children and Broca's aphasics exhibit some interesting similarities in the pattern of their comprehension errors. Rather than explaining their deficit in syntactic terms, I have attempted to account for the observed errors in terms of the lack of processing resources, or energy, necessary for carrying out certain linguistic operations. From an independent linguistic perspective, certain constructions require additional, discourse-related operations. The clearest example is the difference between *who-* and *which*-questions: Only the latter are discourse-linked. As predicted, both populations have more difficulties with these questions demonstrating a chance performance.

Clearly, more research needs to be done both in aphasiology, language acquisition, and neurological development to arrive at a coherent theory of the similarities between children and aphasics. But one claim, it seems, can be made now. Although it is often tempting to come up with a theory of language acquisition or language impairment formulated in purely structural, formal terms, such a formulation may not always reflect the actual state of affairs. Elegant and formal in their formulations, linguistic theories are about the human *knowledge of language.* But speakers must have resources to *implement* this knowledge. The correct explanation of observed errors in children and aphasics, thus, may turn out to be less elegant and formal than one might desire.

ACKNOWLEDGMENTS

First and foremost I thank my teacher, colleague, and friend Edgar Zurif for introducing me to the exciting field of psycholinguistic research and for being so helpful to me throughout the years. I also thank Stephen Crain, Lawrence Horn, David Pesetsky, Lewis Shapiro, Rozalind Thornton, and Ken Wexler, for valuable discussions and comments. I am grateful to Martin Denis for his help with the statistical analyses. Very special thanks are due to Kerry Fisher for her assistance in testing children and to the children, teachers, and parents of Wallingford Daycare Center (Wallingford, CT) for giving us an opportunity to conduct the research reported here. This research was supported in part by National Institute of Health Grant P50 DC 00081, which is hereby gratefully acknowledged.

REFERENCES

Avrutin, S. (1994). *Psycholinguistic investigations in the theory of reference. Ph.D. dissertation,* MIT, Cambridge, MA. Distributed by MIT Working Papers in Linguistics.

Avrutin, S. (1999). *Development of the syntax–discourse interface*. Dordrecht: Kluwer.

Avrutin, S., Lubarsky, S., & Green, J. (2000). Comprehension of contrastive stress by Broca's aphasics. *Brain and Language, 70*, in press.

Berwick, R. (1985). *The acquisition of syntactic knowledge*. Cambridge, MA: MIT Press.

Caramazza, A., & Zurif, E. B., (1978). *Language acquisition and language breakdown*. Baltimore, MD: The Johns Hopkins University Press.

Chomsky, N. (1994). *Bare phrase structure*. Cambridge, MA: MIT Working Papers in Liguistics.

Cinque, G. (1990). *Types of A-bar dependencies*. Cambridge, MA: MIT Press.

Comorovski, I. (1989). Discourse-linking and the Wh-island constraint. In J. Carter & R.-M. Dechaine (Eds.), *Proceedings of the 19th North East Linguistic Society Conference* (pp. 78–97). Amherst: Univ. of Massachusetts.

Crain, S. & Steedman, M. (1985). On not being led up the garden path: The use of context by the psychological syntax processor. In D. R. Dowty, L. Karttunen, & A. M. Zwicky (Eds.), *Natural language parsing: Psychological, computational, and theoretical perspectives*. New York: Cambridge University Press.

Dell, F. (1981). On the learnability of optional phonological rules. *Linguistic Inquiry, 12,* 31–37.

de Villiers, J. (1991). Why questions. In T. Maxfield & B. Plunkett (Eds.), *Papers in the acquisition of wh*. Amherst, MA: University of Massachusetts Occasional Papers in Linguistics.

De Vincenzi, M. (1991). *Syntactic parsing strategies in Italian*. Boston: Kluwer.

Dobrovie-Sorin, C. (1990). Clitic doubling, wh-movement, and quantification in Romanian. *Linguistic Inquiry, 21,* 351–397.

Enç, M. (1991). Anchoring conditions for tense. *Linguistic Inquiry, 18,* 633–657.

Frampton, J. (1991). Relativized minimality: A review. *Linguistic Review, 8,* 1–46.

Friedmann, N., & Grodzinsky, Y. (1997). Tense and agreement in agrammatic production: Pruning the syntactic tree. *Brain and Language, 56,* 397–425.

Goodglass, H., & Geschwind, N. (1976). Language disorders (aphasia). In C. Carterette & J. Friedman (Eds.), *Handbook of perception* (Vol. 7, pp. 257–267).

Grodzinsky, Y. (1990). *Theoretical perspectives on language deficit*. Cambridge, MA: MIT Press.

Grodzinsky, Y. (1995). Trace deletion, theta-roles, and cognitive strategies. *Brain and Language, 51,* 469–497.

Grodzinsky, Y., & Reinhart, T. (1993). The innateness of binding and the development of coreference. *Linguistic Inquiry, 24,* 69–103.

Heim, I. (1982). *The semantics of definite and indefinite noun-phrases*. Ph.D. dissertation, University of Massachusetts, Amherst.

Hickok, G., & Avrutin, S. (1995). Representation, referentiality, and processing in agrammatic comprehension: Two case studies. *Brain and Language, 50,* 10–26.

Jakobson, R. (1941/1968). *Child language, aphasia, and phonological universals*. The Hague: Mouton.

Kroch, A. (1989). *Amount quantification, referentiality, and long wh-movement*. Unpublished manuscript. University of Pennsylvania, Philadelphia.

Kunt, R. D. (1998). *Chronology of speech subsystem development*. Talk given at Haskins Laboratories, New Haven, CT.

Maratsos, M. (1973). The effect of stress on the understanding of pronominal coreference in children. *Journal of Psycholinguistic Research, 2,* 1–8.

Pesetsky, D. (1987). Wh-in-situ: Movement and unselective binding. In E. Reuland & A. ter Meulen (Eds.), *The representation of (in) definiteness*, Cambridge, MA: MIT Press.

Ribot, T. A. (1883). *Les maladies de la memoire*. Paris: Librairie Germain Bailliere.

Rizzi, L. (1990). *Relativized minimality*. Cambridge, MA: MIT Press.

Sarma, J. (1990). *The acquisition of wh-questions in english*. Unpublished doctoral dissertation, University of Connecticut, Storrs.

Stalnaker, R. (1979). Assertion. In P. Cole (Ed.), *Syntax and semantics* (vol. 9, pp. 315–332). New York: Academic Press.

Stromswold, K. (1990). *Learnability and the acquisition of auxiliaries.* Unpublished doctoral dissertation, MIT, Cambridge, MA.

Swinney, D., Nicol, J., & Zurif, E. (1989). The effects of focal brain damage on sentence processing: An examination of the neurological organization of a mental module. *Journal of Cognitive Neuroscience, 1,* 25–37.

Swinney, D., & Prather, P. (1989). On the comprehension of lexical ambiguity by young children: Investigations into the development of mental modularity. In D. Gorfein (Ed.), *Resolving semantic ambiguity.* New York: Springer-Verlag.

Tait, M. E., Thompson, C. K., & Ballard, K. J. (1995). Subject-object asymmetries in agrammatic comprehension of four types of wh-questions. *Brain and Language, 51,* 77–79.

Thornton, R. (1990). *Adventures in long-distance moving: The acquisition of complex wh-questions.* Unpublished doctoral dissertation, University of Connecticut, Storrs.

Thornton, R. (1995). Referentiality and *Wh*-movement in child english: Juvenile *D-* link*uency. Language Acquisition, 4,* 139–175.

Wexler, K. (1995). Optional infinitives, head movement and the economy of derivation in child grammar. In D. Lightfoot & N. Hornstein (Eds.), *Verb movement.* Cambridge: Cambridge University Press.

Wexler, K., & Manzini, R. (1987). Parameters and learnability in binding theory. In T. Roeper & E. Williams (Eds.), *Parameter setting.* Dordrecht: Reidel.

Yakovlev, P., & Lecours, A. (1964) The myelogenetic cycles of regional maturation of the brain. In A. Minkowsi (Ed.), *Regional development of the brain in early life.* Oxford: Blackwell Scientific.

Zurif, E., Swinney, D., Prather, P., Solomon, J., & Bushell, C. (1993). An on-line analyses of syntactic processing in Broca's and Wernicke's aphasia. *Brain and Language, 45,* 448–464.

Chapter 16

Positron Emission Tomographic Studies of Syntactic Processing

David Caplan

In 1976, the honoree of this *Festschrift*, Edgar Zurif, and his student, Alfonso Caramazza, described several aphasic patients who were able to match "semantically irreversible" sentences, such as (1), to pictures but not "semantically reversible" sentences, such as (2):

1. The apple the boy was eating was red.
2. The boy the girl was chasing was tall.

Edgar and Alfonso interpreted this pattern of performance as resulting from an inability of these patients to apply "algorithmic" analyses of these sentences, and a dependency on "heuristics" to understand a sentence. Heuristics assign meaning according to plausible relationships of nouns, verbs, and adjectives. In sentence (1), there are only two plausible sets of relationships—the boy is eating the apple and the apple is red—so these patients could assign these aspects of meaning unambiguously. In (2), either the boy or the girl could be chasing the other and either could be tall, so this "heuristic" route to the meaning of the sentence did not yield a single meaning and patients could not determine the actual meaning of the sentence.

The algorithmic process that Edgar and Alfonso thought was affected in their patients was the ability to assign the syntactic structure of a sentence. At the time, the syntactic level of linguistic representation was considered to be a species- and domain-specific cognitive structure, whose final form in the adult was the result of the unfolding of innately specified neural operations when a child was exposed to a linguistic environment (Chomsky, 1957, 1965). (Though increasingly debated, this view still seems essentially correct.) The neural basis for syntactic processing was therefore of considerable neurobiological interest, and these patients of Edgar's and Alfonso's held a key to this mystery.

Edgar and Alfonso identified two groups of patients who were thought to have this problem. One was a group of "Broca's aphasics"—patients with nonfluent speech often marked by omission of function words and bound morphemes and simplification of syntactic structure. Edgar and Alfonso were struck with the similarity between speech production and sentence comprehension in these patients, both of which appeared to suffer from an abnormality in syntactic processing. Edgar described the deficit in these patients as an "overarching" syntactic deficit, the result of damage to Broca's area.

In this chapter, I will review studies in our laboratory using positron emission tomography (PET) that investigate the neural basis for processing the relative clauses used in the 1976 paper.

METHODS

All studies reported here used the plausibility judgment task. In this task, subject either read or listened to a sentence and made a speeded decision as to whether it was plausible (made sense) or not. In the activation condition, sentences that are syntactically more complex were presented; in the baseline condition, sentences that are less complex were presented. In all experiments, implausible sentences were rendered implausible by virtue of an incompatibility between the animacy or humanness features of a noun phrase and the requirements of a verb, as in the example *The book enjoyed the boy*. Therefore, plausibility judgments did not depend on subjects searching semantic memory for obscure facts but could be made on the basis of readily available semantic information.

In all experiments, sentences were blocked by syntactic type, as is required by the PET technique. To reduce the possibility that subjects might habituate to more complex structures or develop nonsyntactic strategies to make judgments regarding the status of a sentence in these blocks, we varied the animacy of nouns in grammatical positions in the sentences. The more and less complex sentences contained the same words and expressed the same content so that differences in lexical items and propositional meaning were not responsible for any regional cerebral blood flow (rCBF) effects. All nouns were common and were preceded by definite articles so as to make the same referential assumptions in the more and less complex syntactic conditions. The point of implausibility was varied throughout the implausible sentences of each syntactic type to force subjects to read or listen to each sentence in its entirety to make a judgment that it was plausible.

Implausibility points were slightly earlier on average in the more complex sentences, biasing against the simple forms benefiting from the use of a strategy that judges a sentence to be acceptable when a certain point in the sentence had passed. All experiments in the PET scanner were preceded by behavioral testing in the psychology laboratory to ensure that there was behavioral evidence, in the form of longer reaction times (RTs) and sometimes more errors, that the more complex sentences were indeed more complex, and these measurements were repeated in the PET environment to be sure that these differences were obtained there.

Subjects in all experiments were strongly right-handed and had no first degree left-handed relatives. All had normal vision and hearing, and no history of neurological or psychiatric disease.

PET techniques were ones in widespread use. PET data were acquired on a General Electric Scanditronix PC4096 15 slice whole body tomograph in its stationary mode in contiguous slices with center-to-center distance of 6.5 mm (axial field equal to 97.5 mm) and axial resolution of 6.0 mm FWHM, with a Hanning-weighted reconstruction filter set to yield 8.0 mm in-plane spatial resolution (FWHM). Subjects' heads were restrained in a custom-molded thermoplastic face mask, and aligned relative to the cantho-meatal line, using horizontal and vertical projected laser lines. Subjects inhaled C^5O_2 gas by nasal cannulae within a face mask for 90 s, reaching terminal count rates of 100,000 to 200,000 events per second. Each PET data acquisition run consisted of 20 measurements, the first 3 with 10-s duration and the remaining 17 with 5-s duration each. Scans 4–16 were summed after reconstruction to form images of relative blood flow. The summed images from each subject were realigned using the first scan as the reference using a least squares fitting technique (Alpert, Berdichevsky, Levin, Morris, & Faschman, 1996). Spatial normalization to the coordinate system of Talairach and Tournoux (1998) was performed by deforming the contour of the 10-mm parasagittal PET slice to match the corresponding slice of the reference brain (Alpert, Berdichevsky, Weise, Tang, & Rauch, 1993). Following spatial normalization, scans were filtered with a two-dimensional Gaussian filter, full width at half maximum set to 20 mm. Data were analyzed with SPM95 (Friston, Frith, Liddle, & Frackowiak, 1991; Friston et al., 1995; Worsely, Evans, Marrett, & Neelin, 1992).

EXPERIMENTS WITH YOUNG SUBJECTS USING RELATIVE CLAUSES

In the first set of experiments, we contrasted more complex subject object (SO) sentences (e.g., *The juice that the child spilled stained the rug*) with

Table I   RT Results for Subject Object and Object
Subject Sentences: Experiment 1a: Visual Presentation, Eight Young Males

	Subject object	Object subject
Mean RT (Ms)	4230	3719

less complex object subject (OS) sentences (e.g., *The child spilled the juice that stained the rug*). There is considerable behavioral evidence that SO sentences are more demanding of processing resources than OS sentences (Waters, Caplan, & Hildebrandt, 1987; King & Just, 1991). The higher demands made by the SO sentence are thought to be related to maintaining the head noun of a relative clause in memory while the relative clause is being structured, computing the syntactic structure of the relative clause, relating the head noun of the relative clause to a syntactic position in the relative clause, relating the head noun of the relative clause to its position as the subject of the main clause, and interpreting the resulting syntactic structure semantically (Just & Carpenter, 1992; Gibson, 1997).

Eight male subjects (ages 19–28) participated in experiment 1a (Stroms-wold, Caplan, Alpert, & Rauch, 1996). Behavioral results are shown in Table I and PET results in Table II. There was an increase in rCBF in the pars opercularis of Broca's area when PET activity associated with OS sentences was subtracted from that associated with SO sentences.

Experiment 1b (Caplan, Alpert, & Waters, 1998) was a replication of this study with eight female subjects, aged 21–31 years. Behavioral results are shown in Table III and PET results in Table IV. There again was an increase in rCBF in the pars opercularis of Broca's area when PET activity associated with OS sentences was subtracted from that associated with SO sentences. There was also activation in the medial frontal and cingulate gyri.

Table II   Areas of Increased rCBF for Subtraction of PET Activity
Associated with Object Subject Sentences from Subject Object
Sentences: Experiment 1a: Visual Presentation, Eight Young Males

Location	Max Z-score	Number of pixels	Location {X, Y, Z}
L. Broca's area, pars opercularis	2.7	131	−46.5, 9.8, 4.0

Table III Accuracy and RT Results for Object Subject and Subject Object Sentences: Experiment 1b: Visual Presentation, Eight Young Females

	Subject object	Object subject
Percent correct	90.5	94.4
Mean RT (sd), in ms	2886 (1119)	2548 (1011)

Experiment 2 (Caplan, Alpert, & Waters, 1999) was a replication of this study with auditory presentation. Sentences in condition 1 consisted of cleft object sentences (e.g., *It was the juice that the child enjoyed*) and sentences in condition 2 consisted of cleft subject sentences (e.g., *It was the child that enjoyed the juice*). We used cleft object and cleft subject sentences instead of the subject object and object subject sentences used in the previous research because preliminary testing of SO and OS sentences presented auditorily failed to demonstrate differences in RTs for end-of-sentence plausibility judgments. This is probably because the demands made by the embedded clause in SO sentences are over by the end of the sentence when the judgement is made. The cleft object and cleft subject sentences make the same contrast between object and subject relativization that the contrast between SO and OS sentences makes.

Sixteen subjects, eight male and eight female, ages 22–34 years, were tested. Behavioral results are shown in Table V and PET results in Table VI. There was an increase in rCBF in the pars triangulars of Broca's area when PET activity associated with cleft subject sentences was subtracted from that associated with cleft object sentences. There was also activation in the medial frontal gyrus and in the left superior parietal area.

Table IV Areas of Increased rCBF for Subtraction of PET Activity Associated with Object Subject Sentences from Subject Object Sentences: Experiment 1b: Visual Presentation, Eight Young Females

Location	Max Z-score	Number of pixels	Location {X, Y, Z}
Medial frontal gyrus	3.8	131	10, 6, 52
Cingulate gyrus	3.5	173	−2, 6, 40
Broca's area, pars opercularis	3.0	47	−42, 18, 24

Table V   Accuracy and RT Results for Cleft Object and Cleft Subject Sentences: Experiment 2: Auditory Presentation, 16 Young Males and Females

	Cleft object		Cleft subject	
	Plausible	Implausible	Plausible	Implausible
Mean percent errors subject	18.1	7.5	14.7	7.6
Mean RT (sd), in ms	3635 (255)	3717 (268)	3465 (277)	3545 (202)

Experiment 3 (Caplan, Alpert, Waters, & Olivieri, 2000) investigated the possibility that the increases in rCBF in Broca's area in Experiment 1–3 were due to increased rehearsal associated with the more complex sentences. Broca's area is involved in rehearsal (Demonet, Fiez, Paulesu, Peterson, & Zatorre, 1996), so this possibility must be considered. To address this issue, we repeated Experiment 1 under conditions of concurrent articulation. Concurrent articulation engages the articulatory loop and prevents its use for rehearsal (Baddeley, Thomson, & Buchanan, 1975). If the rCBF increase in Broca's area continued to be found under these conditions, it is highly likely that it is due at least in part to abstract psycholinguistic operations, not just to more rehearsal associated with the more complex sentences.

Eleven subjects, five male and six female, ages 19–35, were tested. Behavioral results are shown in Table VII and PET results in Table VIII. There was an increase in rCBF in the pars opercularis of Broca's area when PET activity associated with OS sentences was subtracted from that associated with SO sentences. There were also increases in rCBF in the Dorso-

Table VI   Areas of Increased rCBF for Subtraction of PET Activity Associated with Cleft Subject from Cleft Object Sentences: Experiment 2: Auditory Presentation, 16 Young Males and Females

Location	Max Z-score	Number of pixels	Location {X, Y, Z}
Medial frontal gyrus	4.0	317	–2, 18, 48
Superior parietal lobe	3.3	97	–18, –48, 44
Broca's area, pars triangularis	3.1	48	–52, 18, 24

Table VII   Accuracy and RT Results for Object Subject and Subject Object Sentences: Experiment 3: Written Presentation with Concurrent Articulation, 11 Young Males and Females

	Object subject		Subject Object	
	Plausible	Implausible	Plausible	Implausible
Mean percent errors subject	7.8	7.8	18.3	12.2
Mean RT (sd), in ms	4373 (1215)	4237 (1176)	5168 (1683)	5215 (1685)

medial nucleus of the left thalamus, the posterior cingulate, and the medial frontal gyrus.

These four experiments all showed activation in Broca's area associated with more complex relative clauses. This activation persisted under concurrent articulation conditions. This suggests that Broca's area is the primary locus of some aspects of syntactic processing associated with structuring relative clauses that is more resource-demanding in object- than in subject-relativized structures. No other language regions were activated in these experiments. CBF was also increased in medial frontal lobe structures in several experiments, and in the centromedian nucleus of the left thalamaus in the articulatory suppression experiment, possibly the result of a non-domain-specific arousal and directed attention associated with increases in mental effort (Posner, Inhoff, Friedrich, & Cohen, 1987; Posner, Peterson, Fox, & Raichle, 1988).

Table VIII   Areas of Increased rCBF for Subtraction of PET Activity Associated with Object Subject Sentences from Subject Object Sentences: Experiment 3: Written Presentation with Concurrent Articulation, 11 Young Males and Females

Location	Max Z-score	Number of pixels	Location {X, Y, Z}
Broca's area (Brodmann 45)	3.6	112	−46, 36, 4
Left thalamus (centromedian nucleus)	3.4	62	−14, −20, 4
Cingulate gyrus (Brodmann 31)	3.4	158	−10, −36, 40
Medial frontal gyrus (Brodmann 10)	3.2	113	0, 56, 8

EXPERIMENTS WITH YOUNG SUBJECTS USING ACTIVE AND PASSIVE SENTENCES

Experiment 4 studied the rCBF changes associated with making judgments about passive versus active sentences. Passive sentences are more complex syntactically than active sentences because their structure is more elaborate and the relationship between thematic roles and grammatical positions is noncanonical for English. To control for length, we used both full passive sentences (*The car was admired by the boy*) and truncated passives (*The car was admired*) to compare to the active sentences (*The boy admired the car*). The sentences were presented auditorily. Table XI shows the behavioral results; RTs were longer for passive than for active sentences. However, there were no reliable differences in rCBF associated with processing these two types of sentences. The implication of this study, in combination with the previous ones, is that all syntactic contrasts do not provoke the same patterns of rCBF increases. This suggests a different internal organization of language-devoted cortex for different syntactic operations.

EXPERIMENTS WITH ELDERLY SUBJECTS USING RELATIVE CLAUSES

In the final experiment (Caplan, Waters, & Alpert, under review), we replicated the Stromswold et al. (1996) and Caplan et al. (1998) experiment with 13 elderly subjects, ages 61–70. Results are shown in Tables X and XI. Unlike the young subjects studied in Stromswold et al. (1996) and Caplan et al. (1998; Caplan, Alpert, & Waters, under review), there was no increase in rCBF in Broca's area, but rather in the inferior parietal lobe. There was also an increase in rCBF near the midline of the superior frontal gyrus.

Table IX Accuracy and RT Results for Active and Passive Sentences: Experiment 4: Auditory Presentation, 16 Young Males and Females

	Active		Passive	
	Plausible	Implausible	Plausible	Implausible
Mean RT (sd), in ms, taken from end of sentence or point of anomaly	560	809	617	1051

Table X Accuracy and RT Results for Object Subject and Subject Object Sentences: Experiment 5: Written Presentation, 13 Elderly Subjects, Males and Female

	Subject Object		Object Subject	
	Plausible	Implausible	Plausible	Implausible
Mean percent errors subject	7.9	16.2	7.9	7.0
Mean RT (sd), in ms	4877 (1859)	5279 (1867)	4485 (1619)	4716 (1772)

DISCUSSION

The results of these studies reveal localized increases in rCBF in a variety of locations when subjects made judgments about the plausibility of syntactically more complex sentences with object relativized relative clauses compared to when they made such judgments about syntactically less complex sentences with subject relativized relative clauses. These increases in rCBF can be divided into several groups:

1. Increases in rCBF in Broca's area. This was found in all experiments with young people. It suggests that this region is the primary site of some aspect(s) of processing relative clauses in this population. The relevant aspects are unknown but are likely to be related to maintaining the head noun of a relative clause in a working memory system while its role in the relative clause (and possibly in the main clause) is established.

2. Increases in rCBF in other "language" areas and not in Broca's area. This was seen in elderly subjects, suggesting a reorganization of brain for this aspect of syntactic processing as a function of age. It should be noted that the elderly subjects performed more slowly and less accurately than

Table XI Areas of Increased rCBF for Substraction of PET Activity Associated with Object Subject Sentences from Subject Object Sentences: Experiment 5: Written Presentation, 13 Elderly Subjects, Male and Female

Location	Max Z-score	Number of pixels	Location {X, Y, Z}
Inferior Parietal lobe (Area 40)	3.77	127	–54, –32, 32
Superior frontal gyrus	3.10	73	–22, 56, 8

the young subjects, and that this different localization may reflect differences in syntactic processing ability, not age *per se*. This will require additional experimentation with subjects matched for one of these factors who vary on the second.

3. Increase in rCBF in midline frontal and thalamic structures. This was found in Experiments 1b (written presentation, young females); 2 (auditory presentation, young males and females), 3 (written presentation with concurrent articulation), and 5 (written presentation, elderly males and females). This activation has been attributed to non-domain-specific functions such as arousal and deployment of attention. Of note is that it was often found in more superior structures in these studies than has been the case in previous work raising questions about its interpretation.

4. Other increases in rCBF. There was one other increase in rCBF in the high parietal lobe in Experiment 2 that is unaccounted for.

5. No increases in rCBF. We found that contrasting active and passive sentences was not associated with reliable changes in rCBF despite the presence of behavioral effects in this experiment.

Overall, these results suggest a brain organization for syntactic processing in which:

1. Different syntactic structures activate brain regions in different ways; cf. The difference between relative clauses and the active/passive contrast.

2. There is a preferred site for some aspects of syntactic processing. In young subjects, this appears to be Broca's area for some aspect of the processing of relative clauses.

3. This preferred site may differ in different groups of subjects. For the processing of relative clauses, this site appears to vary as a function of age and/or processing efficiency, but not as a function of sex in young subjects. Whether other factors such as handedness affect it is unknown.

4. Regions of the brain involved in arousal, attention, and motivation sometimes become active during more complex syntactic processing.

These conclusions are highly tentative, and require more research to validate or modify. The research does, however, demonstrate that activation studies of syntactic processing using highly structured materials can yield interpretable results that can form the basis for theory development in this area.

ACKNOWLEDGMENT

This work was supported by a grant from NIH (DC02146).

REFERENCES

Alpert, N., Berdichevsky, D., Weise, S., Tang, J., & Rauch, S. (1993). Sterotactic transformation of PET scans by nonlinear least squares. In K. Uemura (Ed.), *Quantifications of brain functions. Tracer kinetics and image analysis in brain PET* (pp. 459–463). Amsterdam: Elsevier.

Alpert, N. M., Berdichevsky, D., Levin, Z., Morris E. D., & Faschman, A. J. (1996). Improved methods for image registration. *NeuroImage, 3*, 10–18.

Baddeley, A. D., Thomson, N., & Buchanan, M. (1975). Word length and the structure of short-term memory. *Journal of Verbal Learning and Verbal Behavior, 14*, 575–589.

Caplan, D., Alpert, N., & Waters, G. S. (1998). Effects of syntactic structure and propositional number on patterns of regional cerebral blood flow. *Journal of Cognitive Neuroscience, 10*, 541–552.

Caplan, D., Alpert, N., & Waters, G. S. (1999) PET studies of syntactic processing with auditory sentence presentation. *NeuroImage, 4*, 343–351.

Caplan, D., Alpert, N., Waters, G. S., and Olivieri, A. (2000) Activation of Broca's area of syntactic processing under conditions of concurrent articulation. *Human Brain Mapping*, in press.

Caplan, D., Waters, G. S. & Alpert, N. (under review) Localization of syntactic comprehension by positron emission tomography in elderly subjects.

Chomsky, N. (1957). *Syntactic structures*. The Hague: Mouton.

Chomsky, N. (1965). *Aspects of the theory of syntax*. Cambridge, MIA: MIT Press.

Demonet, J. F., Fiez, J. A., Paulesu, E., Peterson, S. E. & Zatorre, R. J. (1996). PET studies of phonological processing: A critical reply to Poeppel. *Brain and Language, 55*, 352–379.

Friston, K. J., Frith, C. D., Liddle, P. F., & Frackowiak, R. S. J. (1991). Comparing functional (PET) images: The assessment of significant change. *Journal of Cerebral Blood Flow and Metabolism, 11*, 690–699.

Friston, K. J., Holmes, A. P., Worsley, K. J., Poline, J. B., Frith, C. D., & Frackowiak, R. S. J. (1995). Statistical parametric maps in functional imaging: A general approach. *Human Brain Mapping, 2*, 189–210.

Gibson, (1997). Syntactic complexity: Locality of syntactic dependencies. Manuscript.

Just, M. A., & Carpenter, P. A. (1992). A capacity theory of comprehension: Individual differences in working memory. *Psychological Review, 99*, 122–149.

King, J., & Just, M. A. (1991). Individual differences in syntactic processing: The role of working memory. *Journal of Memory and Language, 30*, 580–602.

Posner, M. I., Inhoff, A. W., Friedrich, F. J., & Cohen, A. (1987). Isolating attentional systems: A cognitive–anatomical analysis. *Psychobiology, 15*(2), 107–121.

Posner, M. I., Peterson, S. E., Fox, P. T., & Raichle, M. E. (1988). Localization of cognitive operations in the human brain. *Science, 240*, 1627–1631.

Stromswold, K., Caplan, D., Alpert, N., & Rauch, S. (1996). Localization of syntactic comprehension by positron emission tomography. *Brain and Language, 52*, 452–473.

Talairach, J., & Tournoux, P. (1988). *Co-planar stereotaxic atlas of the human brain*. New York: Thieme.

Waters, G., Caplan, D., & Heldebrandt, N. (1987). Working memory and written sentence comprehension. In M. Coltheart (Ed.), *Attention and performance XII* (pp. 531–555). London: Erlbaum.

Worsley, K. J., Evans, A. C., Marrett, S., & Neelin, P. (1992). A three-dimensional statistical analysis for rCBF activation studies in human brain. *Journal of Cerebral Blood Flow and Metabolism, 12*, 900–918.

Chapter 17

Canonicity in Broca's Sentence Comprehension: The Case of Psychological Verbs*

Maria Mercedes Piñango

The work of Edgar Zurif (some of it in cooperation with colleagues) has been crucial in showing that at least certain aspects of syntactic processing depend in a rather direct way on the integrity of the anterior frontal area of the left hemisphere (roughly Broca's area, e.g. Amunts et al., 1997) and certain aspects of semantic composition rely more heavily on Wernicke's area (e.g., Zurif, Caramazza, & Myerson, 1972; Caramazza & Zurif, 1976; Zurif, Swinney, Prather, Solomon, & Bushell, 1993; Swinney, Zurif, Prather, & Love, 1996; Piñango & Zurif, 1999; Grodzinsky, Piñango, Zurif, & Drai, 1999). This has been possible, in large part, because of the lesion localizing value that aphasia syndromes offer. This key property of Broca's and Wernicke's aphasia in particular has allowed the link of patterns of sparing and loss, unified within principled characterizations, to mutually exclusive neuroanatomical regions.

It has been the case that, until recently, lesion studies constituted the main and only source for this kind of investigation. However, the introduction of neuroimaging techniques [e.g., positron emission tomography (PET) and functional magnetic resonance imaging (fMRI)] have not only opened new avenues of investigation, but most importantly, have provided evidence that converges with what was already suggested by lesion studies, particularly with respect to the Broca's area–syntax connection (e.g., Cooke et al., 1999; Caplan, Alpert, & Waters, 1998).

Within this tradition, the present chapter further investigates the Broca's area–syntax connection by putting to the test two linguistically based descriptive generalizations for Broca's aphasia comprehension. It

*Portions of this paper are adapted and reprinted by permission of Maria M. Piñango from Piñango, Maria M. "Some Syntactic and Semantic Operations and Their Neurological Underpinnings." Ph.D. diss., Brandeis University, 1998.

does this by distinguishing, experimentally, two components of sentence representation. One component is order of thematic roles in syntactic representation. The other component is syntactic displacement (i.e., argument movement).[1] These factors are important because they seem to play a part in the widely observed pattern of performance in Broca's comprehension where constructions such as the agentive active (e.g., *The cat chased the dog*), subject relative (e.g., *The cat that chased the dog is big*), and cleft (e.g., *This is the cat that chased the dog*) are comprehended at a level greater than *chance*, and constructions such as the agentive passive (e.g., *The dog was chased by the cat*), object relative (e.g., *The dog that the cat chased is big*), and object cleft (e.g., *This is the dog that the cat chased*) exhibit a performance level within the *chance* range.

One well-known descriptive generalization that makes use of the syntactic movement component is the trace deletion hypothesis (TDH) (Grodzinsky, 1990, 1995). Briefly, the TDH accounts for the above pattern within the government and binding framework (Chomsky, 1981) by positing (1) that traces of moved arguments are deleted in the Broca's agrammatic representation,[2] and (2) that in case the first referential noun phrase of the sentence is left without a thematic role (due to trace deletion), the role of *agent* is assigned to it by default. Predictions for agrammatic comprehension follow from the interaction between an impaired representation (one that lacks argument traces) and the default (agent-first) strategy [see also, Hickok, Zurif, & Canseco-Gonzalez (1993) and Mauner, Fromkin, & Cornell (1993) for different implementations of the same insight].[3]

---

[1]Throughout this chapter whenever I mention argument movement I will be referring only to the overt syntactic displacement of a noun phrase. This is so irrespective of whether it moves to a so-called argument position, or to a nonargument position (A-bar position).

[2]Traces in θ positions are created whenever syntactic movement of a noun phrase (NP) takes place from its base-generated position in underlying representation to its final landing site in surface representation.

In government binding theory (Chomsky, 1981), argument traces are the recipients of thematic information which is assigned structurally by the verb to its arguments. The connection between the object position (where the trace is) and the subject position (where the antecedent has moved to) is established by a so-called argument chain that links the antecedent with its *trace*. The following illustrates the process:

(2)   e   is chased <u>the bird</u> by the cat (underlying representation)

(3)   <u>The bird</u>$_i$ is chased t$_i$ by the cat (surface representation)
        |____ chain ____| move-alpha

[3]Actually this is not the complete story. To derive its predictions (specifically, to derive the predictions for verbs that do not license *agents*) the TDH invokes a secondary mechanism for θ assignment: the thematic hierarchy. In Piñango (1998) I argue against the idea

The necessity to incorporate an extralinguistic element in the generalization, such as the *agent*-first strategy, is given by the fact that not all types of syntactic displacement result in impaired levels of performance. So, even though there is syntactic displacement in both subject relatives and object relatives, *chance* performance surfaces only in object relatives. A similar situation arises in agentive actives and passives and agentive subject clefts and object clefts where *chance* performance occurs only in object clefts and passives even though all four agentive constructions are analyzed as involving some kind of argument displacement (i.e., they involve an antecedent–gap relation).

In Piñango (1999), I directly investigate the question of whether syntactic movement, independent of the order of thematic roles in syntactic

---

that the thematic hierarchy can be used by the comprehension system as an alternative route for θ-marking, that is, as a source of thematic roles, whenever those licensed by the sentential predicate are inaccessible. The reason is straightforward: The thematic hierarchy is only a descriptive generalization that seeks to capture the well attested cross-linguistic regularity of thematic role distribution over grammatical relations (Bresnan & Kanerva, 1989; Grimshaw, 1990; Jackendoff, 1972, 1990). The notion of a thematic heirarchy arises from the observation that there is an interaction between grammatical relations and the thematic role of the arguments of the sentence (as licensed by the predicate) such that whenever there is a verb with an argument structure containing an *agent,* and a *patient*, the *agent* will invariably be linked to the most prominent grammatical function (i.e., subject) and the *patient* will be left to be linked to the next available grammatical function (e.g., direct object).

One important fact that Grodzinsky (1990, 1995) overlooks in his use of this hierarchy is that even though it is a theoretical generalization, it is not and never was intended to be an independent theoretical object. This is so because the thematic hierarchy is a generalization over how thematic roles are organized (for a given predicate) for the purposes of mapping onto syntactic structure.

Thematic roles (the components of the hierarchy) have been defined since their inception (Gruber, 1965) as *semantic relations* established over semantic representation. This means in turn that a thematic role (or the hierarchy) cannot exist without the predicate that licenses it. Hence, the hierarchy as an independent compilation of ordered thematic *labels* (as Grodzinsky invokes it) is an untenable concept. Jackendoff (1990) makes this point very cleary, "[Thematic roles] are not primitives of semantic theory. Rather, they are rational notions defined structurally over conceptual structure, with a status precisely comparable to that of the notions subject and object in many syntactic theories (e.g., extended standard theory, GB)." (p. 49).

This is not a trivial problem for the TDH. On the one hand, as I have shown, the thematic hierarchy as employed in the TDH is not a possible theoretical object. On the other hand, and as we will see very clearly here, without the hierarchy the TDH cannot predict anything but *above-chance* performance for sentential constructions with predicates that do not license an *agent*. This is so because every time the strategy is triggered (as a result of argument movement), it causes semantic incoherence in the interpretation. This in turn, forces the system to ignore the strategically assigned thematic role, and, as a result allows it to infer the "missing" thematic role.

representation, is at the core of the Broca's comprehension deficit, as the TDH claims. There I show—through the phenomenon known as split intransitivity or unaccusativity—that it is possible to obtain *above-chance* performance by Broca's patients despite of the presence of object movement, if the order of thematic roles is not reversed in syntactic representation. In other words, I show that presence of movement of the sort observed in passives and object relatives (i.e., object movement) does not necessarily cause impaired (chance) performance.

This finding led to a new generalization, one that made the focus of the Broca's deficit the *mismatch* between order of thematic roles in argument structure (e.g.,*<agent–patient>* for agentive verbs) and how it is represented in syntactic structure (e.g., *patient* before *agent*, say, for agentive passives), and not inability to represent argument-traces. I call that generalization the argument linking hypothesis (ALH) (Piñango, 1998, 1999).

Nevertheless, that report only dealt with one side of the equation: that presence of object-movement does not necessarily lead to unimpaired performance *if* the thematic roles licensed by a predicate are not reversed in surface representation. Here, I show the other side: that absence of movement can result in impaired performance *if* the thematic roles licensed by the main predicate are reversed in surface representation. This kind of evidence is afforded by investigating Broca's performance in sentential constructions containing so-called psychological verbs.

In what follows I (1) briefly describe the linguistic nature of psychological verbs, (2) present the argument structure hypothesis and its predictions for these verbal constructions (3) summarize the findings published on the comprehension of these verbs (including a discussion on the predictions that the TDH should make for the constructions), and (4) discuss old and new evidence that bears on these two sets of predictions. To forecast, the main conclusion that will arise from those findings is that impaired performance (i.e., *chance* performance) arises only when the order of thematic roles represented in argument structure is reversed in syntactic representation, independent of argument movement.

PSYCHOLOGICAL VERBS

As the name indicates, psychological verbs (psych verbs) denote mental states of an emotional sort (e.g., *love, fear, frighten, worry*). In linguistics, these verbs have been given special attention because they are nonagentive, and as a result constitute an interesting test case for theories on the mapping between semantic arguments and syntactic functions/positions when the *agent*–subject connection is not available (e.g.,

Grimshaw, 1990; Jackendoff, 1990; Pesetsky, 1995). In aphasia research these verbs have become of interest because they offer a potential interaction with *agent*-first strategies—which form part and parcel of movement-based generalizations such as the TDH, and in this way allows us to further probe the virtues of those accounts (Grodzinsky, 1995; Balogh and Grodzinsky, 1996).[4]

Psych verbs divide into two main classes: subject-*experiencer* (*fear*-type) and object-*experiencer* (*frighten*-type). As the labels show, these two types are distinguished by how their respective argument structures map onto grammatical functions in simple declarative active sentences:

Type	Argument structure	Example
Subject-*experiencer* (*fear*-type)	*<exp, theme>*	*John* feared *the gun* *exp* *theme*
Object-*experiencer* (*frighten*-type)	*<theme, exp>*	*The gun* frightened *John* *theme* *exp*

Besides being nonagentive, one subclass of these predicates—object-*experiencer* (*frighten*-type)—has the feature that, in active sentences, it links its "volitional" thematic role (i.e., *experiencer* role) to the object position. This is in fact what makes these types of verbs interesting: they represent a direct counterexample to the overwhelming generalization observed cross-linguistically that the more agentlike argument must be linked to the most prominent grammatical relation (subject) in simple declarative active sentences. In the case of object-*experiencer* verbs, it is the *theme* (least agentlike) and not the *experiencer* (most agentlike) argument that is linked to subject position.

This "mismatch" found between the argument structure and syntactic representation of these verbs (in simple declarative active sentences) has driven considerable debate in the linguistic literature (e.g., Belletti & Rizzi, 1988; Grimshaw, 1990; Jackendoff, 1990; Pesetsky, 1995). At issue is how the linking between argument structure and syntactic representation for these verbs can be reconciled with the widely accepted generalization that at some level of representation, semantic arguments seem to map onto grammatical functions based on a partial "hierarchy" of arguments (e.g., highest role goes to subject). A discussion of the different proposals seeking to answer this question would take us too far afield. I will therefore focus only on the syntactic analysis proposed for psych verbs in

---

[4]Only one type of psych verb license *agents*: agentive *frighten*-type as in the agentive reading of, "John frightened Lou." The type I am concerned with here licenses a *theme* and an *experiencer* as in, "The movie frightened the boy."

active and passive constructions this being the only analysis that has a direct impact on the predictions for Broca's agrammatic comprehension. In a review of the literature on the syntax of psychological verbs, Pesetsky (1995) argues, contrary to previous claims,[5] that object-*experiencer* verbs (*frighten*-type) behave syntactically like subject-*experiencer* verbs (*fear*-type).[6] He does this by showing that whatever difference there is in the semantics of these verbs, it is not reflected in the grammatical functions that the verbs license in underlying representation.[7] In other words, Pesetsky argues that in underlying representation, psych verbs are no different from

[5]Previous proposals [ie., Belleti & Rizzi (1988)] had in fact distinguished these two types of verbs along syntactic lines: *fear*-type verbs licensed a base-generated NP in subject position while *frighten*-type verbs did not. They argued that for *frighten*-type verbs, the understood subject is derived, that is, it is base-generated in object position, and then moved to surface structure to subject position leaving a trace behind as in *The man$_i$ frightened the woman t$_i$*.

[6]The source of the conflict, Pesetsky argues, arises from the fact that the *theme* argument of those verbs encompasses three different semantic relations (causer, target of emotion, and subject matter). It is this difference in thematic relations that motivates the difference in mapping onto syntactic function (*causer* arguments map onto subjects, and *target/subject matter* arguments map onto objects). Whereas this solution is based on the intuition that there must be regularity in the correspondence of thematic roles and syntactic function [as embodied in the uniformity of thematic assigment hypothesis or UTAH, Baker (1988)], it is not necessary for the formulation of predictions for Broca's comprehension.

[7]The following is a technical point that can be skipped for the purpose of following the text. Belleti and Rizzi (1988) argue that *frighten* verbs license only internal arguments and no external arguments. Within GB theory this has direct consequences for the mapping of arguments onto syntactic positions since a classification of internal argument entails base-generation as a complement of the verb. A classification of external arguments by contrast entails within this framework base-generation in the specifier position of the verb phrase (VP).

In order to argue for the internal nature of the *frighten* arguments, Belletti and Rizzi (1988) seek evidence for the "athematicity" of the subject position in active sentences. [The rationale is the following: Establishing that the subject position is athematic means, within GB, that whatever argument(s) is/are licensed by the verb must be internal, since external arguments are licensed in subject position only.] For instance, Belletti and Rizzi point out that arbitrary *pro* reading is impossible for regular unaccusatives [**pro* sono arrivati a casa mia "(somebody) arrived at my place," Pesetsky (1995, ex. 107, p. 38)], but not for unergatives or transitives whose deep subject position is thematic [*pro* hanno telefonato a casa mia "(somebody) telephoned my place" (106 a, p. 38)]. There are indeed examples of *frighten*-type verbs that do not allow arbitrary pro reading [**pro* hanno colpito il giornalista per la gentilezza "(somebody) struck the journalist with his kindness" (108 b, p. 39)]. This is intended to show that just like unaccusativeness, *frighten*-type verbs don't license external arguments.

Pesetsky (1995) determines the invalidity of this argument by showing that arbitrary *pro* is not a diagnostic for *thematicity* of a syntactic position, but rather a diagnostic for *agentivity* (thus implying that external arguments can bear thematic roles other than *agent*). That diagnostic, Pesetsky claims, works for unaccusatives because unaccusatives *by defintion* are nonagentive. However that diagnostic does not say anything about the athematic status of the subject position (for *frighten* verbs and unaccusativeness alike) which is what Belletti and Rizzi (1988) were arguing for. As a result, that test cannot be used as an argument for a specific grammatical configuration.

agentive verbs in the way they link their arguments onto syntactic positions. This conclusion provides us with a straightforward view of the syntactic representation for these verbs which is akin to that proposed for agentive verbs. And, in turn, it allows us to make specific predictions with respect to Broca's comprehension.

The four sentential constructions I will be focusing on are the following:

a. *The dog* feared *the cat*   (active/subject-*experiencer*)
   experiencer   *theme*

b. *The dog* frightened *the cat*   (active/object-*experiencer*)
   theme   *experiencer*

c. *The cat$_i$* was feared t$_i$ by *the dog*   (passive/subject-*experiencer*)
   theme   *experiencer*

d. *The cat$_i$* was frightened t$_i$ by *the dog*   (passive/object-*experiencer*)
   experiencer   *theme*

Belletti and Rizzi (1988) also argue that passives of *frighten* verbs are "adjectival" (i.e., passive morphology on the verb is lexically and not syntactically derived). The motivation behind that argument is the following. It is known that unaccusitives do not passivize (e.g.,*The man was arrived) probably for syntactic reasons. However *frighten* verbs can undergo passivization (e.g., The man was frightened by the woman). If, as Belletti and Rizzi claim, *frighten* verbs are unaccusative then the passive construction those verbs form cannot be syntactically derived. Therefore those passives must be adjectival (i.e., not syntactically derived).

One feature of adjectival passives is that they denote stativity (e.g., they denote a *state* or a *situation* but not an *event*) (e.g., The teacher is worried about the student). Stativity has syntactic reflections in that it allows participle–adjective conversion (e.g., the frightened boy), and in that it allows stative verbs to be compatible with the progressive form (e.g., The man is admiring the picture). Based on these two features, Pesetsky (1995) shows that although there are some *frighten* verbs that denote stativity and therefore have adjectival properties [e.g., (a) and (b)], not all do [e.g., (c) and (d)]:

(a) Sue was very *scared* by noises
(b) Noises were *scaring* Sue
(c) ??Sue was very *depressed* by noises [Pesesky's (1995) judgments (p. 29)]
(d) ??Noises were *depressing* Sue

By showing that the stativity–*frighten*-verb connection is only partial, Pesetsky demonstrates that it cannot be used as a valid argument for their "adjectivalness" and therefore for the unaccusative analysis of those verbs. Moreover, even if that were a strong correlation, it is a well-known fact that whereas adjectival participles are formed from unaccusative verbs (a fallen leaf), not all unaccusatives form participles (* the left traveler). So, to argue that *frighten* verbs form participles is not a complete argument for an unaccusative analysis of *frighten*-verbs. These and other similar arguments lead Pesetsky to the conclusion that the syntactic representation of the passive of *frighten*-verbs is not the same as that of unaccusativeness. Within the GB approach this entails that *frighten*-verbs produce syntactic representations analogous to those of agentive verbs. So, contrary to Belletti and Rizzi's (1988) original proposal the thematic features of these verbs (i.e., *theme* goes to subject position) do not have a syntactic reflection in their base generated representation.

Notice again that in neither of these sentence types do the verbs license an *agent* role. Notice also that even though for actives/subject-*experiencer* passivization reverses the order of roles such that the most *agent*like (the experiencer) is in the by-phase (just like in passives with agentive verbs), the reverse is true for sentences with object-*experiencer* verbs: passivization "fixes" the mismatch between the order of arguments assumed to exist at the level of argument structure, and the order of arguments in syntactic representation (the most agentlike, the *experiencer* role is in first position). This contrast is thus key for the purposes of differentiating syntactic-movement from order of thematic roles; it offers us the condition where there is object-movement and no reversal of roles (frighten-passives), and also the condition where there is no-object movement but there is reversal of roles (frighten-active). In this way, it allows us to investigate the possibility that it is not syntactic movement but the resulting order of thematic roles in syntactic representation that seems to be at the core of the Broca's comprehension problem. I present the argument linking hypothesis, the generalization that embodies this latter possibility, directly below.

THE ARGUMENT LINKING HYPOTHESIS

The argument linking hypothesis (ALH) is based on the notion that in the language system there are two linking mechanisms that can potentially establish correspondence between arguments in semantic structure and grammatical functions in syntactic representation (i.e., surface structure). One mechanism, *semantic linking*,[8] is purely semantically based and establishes correspondence between arguments and *linear positions* in the sentence (first, second, etc. . . .). The other is *syntactic linking* which establishes correspondence between arguments and *syntactic functions* based

[8]*Semantic linking* preserves the intuition, present in all descriptions of Broca's agrammatic comprehension I know, that given two arguments licensed by a predicate, and in the absence of syntactic information, the first argument in a sentence is more likely than not to be interpreted as an actor rather than as an undergoer. Rather than attributing this regularity to extralinguistic knowledge, I follow the intuition that this systematicity in the way semantic roles are organized in syntactic representation is a reflection of syntactically relevant semantic representation that (a) is independent from syntax, and (b) does not go away even after more complex grammatical principles develop. Moreover, given that this organization is independent from syntactic representation, I assume that it can emerge as a system of correspondence whenever syntactic principles of linking fail to be properly implemented (or as I will propose below, fail to be implemented "on time"). Reflections of this mechanism are not easy to come by, however, they can be observed in the process of pidginization (Bickerton, 1981), and in the language of second language learners who acquire the target language in a naturalistic setting (Klein & Purdue, 1998).

on syntactic principles (i.e., correspondence rules). This is the system which theories of syntax–semantics correspondence seek to capture. In the normal case, the system of correspondence is constrained in such a way that *syntactic linking* always prevails over *semantic linking* (I will call the constraint that keeps *semantic linking* from interfering, the *linking* constraint). The *linking* constraint is a temporal constraint whose main effect is to keep a temporal differential in the unfolding of syntactic and semantic representations as comprehension progresses. As a result, in the intact system, syntactic mechanisms (including *syntactic linking*) will be implemented *before* any semantically based mechanism. However, if, for some reason, this temporal constraint is rendered inoperative (say, due to brain damage) or the relevant syntactic information—to complete *syntactic* linking—is somehow delayed, the product of *semantic* linking is left free to emerge alongside with that of *syntactic* linking.

The argument linking hypothesis proposes that in the Broca's system the *linking* constraint is impaired. The direct consequence of this is that even though both, syntactic representation and argument structure are intact, the system now has, instead of one, two active linking mechanisms that, as a result, must *compete* against each other for implementation. This, in turn, means that whenever the two linking mechanisms agree, absence of the *linking* constraint is not apparent (normal-like comprehension will occur). However, whenever the two linking mechanisms yield conflicting correspondences (i.e., whenever semantic roles are reversed in syntactic representation) impaired comprehension, in the form of *chance* performance, will arise.

Evidence for a "slowed-down" lexical processor as a possible source of Broca's aphasia comprehension deficit has been well documented. Building on this, there are accounts proposing that even though Broca's patients are not unable to activate lexical meanings, for these patients, lexical activation in the form of priming seems to be "temporally protracted," that is, it seems to have a "slower-than-normal" time course (e.g., Prather et al., 1992, Prather et al., 1997; Zurif et al., 1993). I propose here that it is the inability to implement a fast acting syntactic representation that allows the product of a semantic mechanism (i.e., linking by linear position) to emerge, off-line, for the purposes of sentence comprehension, and, as a result, to compete with *syntactic linking*. Such competition is only visible when the products of the two linking mechanisms differ (i.e., when the order of thematic roles—in argument structure—is reversed in syntactic representation).

The argument linking hypothesis predicts *above-chance* performance in agentive actives, subject relatives, and subject clefts because in these constructions both linking mechanisms (*syntactic* and *semantic*) coincide.

So, in the sentence *The boy kissed the girl, the boy* (agent) is both first position and subject position, and *the girl* (goal) is both second position and object:

kissed <*agent, goal*>
agent $\longrightarrow$ first position = subject $\longrightarrow$ $NP_{the\ boy}$
goal $\longrightarrow$ second position = object $\longrightarrow$ $NP_{the\ girl}$

The ALH predicts *chance* performance in passives, object relatives, and clefts, because in these constructions, the semantic and syntactic systems give conflicting correspondences. For a passive such as *The girl was kissed by the boy*, for instance, *syntactic linking* yields:

kissed <*agent, goal*>
agent = oblique $\longrightarrow$ (*agent* = $NP_{the\ boy}$)
goal = subject $\longrightarrow$ (*goal* = $NP_{the\ girl}$)

but *semantic linking* yields:

kissed <*agent, goal*>
agent = first position (agent = $NP_{the\ girl}$)
goal = second position (goal = $NP_{the\ boy}$)

Given that the *linking* constraint is not available to force the system to opt for *syntactic linking*, both possibilities are, therefore, equally likely; so competition between these two systems ensues. This, in turn, results in *chance* performance (i.e., sometimes syntactic linking prevails, and sometimes semantic linking does).

For object relatives and clefts a similar situation arises. In the subordinate clause of the sentence, *The girl that the boy kissed is tall*, syntactic linking yields:

kissed<*agent, goal*>
agent $\longrightarrow$ subject $\longrightarrow$ $NP_{the\ boy}$
goal $\longrightarrow$ complementizer $\longrightarrow$ $COMP_{that}$)[9]

but *semantic linking* gives,

kissed<*agent, goal*>
agent = first position (this results in *agent* = COMP)
goal = second position (this results in *goal* = $NP_{the\ boy}$)

---

[9]The complementizer is analyzed as the bearer of the thematic role assigned by the verb in the subordinate clause. The complementizer has to its left an operator (O), which is in fact the bearer of the thematic role assigned by the verb in the relative clause.

And again, it is the conflict between these two competing mechanisms that yields *chance* performance.

So, as we see the ALH offers a view of Broca's agrammatic comprehension that does not capitalize on the presence of syntactic displacement, but that, instead, characterizes the comprehension impairment as an inability to constrain possible correspondences between semantic and syntactic representations.

So far, I have presented both the TDH and the ALH, I have also briefly described the linguistic analysis for psych verbs in actives and passive constructions. I will now turn to the predictions these two generalizations offer.

PREDICTIONS BY THE TRACE DELETION HYPOTHESIS AND THE ARGUMENT LINKING HYPOTHESIS

Table 1 shows the predictions that the TDH made for actives and passives with psychological verbs when the first findings were reported:

In this section I will present arguments against the possibility that the TDH as it is formulated can predict anything but *above-chance* performance for all four constructions with psych verbs. I will show that the semantic incoherence introduced by the application of the *agent*-first strategy interacts with the thematic composition of the sentences in such a way that the system is forced to bypass the strategy in order to achieve semantic well-formedness. This results in normal-like performance across the board. In contrast, I will show that the predictions for the ALH are as follows: above chance whenever the order of thematic roles in argument structure, and the order of thematic roles in syntactic representation agree, and chance, whenever they do not. But before I turn to those predictions I will present the arguments for the predictions by the TDH.

Grodzinsky (1990, 1995) derives the prediction for *fear*-passives in the following manner. He posits that patients make "consistent reversal errors" because they interpret these sentences as if they were actives. This happens, he states, "because the subject of these sentences (agent) would now be higher on the (thematic) Hierarchy than the object (experiencer)." Consistent reversal errors translate into a prediction of *below-chance* performance.

Let us take a closer look at the argument behind this prediction. First of all, it is not clear how compliance with hierarchical order of thematic roles (although see footnote 3 for a brief discussion on why the use of the hierarchy in this manner is problematic) should lead to systematic reversal in Broca's agrammatic comprehension. The implication of stating that Broca's patients understand *fear*-passives like actives because of the

Table 1 Predictions Reported in Grodzinsky (1995) and Balogh and Grodzinsky (1996)

Type	Example	TDH predictions
fear-active	The dog feared the cat *experiencer* *theme*	**above chance** (as presented in Grodzinsky, 1995)
frighten-active	The dog frightened the cat *theme* *experiencer*	**above chance**
fear-passive	The cat$_i$ was feared t_i by the dog *theme* *experiencer*	**below chance** (as presented in Grodzinsky, 1995) **chance** (as presented in Balogh and Grodzinsky, 1996)
frighten-passive	The cat$_i$ was frightened t_i by the dog *experiencer* *theme*	**above chance** (as presented in Balogh and Grodzinsky, 1996)

assignment of agency to the subject-NP misses the point that *fear*-type verbs *do not* license *agents*. So, it cannot be the case that Broca's agrammatic patients interpret *The man is feared by the boy* as *The man fears the boy*, because even in the active construction, the subject-NP is incompatible with a thematic role of *agent* as shown by the sentence **The man fears the boy on purpose* (the adverbial *on purpose* is only compatible with agentive subjects; the ungrammaticality of this sentence then shows that the subject NP cannot be construed as an *agent*). In effect, it is not clear how the agent-first-strategy can be allowed to apply in a situation where assumption of agentivity causes semantic incoherence.[10] In fact, what I will argue for in this and the other cases is that in a situation of thematic incoherence (i.e., when the strategy introduces a thematic role that is incompatible with

[10] This is not the first time this question has been raised. In fact, others have mentioned that a semantic representation of a psych predicate with an *agent* role is incoherent and Grodzinsky (1995, footnote 10) discusses this issue. There he argues that even with an *agent* NP the sentence can be semantically coherent. To support this, he points out that contexts can be construed where an agentive reading is allowed. Consider the sentence *John was misunderstood on purpose*. Grodzinsky (1995) claims that this sentence is grammatical in the reading that, "John got himself misunderstood intentionally." I tested this possibility on four native speakers of English. I utilized the sentences Grodzinsky (1995, p. 495), and added "on purpose" to them (to induce an agentive reading). I asked my informants to create *any kind of context* in which the subject of the sentence could be an *agent*. The seven sentences tested were, *The woman was desired by the man on purpose, The princess was loved by the prince on purpose, The boy was trusted by the girl on purpose, The woman was admired by the man on purpose, The father was heard by the son on purpose, The soldier was hated by the boy on purpose,* and *The woman was understood by the man on purpose.* None of my informants accepted the grammaticality of any of the sentences given with the agentive reading, nor could they come up with a reading in which the sentences could be even somewhat grammatical. This result calls into question Grodzinsky's first argument since it shows that at least for the sentences he utilized in the test reported in 1995, the agentive reading for the *fear*-type passive is not possible.

In that same footnote, Grodzinsky offers two other reasons why the issue of semantic incoherence may not represent a problem. He notes that:

> ". . . even if there is (incoherence in the semantic representation), it is clear that on a forced-choice task, the patient would use whatever information is available to him, and even if the representation is slightly incoherent, he would attempt to use its predicate–argument structure to come up with an answer. In this case there should not be a problem, and he has two distinct theta-roles, which guide his behavior." (p. 486)

Let us consider the first point that, "the patient would use whatever information is available to him." Even though this is a reasonable assumption, it is not at all clear how the forced choice task would lead the Broca's agrammatic patient to make *systematic* mistakes. In particular, if the sentence is semantically ill-formed (after application of the strategy) the patient should feel forced to attend to the meaning of the sentence. If that is the case, agency would be disallowed since the Broca's agrammatic patient knows that *fear*-type verbs do not license agency and, contrary to data, correct inference of thematic roles would follow.

the argument structure that the predicate of the sentence licenses), the assignment of agency is by necessity bypassed, and in its place, the system
is allowed to infer the missing thematic role. This leads consistently to an
above-chance prediction of performance.

Regarding *fear*-type actives, Grodzinsky (1990, 1995) predicts *above-
chance* performance on the grounds that after application of the strategy
the resulting order of θ-roles matches the thematic hierarchical order
which then consistently leads to correct interpretation of the sentence;
hence, *above-chance* performance.[11] But just as with *fear*-passives, this is a
problematic deduction because it violates what we know about argument
structure (i.e., that it is the level where arguments *licensed* by a predicate
are represented) and it overlooks an important empirical fact about what
is preserved in Broca's comprehension (i.e., Broca's patients know what
fear means). However, for the *fear*-type actives the problem with that argument does not cause a change in the prediction. That is because the semantic incoherence created by the application of the agent-first strategy
once again should force the Broca's patient to ignore the ill-assigned
agency and allow him to look at the argument structure of the verb and
correctly infer the "missing" thematic role. This, again, leads to *above-
chance* performance.

---

[10]*cont.* Let us consider now the second point, "even if the representation is slightly incoherent, (the agrammatic patient) would attempt to use its predicate–argument structure
<agent, experiencer> to come up with an answer." As stated, this idea overlooks the fact that
the concept of argument structure, to the extent that it has been discussed in the literature,
refers exclusively to the thematic structure that the verb *licenses*. So the notion that the agrammatic patient *creates* an incoherent argument structure for a verb when the correct one is
readily accessible is not theoretically tenable. To suggest that would be to say that Broca's
agrammatic patients do not know what *fear*-type verbs mean. This we know is not the case.
    Alternatively, we could understand this latter point of Grodzinsky's (1995) as suggesting
that the Broca's patient will examine the verb's argument structure in the presence of an incoherent semantic representation. However that assumption again would imply that
agrammatics patients will be able to *bypass* the assignment of the strategy and correctly infer
the thematic role of the dangling NP, just as they do for nonreferential subjects. Again, this
would lead to *above* not *below-chance* performance. I have shown here that the only possible
prediction that the TDH can offer for sentences with nonagentive predicates (psych verbs),
must be above-chance.
    [11] Grodzinsky (1995) formulated this prediction assuming the VP-internal subject hypoth-
esis (e.g., Burton & Grimshaw, 1992). The VP-internal subject hypothesis proposes that NP-
subjects are always generated in a position internal to the verb phrase (specifier of VP).They
then move to the specifier of CP leaving behind a trace. The direct consequence of this hypothesis, for our purposes, is that even in active sentences there is argument movement
(which in turn triggers the agent-first strategy). Nevertheless, in the end the prediction of
performance by the TDH is not really affected by this assumption. It remains above chance.

As for *frighten*-verbs, the situation is similar. On the assumption that the verb is interpreted as nonagentive, in *frighten*-passives, just like in *fear*-passives, the application of the strategy will cause semantic incoherence which should force the agrammatic patient to bypass the agency assignment by the R-strategy and correctly infer the appropriate thematic role. This would predict *above-chance* performance. Similarly, for *frighten*-actives performance is predicted to be above-chance (see footnote 11).

Let me now summarize the main points of this section so far. First, I have shown that both the TDH and the ALH successfully capture the so-called "core" pattern of performance in Broca's aphasia comprehension: above-chance in agentive actives, agentive subject relatives, and agentive clefts; chance in agentive passives, object relatives, and object clefts. Second, I have argued that the TDH must predict *above-chance* performance for both *fear*- and *frighten*-actives and -passives. It must do so, because in the presence of a nonagentive predicate, application of the agent-first strategy necessarily leads to semantic incoherence. This in turn forces the system to bypass the strategy and thus correctly infer the "missing" thematic role.

At the beginning of the section I mentioned the predictions of the argument linking hypothesis for these four constructions. These are illustrated in more detail in Table II.

With all the predictions in place, I now turn to a discussion of the experimental record that puts to the test these two descriptive generalizations and their respective predictions.

PREVIOUS AND NEW EMPIRICAL EVIDENCE

Previous Evidence

To my knowledge, Grodzinsky (1995) and Balogh and Grodzinsky (1996) constitute the only published studies on the topic of psych verbs in Broca's sentence comprehension.[12] These two studies report on two experiments that investigate comprehension performance on *fear*-type passives and *fear*-type actives (Grodzinsky, 1995) and on *fear*- and *frigthen*-passives (Balogh and Grodzinsky, 1996). I describe each study in turn.

---

[12] This is in large part the reason why I have made the TDH the generalization representative of movement-based accounts. As far as I know, it has been only for the TDH that clear predictions for these constructions have been offered in the literature.

Table II Experimental Sentences and Predictions of Performance by the Argument Linking Hypothesis

Type	Example	ALH prediction
fear-active	The dog feared the cat experiencer · · · theme	**above chance** fear < *experiencer, theme* > syntactic linking yields: experiencer = subject $\longrightarrow$ $(exp = \text{NP}_{the\ dog}$ theme = object $\longrightarrow$ theme = $\text{NP}_{the\ cat})$ and semantic linking yields: experiencer = first position[a] $(exp = \text{NP}_{the\ dog}$ theme = second position $(theme = \text{NP}_{the\ cat})$
frighten-active	The dog frightened the cat theme · · · experiencer	**chance** frighten < *experiencer, theme* > syntactic linking yields: theme = subject $\longrightarrow$ $(theme = \text{NP}_{the\ dog})$ experiencer = object $\longrightarrow$ $(experiencer = \text{NP}_{the\ cat})$ but semantic linking yields: experiencer = first position $(exp = \text{NP}_{the\ dog})$ theme = second position $(theme = \text{NP}_{the\ cat})$
fear-passive	The cat$_i$ was feared t_i by the dog theme · · · experiencer	**chance** fear < *experiencer, theme* > syntactic linking yields: theme = subject $\longrightarrow$ $(theme = \text{NP}_{the\ cat})$ experiencer = oblique $\longrightarrow$ $(experiencer = \text{NP}_{the\ dog})$ but semantic linking yields: experiencer = first position $(exp = \text{NP}_{the\ dog})$ theme = second position $(theme = \text{NP}_{the\ cat})$
frighten-passive	The cat$_i$ was frightened t_i by the dog experiencer · · · theme	**above chance** frighten < *experiencer, theme* > syntactic linking yields: experiencer = subject $\longrightarrow$ $(exp = \text{NP}_{the\ cat})$ theme = oblique $\longrightarrow$ $(theme = \text{NP}_{the\ dog})$ and semantic linking yields: experiencer = first position $(exp = \text{NP}_{the\ cat})$ theme = second position $(theme = \text{NP}_{the\ dog})$

[a] "Position" in this context always refers to a position that a noun phrase can occupy.

In (Grodzinsky, 1995) four Broca's agrammatic subjects were tested using an anagram-with-pictures task.[13] In addition to subject-*experiencer* (*fear*-type) verbs, regular agentive verbs were tested as the control condition. Seven verbs were used per condition, and each verb was presented four times: two in the active form and two in the passive form. These are the findings expressed in terms of mean percentage correct (Grodzinsky, 1995, p. 491):

	Active	Passive
Agentive-type (control condition)	91.07 (above chance)	60.72 (chance)
fear-type	80.37 (above chance)	32.17 **(below chance)**

Statistical analyses on these data reveal that performance in actives was consistently *above-chance*, whereas performance in passives was only at *chance* for the agentive verbs. For the *fear*-type passives, performance was *below-chance* ($p = .02$). As we can see, all, except for one prediction (above-chance in *fear*-passives) were borne out by the results.

Balogh and Grodzinsky (1996) sought to replicate and expand on the previous study by employing a truth-value judgment task.[14] In this study they investigated performance on both *fear* and *frighten* verbs (the latter only in the passive form). A paired t test (comparing each mean to chance) revealed the following:

	Passive ($n = 4$)		
fear-type	$X = 10.25$	$p = .882$	chance
frighten-type	$X = 14.25$	$p = .0425$	above chance

[13] The task is carried out in the following manner. The subject is handed a picture depicting either two people or two objects in some clear relation to each other. At the same time a set of three cards with printed sentence fragments is given to the subject. The cards contain a sentence that describes the action in the picture (the sentence is distributed as NP+was-V-by+NP among the cards). The task of the subject is to organize the cards according to their interpretation of the picture.

[14] In the truth-value task each sentence is preceded by an appropriate discourse context. This is intended to facilitate the response since it saves the subject (with already limited resources) the effort of creating the (pragmatic) context that gives the sentence felicitousness. For this study, all the stories (contexts) and the sentences involved two figurines. Half of the sentences (20 per type) required a "yes" response, and half required a "no" response (with counterbalancing, each verb was in two "yes" and two "no" contexts). The testing procedure was as follows. Each of the figurines was identified for a given story. The story was then played over headphones while the experimenter acted out the scenario using figurines. After the story was played, the experimental sentence was read. Comprehension was measured in the form of a yes or no answer as to whether or not the sentence agreed with the story.

Again, we see that whereas the prediction for *frighten*-passives is borne out by the results, that for *fear*-passives is not. Furthermore, Balogh and Grodzinsky (1996) failed to replicate the findings from Grodzinsky (1995). These shortcomings alone do not constitute reason enough to discard the idea of a movement-based deficit. This is so, because it is still not clear what the preformance for *fear*-passives is, given the conflicting results obtained in the two previous studies and also, because we do not know the performance of *frighten*-actives. It is these two pieces of evidence that will provide the complete picture of performance for this verbal construction and in the progress will allow us to effectively tease apart the components that constitute the focus of the study: order of θ roles and syntactic movement. These reasons represented the main motivation for the next and last study.

New Evidence

To recapitulate, the new study that I am about to present has two main objectives: (1) to determine the correct level of performance for *fear*-passives and (2) determine the level of performance for *frighten*-actives. With these objectives in mind, a total of 58 experimental sentences were constructed distributed among conditions in the following manner: 12 *fear*-type actives, 12 *fear*-type passives, 12 *frighten*-type actives, 12 *frighten*-type passives, and 10 agentive object relative sentences (included as control). All sentences were semantically reversible. In addition 58 different contexts were constructed (one for each experimental sentence) to induce a nonagentive reading (for object relatives the contexts induced an agentive reading). The experimental sentences were each coupled with one set of two pictures, one depicting the correct interpretation, the other the semantically reversed interpretation.

The experimental sentences were presented in a randomized order. Before each sentence was presented, the "context" was provided to ensure the nonagentive reading. Both, contexts and experimental sentences, were recorded by a native speaker of English and presented auditorily over headphones. The following illustrates the procedure:

Presentation of characters: (pointing to the woman in the picture) "This is the mom," (pointing to the girl in the picture) "This is the daughter." This was done for each picture.
Context: "The mom found out that her daughter had been shoplifting at the mall. Because of this" . . . (pause). . . .
Sentence: "The mom was outraged by the daughter."

The above was said while the patient was looking at the corresponding two pictures. The patient was then asked to match his interpretation of the sentence just heard with the picture that best described it. Each subject was tested over four separate sessions. There was no limit set as to the number of times the subject could listen to the sentence or the context.

Subjects

Six subjects participated in the study: two neurologically intact control subjects, and four Broca's agrammatic patients: RD, JC, JB, and HB. All four patients were selected based on a BDAE (Goodglass and Kaplan, 1972) classification which placed them as moderate Broca's aphasics. All patients were medically stable and at least 2 years postonset.

The control subjects matched the Broca's patients in age and level of education. They were all right-handed and native speakers of English.

Results

Both neurologically intact subjects performed at ceiling level in all five conditions. Table III shows the results for the Broca's patients.

A repeated measures ANOVA reveals a significant difference among the four conditions ($F_{(3, 9)} = 7.41$, $p < .01$). Planned comparisons in the form of paired t tests reveal, more specifically, a significant difference only as a function of canonicity: So, even though *fear* actives differed significantly from their passive counterparts [$t_{(3)} = 3.4$, $p = .02$ (one-tail)], *frighten*-actives and their passive counterparts differed from each other *but in the opposite direction* ($t_{(3)} = -4.38$, $p = .01$). *Fear*-actives did not differ from *frighten*-passives ($t_{(3)} = .07$, $p = .25$) nor did *fear*-passives differed from *frighten*-actives ($t_{(3)} = .48$, $p = .33$). Finally, neither *fear*-passives [$\chi^2 (n - 1 = 100) = .02$, $p >> .05$], nor *frighten*-actives differed from chance [$\chi^2 (n - 1 = 100) = .18$, $p >> .05$]. Our control condition, object relatives, did not differ significantly from chance [$\chi^2 (n - 1 = 100) = .1$, $p >> .05$].

DISCUSSION AND CONCLUSIONS

As we can see, these results agree with the findings from Balogh and Grodzinsky (1996): *fear*-type passives elicited *chance* performance. So, again Grodzinsky's (1995) findings were not replicated, nor was the TDH's prediction for *fear*-passives supported. By contrast, all five predictions by the ALH were borne out by the results. The fact that *frighten*-type passives elicited *above-chance* performance and thus replicated the Balogh and Grodzinsky (1996) results further argues for the reliability of the present findings.

Table III Broca's Agrammatic Comprehension of Active and Passive Sentences with Psychological Passives[a]

Order of thematic roles	Canonical	Noncanonical	Noncanonical	Canonical	Noncanonical
Construction and verb type	*Fear*-actives (12)	*Fear*-passives (12)	*Frighten*-actives (12)	*Frighten*-passives (12)	Object relatives (10) control condition
RD	10	5	2	5	4
JB	11	8	7	12	5
JC	9	7	7	9	4
HB	11	3	5	11	5
Mean	10.25	5.75	5.25	9.25	4.5
% correct	85.4	47.9	43.75	77	45

[a]Expressed in numbers and percent correct.

Notice now the performance on *frighten*-actives. As predicted by the ALH, performance for this condition was *chance*. This, together with the *chance* performance in *fear*-passives indicate that movement cannot be the source of the Broca's deficit, since *chance* performance (of the sort found in agentive passives and object relatives) can obtain regardless of whether movement is present or not. Instead, these findings tell us that it is the relative order of thematic roles in surface representation (canonical vs. noncanonical) that seems to matter for correct semantic interpretation. When the order is *experiencer–theme* (canonical order) *above-chance* performance obtains, when the order is *theme–experiencer* (noncanonical order), *chance* performance follows.[15]

Overall, the evidence presented here clearly favors the ALH, an account of Broca's comprehension that focuses on canonicity of arguments over argument movement. Moreover, the evidence presented questions strongly the existence of an agent-first strategy defined as an extralinguistic compensatory mechanism that is triggered in the presence of an incomplete semantic representation. Recall that the original motivation for the introduction of an agent-first strategy was to allow competition between two possible agents (and therefore *chance* performance) in an otherwise intact representation. This tool worked well for passives and object relatives with agentive verbs. However, as it has become apparent, the validity of the strategy becomes untenable once we move away from agentive predicates. Alternatively, it seems to be the case that competition between possible representations, and therefore, *chance* performance arises not from the application of the strategy, but from the creation of competing representations where the choice of thematic roles is circumscribed to those roles represented in the argument structure of the verb. In other words, no third thematic role is ever introduced into the representation. Competing representations, if we have to posit them as such, can only be allowed to arise from alternating assignment of the thematic roles that the verb licenses, and nothing else.

The findings presented here thus support the idea that at the core of Broca's sentence comprehension there is an impaired mechanism that allows otherwise temporally constrained information to arise. Alternating and conflicting representations in off-line comprehension are caused by

---

[15] Admittedly, the data are not all agreeable. There still remains the fact that in one out of the three studies reported, *below-chance* performance for *fear*-passives was reported (Grodzinsky, 1995). I believe that one reason for the disparity is just simple lack of statistical power: In Grodzinsky (1995) only 7 *fear*-passive sentences were tested, as opposed to 20 in the Balogh and Grodzinsky (1996) study, or 12 in the present study. This, coupled with a low subject size (a fact about aphasia research), may have shown a picture of performance that was in fact not representative of the population.

the emergence of the product of *semantic* linking which must then compete with the product of *syntactic* linking.[16] Finally, this type of generalization while being more theory "neutral" (as it does not appeal to one single specific architecture of the language faculty), has direct implications for theories of real-time processing and for inferences regarding the functional commitment of Broca's area (Cooke et al., 1999). It is this kind of bridging that permits further discovery on the architecture of the language faculty both in terms of its computational implementation and in terms of its cortical realization.

ACKNOWLEDGMENTS

The preparation of this paper was supported by NIH Grants DC02984 and DC00081.

REFERENCES

Amunts, K., Klingberg, T., Binkofski, F., Schormann, T., Sitz, R. J., Roland, T. E., & Zilles, K. (1997). The cytoarchitecture of Broca's region and its variability. *NeuroImage, 7*, S353.
Baker, M. (1988). Incorporation: A theory of grammatical function changing. Chicago: University of Chicago Press.
Balogh, J., & Grodzinsky, Y. (1996). Varieties of passives in agrammatic Broca's aphasia: Theta grids, arguments and referentiality. In H. A. Whitaker (Ed.), *Academy of aphasia* (pp. 54–56). London: Academic Press.
Belletti, A., & Rizzi, L. (1988). Psych verbs and theta theory. *Natural Language and Linguistic Theory, 6*, 291–354.
Bickerton, D. (1981). Roots of language. Ann Arbor: Karma Press.
Bresnan, J., & Kanerva, J. M. (1989). The thematic hierarchy and locative inversion in UG. A reply to Paul Schacter's comments. In E. Wehrli & T. Stowell (Eds.), *Syntax and semantics 26: Syntax and the lexicon* San Diego: Academic Press.

---

[16] In this respect, Cooke et al. (1999) report supporting results for this kind of approach, this time from fMRI. The findings they report show that when normal subjects comprehend sentential noncanonical constructions (object relatives) and the antecedent is far away from its gap (a seven-word distance between antecedent and gap), there is extra activation in Broca's area. One way to interpret this finding is by positing that a long antecedent–gap distance permits semantic linking to emerge (if only so briefly). In a noncanonical construction this semantic linking will conflict with syntactic linking. However, since in the normal system the linking constraint is functioning, semantic linking is prevented from fully developing (unlike in the Broca's system where the constraint is not present so semantic linking is free to take place). Nevertheless, this brief emergence of competition forces the system to recover (by favoring syntactic over semantic linking). It is this recovery mechanism that we identify as the "extra-work" associated with Broca's area (a kind of extra work which in Broca's aphasia cannot take place).

Burton, S. & Grimshaw, J. (1992). Coordination and P-internal subjects. *Linguistic Inquiry*, 305–312.

Caplan, D., Alpert, N., & Waters, G. (1998). Effects of syntactic structure and propositional number on patterns of regional cerebral blood flow. *Journal of Cognitive Neuroscience, 10*, 541–552.

Caramazza, A., & Zurif, E. (1976). Dissociation of algorithmic and heuristic processes in language comprehension: Evidence from aphasia. *Brain and Language, 3*, 572–582.

Chomsky, N. (1981). *Lectures on government and binding*. Dordrecht: Foris.

Cooke, A., Zurif, E. B., DeVita, C., Alsop, D., McSorly, C., Koenig, P., Piñango, M. M., Detreg, J., Gee, J., Glosser, G., Balogh, J., & Grossman, M. (1999). *The neural basis for grammatical and short-term memory components of sentence comprehension*. Presentation, Cognitive Neuroscience Society Meeting, Washington, DC.

Goodglass, H., & Kaplan, E. (1972). *The assessment of aphasia and related disorders*. Philadelphia: Lea & Febiger.

Grimshaw, J. (1990). *Argument structure*. Cambridge, MA: MIT Press.

Grodzinsky, Y. (1990). *Theoretical perspectives on language deficits*. Cambridge, MA: MIT Press.

Grodzinsky, Y. (1995). Trace deletion, theta roles and cognitive strategies. *Brain and Language, 51*, 469–497.

Grodzinsky, Y., Piñango, M. M., Zurif, E. B., & Drai, D. (1999). The critical role of group studies in neuropsychology: Comprehension regularities in Broca's aphasia. *Brain and Language, 67*, 134–147.

Gruber, J. (1965). *Studies in lexical relations*. Doctoral dissertation, MIT, Cambridge, MA.

Hickok, G., Zurif, E., & Canseco-Gonzalez, E. (1993). Structural description of agrammatic comprehension. *Brain and Language, 45*, 371–395.

Jackendoff, R. (1972). *Semantic interpretation in generative grammar*. Cambridge, MA: MIT Press.

Jackendoff, R. (1990). *Semantic structures*. Cambridge, MA: MIT Press.

Klein, W., & Perdue, C. (1998). *The basic variety (or: couldn't languages be much simpler?)*. Manuscript. Max Planck Institute for Psycholinguistics, Nijmegen, The Netherlands.

Mauner, G., Fromkin, V., & Cornell, T. L. (1993). Comprehension and acceptability judgements in agrammatism: Disruptions in the syntax of referential dependency. *Brain and Language, 45*, 340–370.

Pesetsky, D. (1995). *Zero-syntax*. Cambridge, MA: MIT Press.

Piñango, M. M. (1998). *Some syntactic and semantic operations and their neurological underpinnings*. Doctoral dissertation, Brandeis University, Waltham, MA.

Piñango, M. (1999). Syntactic displacement in Broca's aphasia comprehension. In R. Bastiaanse & Y. Grodzinsky (Eds.), *Grammatical disorders in aphasia: A neurolinguistic perspective*. London: Whurr.

Piñango, M., & Zurif, E. (1999). *On the semantics–Wernicke's area connection: Comprehension at the sentence level*. Manuscript. Brandeis University, Waltham, MA.

Prather, P., Zurif, E., Stern, & Rosen, T. (1992). Slowed lexical access in nonfluent Broca's aphasia and fluent Wernicke's aphasia. *Brain & Language 59*, 391–411.

Prather, P., Zurif, E., Love, T., & Brownell, H. (1997). Speed of lexical activation in nonfluent aphasia. *Brain and Language 45*, 336–348.

Shapiro, L., Gordon, B., Hack, N., & Killackey, J. (1993). Verb–argument structure processing in complex sentences in Broca's and Wernicke's aphasia. *Brain and Language, 45*, 423–447.

Stromswold, K., Caplan, D., Alpert, N., & Rauch, S. (1996). Localization of syntactic comprehension by positron emission tomography. *Brain and Language, 52*, 452–473.

Swinney, D., Zurif, E., Prather, P., & Love, T. (1996). Neurological distribution of processing resources underlying language comprehension. *Journal of Cognitive Neuroscience, 8*, 174–184.

Zurif, E., Caramazza, A., & Myerson, R. (1972). Grammatical judgements of agrammatic aphasics. *Neuropsychologia, 10,* 405–417.

Zurif, E., Swinney, D., Prather, P., Solomon, J., & Bushell, C. (1993). An on-line analysis of syntactic processing in Broca's and Wernicke's aphasia. *Special Issue on Syntactic Analyses, Brain and Language, 45,* 448–464.

Chapter 18

A Simple Argument
for Subject Gaps

Joan Maling

Relative clauses have figured prominently in the research on real-time language processing. How is it that speakers are able to identify a verb's arguments so quickly and effortlessly, even when these arguments are not overtly present in the sentence or when they are not in the canonical word order? How do speakers recognize the presence of gaps in constructions like relative clauses and *wh*-questions, and how do they go about filling them? I will not address these questions directly in this paper. I will focus here on the syntactic properties of these constructions. In particular, I argue that even when there is no overt change in word order, subject relatives contain a gap that must be filled by *wh*-movement.

The derivation of relative clauses in English, as in many languages, is standardly assumed to involve movement of the *wh*-word or phrase from its underlying position to [Spec,CP] as sketched in (1).

(1) The gymnast admired the professor [$_{CP}$ [$_{NP}$ whose bad jokes]$_i$ [$_S$ students complained about e_i]]

The moved *wh*-phrase leaves behind an empty category *e* called a trace in the position from which it moved; the (potentially long-distance) dependency between the moved consituent and the trace is formally represented by co-indexing, as shown by the subscript *i*.

When the *wh*-phrase is the complement of a verb or a preposition, as in object relatives, *wh*-movement is overt. Suppose, however, that the *wh*-phrase is the grammatical subject of the matrix verb in the relative clause, as in the sentence in (2).

(2) The gymnast admired the professor whose students complained about his bad jokes.

For subjects relatives, there is no overt change in word order, since English lacks an overt relative complementizer in C. Nonetheless, it is standard to assume that *wh*-movement effects the same structural change in subject relatives as it does in object relatives, even though in the case of subject relatives such movement is string-vacuous (Balogh et al., 1998; Swinney & Zurif, 1995; Swinney et al., 1996; Zurif et al., 1993). Thus the sentence in (2) is assumed to have the syntactic representation sketched in (3), where the *wh*-phrase has moved to [Spec,CP] leaving behind a trace in its underlying position as subject of the verb *complained*.

(3) a. The gymnast admired the professor [$_{CP}$ [$_{NP}$ whose students]$_i$ [$_S$ e_i complained about his bad jokes]]

b.
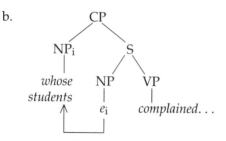

The assumption that *wh*-movement always has the same structural effect regardless of the extraction site may be considered the null hypothesis. But is there theory-independent, empirical evidence for such string-vacuous movement? In his papers, Zurif refers to Clements, McCloskey, Maling, and Zaenen (1983), who provide cross-lingusitic evidence for string-vacuous movement based on data from three "exotic" languages: Icelandic, Kikuyu, and Irish. Icelandic for example has a movement rule known as stylistic fronting (SF) which optionally preposes nonfinite verb forms (inter alia) from their normal position after the finite verb to "first position" in the clause:

(4) a. Verðbólgan varð verri, en [hafði verið *búist* við]
    inflation   was worse, than had   been expected Prt

   b. Verðbólgan varð verri, en [*búist* hafði verið við]
    inflation   was worse, than expected had   been Prt

This preposing of nonfinite verb forms applies only in clauses which lack subjects (Maling, 1980). The relevant question, then, is whether it can apply to clauses in which the subject has been questioned or relativized. If *wh*-movement applies string-vacuously to subject noun phrases (NPs), removing them from their clause, then we predict that SF will be able to apply; however, if syntactic theory rules out string-vacuous movement, we predict that SF will not apply. It is the first prediction which turns out to be correct:

(5) a. Lögreglan veit ekki, hver [*framið*   hafi glæpinn]
the.police know not, who committed has the.crime
Embedded question

b. þetta er maðurinn, sem [*framið*   hafi glæpinn]
this is the.man, that committed has the.crime.
Relative clause

For those who are suspicious of data from other languages, I would like to provide here a simple argument using empirical evidence from English, which demonstrates just as clearly the need for string-vacuous *wh*-movement in the case of subject relatives. There are certain adverbial phrases which can be fronted to clause-initial position, but which cannot occur between the subject and the finite verb, as illustrated in (6). This judgment is even sharper when the subject NP is a pronoun, as in (6d).

(6) a. This heat wave would be considered cold *in Tucson*.
b. *In Tucson*, this heat wave would be considered cold.
c. *London's heat wave *in Tucson* would be considered cold.
d. **It *in Tucson* would be considered cold.

Where does the frontal adverbial move to? As illustrated in (7), the fronted adverbial must follow the complementizer *that* in an embedded clause.

(7) a. I guess that *in Tucson*, this heat wave would be considered cold.
b. *I guess *in Tucson* that this heat wave would be considered cold.

I assume, therefore, that the fronted adverbial is not moved to [Spec,CP],[1] but remains inside the embedded S, perhaps adjoined to S. Whatever one assumes about the attachment of the fronted adverbial, it is clear that it must precede the subject NP.

Now suppose that such an adverbial phrase occurs inside a relative clause. Several papers have discussed that fact that the presence of a sentential adverbial between a complementizer *that* and its complement S (or IP) leads to a suspension of the *that*-trace effect (Culicover, 1993;

---

[1]As assumed by Browning (1996), among many others.

Deprez, 1994; Browning, 1996). However, these papers do not mention the consequences of adverbial fronting for string-vacuous movement. This even simpler "adverb effect" is illustrated in (8):

(8) a. London was experiencing a heat wave [which would be considered cold *in Tucson*].
    b. London was experiencing a heat wave [which *in Tucson* would be considered cold].
    c. *London was experiencing a heat wave *in Tucson* [which would be considered cold].

The fact that the relative pronoun must precede the fronted adverbial phrase indicates that *wh*-movement not only can, but *must* move the subject NP from its underlying position to a position to the left of the fronted adverbial, a position which under current theoretical assumptions is identified as [Spec,CP].

(9) London was experiencing a heat wave $[_{CP} [_{NP}$ which$]_i [_S$ in Tucson e_i would be considered cold]]

It seems clear, therefore, that syntactic representations must allow for string-vacuous movement.[2] Even subject relatives contain a relative gap which must be filled by the moved *wh*-constituent.

ACKNOWLEDGMENT

Thanks to my students in Ling 8b (Structure of the English Language) for asking the "stupid" questions which force us to look for simple yet elegant answers.

REFERENCES

Balogh, J., Zurif, E. B., Prather, P., Swinney, D., & Finkel, L. (1998). Gap-filling and end-of-sentence effects in real-time language processing: Implications for modeling sentence comprehension in aphasia. *Brain and Language, 61,* 169–182.

Browning, M. A. (1996). CP recursion and *that-t* effects. *Linguistic Inquiry, 27,* 237–255.

---

[2]After writing this article, I discovered that McCawley (1998, pp. 444 and 481, n. 11) independently makes the same argument, namely, that a relative pronoun may be "followed by a consituent which can be a left modifier of S but not of V'":
  (i)   a person who for years has been harassing me (=50a)
  (ii)?? He for years has been harassing me. (=50b)
  (iii) For years he has been harassing me. (=50b)

Clements, G. N., McCloskey, J., Maling, J., & Zaenen, A. (1983). String-vacuous rule application. *Linguistic Inquiry 14*, 1–17.

Culicover, P. (1993). Evidence against ECP accounts of the *that-t* effect. *Linguistic Inquiry, 24*, 557–561.

Deprez, V. (1994). A minimal account of the *that-t* effect. In G. Cinque, J. Koster, J.-Y. Pollock, L. Rizzi, & R. Zanuttini (Eds.), *Paths towards universal grammar. Studies in honor of Richard S. Kayne,* (pp. 121–135). Washington, DC: Georgetown University Press.

Maling, J. (1980). Inversion in embedded clauses in modern Icelandic. *Íslenskt mál, 2*, 175–193.

Maling, J. & Zaenen, A. (1981). Germanic word order and the format of surface filters. In F. Heny (Ed.), *Binding and Filtering* (pp. 255–278). London: Croom-Helm.

McCawley, J. (1998). *The syntactic phenomena of english,* 2nd ed. Chicago: University of Chicago Press.

Swinney, D. & Zurif, E. B. (1995). Syntactic processing in aphasia. *Brain and Language, 50*, 225–239.

Swinney, D., Zurif, E. B., Prather, P., & Love, T. (1996). Neurological distribution of processing resources underlying language comprehension. *Journal of Cognitive Neuroscience, 8*, 174–184.

Zurif, E. B., Swinney, D., Prather, P., Solomon, J., & Bushell, C. (1993). An on-line analysis of syntactic processing in Broca's and Wernicke's aphasia. *Brain and Language, 45*, 448–464.

Chapter **19**

Some Recent Investigations of Gap Filling in Normal Listeners: Implications for Normal and Disordered Language Processing

Lewis P. Shapiro

In this chapter I describe two on-line studies investigating the time-course of comprehending structures involving *chains;* those that require a listener to connect two nonadjacent positions that co-refer. In the first study we examine *verb phrase (VP)–ellipsis* structures that contain verbs whose lexical properties severely restrict interpretation. We find that listeners initially ignore such lexical properties and defer to the syntax. In the second study we examine *Wh-questions* that are discourse-linked. We find that the time-course of interpretation is influenced by these discourse-linked properties. Both studies are interpreted with reference to current accounts of normal and disordered language processing.

STUDY 1: VP–ELLIPSIS

Consider:

(1) Dillon likes apples, and Paul does too.

The second clause contains a bare auxiliary—*does*—that signals the elision of a VP. We assume that the missing VP is represented by an empty category (Lobeck, 1992):

(2) Dillion likes apples, and Paul does [e] too.

At the level of logical form (LF is considered the conceptual–intentional interface, concerned with semantic interpretation), the empty VP is replaced with material as a function of a dependency on the VP in the preceding clause:

(3) Dillion likes apples, and Paul does [like apples] too.

The LF representation in (3) is input to interpretational processes and accounts for why the elliptical sentence in (2) is interpreted in the same way as a similar sentence without ellipsis, such as "Dillion likes apples and Paul likes apples too." This process of filling in the elided material at LF is referred to as *syntactic reconstruction;* see Kitagawa (1991) and Fiengo and May (1994) for versions of such a theory.

Anaphoric elements can also enter into elided constructions. We assume that pronouns and reflexives have indices that indicate their interpretation (i.e., the NP to which they are interpreted as identical); co-indexing indicates co-reference (while non-co-indexing indicates distinct reference), as illustrated below:

(4) Dillion-1 likes himself-1 (i.e., Dillon likes Dillon).

(5) Dillon-1 likes his-1 mother (i.e., Dillon likes Dillon's mother).

Such co-reference relations are relatively straightforward, set by the properties of anaphors. But what happens when an empty VP is reconstructed on the basis of an overt VP that contains anaphoric elements? The simplest possibility is that the pronoun gets copied along with the index it carries in the preceding VP—as illustrated below—where (7) is the reconstructed representation of (6):

(6) Dillon-1 likes his-1 mother, and Paul does [e] too.

(7) Dillon-1 likes his-1 mother, and Paul does [like his-1 mother] too.

The resulting interpretation is that "Dillon likes his own mother," and that "Paul also likes Dillon's mother"—the *strict* reading. However, there is another interpretation of (6), namely, "Dillon likes his own mother and Paul likes HIS own mother"—the *sloppy* reading. In the account we are assuming, this reading comes about as follows: A pronoun, when copied, is allowed to change its index to that of the local subject on the condition that the two binding relations are *parallel* in structure. That is, each pronoun is bound to the subject of its own clause, so the structural position of the antecedent relative to the pronoun is identical in the two clauses (see Fiengo & May, 1994, for detailed discussion about the nature of this parallelism requirement). Thus, an alternative LF representation of (6) is (8):

(8) Dillon-1 likes his-1 mother, and Paul-2 does [like his-2 mother] too.

This representation then yields the sloppy interpretation.

When we turn to reflexives, the sloppy reading is derived in the same way since the index change option used with a pronoun can be exercised with a reflexive as well. To illustrate, consider an example like (9):

(9) Dillon-1 likes himself-1, and Paul does [e] too.

The index change reconstruction yields (10), which, when interpreted is equivalent to "Dillon likes Dillon and Paul likes Paul":

(10) Dillon-1 likes himself-1 and Paul-2 does [like himself-2] too.

With strict readings, however, the situation gets a bit more complex. A reflexive has the property that it must find an antecedent in the minimal clause that contains it. To illustrate, in (11) the reflexive can only get its reference from the subject *Paul* and not from the nonlocal subject *Dillon*:

(11) Dillon-1 likes his mother, and Paul-2 likes himself-2.

Given this constraint on the distribution of reflexives and their antecedents, if an elided VP that is reconstructed on the basis of a VP that contains a reflexive simply copies the preceding VP and the reflexive with its index, an ill-formed representation will result. To illustrate, consider again the VP–ellipsis in (12) reconstructed in this way:

(12) *Dillon-1 likes himself-1 and Bill-2 does [likes himself-1] too.

Though the indexation in (12) would correspond to a strict reading that is "Dillon likes Dillon and Bill likes Dillon too," this representation violates the requirement that reflexives have local antecedents, since the reconstructed reflexive in the second clause is not locally bound to its subject NP "Bill"; this representation therefore cannot be the source of this interpretation. Since the strict reading is nevertheless acceptable to many speakers, we assume that a reflexive can alternatively be reconstructed as a *pronoun;* such a process has been called *vehicle change* (Fiengo & May, 1994; see also Kitagawa, 1991). This means that the ellipsis in (12), if reconstructed with the same index as in the overt VP in the source clause, must be reconstructed as in (13):

(13) Dillon-1 likes himself-1 and Bill-2 does [likes him-1] too.

Vehicle change thus allows the strict reading with reflexives by reconstructing the reflexive that is copied from the first to the second clause as a pronoun, which has the property that it cannot be locally bound. That is, in (13) the pronoun *him* can refer back to the nonlocal subject *Dillon*, unlike the reflexive in (12).

THE PRESENT STUDY

Consider, now, the following:

(14) The *policeman*$_i$ defended himself$_i$, and *the fireman*$_j$ did
____(?) too, according to someone who was there.

The *sloppy* interpretation is that the "fireman defended *himself*," where *himself* co-refers with the *fireman;* this interpretation is typically generated first by approximately 80% of normal listeners during an off-line judgment task and is set by the properties of anaphors: An anaphor must be locally bound. The *strict* interpretation is that the "fireman defended *him*," where *him* co-refers with the *policeman*—the subject of the initial clause; this interpretation is often more difficult to generate off-line (a majority of listeners indeed make such an interpretation, though it is certainly not the first interpretation to come to mind; see Shapiro & Hestvik, 1995; Shapiro, Swinney, & Borsky, 1998) and is set to the properties of personal pronouns; A pronoun cannot be locally bound.

In an on-line examination of such VP–ellipsis understanding, Shapiro and Hestvik (1995) found that normal listeners (re)activate the subject NP from the first, source clause (e.g., *the policeman*) at the elided VP position of the second clause (i.e., the gap). Because such an interpretation is obviously the less-frequent one that is available to listeners, we interpreted our results as reflecting the operation of an automatic parser that is initially insensitive to such probabilistic information.

In our most recent study that we describe here we conducted a stronger test of how lexical properties influence gap filling. Specifically, we used verbs that allow *only* the sloppy interpretation. Consider:

(15) The optometrist who had signed the release [1] form asserted herself [2], and the pilot who needed to pass [3] the training exam did [4] too. . . .

(16) The gambler who won ten hands in [1] a row winked his [2] eyes, and the pit boss who was in on [3] the elaborate scheme did [4] too. . . .

In (15) the verb *assert* allows only the reflexive reading; that is, only the "sloppy" interpretation is allowed in the second clause (the "pilot" can only assert herself, and not the "optometrist"). Similarly, in (16) the verb *wink* requires an object (a body part) that is possessed by the subject NP (the "pit boss" cannot typically wink the "gambler's" eyes). Though other continuations exist ("assert control," "wink" as intransitive), we found that off-line judgments from an independent subject group presented with sentences like (15) and (16) revealed that only the sloppy interpretation was available. Thus, the lexical properties of these "reflexive" and "inalienable body-part possession" verbs (see, e.g., Levin, 1993) place obvious constraints on the interpretation of VP–ellipsis constructions.

We investigated whether on-line gap filling would respect these lexical constraints. This issue reflects on the basic nature of sentence processing. For example, in the constraint–satisfaction framework, probabilistic information (e.g., frequency-of-use), context, and lexical properties work together to constrain interpretation (e.g., MacDonald, Pearlmutter, & Seidenberg, 1994). Such an account would predict that only the sloppy reading would be active on-line, since it is (a) substantially more frequent overall in ellipsis constructions, and (b) the lexical properties of the verb only allow the sloppy interpretation. However, a strongly form-driven account of gap filling—one that claims that there is an "automatic" syntactic processor—would predict that gap filling is a reflexive, form-driven process that initially ignores probabilistic and lexical constraints; such constraints are said to exert their influence after-the-fact (see, e.g., Shapiro et al., 1998). On this latter account, then, both the sloppy and strict interpretations should be available in the immediate temporal vicinity of the gap. And, it should only be after-the-fact that the context-appropriate interpretation is available.

We used the cross-modal priming (CMP) task. Sentences were presented to listeners over headphones. During the temporal unfolding of each sentence, a visual lexical decision probe (WORD/NONWORD) was presented for 500 ms at a strategically located probe position. When the probe formed a word, it was related to either the subject from the first clause (strict interpretation), the subject from the second clause (sloppy interpretation), or was an unrelated control probe, matched to its related counterpart in terms of number of letters/syllables, frequency of occurrence, and base reaction times (RTs) (gathered from an independent group of subjects during a standard visual lexical decision task). When RTs to the related probes are significantly faster than RTs to the control probes, priming is said to have occurred, which suggests that a meaning related to the probe has been activated.

Predictions

Reflexive or inalienable possession verbs that only allow the sloppy interpretation off-line were inserted into VP–ellipsis constructions. We repeat here sentence (15):

The optometrist who had signed the release [1] form asserted herself [2], and the pilot who needed to pass [3] the training exam did [4] too. . . .

In one experiment we examined whether listeners would reactivate the subject NP from the *first* clause (e.g., *the optometrist*). This pattern—priming for *the optometrist* at the gap [4] but not at the pregap [3] position—would indicate that listeners generate the strict reading on-line. Additionally in this experiment we examined whether listeners access the locally bound antecedent for the reflexive. In this case, we should observe significant priming for *the optometrist* at the reflexive [2], yet find no priming at the prereflexive position [1]. In a second experiment we considered whether listeners would reactivate the subject NP from the *second* clause in the test sentences (i.e., the sloppy interpretation). Thus, if we observe priming for, for example, *the pilot* at the elided VP position [4], yet observe no priming at the pregap position ([3]), then the subject NP from the second clause will have been *re*accessed at the gap.

Subjects included 96 college-age neurologically intact adults; 16 each were randomly assigned to each probe position for each experiment (strict interpretation, sloppy interpretation). Each subject received both a control and related probe for each sentence (nested, and presented 2 weeks apart). All probes (word and nonword) except those associated with the test sentences were randomly distributed across different temporal positions in the sentences. For the test sentences of Experiment 1 (strict interpretation), there were four probe positions; for Experiment 2 (sloppy interpretation) there were two probe positions. The sentences were presented over headphones. During the course of each sentence, a lexical decision probe appeared momentarily on the screen. Subjects were required to attend to the sentences and make a lexical decision quickly and accurately by pressing one of two response keys (WORD, NONWORD); RTs to this decision were recorded by the computer. In approximately 20% of the trials, the tape was stopped and subjects were asked to paraphrase the sentence that they had just heard.

Results and Discussion

Only correct responses to the real word probes presented with test sentences were used in the analyses. RTs greater than 2000 ms were discarded as errors. We first present the data from Experiment 1 (strict interpretation), shown in Table I.

These data show the following patterns: At position 1—the prereflexive probe point—no significant priming was observed; that is, RTs to the re-

Table I   Results from Experiment 1: Strict

Position	Control (ms)	Related (ms)
1 (preref.)	722	712
2 (reflexive)	755	721[a]
3 (pregap)	719	710
4 (gap)	801	769[a]

[a]($p < .01$).

lated probes (related to the subject NP from the first clause) were not significantly faster than to their controls. However, at position 2—the reflexive—significant priming was observed. Thus, when a reflexive is encountered in a sentence, the locally bound NP to which it co-refers is reactivated (see also Nicol, 1988). More to the purposes of the experiment, at position 3—the pregap position in the second clause—significant priming was not observed. However, at position 4—the gap or elided VP position—significantly faster RTs to the related probes (related, again, to the subject NP from the first clause, i.e., the strict interpretation) was observed relative to the RTs for the control probes.

We now present the results from Experiment 2 (Table II):

The data from this experiment show that at position 3—the pregap position—no significant priming was observed. That is, the RTs for the control probes and for the related probes (related to the subject NP from the second clause; i.e., the sloppy interpretation) were not significantly different. However, at probe position 4—the gap or elided VP—RTs to probes related to the subject NP were, again, significantly faster than RTs to controls.

Putting the data from both experiments together, listeners apparently reaccess the subject NP from both the first and second clauses at the elided VP position in the second clause. Thus, they have available *both* the sloppy and strict interpretation on-line (see Hickok, 1993, and Nicol & Pickering, 1993, for further evidence suggesting multiple access of *structural* possibilities). The implications for accounts of sentence processing are clear. Given that (1) the verbs inserted into these constructions were highly constrained toward only the sloppy interpretation, and that (2) off-line judgements suggest that only the sloppy interpretation is available to listeners (note that even with verbs that allow both interpretations, the sloppy reading is chosen initially by a wide majority of listeners; Shapiro & Hestvik, 1995), immediate structural processing appears to ignore such constraints, initially. Yet, because listeners indeed generate solely the sloppy interpretation off-line, at a point between the gap and final interpretation listeners discard (or suppress) the strict reading. We

Table II   Results from Experiment 2: Sloppy

Position	Control (ms)	Related (ms)
3 (pregap)	808	801
4 (gap)	855	829[a]

[a]($p < .01$).

suggest, therefore, that theories of sentence processing will have to include operations geared to (1) initial activation driven by syntactic considerations only and (2) multiple interpretations. A "constraint satisfaction" account that claims that multiple constraints initially converge on a single interpretation will need to be revised.

A Note on Language and Brain

The independence of structural processing from lexical influences fits quite nicely with some previous work examining on-line sentence comprehension in Broca's and Wernicke's aphasic individuals. Briefly, Zurif and colleagues (Swinney, Zurif, Prather, & Love, 1996; Zurif, Swinney, Prather, Solomon, & Bushell, 1993) have shown that Wernicke's aphasic patients evince normal gap-filling patterns, while Broca's aphasic patients do not. However, Shapiro and Levine (1990) and Shapiro, Gordon, Hack and Killackey (1993) found an opposite pattern so far as activating the argument structure properties of verbs during on-line sentence comprehension is concerned: Broca's aphasic patients, but not Wernicke's individuals, were normally sensitive to these lexical properties (see also Canseco-Gonzalez, Shapiro, Zurif, & Baker, 1990). Thus, the failure of Broca's aphasic individuals to fill gaps cannot be because they are insensitive to the lexical properties of verbs—those properties that might "signal" that a verb licenses a direct object position. These patterns suggest then that the activation of lexical properties is independent from structural processing, and that this independence is respected by brain–language relations.

STUDY 2: WH-QUESTIONS

We now describe two experiments that extend the investigation of long-distance dependencies by examining the on-line processing of two different types of *Wh*-questions: questions headed by *who* or *what* (e.g., Who did the policeman push ____ into the street?) and questions headed by *which*-NP (e.g., Which student did the policeman push ____ into the street?). These two types of *wh*-questions can be distinguished on linguistic grounds. For example, *which* phrases are considered *referential* (i.e., they include participants taking part in the event described, e.g., *student*) while *who* and *what* questions are considered *nonreferential*. Related to their referentiality, *which* phrases pick out an individual from a set of individuals explicitly mentioned or inferred from the discourse and are therefore considered *discourse-linked* (*D-linked*), whereas *who* and *what* phrases do not have to be.

We summarize these differences and examine their implications for sentence processing. De Vincenzi (1996) and Hickok and Avrutin (1996) have shown that these two question types are, indeed, differentiated in off-line sentence interpretation (but see Thompson et al., 1998). Unlike their efforts, however, we focus on the processes that occur *prior* to final interpretation; we investigate on-line performance. In doing so, we interpret our data in terms of a sentence processing account that integrates discourse representations in putatively automatic operations of the parser.

A Brief Linguistic Background

Consider the following:

(17) Who-1 did Dillon push e-1?

According to the linguistic theory we are entertaining here (a form of *minimalism*, which is a major revision of the principles-and-parameters framework), and skipping many details, the *wh*-word *who* moves from its canonical postverb direct object position to a preverb specifier position of CP (Spec-CP), leaving behind a *trace* (i.e., empty category) or copy of the moved element. This operation is motivated by a need for constituents to move in order to check their own features (enlightened self-interest; Lasnik, 1995). In this case, the head of the CP (that is, COMP) has the interrogative feature [*wh*], and the *wh*-word moves to the Spec-CP position (i.e., subject position) to *check* the features under CP. Once checked, the features are *erased* and can be interpreted at LF. The trace and moved category form a *dependency* relation (note that we are using numerals attached to positions to indicate that the positions relate to each other). Consider, now:

(18) Dillon pushed Joelle.

(19) Who did Dillon push?

The argument *Joelle* in (18) has an exact interpretation; it has one and only one referent (*Joelle*). However, the *wh*-phrase *Who* in (19) has a *variable* interpretation; it does not, in principle, have a specific referent.

Borrowing from standard logic, *who* is said to be an *operator* that binds a variable, *x*, as in:

(20) Who$_i$ did Dillion push x_i ?

(20) is a semantic representation (the trace is signified by a variable, *x*). In standard logic the operator takes *scope* over its domain; that is, operators can affect the interpretation of other elements. In this case, the *wh*-word— the operator—determines the interpretation of the entire sentence (that is, the sentence is an interrogative just because the operator is a *wh*-word). The scope domain of the operator is the domain which it c-commands (the CP, or clause). Hence, positions occupied by operators are left-peripheral since they must take scope over their domain. This means that every operator will need to move out of an argument position to a scope position (*wh*-movement is also known as *operator movement*). For *wh*-questions in English, this forces leftward movement of the operator (e.g., *who*).

The distinction between who/what and which-np questions

With this background in mind, in this section we briefly review linguistic evidence that supports a distinction between *who/what* questions and *which*-NP questions.

D-linking. We begin with Pesetsky's (1987) observation that the two question types pattern differently in terms of a *Superiority Condition*—a constraint on movement. Briefly, the condition involves constructions with multiple *wh*-phrases, where, for example, one *wh*-phrase has undergone movement and the other is considered *wh-in-situ* (that is, a *wh*-phrase that stays in place). This condition (on grammaticality) requires that the trace of the moved *wh*-phrase must *c-command* the position of the *wh*-in-situ (the *wh*-phrase that does not undergo movement). C-command, for our purposes, is a "precedence" relation where one node precedes another in a particular way in the phrase structure tree. For example (adapted from Pesetsky, 1987):

(21) a. *Who*-1 did you persuade *trace*-1 to read *what*?
     b. ??*What*-1 did you persuade *who(m)* to read *trace*-1?

(Note: * = ungrammatical; ?? = suspect grammaticality. Also, as is currently standard in theoretical linguistics, it is the *relative* grammaticality between two structures that is at issue, not the absolute grammaticality of one or the other).

In (21a) the trace of the *wh* c-commands (i.e., "precedes") the position of the *wh*-in-situ, *what*. In (21b), the trace of *wh* does not c-command the *wh*-in-situ (it's actually the other way around), hence violating the superiority condition and explaining the relative ungrammaticality.

However, *which*-phrases appear to violate the condition yet remain well formed:

(22) a. *Which man*-1 did you persuade *trace*-1 to read *which book*?
b. *Which book*-1 did you persuade *which man* to read *trace*-1?

In (22b)—like its counterpart in (21)—the *wh-trace* does not c-command the *wh*-in-situ, violating the superiority condition, yet it is well formed, as is (22a) that does conform to the condition. That is, this constraint explains the distinction between grammatical and ungrammatical sentences containing multiple dependencies where *what* and *who* phrases are involved, yet does not explain why *which*-NPs can violate the constraint and keep their grammaticality intact.

Pesetsky's (1987) solution to this discrepancy involves the following: The superiority condition can be derived from a condition on movement—the *nested dependency condition*—that states that if two *wh*-trace dependencies overlap, one must contain the other. Furthermore, it is standardly assumed that *wh*-in-situ moves at LF (because operators must occupy scope positions). Consider the abbreviated LF representations for (21a) and (21b):

(23) a. *What*-1 *who*-2 you persuade x-2 to read x-1?
b. ??*Who*-1 *what*-2 you persuade x-1 to read x-2?

Note that in (23a), the two trace (that is, x)-antecedent dependencies are nested; *who* and its trace are nested within the boundaries of *what* and its trace. Yet in (23b), this *nested dependency condition* is violated, rendering the question ill-formed.

What about *which*-NP questions? As shown above, superiority effects do not show up with these constructions. According to Pesetsky, *which*-phrases, unlike *who* or *what*, are *discourse-linked* (*D-linked*), while *who* and *what* are *not required* to be. What does "D-linked" mean, in principle? Consider:

(24) Which woman did the soldier push into the street?

(25) Who did the soldier push into the street?

The question in (24) presupposes a set of women, one of whom was pushed into the street. In (25) no such presupposition is required for interpretation. Thus, (24) would be infelicitous without a discourse (overt, or covert) to pick an individual out from a set of individuals; in (25) no set of individuals need be presumed.

Pesetsky (1987) goes on to claim that *D-linked wh-phrases are not operators*. Recall that every operator moves at LF. Because movement is not required for nonoperators, it follows that *which*-phrases escape the *nested dependency condition* and thus do not exhibit *superiority effects*. The claim that referential, D-linked *which*-NPs are not operators makes sense given that operators bind variables that have *nonreferential* interpretations. NPs that pick out a referent from the universe of discourse [*Dillion*, in (4), e.g.] do not enter into the operator-variable dependency, and thus, neither should *which*-NPs.

Thus, whether or not a phrase is D-linked is concomitant with whether or not the phrase is considered referential. Again, a phrase is considered referential if it refers to a specific member of a set, established either in the mind of the speaker or overtly established in the discourse. As Cinque (1990) points out, the relation between D-linked phrases and referentiality can be seen with co-reference relations:

(26) Which boy-1 started a fight with which girl-2 wasn't even clear to them-1+2.

(27) *Who-1 started a fight with whom-2 wasn't even clear to them-1+2.

In this case, (26) shows that the two *which*-NP phrases and the anaphor *them* co-refer, yet in (27) the two *who* phrases and the anaphor cannot co-refer.

Linguistic distinctions and their relevance to processing

What are we to make of the linguistic work that suggests various ways to cut the pie regarding *which*-NPs and *who* and *what* phrases? To review, *which*-phrases are referential and therefore do not enter into operator-variable dependencies at LF; *who* and *what* questions are potentially not referential and therefore are operators that do bind variables. *Which*-NPs are D-linked; *who* and *what* questions are potentially not. Finally, *Which*-NPs are phrases that contain both a head (*which*) and a noun complement; the noun complement moves with the head in what has been called *pied piping; who* and *what* are"bare"lexical heads(Chomsky, 1995; Radford, 1997).

Our concern here is, of course, with language processing. Given, however, that there are several linguistic facets to the distinction between *which*-NPs and *who* and *what* questions, we might ask which—if any— could be relevant to any predicted distinction in terms of on-line processing. Our intuitions—buttressed by some psycholinguistic evidence (see below)—suggest that the relevant notion that distinguishes these two types of *wh*-questions has to do with the discourse-linking properties of *which*-NPs and their referential quality. That is, it is the fact that *which*-NPs refer to selected individuals picked out from a set of individuals set up in the discourse—while *who* and *what* NPs do not have this property—that may have important implications for processing.

Let us be a bit more clear here about the distinction: *Which*-NP questions are referential and carry an existential presupposition that requires a connection to the discourse. Based on the linguistic literature we have been claiming that *who* and *what* questions are not referential and are not D-linked. Yet, on simple reflection *who* and *what* questions can, indeed, refer to a set of individuals constructed on the basis of the discourse, just like *which*-NP questions. For example, if we ask a particular group of people, "Who wants ice cream?" we likely don't mean something like, "Who in the world wants ice cream?" Instead, we mean, "Of this group of people stipulated in the world of discourse, who among this group wants ice cream?" However, our review suggests that the grammar *requires* that *which*-NP questions be D-linked (indeed, *which*-NP questions are infelicitous without a discourse), while *who* and *what* questions *may or may not be*. To forecast our case, then, we assume that if the grammar *requires* a link to the discourse, this will add a burden to the sentence processor (see also Shapiro & Hestvik, 1995); that burden will be reflected in a particular pattern of results that differentiates *which*-NP constructions from their *who* and *what* counterparts on-line.

We now report on two experiments. The first involves *who and what* questions, the second, *which*-NP questions. The initial hypothesis is that the sentence processing system will respect the grammar in the following way: Based on past gap-filling work, we predict that immediate gap-filling effects will be observed with *who and what* questions. However, with *which*-NP constructions, we will observe a different, delayed, time-course of gap filling. This prediction is based on the structural differences between the two types of dependencies outlined in the introduction, and, in particular, the D-linking and referential nature that is required of *which*-NP constructions. That is, we predict that required contact with the discourse will add to the computational burden of the parser.

EXPERIMENT 1: *WHO* AND *WHAT* QUESTIONS

Consider the following example from our first experiment:

(28) The soldier is pushing the <u>unruly student</u> violently into the street? <u>Who</u> [1] is the soldier [2] pushing _____ [3] violently [4] into the street?

Note that there is a gap in the direct object position occurring after the verb "pushing." The gap gets its reference from the *wh*-word "who," which, in turn, depends on the explicitly mentioned direct object from the first sentence, "the unruly student." Thus, to understand the discourse, a listener must connect the empty direct object position after the verb in the question to the *wh*-word that comes before it, and must also connect the *wh*-word to the direct object from the initial sentence. To the best of our knowledge, there have been no published reports on how listeners process such constructions on-line. How listeners do this, of course, will have important implications for accounts of normal sentence processing. For example, the gap (position [3]) is a long distance from the explicit referent; indeed, the referent and gap are separated by a sentence boundary, and a few phrasal and clausal boundaries as well. One can imagine that the referent is simply too far away to be activated at the gap. However, note that there is a *wh*-word (a proform) at the beginning of the question that in fact gets its reference from the direct object in the first sentence. And by various syntactic accounts, we know that the *wh*-word and the gap also co-refer. Thus, in essence, there are three elements—the explicitly mentioned direct object in the first sentence, the *wh*-word, and the gap (both in the second sentence)—that form an interpretive *chain*. The question is, will we observe activation of the referent through the links of that chain?

We used the CMP task. Listeners were presented with spoken sentences like (28). The listener—while attending to the sentences—had to decide rapidly and accurately whether a visually presented lexical decision probe formed a word or nonword. Reaction times (RTs) to this lexical decision were recorded. The lexical decision probes were either (a) semantically related to the direct object of the initial sentence (in the example above the related probe was SCHOOL, related to the direct object, *student*), (b) an unrelated control probe—controlled for frequency of occurrence, number of letters/syllables, and base RTs, or (c) nonwords that conformed to orthographic rules of English.

In this experiment there were four probe positions, one occurring at the *wh*-word, one before the *wh*-gap, one occurring at the gap, and one occurring downstream from the gap. Normal listeners (15 subjects each) were randomly assigned to one of each probe position. Again, when RTs to the related probe are significantly faster than the RTs to the unrelated, control probes, *priming* is said to have occurred, which is evidence that the sense of the target word (in this case, *student*) has been activated in the immediate temporal vicinity of the probe.

Specifically, then, in this experiment we predicted the following patterns: Because *who* functions much like a pronoun, we predicted activation of the referent of that "pro-form" at who [1]—for example, the direct object from the preceding sentence. However, given that there is no apparent way for the processor to "know" that *who* indeed refers to something mentioned in the previous sentence at the temporal point when *who* is encountered, it is possible that no priming would occur for probes related to the direct object. No significant differences between the related and control probe were predicted at the pregap position [2], yet significantly faster RTs to the related probe relative to the unrelated probe at the gap position [3]. Such a pattern would indicate *reaccess* of the gap's filler.

Results and Discussion

We found significantly faster RTs to probes related to the direct object from the carrier phrase (764 ms) than to control probes (847 ms), at the *wh*-word (Table III). No priming was observed at the pregap position. Significantly faster RTs to the related probe (734 ms) were again found relative to control probes (793 ms) at the gap position. And, at the postgap position, though probes related to the direct object were faster (769 ms) relative to the control probes (809 ms), this difference was not significant. Note also that RTs to the control probes presented at the pregap position (747 ms) were significantly faster than the RTs to control probes presented at the gap position (793 ms).

The data, then, show that at position [1]—the *wh*-word—activation for the direct object from the preceding sentence was observed, suggesting that the *wh*-word acts like a pronoun and reactivates its possible antecedents. There are two limitations to this interpretation, however. First, note that we did not have a pre-*wh*-word probe position, so we cannot be sure that the direct object simply continues to be activated *across* the sentence boundary, and we fortuitously captured this continuous activation by probing at the *wh*-word. Second, if the *wh*-word indeed functions like a pro-form, then we would also expect activation of *any* NP (e.g., the subject NP from the first clause); we are currently assessing both possibilities in further experimentation.

Table III   Mean RTs (and SDs) to Cross-Modal Lexical Decision, *Who-What*

	Probe position			
Probe	*Wh*-word	Pregap	Gap	Postgap
Control	847 (134)	747 (106)	793 (87)	802 (109)
Related	764 (162)	758 (99)	734[a] (76)	769 (152)

[a]Significant for both subjects and items, $p < .01$.

More pertinent to the focus of this chapter, however, are the patterns observed at both the pregap and gap positions. At the pregap position significant differences between the related and control probes were not observed, suggesting that the probes were well controlled for base RTs. At the gap position we observed significantly faster RTs to the related compared to the control probes, strongly suggesting that when a listener encounters a direct object gap in a wh-question, that gap is filled immediately by the grammatically appropriate antecedent. Furthermore, such gap filling occurs across sentential boundaries. That is, when the NP to which the *wh*-gap refers [e.g., *the student* in example (28)] is located in a sentence that occurs prior to the *wh*-question, that NP is *reaccessed*. This gap-filling effect also appears to result in a larger interference effect when considering RTs to the control probes only; RTs to the control probes were significantly longer when the probes were presented at the gap than when presented at the pregap position. We will reserve further interpretation of these data until after we present our next experiment.

EXPERIMENT 2: *WHICH*-NP QUESTIONS

In this experiment we changed the question form to *which* NP; the NP referred to was in the direct object position of the declarative sentence. For example:

(29) The soldier is pushing the unruly student violently into the street? *Which student* [1] is the soldier [2] pushing _____ [3] violently [4] into the street?

In this experiment there were again four probe positions: One at the *wh*-word, at a pregap position, gap position, and postgap position. Fourteen subjects each were randomly assigned to each position. The first prediction is straightforward: At the *wh*-word we should observe significantly faster RTs to probes related to the *which*-NP (and thus to the direct object from the first sentence) relative to control probes. Next, if, when encountering a gap in a *which*-NP question, the antecedent to the gap is immediately reaccessed, then significantly faster RTs to the related relative to the unrelated control probes should be observed at the gap, but not at the pregap, position. Such a result would suggest that thought there is linguistic evidence that *who* and *what* questions are dissimilar to *which*-NP questions, the parser treats them as similar objects. Another possibility makes a more direct connection to the grammar: If *which*-NP questions are indeed unlike *who* and *what* questions, then the time-course of activation of the antecedent may be different in the two cases. Specifically, if we assume that

D-linking is required to connect the gap with its antecedent, and the antecedent to the direct object mentioned in the discourse, then gap-filling will be delayed because of the increased use of processing resources (see also Avrutin, 2000; Frazier and McNamara, 1995; and Kluender, 1998, for similar arguments involving increased load for "referential" processing).

Results and Discussion

First, we observed significantly faster RTs to the related (709 ms) as compared to the control probes (798 ms) at the *which*-NP probe position, signifying lexical activation. Next, at the pregap position, no priming was observed. At the gap position, RTs to the related probes (772 ms) were faster than RTs to the unrelated control probes (795) ms), though this difference was significant at the .06 level. Finally, at the postgap position significantly faster RTs were observed for related (758 ms) compared to the control (820 ms) probes.

The data from Experiment 2, then, showed that at the gap position there was a "near-significant" trend. Yet, at the postgap position significant RT differences were observed. Thus, at the downstream postgap position there was unambiguous evidence that listeners reaccessed the antecedent to the gap. These patterns, then, were unlike those found in Experiment 1, where significant priming was found, unambiguously, at the gap. We interpret these data as evidence for delayed gap filling in certain constructions; in the present case listeners fill *which*-NP gaps later in the temporal unfolding of the sentence than they fill *who and what* gaps. The question, of course, is why? Our initial answer has to do with the fact that *which*-NP constructions are required to be referential and D-linked; *who* and *what* questions are not. We assume that making contact with a discourse level of representation takes time and effort—perhaps extending the time-course of reaccess of the antecedent.

Table IV   Mean RTs (and SDs) to Cross-Modal Lexical Decision, *Which*-NP

Probes	Probe position			
	Which-NP	Pregap	Gap	Postgap
Control	798 (97)	772 (93)	795 (52)	820 (139)
Related	709 (92)[a]	779 (93)	772 (66)	758[b] (81)

[a]Significant ($p < .01$) for both subjects and items.
[b]Significant ($p < .05$) for both subjects and items.

Before we continue with this interpretation—and consider additional supporting evidence—we need to consider the following apparent caveat: Both experiments used a carrier phrase that set up a discourse to which the *wh*-gap (*who-*, *what-*, or *which*-NP) could refer (e.g., "The soldier is pushing the unruly student violently into the street? Who/Which student is the soldier pushing violently into the street?"). And, we found immediate reaccess in *who* and *what* questions of an NP that occurred in that discourse. Thus, it could be argued that in practice, both types of *wh*-questions are discourse-linked (as we stated earlier). However, we assume that it is the grammatical distinction of the *wh*-questions that is at issue here, and not solely whether a discourse is presented. That is, *which*-NP questions are required to be D-linked because of their referential nature. Though *who* and *what* questions can refer to an entity mentioned in the discourse, in principle they are nonreferential and thus do not have to be discourse-bound. It is this unmarked case—that *which*-NP questions must be D-linked but *what* and *who* questions do not have to be—that the parser appears to respect.

Our interpretation is supported by evidence from studies of both normal and brain damaged subjects. For example, in our set of experiments examining gap-filling in complex VP–ellipsis structures, Shapiro and Hestvik (1995) showed that in coordinated ellipsis ("The policeman defended himself, *and* the fireman did _____ too, according to someone who was there"), gap filling was observed in the immediate vicinity of the elided VP (after *did*). However, in subordinated ellipsis ("The policeman defended himself *because* the fireman did _____, according to someone who was there"), delayed gap filling was observed (after *someone*). We suggested that in the coordinated case, gap filling is driven by the syntactic nature of the trace–antecedent relation. In the subordinated case, however, to locally interpret the second, target clause, a causal relation must also be computed between the two clauses; that is, X happened just *because* Y happened. Computing this causal relation stems from either a semantic or discourse representation (see, e.g., Dalrymple, 1991; Kehler, 1994).

In effect, then, we are suggesting that when gap filling is driven solely by syntactic considerations, immediate effects are observed. But when extrasyntactic information is involved, gap filling is delayed. Our interpretation is buttressed by the work of De Vincenzi (1996) who found a processing distinction between *who* and *which*-NP questions using a self-paced reading task. Relatedly, Hickok and Avrutin (1995) found that their agrammatic aphasic patients showed a subject–object asymmetry only for *which*–NP questions, and not for *who* questions. And, Avrutin (2000), examining both children and aphasic patients, has more recently suggested that the most "energy consuming" operations are those that involve the interface between the syntactic and discourse modules of the language faculty, just the sort of suggestion we are making here. And finally, Frazier and McNamara (1995), using a grammaticality judgement rating task, found some indication that *which* and *who* questions are treated differently by aphasic patients. Their patients accepted significantly less grammatical object-gap *which* questions than normal controls, yet showed no difference in this regard with grammatical object-gap *who* questions. Also, these patients showed an asymmetry between subject- and object-extraction for *which* questions, but not for *who* questions. They suggest a "favor referential principle" in agrammatic aphasia, whereby these patients have a resource capacity limitation. When encountering both the computational syntactic demand of a complex sentence and the referential demands imposed by the content of the sentence, the aphasic listener favors the referential over the syntactic. This means that because they have both the referential and syntactic demands of the *which*-NP constructions to deal with—and assuming that the syntactic representation normally degrades rapidly—they will do worse than with nonreferential *who* questions, those that must be represented syntactically.

ACKNOWLEDGMENTS

I thank my mentor and friend, Edgar Zurif, for showing me the importance of integrating linguistic theory into work on normal and disordered language processing, and for training me in the fine details of doing such work. His influence on the fields of psycholinguistics and neuropsychology not only is evinced by his own important accomplishments, but has also been shown by those students and colleagues who have had the pleasure of working with him. Thanks also to the following for directly contributing to the studies described in this chapter: Rachel Garcia, Arild Hestvik, Andrea Massey, Elizabeth Oster, and Cynthia Thompson. This work was supported in part by a grant from NIH-NIDCD (DC00494).

REFERENCES

Avrutin, S. (2000). Comprehension of discourse-linked and non-discourse-linked questions by children and Broca's aphasics. To appear in Y. Grodzinsky, L. P. Shapiro, & D. Swinney (Eds.), *Language and the brain: Representation and processing.* San Diego: Academic Press.

Canseco-Gonzalez, E., Shapiro, L. P., Zurif, E. B., & Baker, E. (1990). Predicate–argument structure as a link between linguistic and nonlinguistic representations. *Brain and Language, 39,* 391–404.

Chomsky, N. (1995). *The minimalist program.* Cambridge, MA: MIT Press.

Cinque, G. (1990). *Types of A-dependencies.* Cambridge, MA: MIT Press.

Dalrymple, M. (1991). *Against reconstruction in ellipsis.* (Technical report No. SSL-91-114). Xerox.

De Vincenzi, M. (1996). Syntactic analysis in sentence comprehension: Effects of dependency types and grammatical constraints. *Journal of Psycholinguistic Research, 25,* 117–133.

Fiengo, R., & May, R. (1994). *Indices and identity.* Cambridge, MA: MIT Press.

Frazier, L., & McNamara, P. (1995). Favor referential representation. *Brain and Language, 49,* 224–240.

Hickok, G. (1993). Parallel parsing: Evidence from re-activation in garden path sentences. *Journal of Psycholinguistic Research, 22,* 239–250.

Hickok, G., & Avrutin, S. (1995). Representation, referentiality, and processing in agrammatic comprehension: Two case studies. *Brain and Language, 50,* 10–26.

Hickok, G., & Avrutin, S. (1996). Comprehension of wh-questions in two Broca's aphasics. *Brain and Language, 52,* 314–327.

Kehler, A. (1994). Common topics and coherent situations: Interpreting ellipsis in the context of discourse inference. In *Proceedings of the 32nd Conference of the Association of Computational Linguistics.*

Kitagawa, Y. (1991). Copying identity. *Natural Language and Linguistic Theory, 9,* 497–536.

Kluender, R. (1998). On the distinction between strong and weak islands: A processing perspective. In *Syntax and semantics: The limits of syntax.* San Diego: Academic Press.

Lasnik, H. (1995). Case and expletives revisited: On greed and other human failings. *Linguistic Inquiry, 26,* 615–633.

Levin, B. (1993). *English verb classes and alternations.* Chicago: University of Chicago Press.

Lobeck, A. (1992). Licensing and identification of ellipted categories in English. In S. Berman & A. Hestvik (Eds.), *Proceedings of the Stuttgart Ellipsis Workshop (Arbeitspapiere des Sonderforschungsbereich 340, Bericht Nr. 29, 1992).* Heidelberg, IBM Germany.

MacDonald, M. C., Pearlmutter, N. J., & Seidenberg, M. S. (1994). Lexical nature of syntactic ambiguity resolution. *Psychological Review, 101,* 676–703.

Nicol, J. (1998). *Coreference processing during sentence comprehension.* Unpublished doctoral dissertation. MIT, Cambridge, MA.

Nicol, J., & Pickering, M. (1993). Processing syntactically ambiguous sentences: Evidence from semantic priming., *Journal of Psycholinguistic Research, 22.*

Pesetsky, D. (1987). *Wh*-in-situ: Movement and unselective binding. In A. Ter Meulen & E. Reuland (Eds.), *Representation of (in)definateness.* Cambridge, MA: MIT Press.

Radford, A. (1997). *Syntax: A minimalist introduction.* New York: Cambridge University Press.

Shapiro, L. P., Gordon, B., Hack, N., & Killackey, J. (1993). Verb–argument structure processing in complex sentences in Broca's and Wernicke's aphasia. *Brain and Language, 45,* 423–447.

Shapiro, L. P., & Hestvik, A. (1995). On-line comprehension of VP–ellipsis: Syntactic reconstruction and semantic influence. *Journal of Psycholinguistic Research, 24,* 517–532.

Shapiro, L. P., & Levine, B. A. (1990). Verb processing during sentence comprehension in aphasia. *Brain and Language, 38,* 21–47.

Shapiro, L. P., Swinney, D. A., & Borsky, S. (1998). On-line examination of language performance in normal and neurologically-impaired adults. *American Journal of Speech-Language Pathology.*

Swinney, D. A., Zurif, E. B., Prather, P., & Love, T. (1996). Neurological distribution of processing operations underlying language comprehension. *Journal of Cognitive Neuroscience, 1,* 25–37.

Thompson, C. K., Tait, M. E., Ballard, K. J., & Fix, S. C. (1999). Agrammatic aphasic subjects' comprehension of subject and object extracted Wh questions. *Brain & Language, 67,* 169–187.

Zurif, E. B., Swinney, D. A., Prather, P., Solomon, J., & Bushell, C. (1993). An on-line analysis of syntactic processing in Broca's and Wernicke's aphasia. *Brain and Language, 45,* 448–464.

Index

377

Wh-questions (*continued*)
  which, 298–299, 301–308, 311, 365,
    367–369, 372–375
  who, 298–299, 301–307, 311, 366–375
Word
  deafness, 91, 94, 101, 204
  order, 15, 105, *see also* Canonical order
Word-finding difficulty, 159
Working memory, 42, 118, 145–147, 149–150,
    152, 197–198, 235, 260–262
  component of, 127

interference in
  phonological similarity, 130–131,
    135
  word length effect, 130–132, 135
load, 235
phonological, 97, 99,
rehearsal, 117–118, 124–127, 138
retrieval from, 235
semantic, 135–137, 139
storage in, 235
verbal, 118, 123–124, 126–135, 138